"Ben Edge is a natural-born storyteller. His fascinating blend of art, archive and anecdote opens a portal into the world of British folk customs, revealing an entire universe beyond."

– Holly EJ Black, writer, arts journalist
and author of *Artists on Art*

"A very timely book. Ben Edge weaves his personal story in with the traditional rituals of the British Isles. It's time to rediscover the real and this book tells you where to find it. Indispensable."

– Jarvis Cocker, musician and author of the
The Sunday Times bestseller *Good Pop, Bad Pop*

"Full of stunning images and rich with first-hand experience of Britain's folk customs, this is a potent tome indeed from an authentic voice within the folkloric realm."

– *Weird Walk*

"A book that positively glows with the magical luminance of the deep past. Ben writes with a unique love, sensitivity and wonder for the folk traditions and ancient monuments of Britain. A beautiful book from a trailblazer of folklore reborn and reimagined."

– Dr Jennifer Wexler and Dr Neil Wilkin, archaeologists and
curators of The World of Stonehenge, British Museum

"A vibrant celebration of all that the establishment do not control or understand."

– John Higgs, novelist, cultural historian and author of books
including *William Blake vs the World* and *Watling Street*

"A fascinating and engaging first-hand account of our ancient customs by the grandmaster of folk art."

– Charlotte Mullins, art critic, broadcaster and
author of books including *A Little Book of Art*
and *Painting People: Figure Painting Today*

"In his deeply squirrelly, edgy, almost mystic paintings, Ben Edge tries to ask where we all come from and why we tell ourselves the stories we tell ourselves."

– Jerry Saltz, Senior Art Critic for *New York Magazine*,
2018 Pulitzer Prize for Criticism, author of
The New York Times bestseller *How To Be An Artist*

"Being connected to each other and to the world of which we are a part is fundamental to our wellbeing and is an aspect of our humanity that has endured in multifarious, extraordinary and somewhat bizarre traditions. I travelled in these pages from one end of Britain to the other immersed in Ben Edge's storytelling and his art, and I've learning as much about my contemporaries as I have about the roots of folklore.

There are others who are witness to the folklore that stitches our lives today to those of our ancestors and others who have taken on the responsibility of creating the catalogue, but it's through Ben's artist response that the meaning of each tradition has an incredible contemporary potency. From the Burryman of South Queensferry standing before the council estate housing of my childhood to the Druids by the Tower of London, we cut through time and space and become a little more reconnected than we were."

– Sharon Ament, Director of the Museum of London

"Ben's exquisite artwork adorns each page of this magnificent journey through the folk traditions of Britain. Ben has not only been instrumental in painstakingly recording folk history for prosperity but also in opening up its magic to a new generation, allowing it to continue to flourish and ignite imaginations to come!"

– Maxine Peake, actor

Folklore Rising

An Artist's Journey through the British Ritual Year

BEN EDGE

WATKINS

Folklore Rising

Ben Edge

First published in the UK and USA in 2024 by
Watkins, an imprint of Watkins Media Limited
Unit 11, Shepperton House,
83–93 Shepperton Road,
London
N1 3DF

enquiries@watkinspublishing.com

Publisher: Fiona Robertson
Managing Editor: Daniel Culver
Copyeditor: Sue Lascelles
Designer: Alice Claire Coleman
Cover Designer: Rebecca Wright
Head of Design: Karen Smith
Proofreading: Steve Williamson
Indexing: Lisa Footit
Production: Uzma Taj

A CIP record for this book is available from the British Library

ISBN: 978-1-78678-874-0 (Hardback)
ISBN: 978-1-78678-912-9 (eBook)

10 9 8 7 6 5 4 3 2 1

Typeset in Brandon Grotesque
Printed in Bosnia and Herzegovina
Colour reproduction Rival Colour LTD

Abbreviations used throughout this book:
CE Common Era (the equivalent of AD)
BCE Before the Common Era, (the equivalent of BC)

www.watkinspublishing.com

Contents

Introduction

You could say that it all began with a chance encounter. One day in March, I was on my way to the Tower of London to talk to the Ravenmaster about possibly painting his portrait. Legend has it that six ravens must be kept at the Tower at all times and if any were to escape "the Crown would fall and the kingdom with it". The Ravenmaster's job is to ensure that this doesn't come to pass. It was midday as I came out of Tower Hill tube station, when I noticed a group of figures in white processing in the distance. Intrigued, I ran across the road and watched as they gathered in a circle and began enacting what seemed to be some kind of ancient rite.

As I stood on the edges of the circle, I noticed the group included all sorts: tall people, short people, elderly and young, with their faces sticking out from their hoods like the beaks of birds. Their footwear ranged from Nikes and Reeboks to plimsolls and sandals, but this was the only individual aspect of their clothing, as in other respects they seemed to morph into the collective identity of the sheet-like robes draped over them.

"Who are they?" I asked a photographer next to me.

"Druids," he replied, before moving on to take another shot.

In the ceremony, there was mention of William Blake, the use of a sword and trumpet, and talk of spring equinox, spiritual harvest and of London one day being reclaimed by Mother Earth. I would later find out that these were members of London's very own Druid Order.

Witnessing a ritual like this taking place in Britain – against the backdrop of Tower Bridge, a phone box, a KFC and the "Walkie-Talkie" building gleaming in the distance, juxtaposed with the ancient Church of All Hallows-by-the-Tower, the Tower of London itself and remnants of the Roman city wall – awoke something within me, something that had been lost. It felt as if time had merged into one, with the ancient and the contemporary walking side by side, coexisting in a single moment. A sense of eternity itself came over me and I felt connected to something larger than myself – to the ancestors, to Nature. Looking back, you could say it was a kind of awakening, an epiphany.

Although I would later fulfil my original ambition of painting a portrait of the Ravenmaster, I never made it to the Tower that day, but instead went home and spent hours googling the Druid Order and their seasonal rituals. I was amazed to discover that similar folk customs take place through the year all across Britain. I hadn't realized it at the time but a new obsession had been born within me, and I felt compelled to visit these remarkable rituals for myself, travelling by train, bus and on foot, often finding myself being rattled into the hedges by passing cars and lorries as I walked along the country roads that led from rural train stations to the spots in which these peculiar customs were most commonly found. These are home to communities where I have been shoved, kicked, threatened, crushed, burned and drenched to the bone, as well as being welcomed in with open arms by the local people, whom I have eaten with, drunk with and laughed with, welcomed in the seasons alongside, watched the sunrise and sunset, and inherited the wonderful stories that can now be told and retold within the narratives of my paintings.

Not long before that life-changing moment at Tower Hill, which I now refer to as my "Druidic epiphany", I had been going through an extremely dark period in my life, during which my grandfather had died in a house fire, followed soon after by the death of my wife Rose's grandparents, who also unbelievably died in a house fire. My band, Thee Spivs, to which I had given my all, had fallen apart, and in hindsight I was absolutely exhausted. To add insult to injury, on New Year's Day that year, I was sacked from my job as a labourer, which had been the last in a long line of jobs that I'd had over the years to pay the rent and make sure I'd enough time for making art. But despite managing to maintain my art practice through it all, I felt a million miles from where I truly wanted to be. With all of this taking its toll on me, I became clinically depressed, trapped in a constant loop of negativity, self-hatred and suicidal thoughts, and I had a nervous breakdown. I had reached rock bottom, everything felt so dark, and I had forgotten who I was.

The thought of continuing down this torturous path was now far more terrifying to me than the possibility of failing at doing what I actually wanted to do. Decision made, there was no going back: I was going to be a full-time artist. Even though I had nothing lined up, no financial support and just blind faith, I gave myself over to the great unknown.

Around this time, I had painted a self-portrait in which I was standing in a distressed and contemplative state on top of Primrose Hill, with the view of the London skyline behind me. The painting encapsulates this period of inner conflict, where I had begun taking long walks across London in an attempt to escape my depression, inspire new work and re-engage with the outside world in general. These walks, in which my passion for the city and its folklore were reignited, would ultimately lead to me being in the "right place at the right time", in which I would find my life's purpose and some much-needed light.

Despite this new lease of life, these were still the very early days in my recovery, and the thought of arriving somewhere alone to take pictures of strangers performing some kind of ancient ritual often absolutely terrified me. I had seen the folk-horror film *The Wicker Man*, of course, and it's hard not to feel like you've just arrived in Summerisle when you first rock up, standing out like a sore thumb in communities dressed up in their ritualistic attire. You'd feel their eyes on you and can imagine them thinking: *Who's this? Probably an art student from London. We've seen his type before.* They'd not be too far off the mark either, although I quickly realized that my preconceptions were only partly rooted in reality and that the majority of people seemed to enjoy the fact that I was interested in their cherished local customs and, most importantly, was there to have a good time. I soon made some good friends along the way and gradually developed a new sense of self-confidence.

As I immersed myself in the cyclical seasons of Nature and the very human celebrations that surrounded them, my view of the world began to change. The shackles of my urbanized existence were loosened and the darkness of my depression lifted as I watched the flowers blooming while the 'Obby 'Oss performed his fertility dance through the streets of Padstow on May Day morning. I felt the crunch of fallen leaves underfoot as I found myself back on London's Primrose Hill, this time not in a state of despair, but on the trail of the Druids as they performed their autumn equinox ceremony at the summit. I inhaled the stench of the singed hair of the Flaming Tar Barrel runners of Ottery St Mary (as well as my own) as they chased away evil spirits beneath the cold, dark skies of approaching winter. I marvelled at the budding leaves as I found myself once more on Tower Hill at the spring equinox and thought back over the incredible year, the places and the people that I had encountered, knowing that I was ready to do it all again.

As an artist who draws inspiration from oral storytelling, I was spoiled for choice by the incredible wealth of stories surrounding the speculated origins of each custom. More often than not, locals believed that the seasonal customs they were celebrating had roots that went all the way back to Pagan times. One thing that you soon discover when delving into the world of British folk customs is that there are often few hard historical facts to back up local beliefs. Depending on your school of thought, this could be down to the fact that the customs were practised by illiterate peasants, whose festivals were once so commonplace that none of the gentry knew about them or was interested or bothered enough to write about them. Or you could be of the school of thought that they began in and around the times of the earliest known records. There are some academics who have dedicated their whole lives to researching the historical origins of folk customs, only to be left with more questions than answers. This is what I love about British folklore: there is space for us all within it, and a whole world of speculation in which you can get lost and found in creativity.

Whatever the truth is, what struck me straight away was that, as the local stories were told and retold, they kept on growing, changing and evolving, much like a living, breathing entity. This connected me to the colourful characters of my own family who'd passed down stories to me, such as my grandfather's tales of old London life at Smithfield market, of colleagues losing fingers and the practical jokes they used to play on each other, and of guns and gangsters. His council flat was home to a vast collection of exotic pets, including on one occasion a tiger lent to him by a friend who worked in the circus, and a chimpanzee called Primo, who would dive from the Brixton council-flat balcony onto the passing milk float, scaring the life out of the milkman.

My grandfather's passion for animals led to him working on films such as *Raiders of the Lost Ark*, which my father also worked on in the art department. When the leading actress refused to walk through a snake pit, Dad shaved his legs and became her stunt double, making a now legendary cameo appearance in the film and a much cherished family story in the process.

There were also tales of more distant relatives, such my third great-grandfather, who was a slaughter man who was ripped apart by a bull, and the factory worker in Salford who refused to wear shoes until the day came that there were no longer any street children. As with folk customs, over time, the characters might change and narratives evolve, taking parts from this and adding to that, until you're left with a mishmash of experiences and the story itself becomes part of the family's collective identity. This, for me, is what folklore is all about, too: it's not to do with historical facts, it's about the passing down of stories, traditions and creativity from generation to generation, which encapsulate the voices, personalities and the ephemeral remnants of everybody who's played a part in that lineage, giving rise to something far greater than ourselves as individuals.

I also thought about my own childhood. I grew up in Southborough in Kent, and was surrounded by woodlands and countryside, where I felt an early connection with the natural world. But I would also go and stay with my dad in Shoreditch, East London, right in the heart of the City. At weekends, it was like a ghost town: one minute you'd be in the Jack the Ripper-esque streets of Norton Folgate; then a street away, you'd be among the ruins of the old Roman wall and gigantic building projects, in which the foundations for huge, new glass buildings were being laid, and where plague pits, Roman ruins and many other significant archaeological discoveries were being unearthed, with the details of each find appearing on the hoardings of the building sites. It was as if the history of London had been blended into a single era unfolding right there and then. This, in hindsight, most certainly had a profound influence on the way that I both look at and experience the world.

I also remember the impact of time spent with my Native American cousins of the Tsleil-Waututh First Nation, who would visit us from Canada and sing us tribal songs, tell mythological stories from their ancient culture and bless our house with prayers. I always felt in awe; it was so magical, sincere, spiritual and connected to Nature. I yearned for something like that of my own and little did I know that it was there on my own doorstep all along, or that I would one day embark on a life-changing journey across Britain, in which I would delve deep into my own folk culture and discover a magical, hidden world that I'd had no idea even existed until then.

As we struggle as a nation with the darker elements of our history, I have found folklore to be a breath of fresh air and something of an antidote to the legacy of our colonial past. That's not to say our folk culture is perfect: women are still underrepresented and there is a lack of diversity, although that's beginning to change. However, despite all this, its greatest appeal to me is that folk customs often arose from the ways in which peasants used their ritual practices, superstitions, storytelling and creativity to take back control of their lives and destinies from the oppressive regimes of the ruling classes. British folklore doesn't filter down from the top, from palaces or stately homes; it's not tied up with the empire or the slave trade;

it sincerely connects us to a time in which we honoured our ancestors, celebrated the seasons, welcomed in the harvest and lived in harmony with the land.

I was inspired, too, by the universality of seasonal customs, variations of which are practised around the world, and which are a manifestation of our shared humanity, while also celebrating the individuality of regional cultures and the never-ending uniqueness and creativity found at the heart of the human spirit. Whether it's a huge garland crowning a man on horseback, aka the Garland King of Castleton, or the Rushcart of Saddleworth, where rushes are piled incredibly high on top of a cart and dragged through the streets, as I looked at the incredible outfits, props and costumes, it got me thinking about the creative impulse: these traditions often involve people who'd never consider themselves to be artists and yet, without even realizing it, they are engaging in a pure kind of folk art, creating beautiful things for their traditions and rituals. This made me feel like I was right back to the birth of art, reinforcing my belief that we are all creative as human beings, and reminded me again of my own family, who despite holding down regular jobs all seemed to practise some form of creativity in their spare time. My grandfather, for example, was a woodcarver, and it was here that I would first come familiar with the symbol of the Green Man, sparking my life-long interest in this mysterious figure, who we will meet on many occasions in this book.

Before we set out on this folkloric adventure together, I'd like to thank you for joining me on this quest of serendipity, recovery, re-enchantment and self-discovery, a path that I continue to walk to this day.

Ben Edge
2024

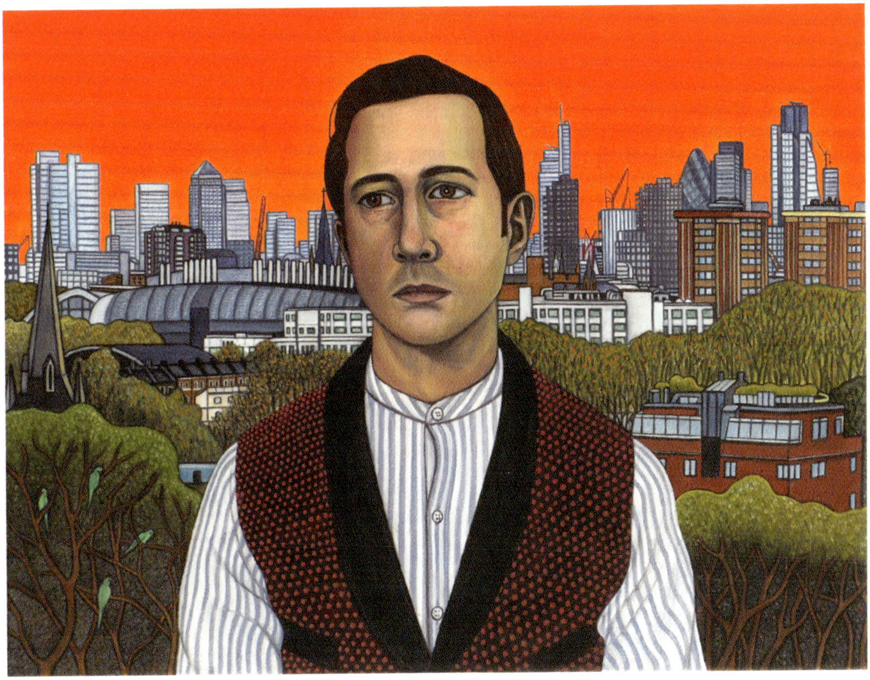

SELF-PORTRAIT WITH LONDON SKYLINE

Oil on Canvas, 30cm × 40cm

2017

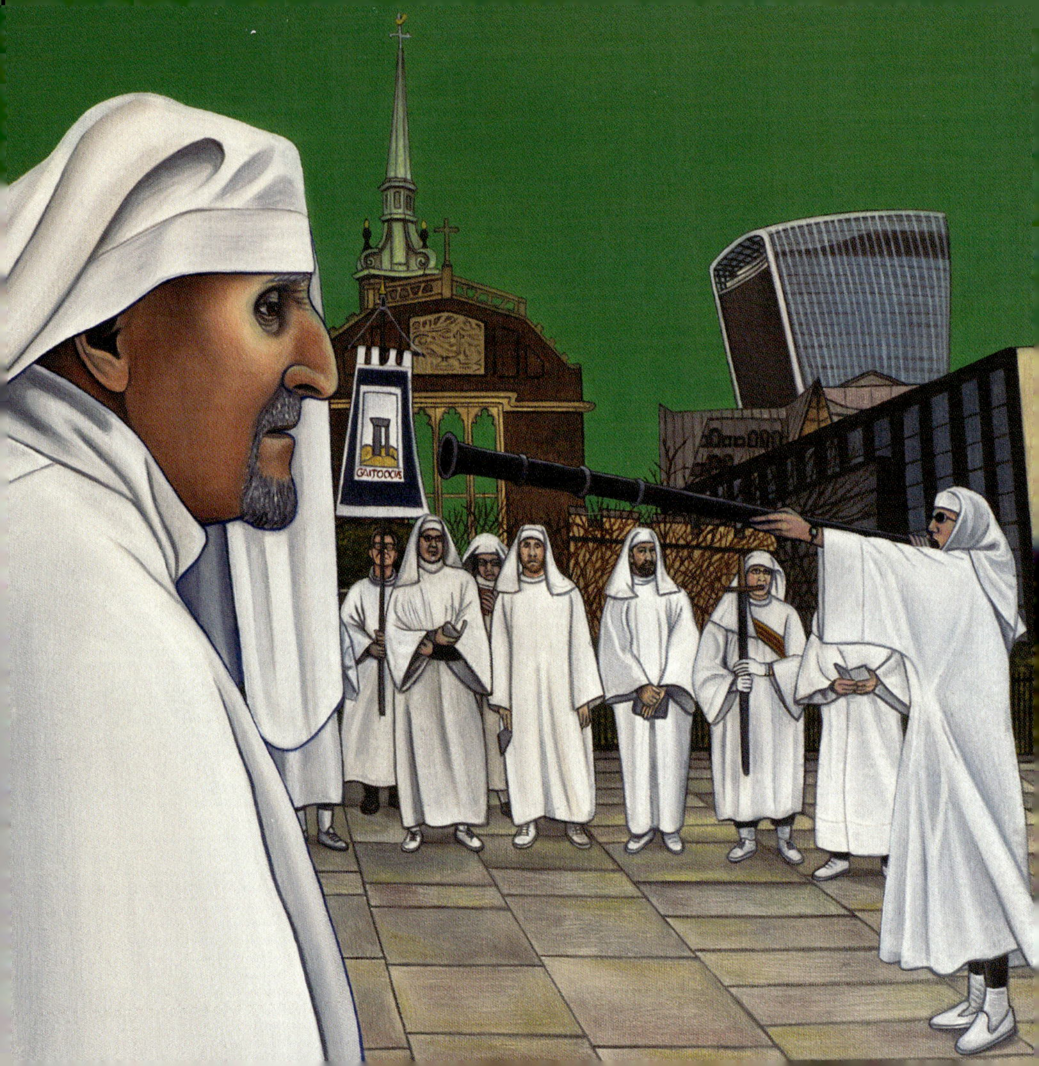

THE SPRING EQUINOX

Oil on Canvas, 45cm × 45cm

2017

Spring Equinox, Tower Hill

LONDON

MARCH 20 OR 21 (NORTHERN HEMISPHERE)

A year passed after my Druidic epiphany. I spent the time reading up on folk customs and felt compelled to visit as many of the sites as I could. My first point of call was the celebration of the spring equinox by the Druid Order at Tower Hill in London, and to begin my new artistic journey from there.

When I went to watch the ceremony, one of the most surprising things was that the Druids assembled in a church before the procession. However, when I delved into the history connected to the Church of All Hallows-by-the-Tower, it seemed a fitting location. Tower Hill was once known in Welsh as "Bryn Gwyn", meaning a white or holy hill, and suggesting that the place held religious significance for the Celts and the ancient tribes in the area. All Hallows itself is the oldest church in the City of London and there's a Roman mosaic floor in the crypt that might have been the site of a Pagan temple. The church also has Saxon foundations and Norman and medieval elements, and the diarist Samuel Pepys climbed its tower in 1666 to watch the Great Fire of London. While surrounding buildings were being blown up during the Blitz in World War II, the church survived, albeit damaged: hardened drips of melted lead roof can still be seen in the crypt. A complete history of London can be found on a site that has been continuously significant for over two thousand years, so where better for contemporary Neopagan worship to take place?

SPRING EQUINOX,
TOWER HILL

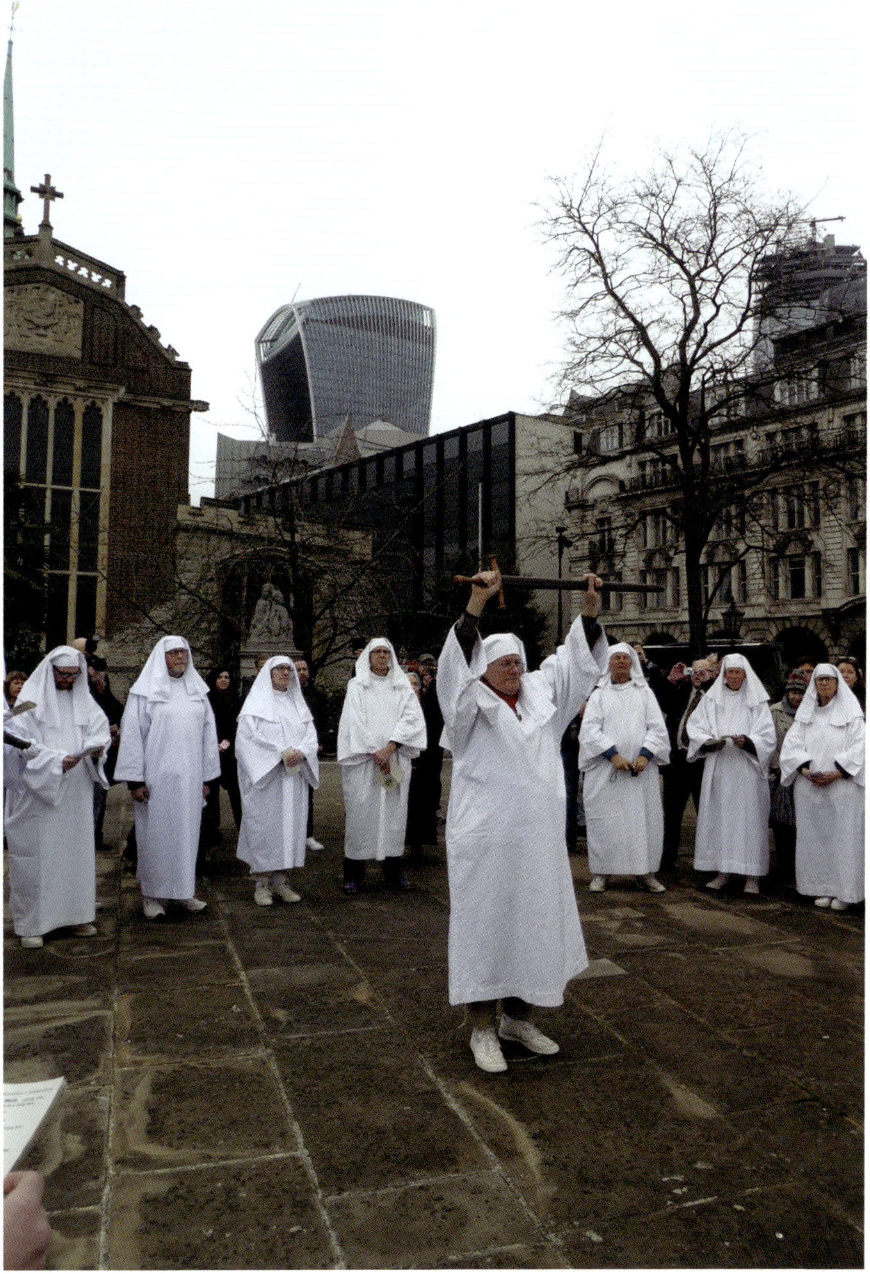

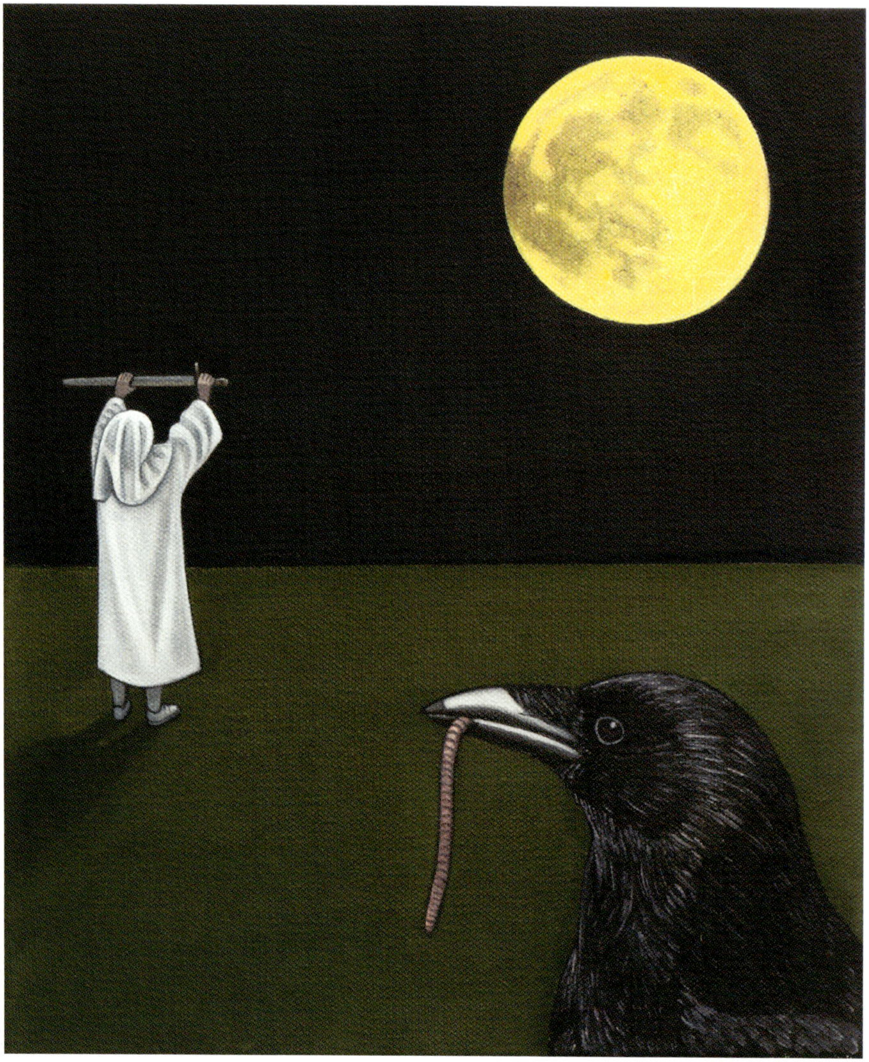

SPRING EQUINOX AT WORM MOON

Oil on Canvas, 30cm × 25cm

2019

Once the procession began, about thirty white-gowned Druids appeared through the glass door of a contemporary extension attached to the church building. There was a remarkably meditative and peaceful atmosphere, despite the location being slap-bang in the middle of the City. Outside, on Byward Street, grotesques and corbel carvings, including a Green Man, watched on from the church, while people gawped in disbelief from car windows, puzzled-looking tourists and city professionals ambled by, and laughing teenagers took photos with their smart phones. I was struck by the footwear of the participants: like the last time I'd seen them, most of them were in white trainers and everyday shoes, which somehow made it clear that this was no re-enactment fantasy; this was a genuine contemporary ritual in which modern people were taking the time to reconnect with Nature, the wheel of the year and the natural rhythms of being alive.

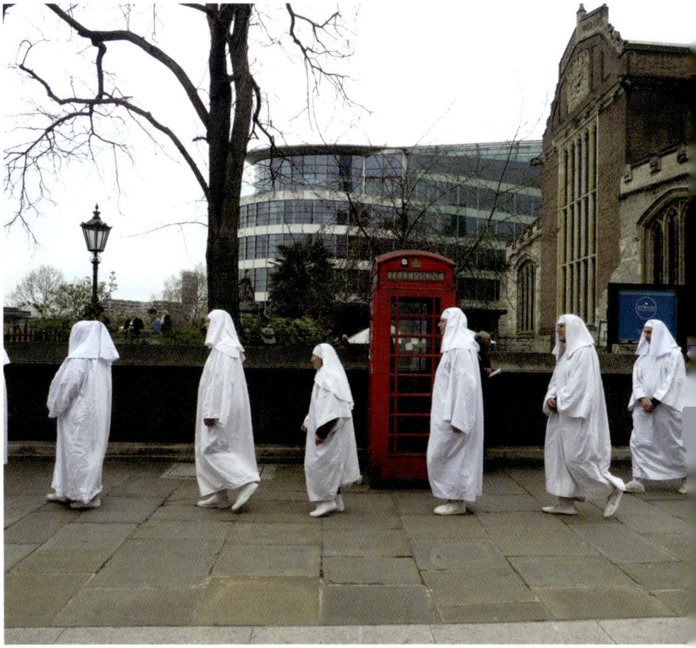

The group processed with a seriousness and dignified focus, ending up in a small square close to the church. Here, the ceremony began. Throughout, the roaring traffic and passing sirens did nothing to detract from the feeling that we were part of something powerful. A sword was partially removed from its scabbard and held up to the sky, a sacred horn blown and the names of past Druids read out, including those of the artist William Blake and the antiquarian William Stukeley. There were readings about reconnecting to Nature, wishing peace and harmony throughout the world and planting the seeds for a flourishing future, along with the idea that London itself will one day be reclaimed by Nature. I couldn't help but feel inspired; maybe we aren't too far gone as a species after all?

The spring equinox is perhaps the most hopeful, forward-thinking time in the wheel of the year, where the dark days of winter are behind us and the long summer nights and the fertility of spring are on their way; a time of balance where night and day are of equal length.

One of the Druids explained to me that they come to Tower Hill because it's sacred ground, and added, "The whole purpose of the spring equinox is to remember that there's a place and there's a season, which is the beginning of the rest of the seasons, so if it were a seed, it's just about to give birth and to spring into life."

This celebration had been exactly what I was looking for; it felt like my own dark days of depression were falling behind me and I was having a kind of inner rebirth. I felt lighter, part of this world again, no longer stuck inside my head. Witnessing the Druids celebrate the spring equinox felt like serendipity instead of coincidence; like I was meant to be there and this was the natural path for me take.

When making the painting that would become the first of my *Frontline Folklore* series, while admittedly I didn't quite understand yet why I felt so compelled to paint British folk customs, I did know from past experience that through the act of making the work and undertaking this folkloric journey, all would eventually be revealed. Later, I would paint a small piece inspired by this event titled *Serendipity*, in which you can see an oak tree emerging from an acorn on Tower Hill. This first experience was very much like that: it was like an acorn was planted in my mind that day that would later flourish into a great oak.

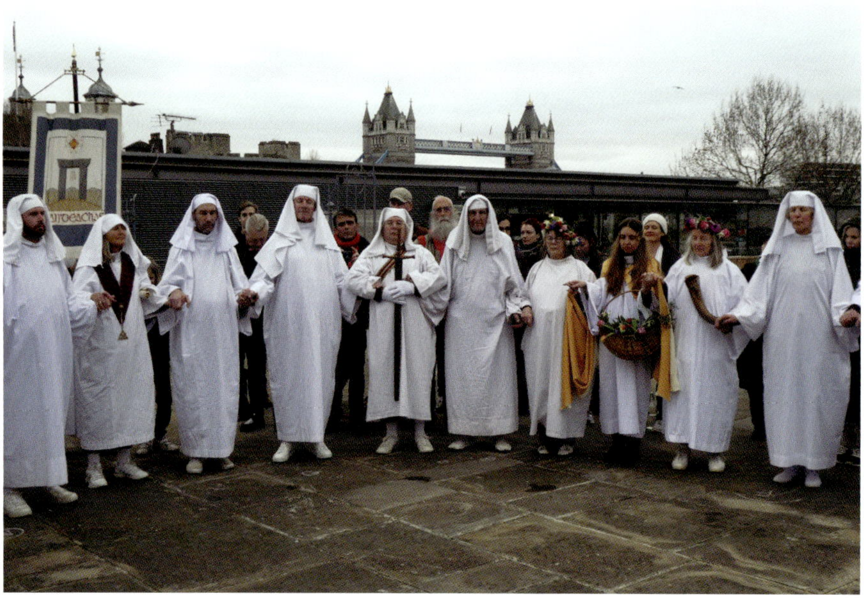

SPRING EQUINOX,
TOWER HILL

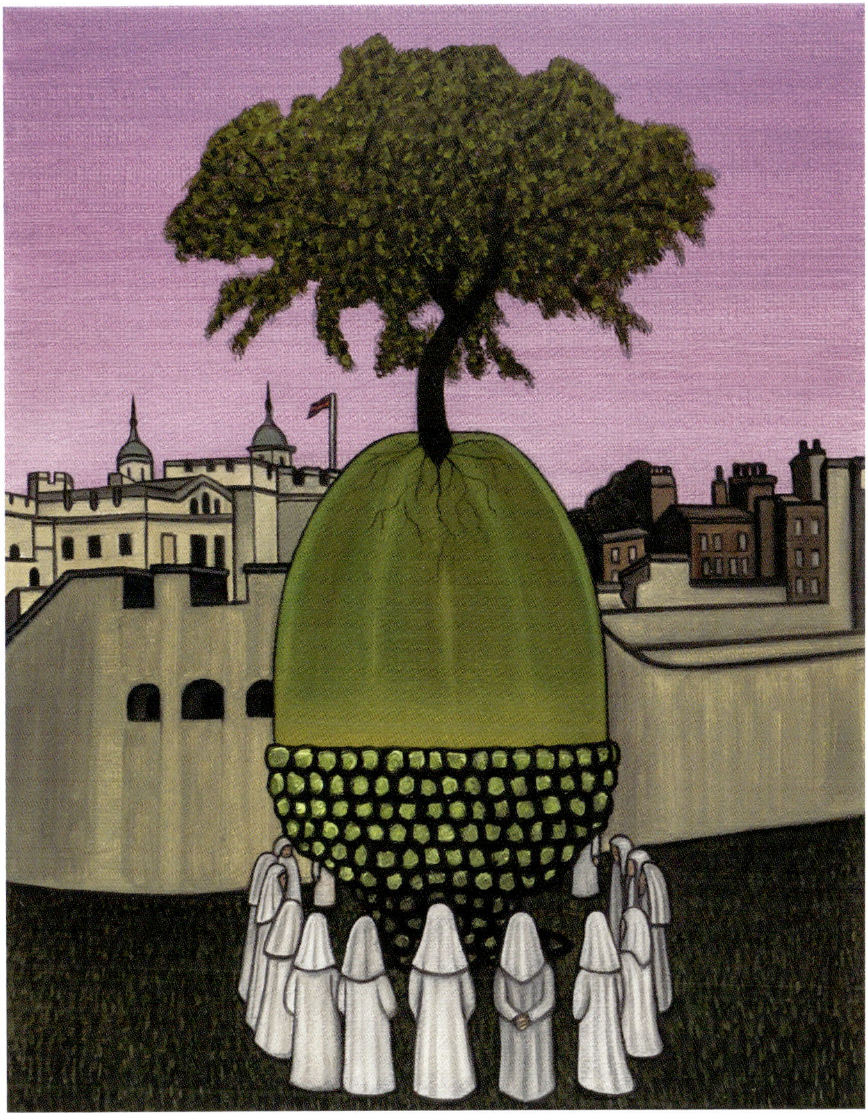

SERENDIPITY

Oil on Canvas, 45cm × 45cm

2021

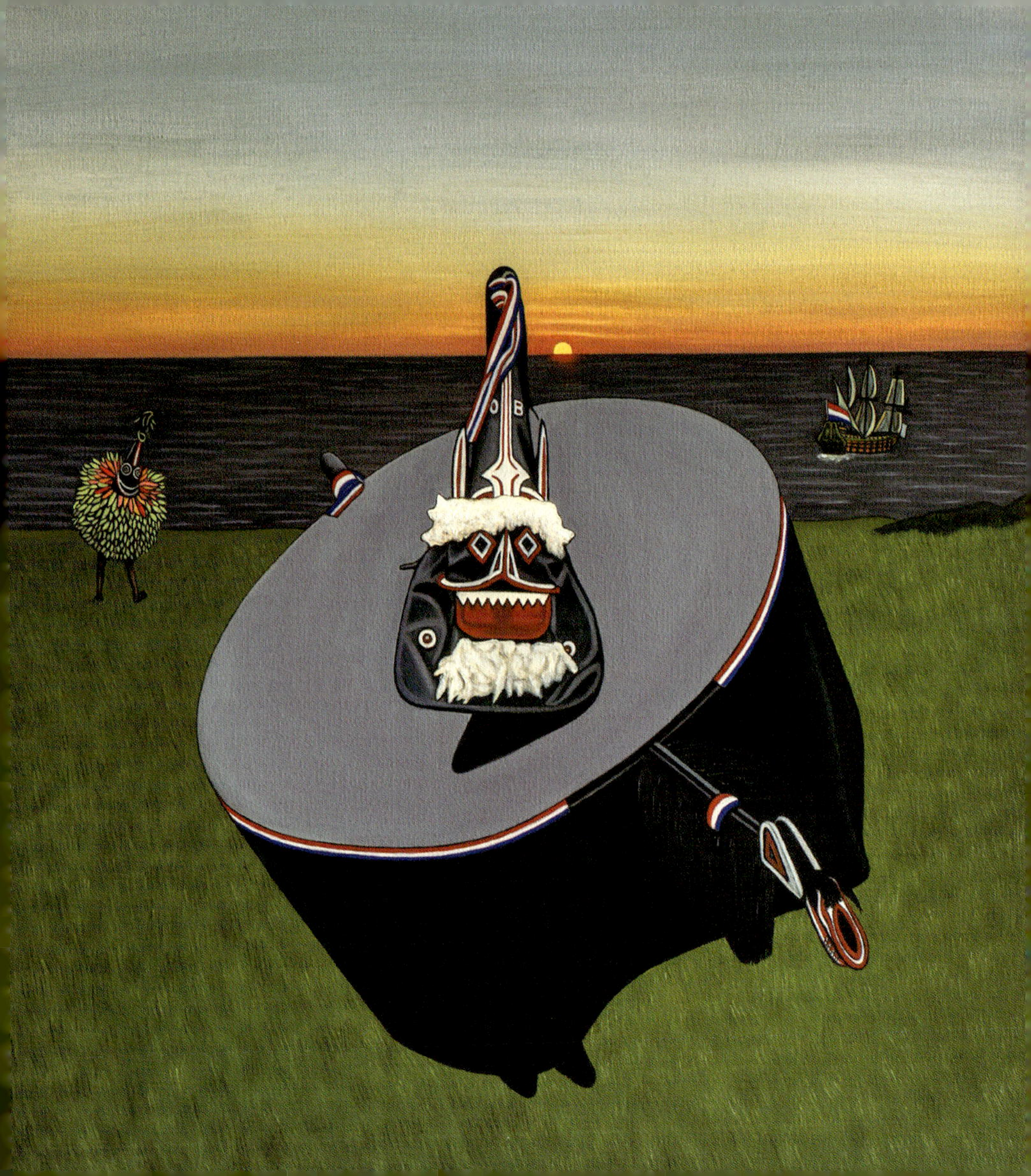

THE 'OBBY 'OSS OF PADSTOW

Oil on Canvas, 50cm × 44.5cm

2017

The 'Obby 'Oss of Padstow

CORNWALL

APRIL 30–MAY 1

While I was researching the folk customs of Britain, I discovered Sara Hannant's mind-blowing book *Mummers, Maypoles and Milkmaids*, about all the contemporary rituals that take place across the country. Flicking through the photographs, I was particularly struck by a strange hybrid creature with a horse's mane and a shiny black cylindrical body topped with a ferocious, beast-like mask, dancing in the middle of a huge crowd of people wearing red neckerchiefs and white clothes. I couldn't quite believe what I was looking at. The image was at once familiar, the Cornwall of my childhood camping holidays, and at the same time totally alien, like something from another century or a far-away land, but happening right now, part of my own culture.

I decided I'd go to Cornwall with my friend Anton, who has a campervan, and that we'd make a holiday out of it, camping along the coast and stopping off at Padstow for May Eve and May Day. After a week on the road we arrived in Padstow somewhat dishevelled, our faces stubbly and our clothes crumpled and unwashed. We parked up above the harbour and fun fair, with the thick smell of the sea and fish-and-chips in the air. Then we wandered through streets draped with flags, stopping off at a bakery for some Cornish pasties, and looking at the May Day posters in all the shop windows. You could feel the excitement almost dripping off the buildings and electrifying everyone in town!

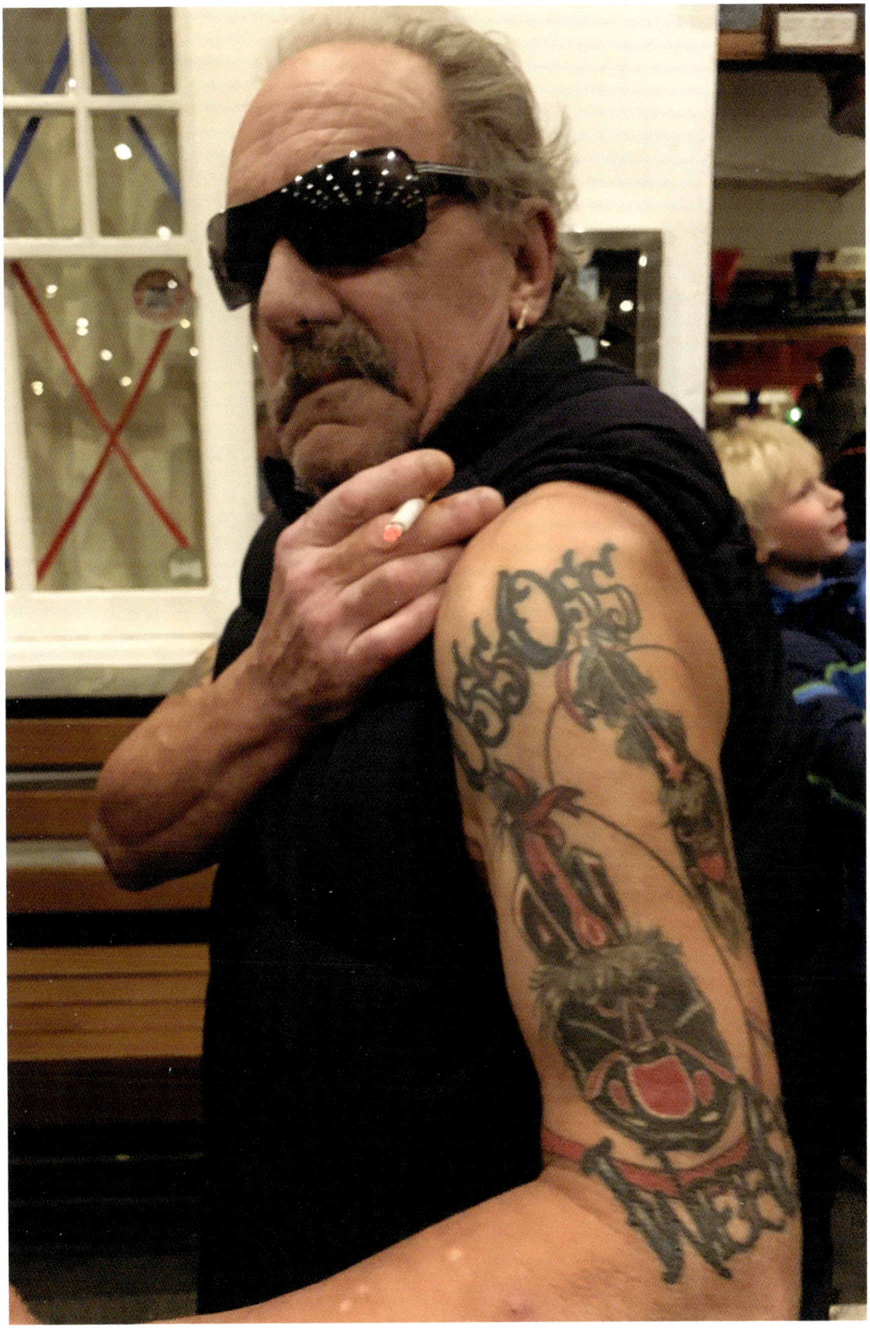

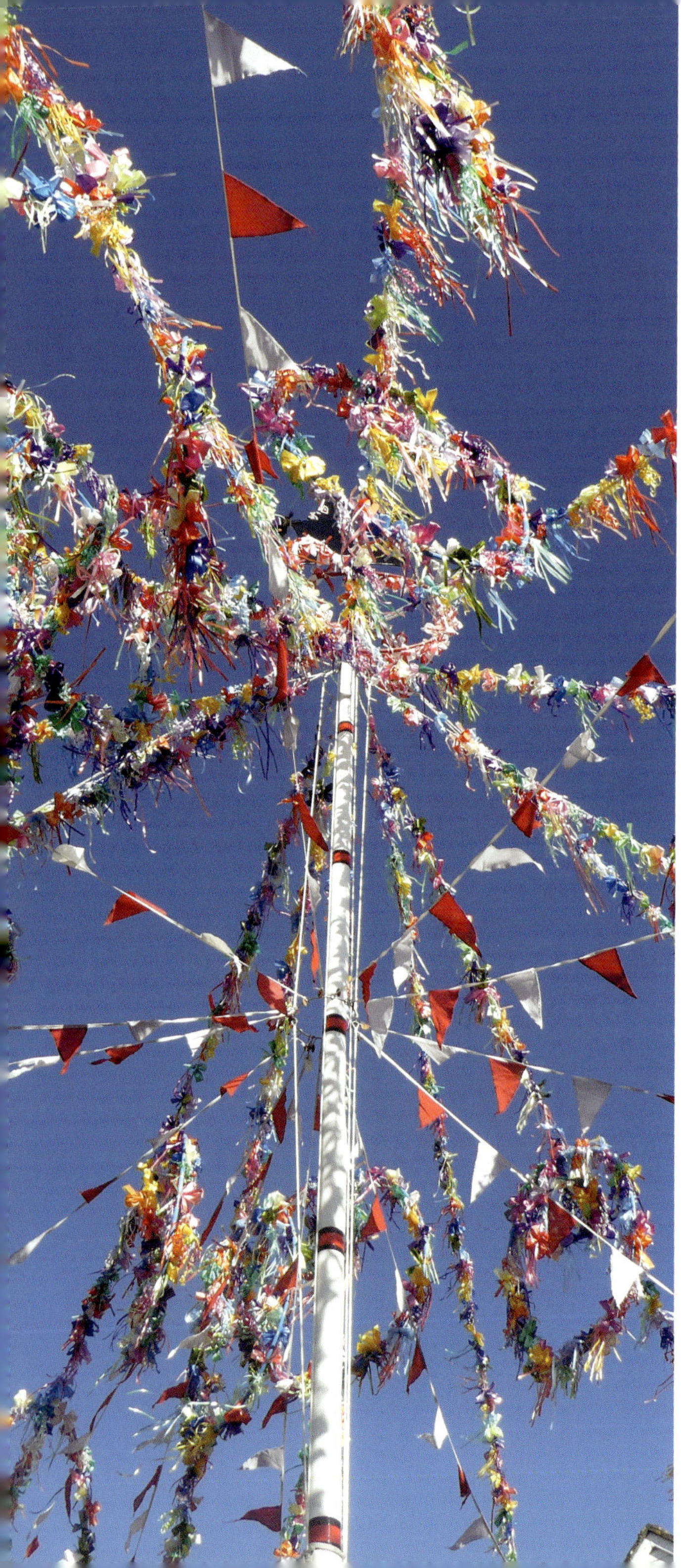

The posters in the windows announced the times the 'Obby 'Osses would be coming out of their stables on May Day: the Blue Ribbon 'Oss would emerge from its stable – the Institute on Market Street – at 10am; the original Old 'Oss from the Golden Lion Pub at 11am. I would later find out that the Blue Ribbon 'Oss, also known as the Peace 'Oss, was created in 1919 by World War I veterans, members of a temperance group who wanted to raise money for charity and to discourage the drunken and disorderly behaviour of the Old 'Oss and its followers.

Me and Anton roamed the streets with pasties in hand, soaking up the atmosphere and stopped off in a few pubs before reaching the Golden Lion, painted bright yellow with its sign proclaiming it the "Stable of Padstow's Original 'Oss". The low-ceilinged, wooden-beamed pub was buzzing with excitement. We bought our first drink and managed to find a free bench among all the full tables.

We got chatting to a man with an 'Oss tattooed on his arm who warned us, only half-jokingly, that "The Old 'Oss party can be a bit aggressive." The Old 'Oss party consists of the musicians who follow that 'Oss throughout May Day, along with their family and friends of "Teasers" who dance and provoke the beast. While the beginnings of the tradition are unknown, family heritage and allegiance determines which 'Oss you follow today, much like the tradition of choosing what football team you support. As with any team rivalry, tensions exist between the different parties, and I even heard stories of families falling out over which 'Oss they support.

While we were talking, a group of accordion players made their way toward the bar, weaving around tables stacked with glasses. It was rammed in there and the low ceiling made it feel even more claustrophobic, like being in a cave, but when the music began, the sound of the accordions all together and the songs of old Cornwall made the hairs on my neck stand up. I felt like I was in some kind of dream, seeing this incredible folk culture connected to the deep past yet living and thriving today.

I tried to get closer, pushing through the crowd to the bar where the musicians were assembled, but I found myself blocked by someone's arm. The man looked me right in the eyes and said, "You're not coming any closer!"

"Are you serious?" I asked, and he said it again, so I retreated. A woman with tattoo-covered arms cackled with laughter. She leaned over and shouted in my ear, "Don't worry about them, they'll soon cheer up!" We got chatting and she told me she'd been going to the Padstow May Day celebrations since she was a baby. I asked her about the origins of the tradition and she told me the story she'd always known. During the French wars when all the men were away fighting, an enemy ship was spotted approaching Padstow and a quick-thinking local named Aunt Ursula gathered the women of the town, dressed them in scary masks and led them up to the cliff tops where they set about banging pots and pans. The French took them for a heathen army with the Devil at its head and quickly turned back! "But the tradition goes back much further, to Pagan times," the woman said. "It was a fertility rite once."

As I headed away from the musicians, I got chatting to a white-haired gent with a cast on his arm and a cockney twang to his voice; it turned out he was a fellow artist called Chris, who had moved to Padstow in his late adolescence and never lost his London accent. This year he wouldn't be playing the accordion due to his broken arm, he told me. I have got to know Chris and his family well since then. On a later visit to Cornwall, he shared with me some particularly fascinating thoughts on the origins and evolving nature of the tradition.

He said, "I think there has always been a festival here in Padstow, to celebrate the coming of summer, but I don't think it's always been in this form. I think the present manifestation is a hybrid of many things: it's not like a thoroughbred race horse, it's been crossbred with so many different influences, imposed contexts and existing contexts." He concluded, "There're all sorts of reasons it's survived here – its geography, the tenacity of its people, a hundred and one reasons."

As the night progressed, voices got louder and the musicians sang and played until midnight, when everybody gathered outside the pub, with more and more people streaming in from all directions. All the Padstownians had come together to sing the "Night Song" to the landlord and lady, who were listening from the upstairs window. Another spine-tingling moment, with emotion in the eyes of everyone as they sang together:

Unite and unite and let us all unite,
For summer is acome unto day,
And whither we are going we will all unite,
In the merry morning of May.

It felt so ancient, lines that could have been sung for hundreds of years, but this was a living ritual, a ceremony to connect everyone who took part and make us feel gratitude for the approaching warm and abundant days of summer.

We sat by the harbour watching the crowds disperse with laughter, shouting and excitement. The atmosphere was intoxicating. We overheard one group talking about heading to the "night singing", so we followed them through the narrow streets to the Old Ship Hotel. It looked closed, but people were gathering outside and they soon broke out in song. The landlord appeared with trays of half-pints of beer that he gave out to the singers and spectators alike. We couldn't believe it. There was so much joy in the air and the singing was so moving. It really meant everything to those singing.

The singing ended, people drank up and moved on. We discovered that the scene would be repeated throughout the night and continue into residential areas through the early hours, with the night singers performing outside houses, in some cases to be rewarded with whisky, cider or beer (though some people did choose to just stay in bed and not even peek out of their windows). We stuck with the party for a while but eventually, after a long day and night, headed back to the campervan to crash.

In the morning, we were woken by drumming and followed the sound to find a group of kids out celebrating May Day in a town now draped in greenery associated with springtime, such as catkins and sycamore twigs, which had been collected during the night by locals. Theirs was one of the smaller children's 'Osses that start out early on May Day morning from a housing estate now known as Natives' Hill; it has been given this sarcastic nickname due to it being where many locals who take part in the festivities now live, having been forced out of the town centre by rocketing house prices caused by gentrification and second-home ownership. We followed the group and to our amazement the pubs were already packed with crowds, pints in hand, as the Wee 'Oss entered each establishment, dancing while everyone joined in singing.

I can't overstate the atmosphere of joy and excitement that built through the morning, exploding as the Blue Ribbon 'Oss came out of its stable. I'll never forget the moment I saw it for the first time as it came swirling out into Market Street among a huge crowd of "Mayers" – people singing the "Day Song", banging drums and playing accordions.

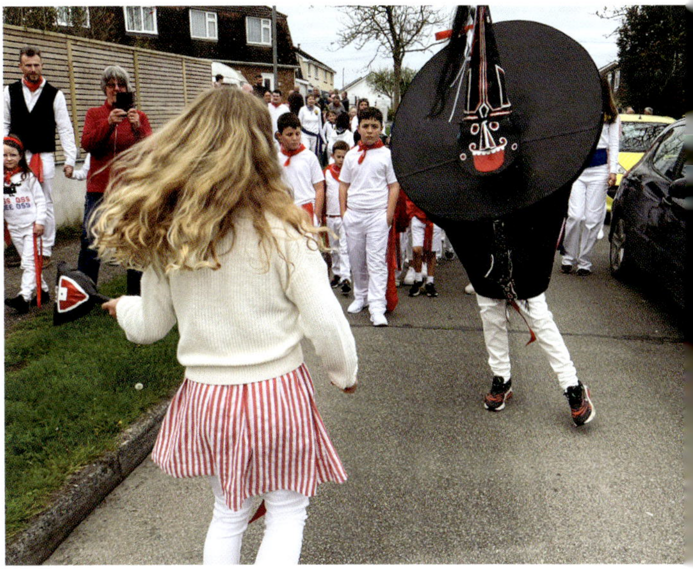

The words "unite and unite" echoed through the streets, people leaned from windows among the draped flags, families gathered round to see the spectacle. The chant of "'Oss 'Oss, Wee 'Oss", the tears of emotion, the townsfolk dressed all in white with blue neckerchiefs to symbolize their loyalty to the Blue Ribbon 'Oss; the Teaser waving a club while dancing around the 'Oss and tenderly orchestrating its symbolic death and rebirth to represent the death of winter and rebirth of summer. The 'Oss collapses as if exhausted. The singing slows down and an emotion verging on mourning can be heard in the voices of the singers, before the drums beat and the 'Oss springs back to life and a more joyful celebration resumes. There is also a tradition whereby women are caught beneath the black tarpaulin of the 'Oss's skirt, which is said to mean that they will become pregnant by Christmas.

Inspired to make a painting of the 'Oss, I tried to get some photos and nearly went flying as two hands on my back shunted me out of the way. One thing I soon learned in Padstow was that the tradition is about local people, not outsiders. For me this made it seem all the more special, authentic and sacred, but admittedly also unnerving. The rain began pouring down but the crowd were not deterred. After some time we realized we'd missed the Old 'Oss coming out of his stable. I was gutted not to have seen that part of the tradition, but I'd already decided I'd be back next year.

So the following year I returned on my own. Starving hungry on arrival, I bought some chips. As I walked up the road I felt a thud on the back of my head – a seagull. It knocked the chips out of my hand and a flock of birds swooped down and devoured them. Welcome to Padstow, I thought – even the seagulls aren't keen on outsiders.

This time, I wanted to focus on the Old 'Oss parade. At the Golden Lion, a bunch of men wearing pirate-style bandanas and red neckerchiefs had gathered, and sailors playing accordions lined up along one side of the street. One of the leading figures of the Old 'Oss party, a man with a long bandana round his waist tied with a small bunch of flowers, and large hooped earrings, entertained the crowd, revving everyone up. When I had the opportunity to interview him later in the day, he told me his family "the MacCowans, were one of the original families to start it off [as it is today] about a hundred and fifty years ago". He added, "I think it started from somewhere else, then merged and stuff, and it could be two hundred, three hundred years old, older – who knows."

Then out came the 'Oss, swaying and dancing, pushing the crowd back and forth as the emotion of the May Song roared through the air. I loved the homemade sweaters with images of the 'Oss that many people were wearing and kept an eye out for any merchandise I could buy, but there was nothing, no 'Oss ornaments, no 'Oss clothing. Perhaps his image is too sacred to use in a commercial way.

As this was my second visit, some people recognized me, which made it a lot easier for me to take photographs. I was even allowed to stand at the bar in the Golden Lion as the accordionists performed. It was as if I'd proven myself on some level. I followed the 'Oss throughout the day and by the afternoon things were getting rowdy. A fight broke out in the town centre. But by the time the two 'Oss parties had come together under the huge maypole in the town centre, things had settled down, and as the words "unite and unite" were sung a sense of unity did seem to come over everyone. The 'Osses danced until dark and were then put to bed in their stables. There was a sense of heightened emotion as the day neared its end. Tears were flowing down the cheeks of many.

For my painting of the 'Obby 'Oss of Padstow, I chose to depict the Blue Ribbon 'Oss as the most recent of the figures and the most representative of the creativity and ever-evolving nature of these traditions, which are kept alive from generation to generation and keep on changing to remain relevant and authentic in each era. I was also inspired by a story about the 'Oss's mask in Donald R. Rawe's pamphlet *Padstow's 'Obby 'Oss and May Day Festivities*. This, according to one local legend, had been introduced by Octavius Branton, a sailor who'd seen the Duk-Duk dancers of Papua New Guinea and, perhaps noticing a resemblance with his own tradition, had taken the mask back to Padstow and added it to the costume. The initials O.B. can be seen on the mask to this day, possibly copied from the original mask marked by Octavius Branton and reproduced in subsequent versions.

I love the idea of the 'Oss being a kind of hybrid mongrel creature that is local to Padstow but also connected to Papua New Guinea; for me this reflects the mongrel nation that Britain is and has always been through thousands of years of movement of people across the globe, coming, going, trading and settling on these isles. This idea is symbolized by the Duk-Duk dancer in the painting. I wanted to emphasize the universality of community rituals, which are practised around the world and are a manifestation of our shared humanity and individual creativity. I also painted the legend of the French ship and Aunt Ursula, which was the 'Oss tale that I came across most often in Padstow.

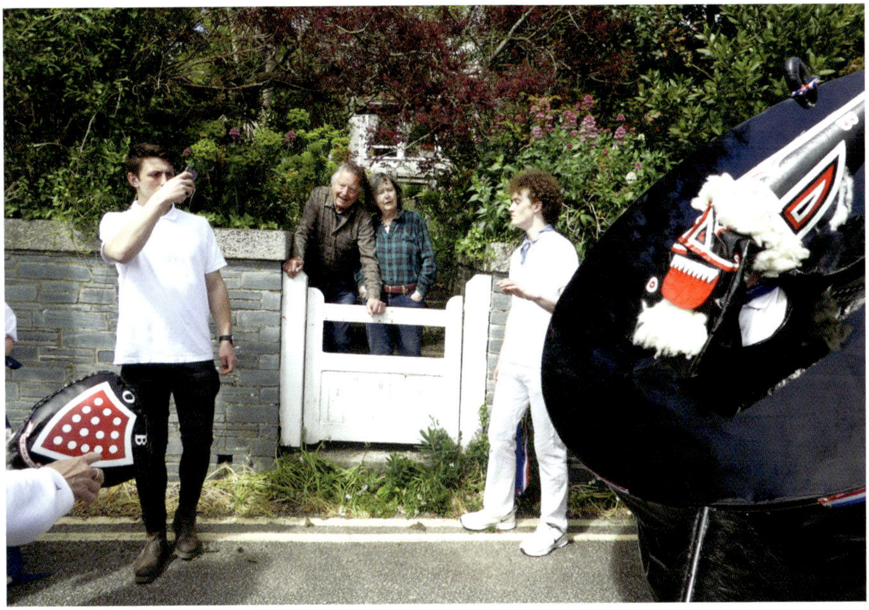

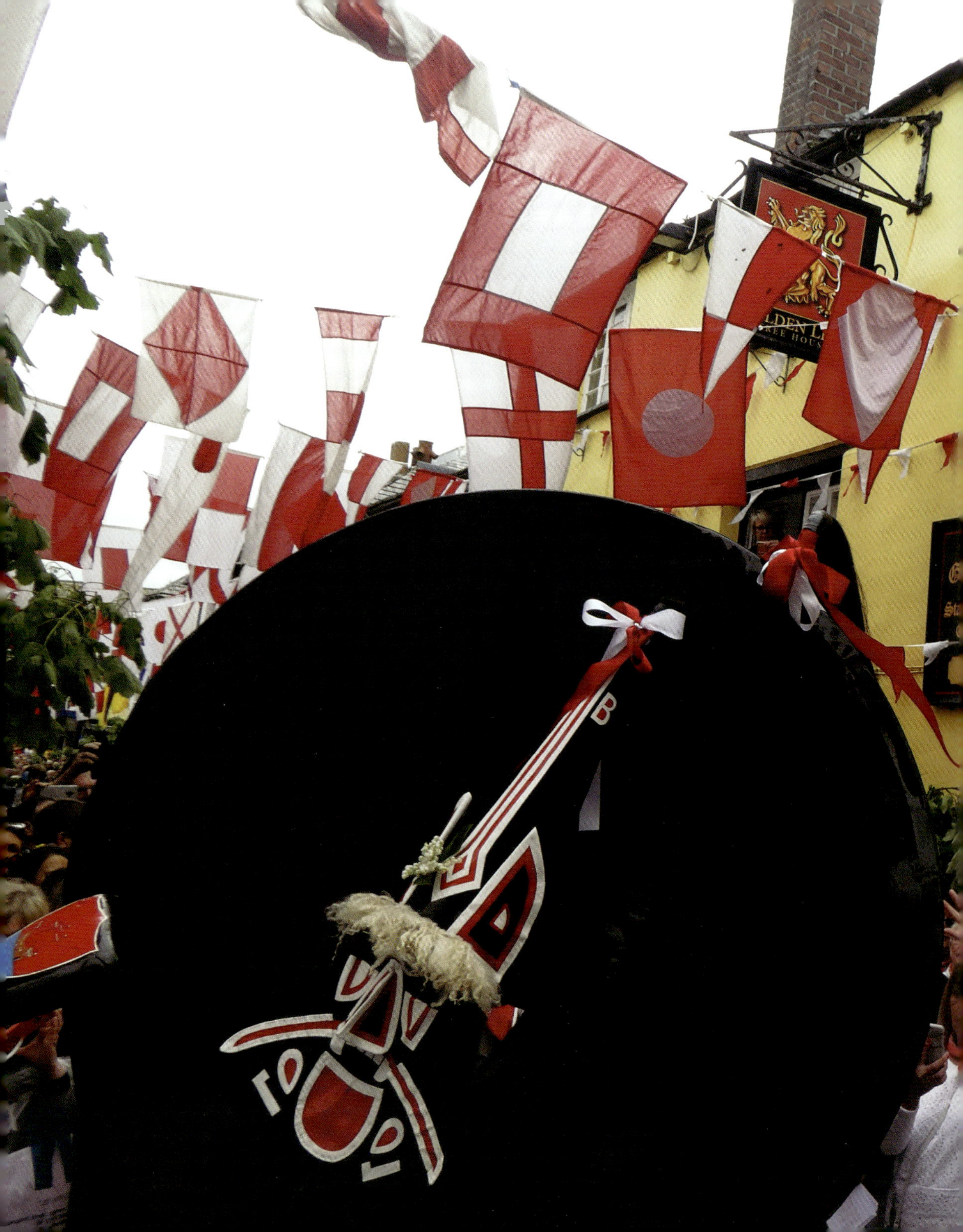

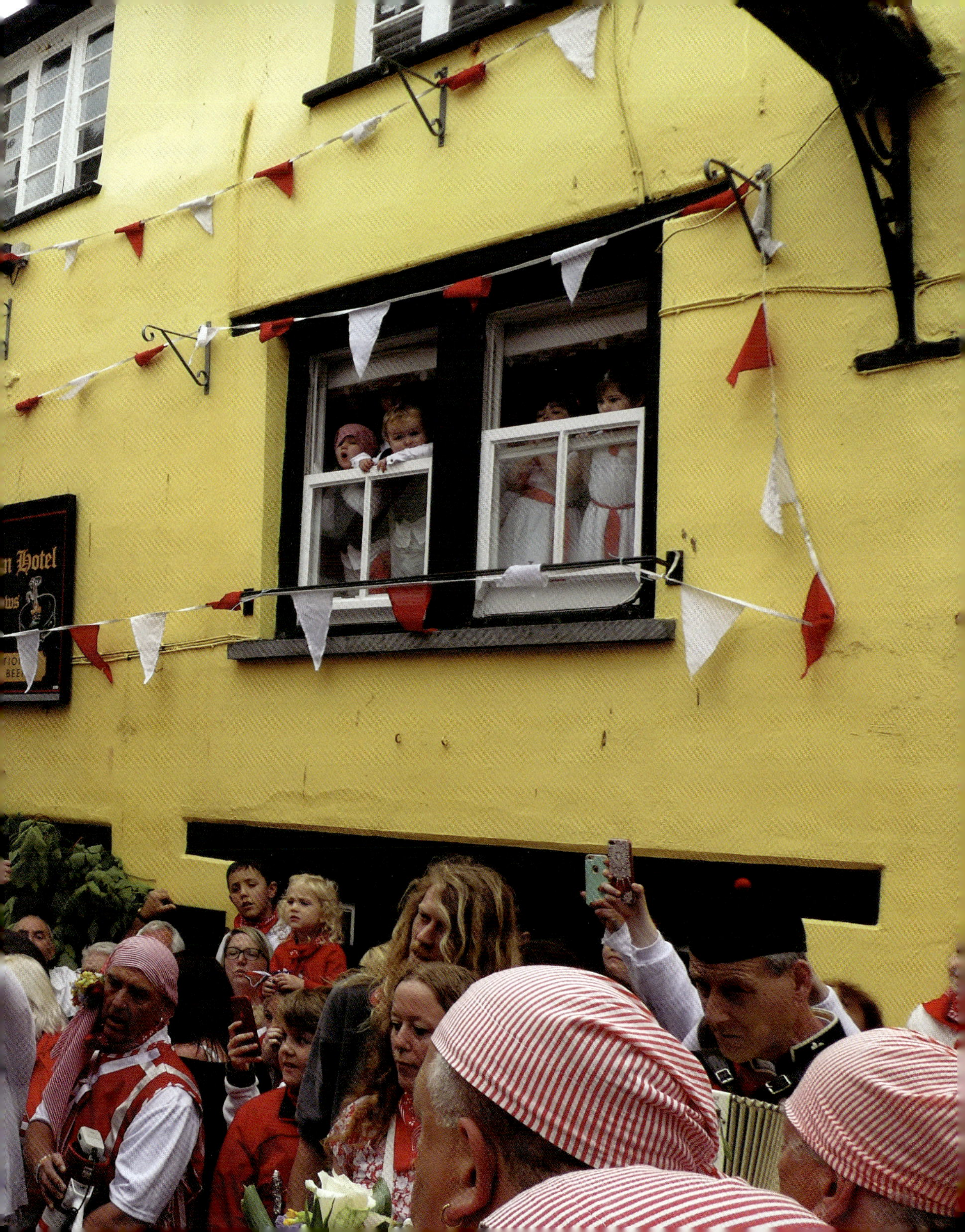
n Hotel

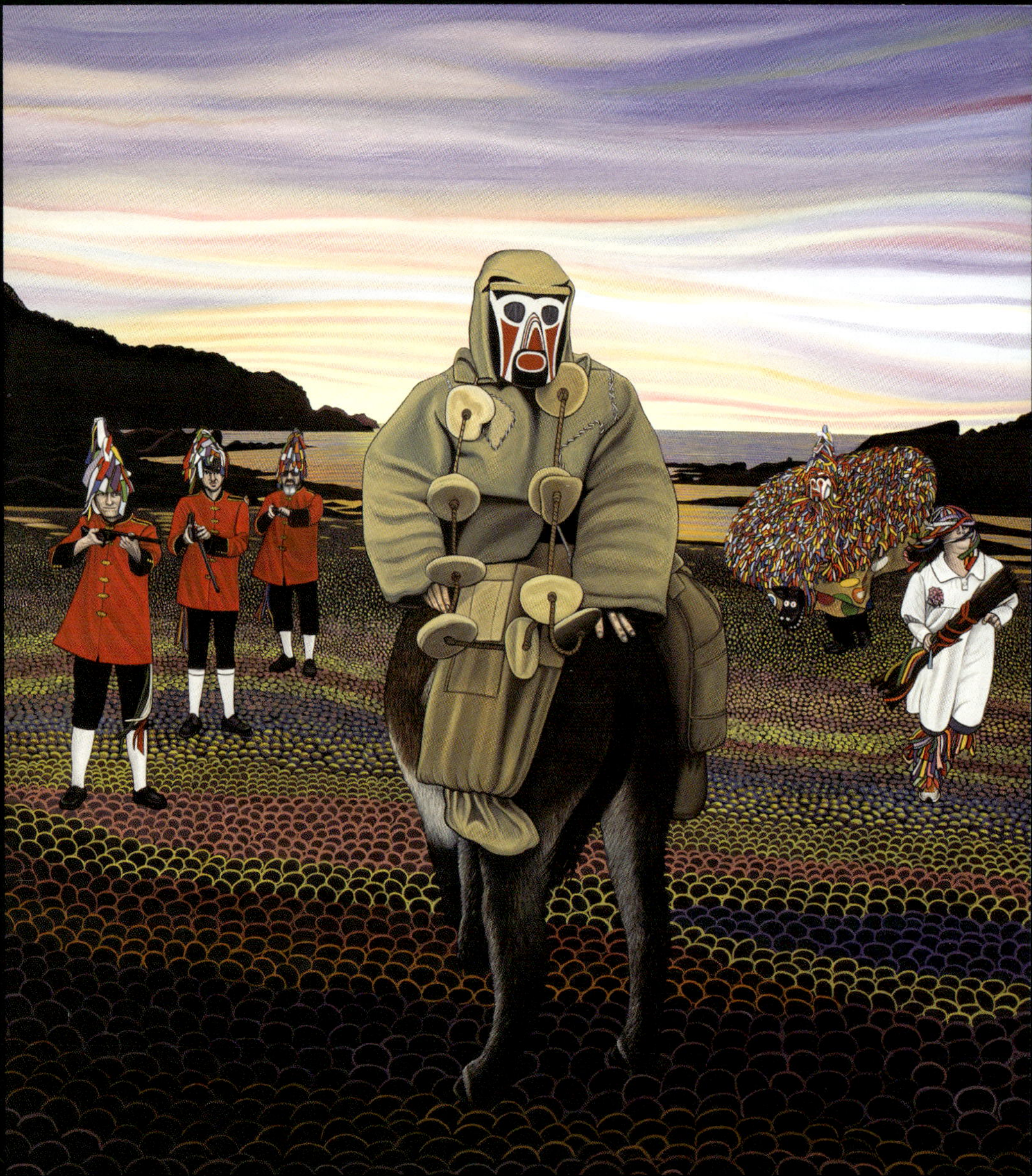

HUNTING THE EARL OF RONE

Oil on Canvas, 100cm × 90cm

2020

Hunting the Earl of Rone

DEVON

SPRING BANK HOLIDAY WEEKEND

It was late May and the rain was hammering down in north Devon. When I checked into my B&B in the village of Combe Martin, the owner informed me that the best place to go would be the Castle Inn pub, the "stable" of the hobby horse, where the pre-celebrations would be taking place before the procession the next day. I'd already discovered, albeit by accident, that finding the pub at the heart of a local custom is a good idea, as not only do you get to meet the people involved beforehand, but you have the opportunity to join in properly with the festivities – rather than just turning up on the day with your camera flashing, which doesn't always go down well.

As soon as I arrived at the pub, I could hear the sound of drums and accordions. I wandered through, slightly timidly, to a packed back room, filled with music, clinking glasses, roaring laughter and singing. There were some spectacular paintings on the walls and I was particularly taken with one of the Earl of Rone being executed and falling from his donkey. The fine paintings and the room had a slightly intimating atmosphere; this community seemed to be very close-knit – would they even want me here?

A kind-faced gentleman clutching an accordion seemed interested in what I was up to. We got chatting and he explained that he and his family had been coming to the event for about forty years and while they were not from Combe Martin but in fact from

Southend-on-Sea, in Essex, today they played a large part at the heart of the festival. All the same, not everyone seemed happy about my presence – and to my surprise I recognized the man from Padstow who'd shunted me out of the way of the 'Oss – but I soon got caught up in the excitement. The evening went on into the early hours, with an enormous cake and lots of pink gin being consumed, and incredible acapella songs sung with lyrics like "We need the Old 'Oss to catch the Earl of Rone and throw him in the sea ..."

The following afternoon, it was time for the procession in which the hobby horse is paraded through the village, starting at the holiday park on top of the hill. Still hungover from the night before, and now accompanied by my film-maker friend Angelica Jopson, I approached the clubhouse in the pouring rain, where I noticed the mask of the hobby horse propped on a metal chair, with its large cylindrical body (similar to the Padstow 'Oss) leaning against a wall under the eaves. Until then I'd only ever seen it in photographs and I was immediately struck by the otherworldly feeling the costume gave me.

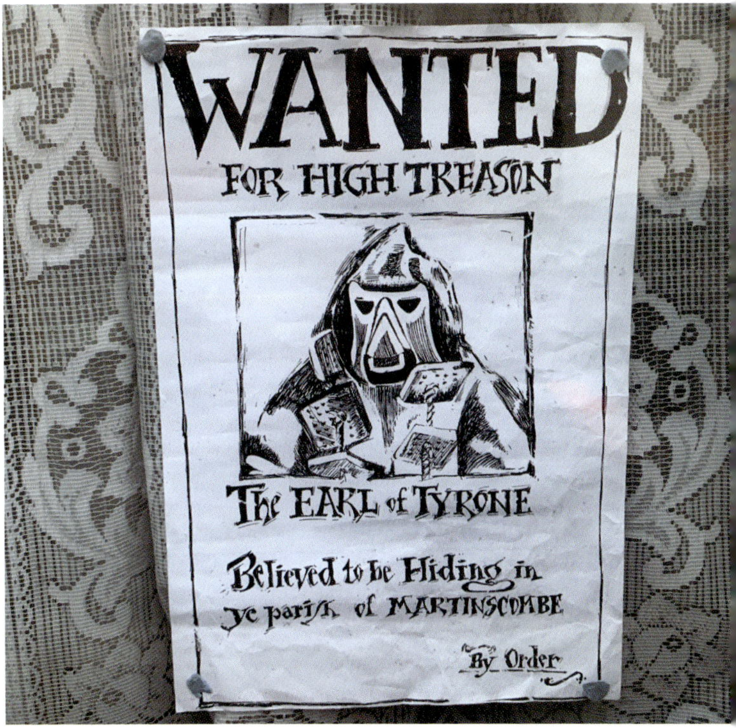

The multicoloured tassels of fabric had been lovingly and individually sewn on by hand, while the face of the mask itself appeared shamanic and ancient with its bold coloured lines. The sense that we are no longer connected to the land and the practices of our ancestors was immediately shattered when I looked at this remarkable costume. It really does give you a sense that not much has changed and reframes and re-enchants your own appreciation of British culture.

When we headed inside the clubhouse, the drinks were already flowing, as were the songs. I was welcomed warmly and some laughs were had about last night. However, there were still a couple of people, including the man who'd shunted me out of the way in Padstow and his

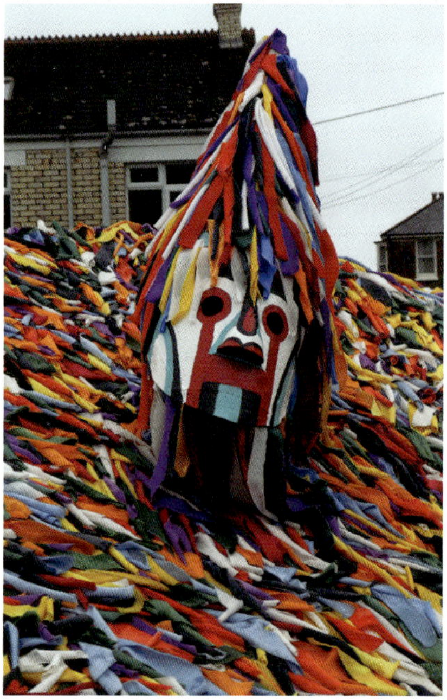

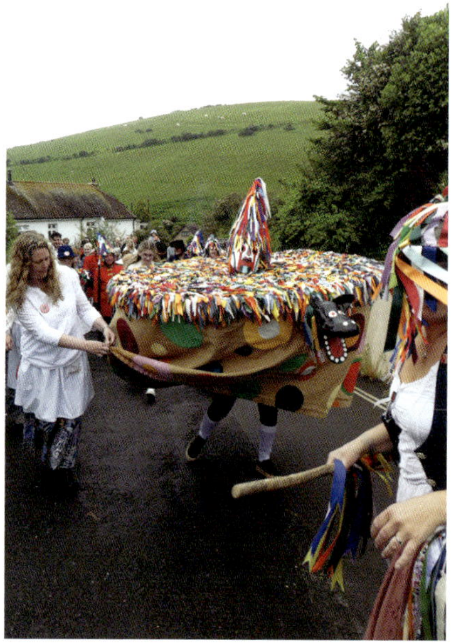

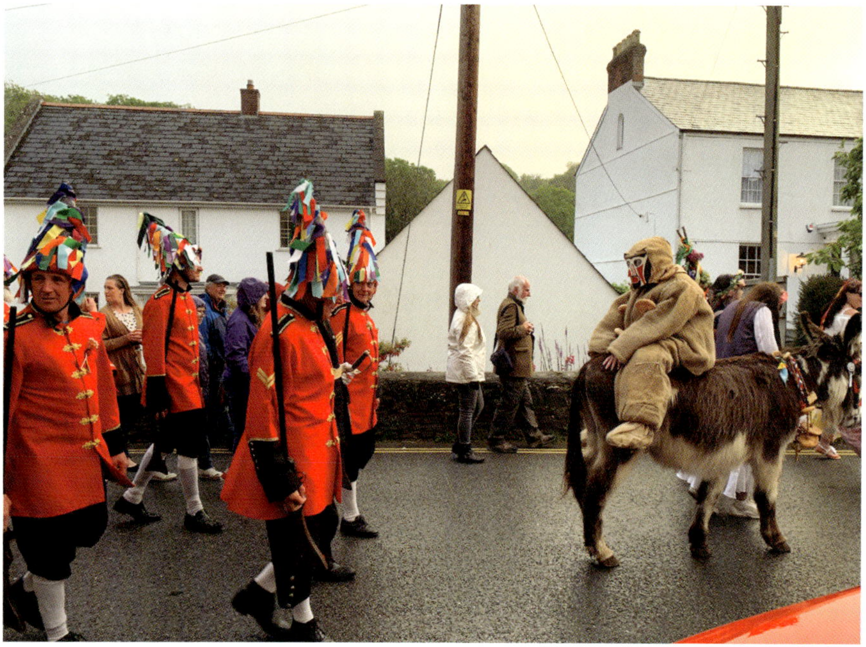

companion, from whom I could still feel a less welcoming energy, which made me slightly anxious while also adding to the sense of adventure and excitement. The couple eventually summoned me over. "Why are you here?" they wanted to know. I explained I'm an artist interested in local stories, to which they replied that the stories just happen and don't need to be analysed. The interrogation went on until thankfully a younger woman intervened and said to leave me alone, "You're terrifying him!"

While it can be intimidating when locals don't take to you being there, I get it: every year outsiders with artistic projects impose their own agendas on to what is sacred to those people who keep the traditions alive. Later that day, Angelica and I spoke more with the couple, who lightened up on discovering that she has family connections to Cornwall. Common ground was found and since then the couple have been very supportive of my work, so you could say I passed the authenticity test.

Now, the rain kept falling as the procession began to wind down the hill, with drummers leading the way, playing the Earl of Rone tune, while a "fool" with a veil of tassels over her face and broomstick in hand, giving her a witchy vibe, danced and kept the hobby horse moving. A group of women in white danced from side to side, almost skipping. Behind them followed grenadiers in red coats and armed with guns that fired blanks. It was a sinister yet magical sight; if you knew nothing about the custom and happened to be passing through, you might think you've stumbled into a real-life folk horror film and best to get the hell out of there, quickly! However, the more you stick around, the more the hypnotic nature of the procession takes you over.

The master of ceremonies was dressed in a top hat and waistcoat. When I spoke to him later, he described how his relationship with the tradition had changed over the years, telling me, "I was probably about two when I first got dragged around by my mum in the pram; I was scared of the 'Oss to start with, and then all I wanted to do was carry the 'Oss, and dance her in – and I've got the privilege now of putting her to bed every year, which I've done for the past thirty years."

The procession continued to various sites during the day, including the local football ground, where I met two Germans who'd stumbled on the custom while holidaying and who'd returned every year since. They insisted upon giving both myself and Angelica a shot of strong liquor.

I also met someone who I presumed to be one of the festival organizers, who told me, "The Earl of Rone was banned in 1837 for excessive drunkenness and licentiousness, and revived in 1970, so we've got a lot of drunkenness and licentiousness to make up on. On Friday night, we go out with just the drums, to hunt the Earl – never find him, for some strange reason, but we do have to visit every pub. And then Saturday is kids' day, which is a complete recreation of the whole thing. Sunday is fun day, which is where we hunt every single corner of the village. Monday, it's the real business: we find him, take him down to the sea sat on the back of a donkey, shoot him lots of times, throw him in."

I asked who the Earl of Rone is and learned, "The Earl of Rone is a character based supposedly on the Earl of Tyrone, who was going to be the next king of Ireland – when there was the Flight of the Earls, who turned up in France and Spain. But there is a month missing in his life history and local historians think that's when he was cast ashore, because there was a shipwreck in Rapperee Cove; he survived on ship's biscuits, which is why you see biscuits hung around the donkey's neck, and that's where it started. But then, like any proper living tradition, it's evolved and it's now Combe Martin celebrating being Combe Martin."

Before moving on to the next stop I also spoke to Mark Norman, writer, folklorist and founder of the Folklore podcast. Mark takes part in the procession and told me, "The festival has got a lot of different components to it. The idea of the Earl being captured, as the ceremony portrays it, ritually shot and revived before finally being thrown into the sea – that element draws from a lot of traditional folklore.

"The ceremony in its original form used to take place around Ascension Day, so you're looking at the coming of spring: this idea of the hobby horse and fool character, resurrecting if you like, ties in with those rites of spring and the coming of the seasons. And again, at the end of the ceremony, where the effigy of the Earl is thrown into the sea, that reflects the sacrificial element and the want for spring."

This made sense to me as a spectator; the themes of death and resurrection seem to be present in all religions and ritual practices, and deeply engrained within the human psyche.

The final day of the custom begins with the grenadiers hunting the Earl in the woods, where you can hear the snapping of branches beneath the feet of the search party from afar, before he is eventually discovered, captured and brought forth to an awaiting crowd. The Earl was a short figure and I was told that he is usually played by a child. His costume is made of sackcloth with stuffing inside, while his mask is reminiscent of the one worn by the hobby horse, with similar strong lines, and round his neck hang ship's biscuits on string, as they do from the donkey. Again, the spectacle has a slightly sinister, almost nightmarish quality and a surrealness that strangely makes total sense and feels quite normal here in Combe Martin.

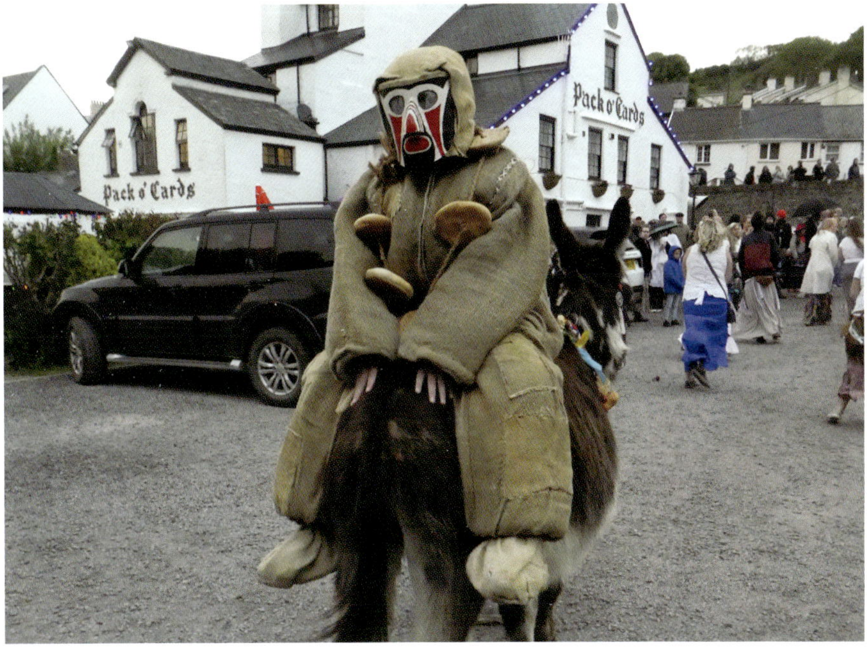
Pack o' Cards
Pack o' Cards

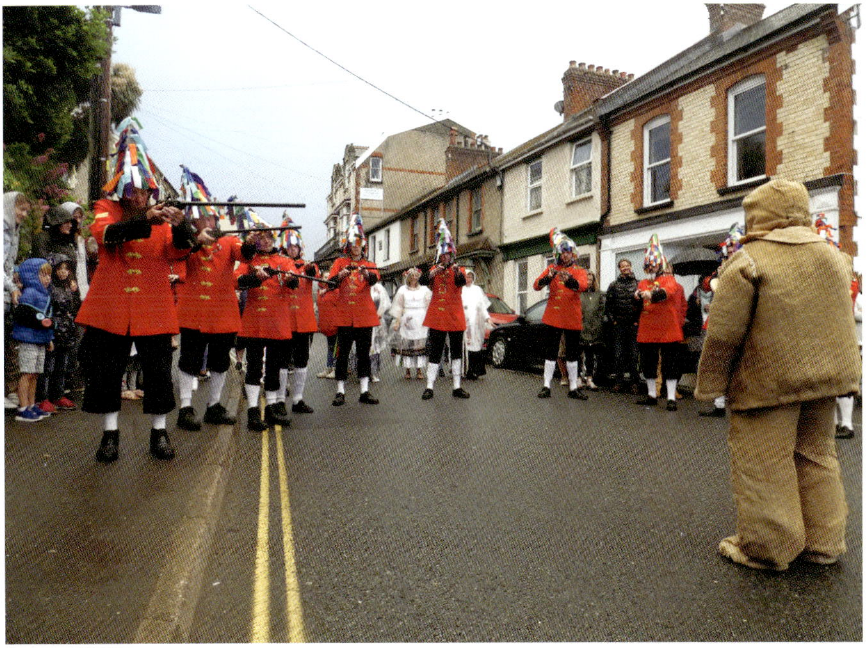

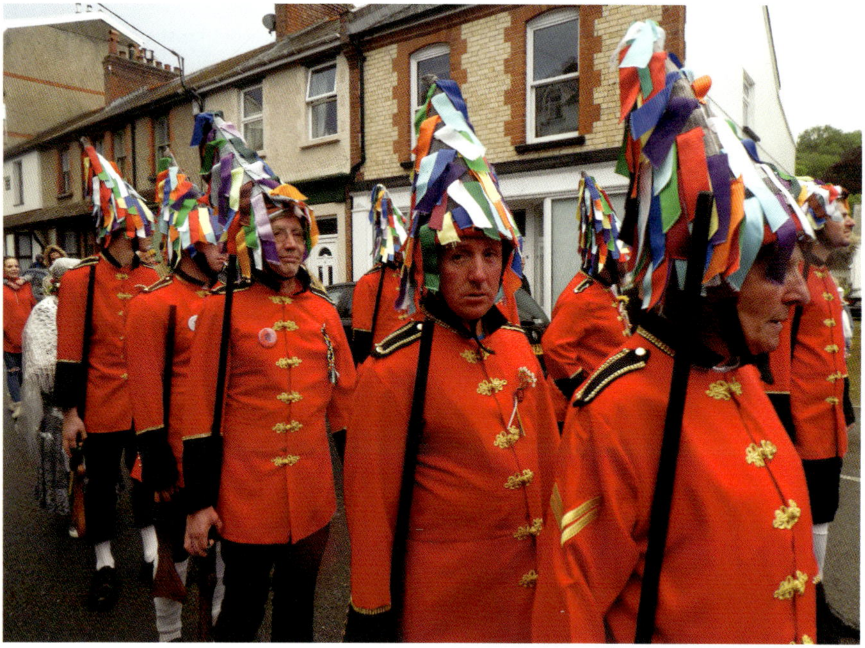

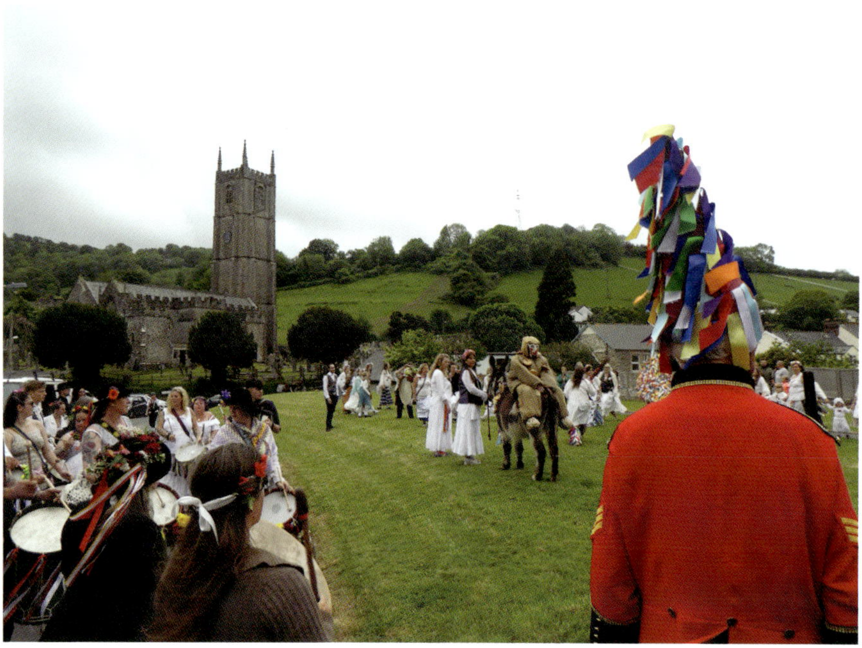

The awaiting crowd then boos and mocks the Earl. Next, he is shot by the grenadiers and shortly afterwards brought back to life by the hobby horse and fool. The Earl is then placed back to front on a donkey and paraded through the village. This ritualistic execution and revival of the Earl happens repeatedly throughout the day, before the procession eventually ends up on the seafront, Rapperee Cove, where the grand finale takes place and the legend of the Earl of Rone is said to have originated.

Watching the crowds during the procession and seeing what the festival means to them was incredibly moving and life-affirming. The idea of the rhythm of life came to the fore as we stopped at the houses of people who had died and who were once at the heart of the celebrations, where everyone removed their hats as a mark of respect; while mothers looked on proudly as their children took part in the ceremony perhaps for the first time. You could feel the connection of past, present and future and the community-binding nature of the folk custom.

This became even more apparent when the whole community gathered at the end and formed a huge circle on the beach, where everybody danced in unison, drums were banged and the hypnotic Earl of Rone tune haunted the atmosphere, as the hobby horse danced even more ferociously on sand illuminated by the setting sun. It was something I never dreamed I'd be witnessing on the shores of north Devon.

Unlike other May-time customs that I've seen, this one didn't end with a feeling of hope and renewal: after his final "execution", the living Earl was (thankfully) replaced by an effigy, which was marched off and thrown into the sea, as a group of ecstatic children ran after him and pelted him with stones. It was like witnessing an angry mob when they pulled him from the water, de-masked him and stamped on him. A grenadier spotted what was happening and returned him to the water, so the drowned figure could drift out to sea.

Watching this humorous yet harrowing scene, and considering it from the perspective of death and rebirth in nature and the wheel of the year, it felt to me like a warning: a reminder that we are taking too much from the land, and that the natural resources which we rely upon seasonally will run out unless we correct the error of our ways. As the sun sank lower and the psychedelic colours intensified, illuminating the wet pebbles on the shoreline, I felt as though I was locked within an Edvard Munch painting like *The Scream* – as if the Earl represented a scream in nature; and these images and feelings became the initial inspiration for my own representation of the tradition of Hunting the Earl of Rone.

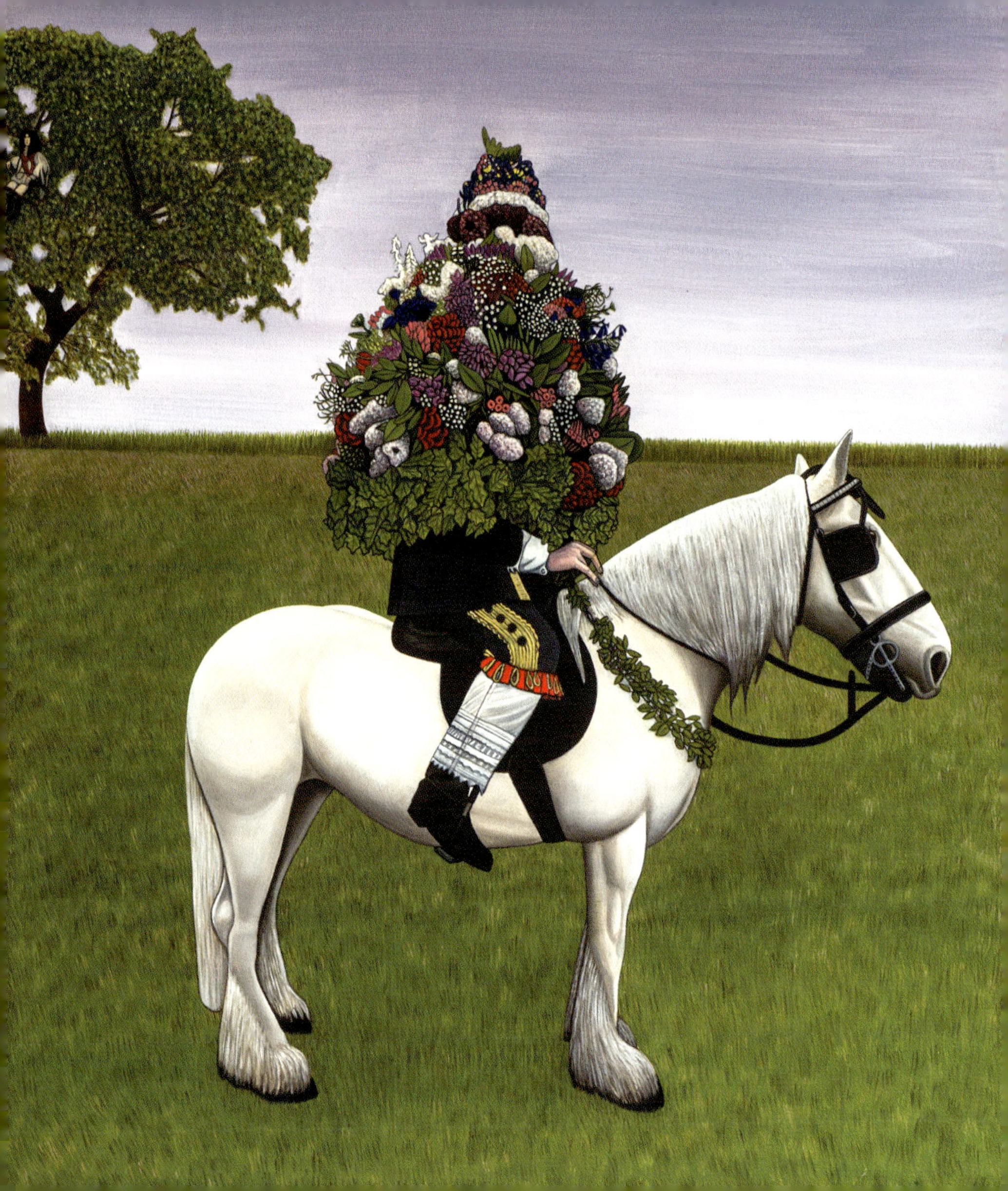

THE GARLAND KING

Oil on Canvas, 75cm × 65cm

2017

Castleton Garland Day

DERBYSHIRE

MAY 29 (UNLESS A SUNDAY, WHEN IT TAKES PLACE ON THE SATURDAY OR MONDAY)

One tradition that quickly captured my visual imagination is that of the dream-like, hybrid half-man, half-flower being who is dressed in Stuart attire and rides on horseback along the pale, stone streets of the village of Castleton in Derbyshire. As soon as I saw images of this festival, I knew I had to paint it.

After catching a train via Sheffield to the Hope Valley, surrounded by the hills of the Peak District, whose silhouettes sat fuzzily within rolling fog and drizzling rain, I made my way past fields of sheep, charming villages and old phone boxes now containing defibrillators instead of telephones, before eventually arriving in Castleton. Here, I spotted a man in the distance, wearing a rain mac and a leather-brimmed hat covered with leaves, and handing out sprigs of oak. Without pausing to find out more, I carried on to my B&B, Ye Old Cheshire Cheese, an old pub with wooden beams and a medieval feel, much like the rest of the village.

There was already a growing buzz as I headed to the old garage where the creation of the Garland was taking place. Upon entering, I came across two groups of locals, one of men and the other of women, who were making sections of the Garland. The women were working on a small posy known as the "Queen", which is added as a topknot at the end. One of them told me that she had been involved in the ceremony pretty much all her life.

"Well," she explained, "I actually started about forty-five years ago, as a dancing girl, but I've been doing this about fifteen, twenty years."

On the other side of the garage, the men were decorating the main body of the Garland, built from a bell-shaped metal frame suspended from the ceiling by rope, which was being covered with vegetation and flowers collected from village gardens. While the group carefully considered the colours of each flower as they attached it to the metal frame, I asked them what the origins of the tradition were.

One of the men, who'd helped to make the Garland for forty-nine years, informed me, "It's supposed to have been a celebration of Oak Apple Day, when King Charles II hid in an oak tree." He was referring to what was once a nationwide holiday, held to commemorate the restoration of the Stuart monarchy. The oak apple was a symbolic reference to when Charles II hid in an oak tree to avoid capture by Cromwell's Roundhead rebel army. Following the beheading of his father, King Charles I, the monarchy had fallen and Britain became a republic between 1649 and 1660, before Charles II regained the throne.

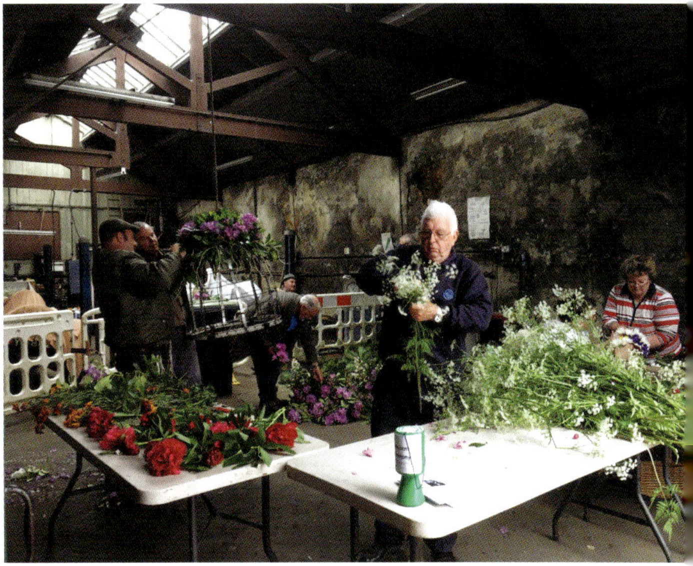

Heading into the streets, I caught up with the man I had seen earlier, giving out sprigs of oak, and learned that anyone found not to be wearing a sprig of oak in honour of the King could be egged, pinched or whipped with stinging nettles. While I didn't see that being practised today, the wearing of the oak was still very much alive.

The man handing out sprigs told me his belief that, "The Garland festival has been going on for thousands of years, pre-Christianity. It's a Pagan event, but when Christianity came in, they had to blend Paganism with Christianity. Then you have the Oak Apple side of things, when Charles II hid in the oak tree, so it's all the same day – Garland festival, Green Man, Christianity."

Another local joined in the conversation as he was receiving his sprig of oak and further enlightened me: "During the period where Britain became a commonwealth under

Cromwell, all the much-loved May Day festivals were banned because they were thought of as Pagan, so here in Castleton, when the monarchy was reinstated we could celebrate it again: we merged it with the new Oak Apple festival and celebrated everything at once." This theory could certainly explain the strange hybridity of the festival that you see today.

The festival starts when the Garland King, dressed in full Stuart costume, rides the village boundaries on horseback while accompanied by his "consort" or "lady", also in traditional Stuart dress. Although the Garland King's consort is today enacted by a woman, the role was traditionally played by men in drag up until the late 1950s. Once the bounds have been ridden, the King arrives at the garage to be dressed in the completed Garland, which is lowered over his head and shoulders, leaving only the lower half of his body visible.

Now the procession begins. Behind the Garland King and his consort, a brass band, followed by dancing girls, make their way through the village. Formed from local schoolgirls dressed all in white, the dancing girls do the "Garland Step" and hold what is known as a Garland stick, representing a miniature maypole. The procession stops at various pubs, where trays of beer are brought out to refresh the villagers.

I got as close as I could to take pictures, but tiny droplets of rain keep finding their way into my camera, making the pictures blurred, so I put away my camera and hoped the rain would ease up. There's something about the raindrops in the Peak District, which seemed to find their way into absolutely everything, including my bag and pockets, soaking my trousers through.

I spoke to a man in a high-vis yellow jacket and large-brimmed hat, who seemed to be leading the festival and keeping the timings running smoothly, and asked him his thoughts on the festival's origins. He told me, "Nobody knows – each year we have to adapt a little bit and change it slightly; we just missed a dance out on the corner because it's so wet tonight, so we don't know", highlighting that this is still very much a living tradition and how all the later changes add up over the years.

Despite the weather, the Garland King continued to lead the procession as it headed out of the village before turning back, while people emerged from their houses or appeared at windows to get a glimpse of the passing spectacle. I watched the dancing girls perform the "Garland Step" to the accompaniment of a catchy marching tune, in the knowledge that some of these young girls would one day be making the Garland themselves, and their grandchildren would be filling their roles.

In the nearby hills are old caverns where the local stone, Blue John, is still mined, where troglodytes once made rope and where the Devil's Arse cavern – so-called because it makes

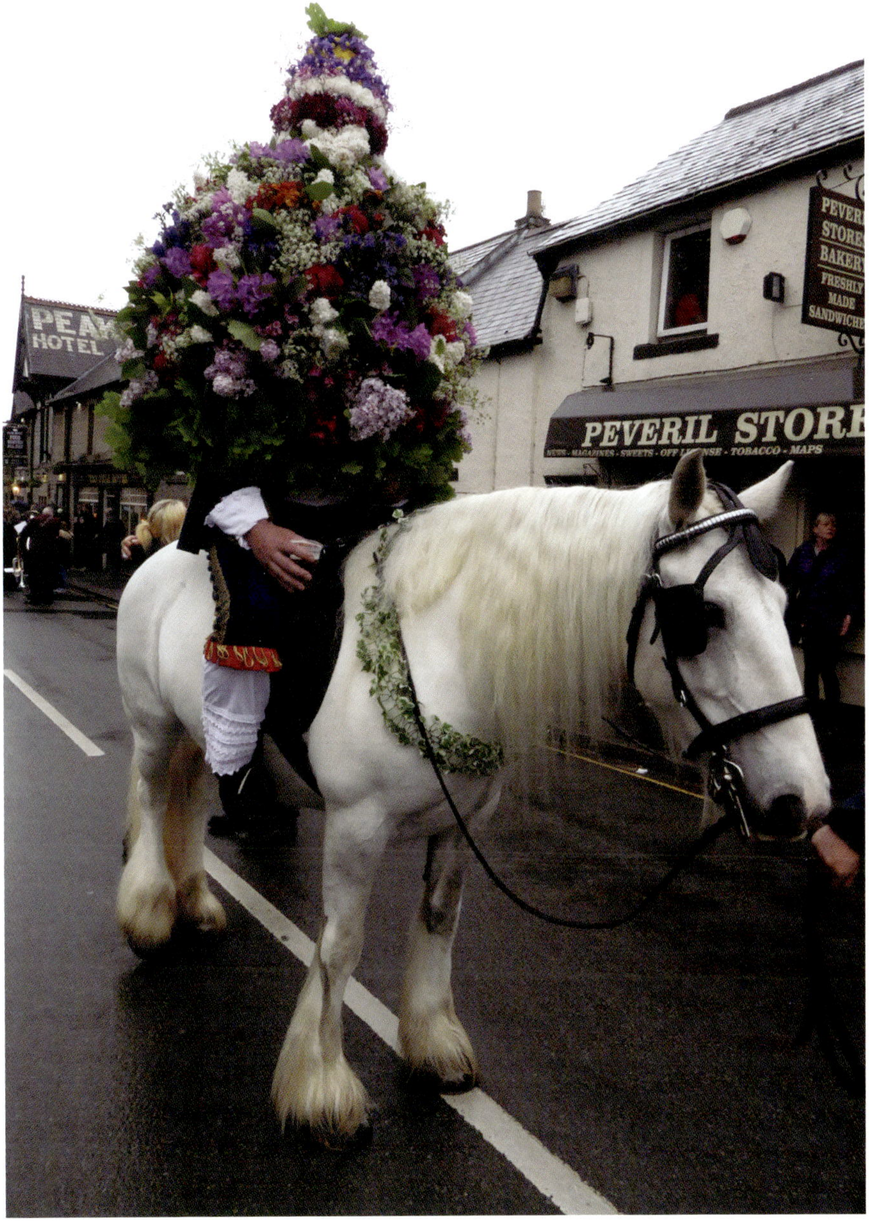
HOTEL
PEVERIL STORE
FRESHLY
MADE

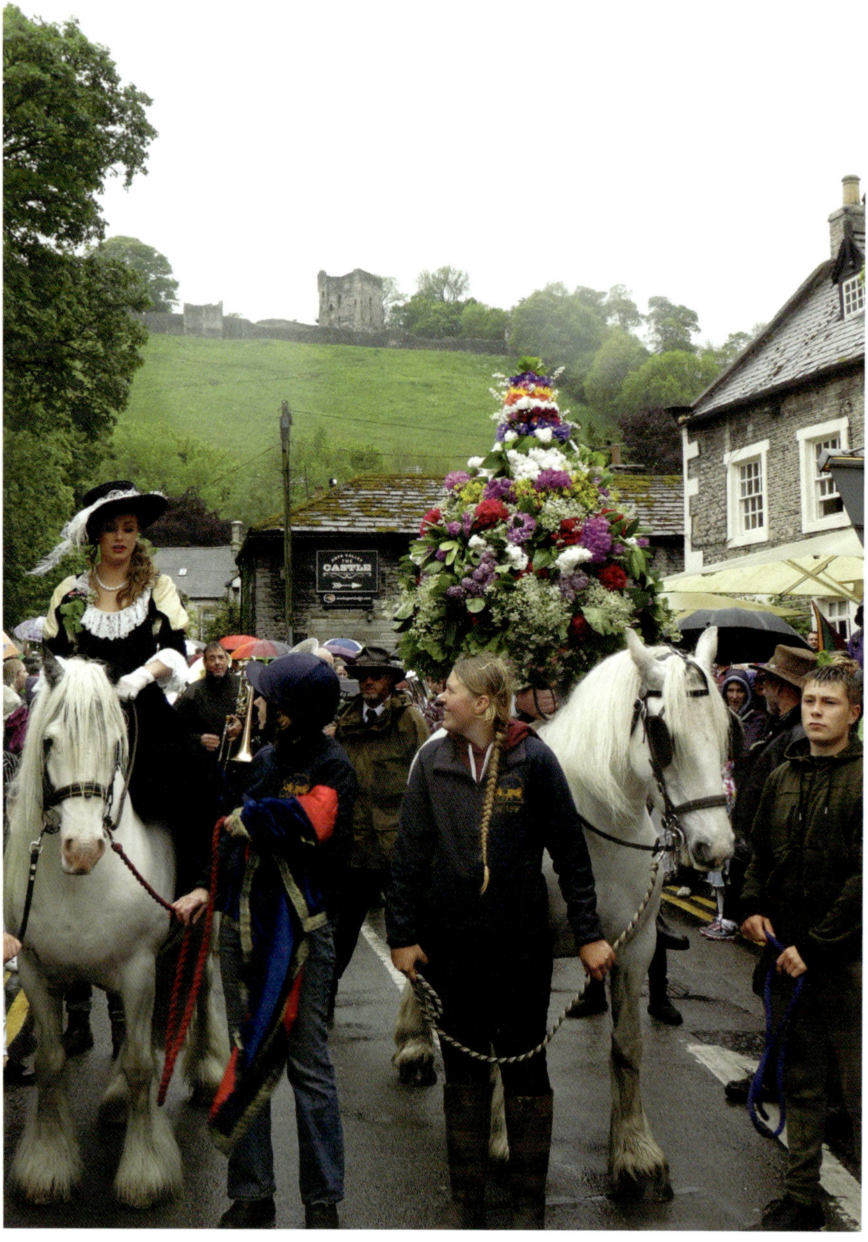
THE
CASTLE

a farting sound on windy occasions – can still be heard erupting during stormy nights. We were getting close now to the final destination, as we passed underneath a steep hill where the ruins of Peveril Castle remain, reminding me of the Norman Conquest, and the sense of the passing of centuries that can be felt throughout both the village and the tradition.

We reached the final pub stop, next to St Edmund's Church – here the Garland was tied to a spindly rope and hoisted to the top of the church tower, where it would replace last year's withered Garland and remain until the following year. This evoked the same feeling of death, rebirth and seasonal renewal that can be felt consistently throughout May customs, leaving me in agreement with the man handing out oak sprigs – that there could be more to all this than just the story about Charles II hiding in an oak tree. Interestingly, in the Peak District and Derbyshire, the tradition of well dressing takes place between May and September, in which intricate works of art are created using natural materials such as moss, leaves and flowers to give thanks to the holy wells. All of which made the beautifully crafted halo of flowers, now perched amidst the peaks and caverns of the Hope Valley, hovering above the damp village, seem very much at home here in this part of the country.

The Garland having reached its final destination, the topknot section, the "Queen", was placed on the war memorial and children danced around the maypole. With ideas of death, rebirth and seasonal renewal still running through my mind, I headed back to my room at Ye Old Cheshire Cheese to change and warm up, as around me people carried on dancing through the streets.

What particularly fascinated me about the Garland King as a symbolic figure is that he can be looked at as both a king disguised as Nature, or as Nature disguised as a king. I couldn't help but view him somewhat romantically as a lost Pagan god from times of Nature worship, who had to take on the role as a resurrected king for a day to ensure his survival. Perhaps he wasn't hiding in the oak after all, but in fact it was within the Stuart costume that he was actually hiding.

When making my painting, I liked the idea of placing the figure within a mysterious yet open natural setting, where against the greenery of grass, the colours of the Garland can be seen springing to life and dominating the foreground of the composition, while Charles II and his oak remain almost hidden within a corner; echoing my thoughts that this is a multifaceted tradition with an evolving symbolism that can only leave us filling in the gaps and unable to ever really know what the true meaning and mystery of the Garland King truly is.

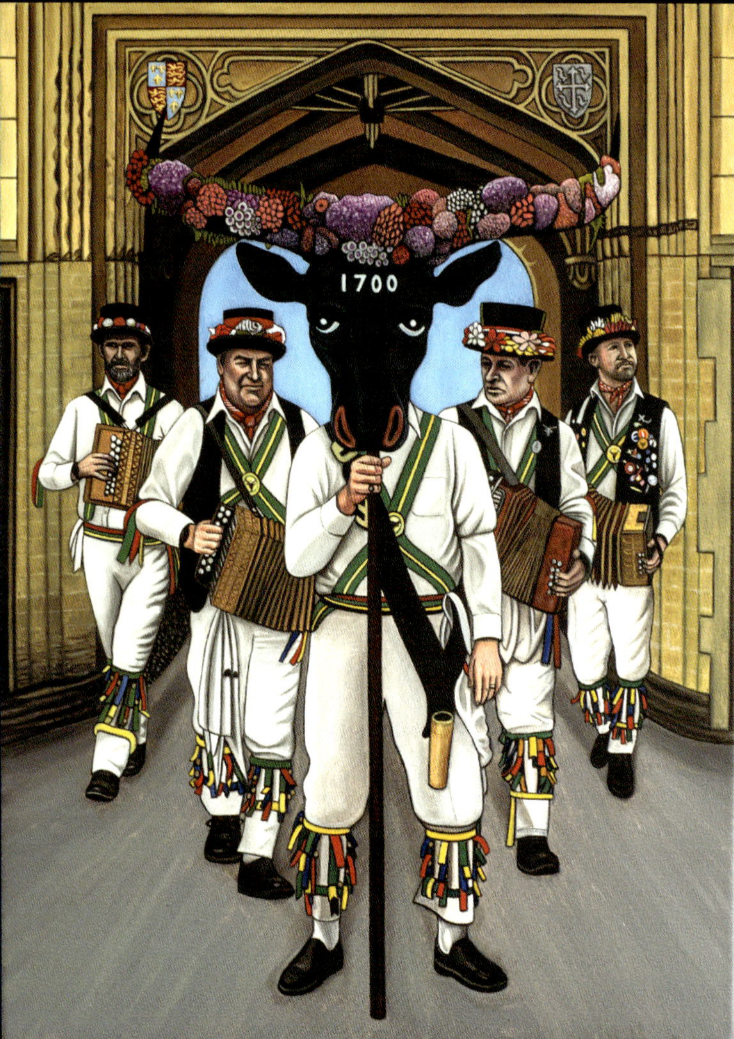

THE HORNS OF OCK STREET

Oil on Canvas, 50cm × 45cm

2017

The Horns of Ock Street

OXFORDSHIRE

SATURDAY CLOSEST TO JUNE 19

Every year in the middle of June, a mock mayor is elected in the town of Abingdon, Oxfordshire and the Horns of Ock Street are paraded by the Abingdon Traditional Morris Dancers. The tradition of electing a mock mayor was once common nationwide as a way of poking fun at the establishment, but now only survives in a handful of places.

I arrived in Abingdon with the beaming sun bleaching my vision and making it hard to see, even with sunglasses on, as I wandered along the High Street. When I found myself on Ock Street, I followed the road to the Brewery Tap pub. Here, a homemade flag depicting the Horns of Ock Street had been raised above a small platform where the identity of the new Mayor of Ock Street would later be revealed. Some of the Abingdon morris men were already gathered, dressed in white with yellow and green sashes, red neckerchiefs and, of course, bells; the brims of their black hats were decorated with bright flowers.

Despite only standing in the sun for a while, I could tell I was going to burn if I wasn't careful and that I'd better find some sun cream quickly. However, I stopped in my tracks when I saw the Horns being brought out and carefully propped against a wall next to the makeshift election platform. They had a remarkable presence; it was as if the painted eyes beneath the Horns were gazing up toward the burning sun, and the charming and slightly haunting, hand-carved face with the date 1700 painted on its forehead gave them an extra preciousness. The Horns themselves were covered with colourful flowers, and the piece as a whole was mounted on a pole, making me feel that I was in the vicinity of an anthropomorphic, shape-shifting, holy object. It was no surprise to find out later that locals touched the Horns throughout the day for good luck.

The man who'd carefully placed them against the wall explained to me, "These are the original horns from the ox that was roasted in 1700; this is the original mask made. We do have a replica set, which was carved for us in 1976 – well, obviously, as these are now 319 years old, they're a little bit precious and we're very protective of them, as you can well imagine." The replicas were made so the original horns never have to leave the town when the Abingdon Traditional Morris Dancers are invited to dance at other events.

When I started taking photos of the Horns, a morris dancer with a youngish, thin face and well-trimmed beard took an interest in what I was doing; it turned out he was the only man in history to have been both the mock mayor and the actual mayor of Abingdon. He also excitedly told me that Doc Rowe would be attending today's event. Doc Rowe has been documenting British folk customs for over fifty years; I had come across his name in books, where I'd seen photos credited to him, and had already looked into his incredible archive on British folk customs, which is finally beginning to be celebrated and honoured as culturally significant. So this was really exciting news to hear.

When David "Doc" Rowe arrived, I was introduced and we immediately got on; he has since become something of a mentor who has introduced me to many people within folk traditions and helped me with my journey through the ritual year of Britain, for which I'm very grateful. On that first meeting at the Brewery Tap, once I had finally managed to get my hands on some sun cream, he and I huddled in the shade of Doc's small umbrella, smothering our sunburned faces with the lotion.

The Horns of Ock Street procession always begins from the Brewery Tap pub, where accordion players and fiddlers, followed by the rest of the morris dancers, walk behind the fool – a man in a dress, carrying a pig's bladder – and a senior member of the group, who carries the Horns in a harness connected to his belt to help him bear their weight. The procession passes redbrick new-builds, fish-and-chip shops and old pubs, before stopping off in the pedestrianized streets of the main shopping area, where they dance while watched by shoppers against the backdrop of a Boots Opticians, a Holland & Barrett health food shop and a Superdrug store, before marching on to more stops and ending up in the town square. It's here that the tradition of the Horns is said to have originated.

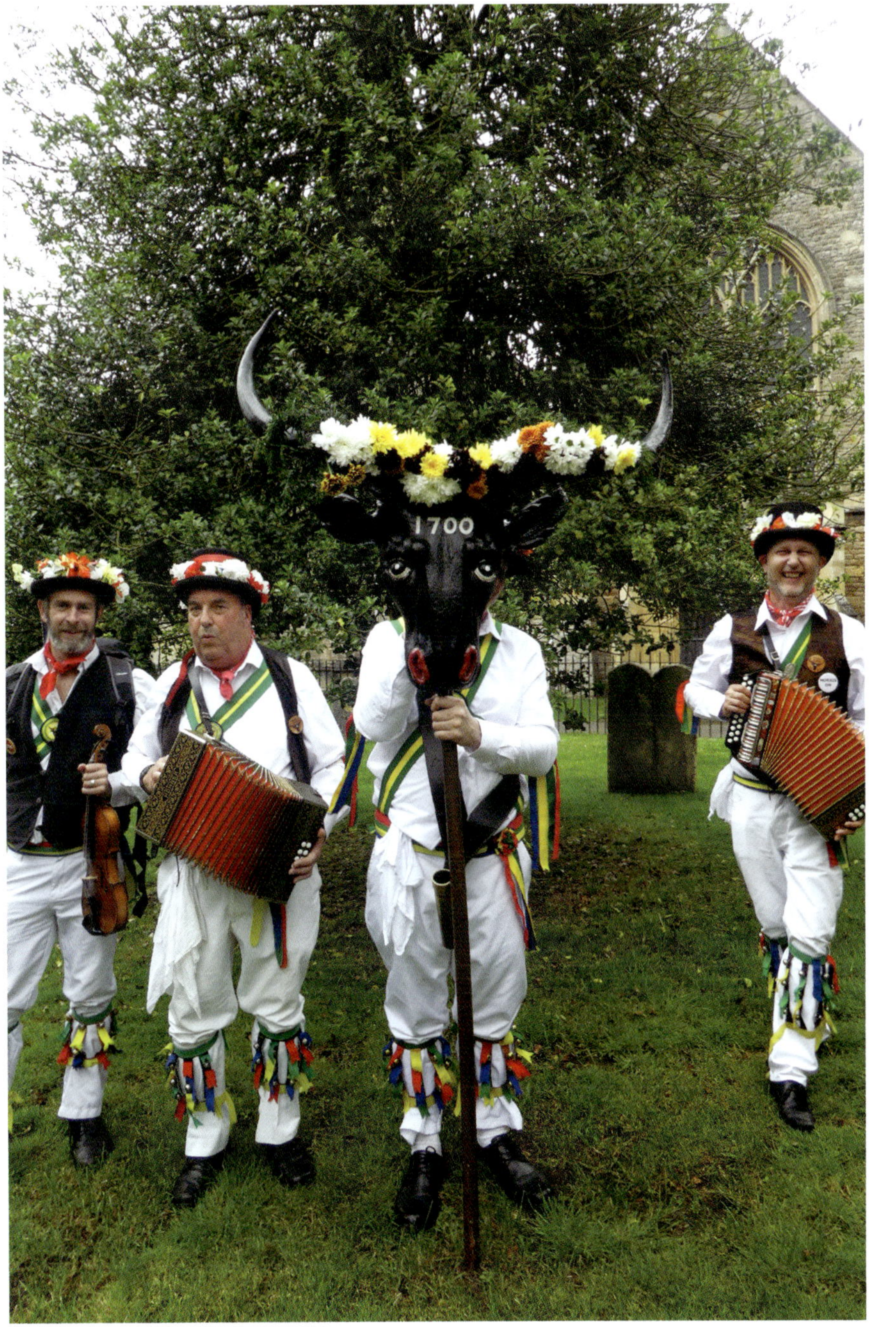
1700

The story that I was told repeatedly by morris dancers and locals alike was always the same: that there used to be a famous horse fair in the town, where traditionally there was an ox roast at which the horns were always presented to the men of the vineyard, which was on the well-to-do side of town. However, in 1700, during a period of civil unrest and resentment at the harsh treatment of the poor, the men of Ock Street rebelled and an enormous fight broke out in the town square, in which they eventually triumphed. To mark this occasion, they have paraded the Horns ever since as an act of working-class defiance, celebration and victory.

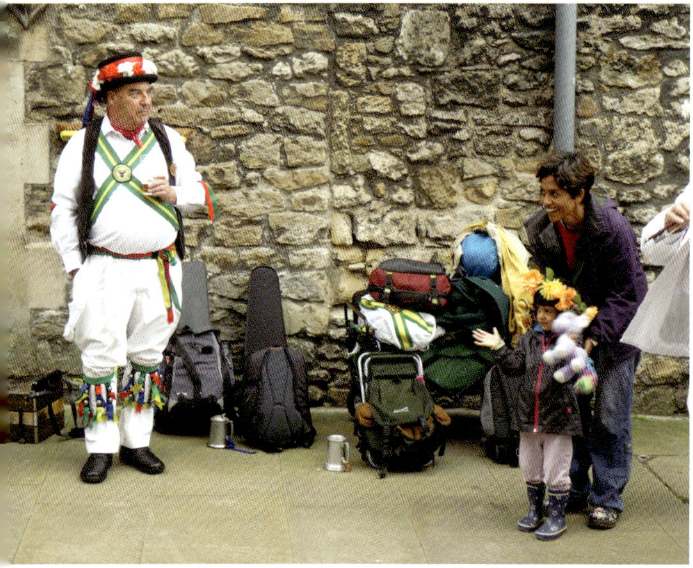

As the day continued, there were various other stop-offs for morris dancing, including at pubs and houses, with one in particular standing out: I was informed that the owners had recently won the lottery and had been supplying drinks for the procession's participants ever since. There was also a stop at an incredible medieval archway attached to a church, where the stone had a golden glow and the grotesques and gargoyles, thought to protect the church from evil spirits, appeared temporarily relieved by the sound of morris bells, also believed to move on evil spirits and thereby redoubling their efforts. One of the fiddle players told me the superstition that it's "bad luck to walk through the arch without holding your breath".

Toward the end of the day, we found ourselves back at the Brewery Tap, where the mayoral election would now take place. I went inside where four serious-looking men were sitting round a table and counting the votes. After I'd gone back out, the announcement came that the new Mayor of Ock Street had been elected. Speeches were given, and a cup, also said to date back to the original fight of 1700, was presented, along with a ceremonial sword. This was followed by a parade in which the newly elected Mayor of Ock Street was seated on a sedan-like chair, made of scaffolding poles covered in flowers, which was hoisted up by the rest of the Abingdon morris dancers and paraded up and down Ock Street.

When planning my composition for my painting, I reflected on what had inspired me the most about the day and without doubt it was the Horns themselves; they are such a beautiful piece of folk art in their own right and represent so many things on so many levels. Among these was the idea of turning the system on its head, like a Lord of Misrule, whereby the people of the lower classes can play king (or mayor in this case) for the day, mock the patriarchy and highlight the absurdity of the political system, showing that just like official elections, it's literally a case of people choosing names with random bits of paper and then handing the winner a ceremonial object that says they're now king or boss.

Combined with the story of the defeat of the well-to-do men in a fight, to me, the Horns really do symbolize working-class defiance and mockery of the establishment. This is why I've positioned them at the heart of the painting, disguising the face of the central figure, who stands holding them like a shaman. This figure is followed by a group of defiant men, passing through the medieval archway, which I included to symbolize my belief that rituals such as these act as a kind of portal whereby, through the wearing of costumes, singing and dancing, and other symbolic behaviours, human beings are able to step into different psychological spaces that can help us deal with the uncertainties and anxieties of everyday life.

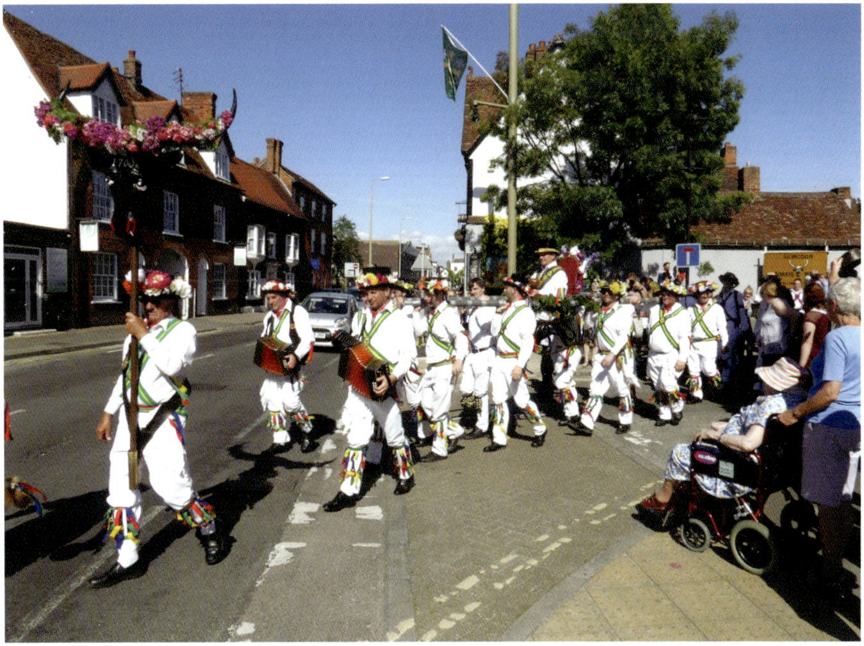

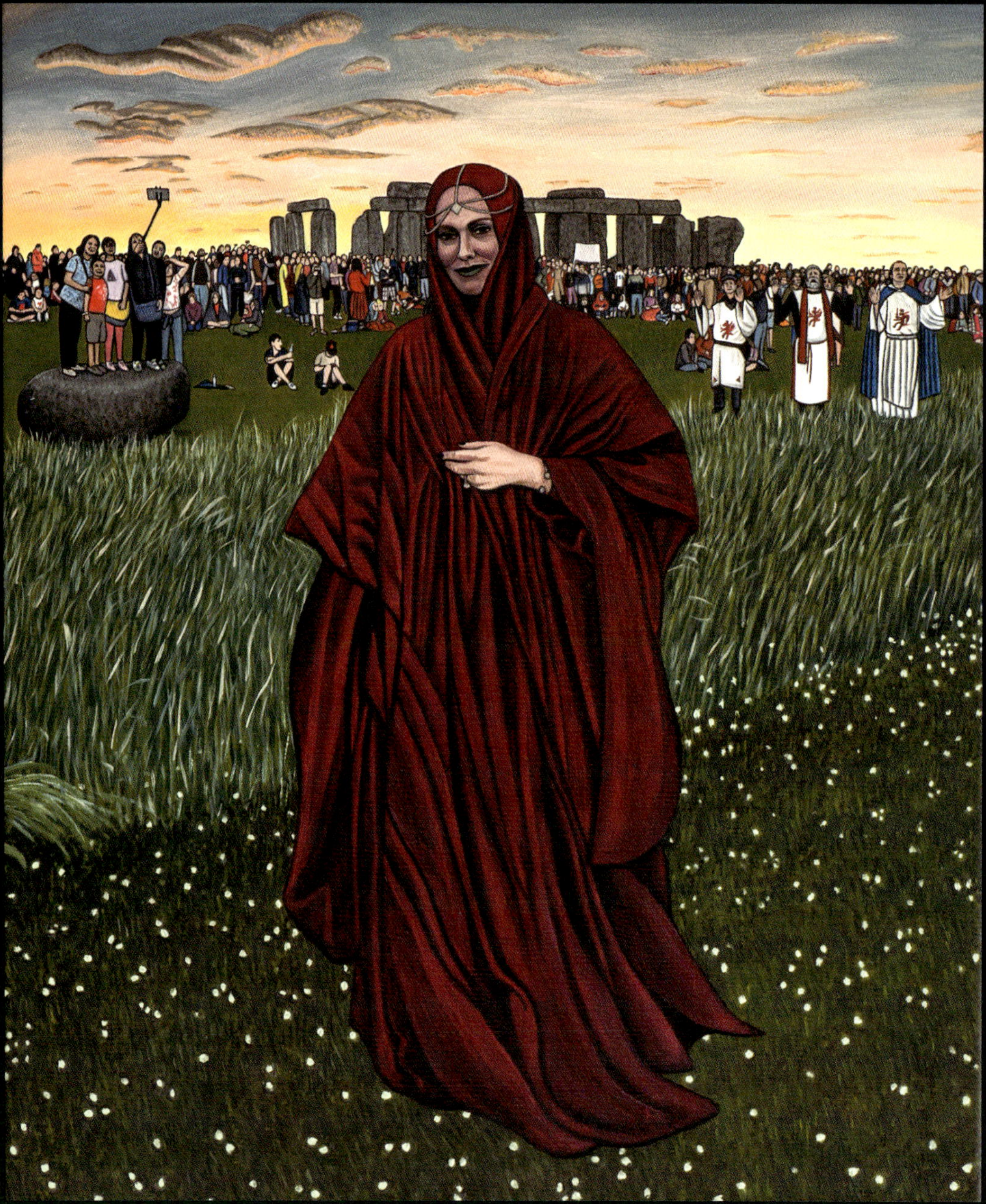

THE SUMMER SOLSTICE

Oil on Canvas, 50cm × 42cm

2018

Summer Solstice, Stonehenge

WILTSHIRE

JUNE 20 OR 21 (NORTHERN HEMISPHERE)

The summer solstice is when the earth's tilt toward the sun reaches its climax, causing the sun to reach its highest point in the sky and giving us maximum sunlight and the longest day of the year. It occurs in late June in the northern hemisphere and people have gathered for millennia to mark and celebrate it, with Stonehenge being one of the most iconic of all locations to do so.

On this occasion, I began my summer solstice eve in Salisbury, Green Man hunting in the cathedral before catching a bus to Stonehenge. As I approached the bus stop, I noticed a figure dressed in a long cloak, with a ceremonial staff and what appeared to be a sword. The mysterious figure was wearing a headband reminiscent of a crown, his eyes had a bright glint and there was a cheeky half-smile buried within his white beard; this was no ordinary summer solstice pilgrim: I recognized Arthur Pendragon – one of the most famous Druids in Britain.

We boarded the bus together and he sat with his sword at hand, gazing out at the Wiltshire landscape as the bus rattled over the well-worn route to the stone circle. After we'd politely chatted for a while, I asked him why he was called Arthur Pendragon. His eyes turned to meet mine and he told me that he was the modern-day King Arthur reincarnated; and that "instead of riding a horse, I ride a motorbike, because that's what Arthur would have done today".

He was a warrior druid, he explained, and had been arrested thirty-eight times for his ongoing campaigning activities, which were currently focused on the building of the Stonehenge tunnel. He was attempting to stop plans to build a tunnel directly beneath the world heritage site, which he described as being "catastrophic" for the future of the monument. He also told me of his ongoing campaign to have the remains of the people buried at Stonehenge "returned to the earth": that if they were Christian bones they'd be respected by law, "but when they're Pagan bones they're kept in little boxes in dusty cabinets in museum corners".

As we approached the Stonehenge complex, the excitement on the bus was building. Two teenagers with a plastic bottle containing what looked to be some kind of homemade vodka-lemonade mix started chatting to Arthur, and once we'd been dropped off in the carpark, I split off on my own. I wandered past motorhomes, the air thick with the aroma of weed and the sound of thudding bongos, while people drank from bottles of alcohol and dipped their fingers into little plastic bags, there being a strict policy of no drink or drugs within the actual enclosure.

When I reached the cursus earthworks, scoured into the earth thousands of years ago and predating the stones themselves, I

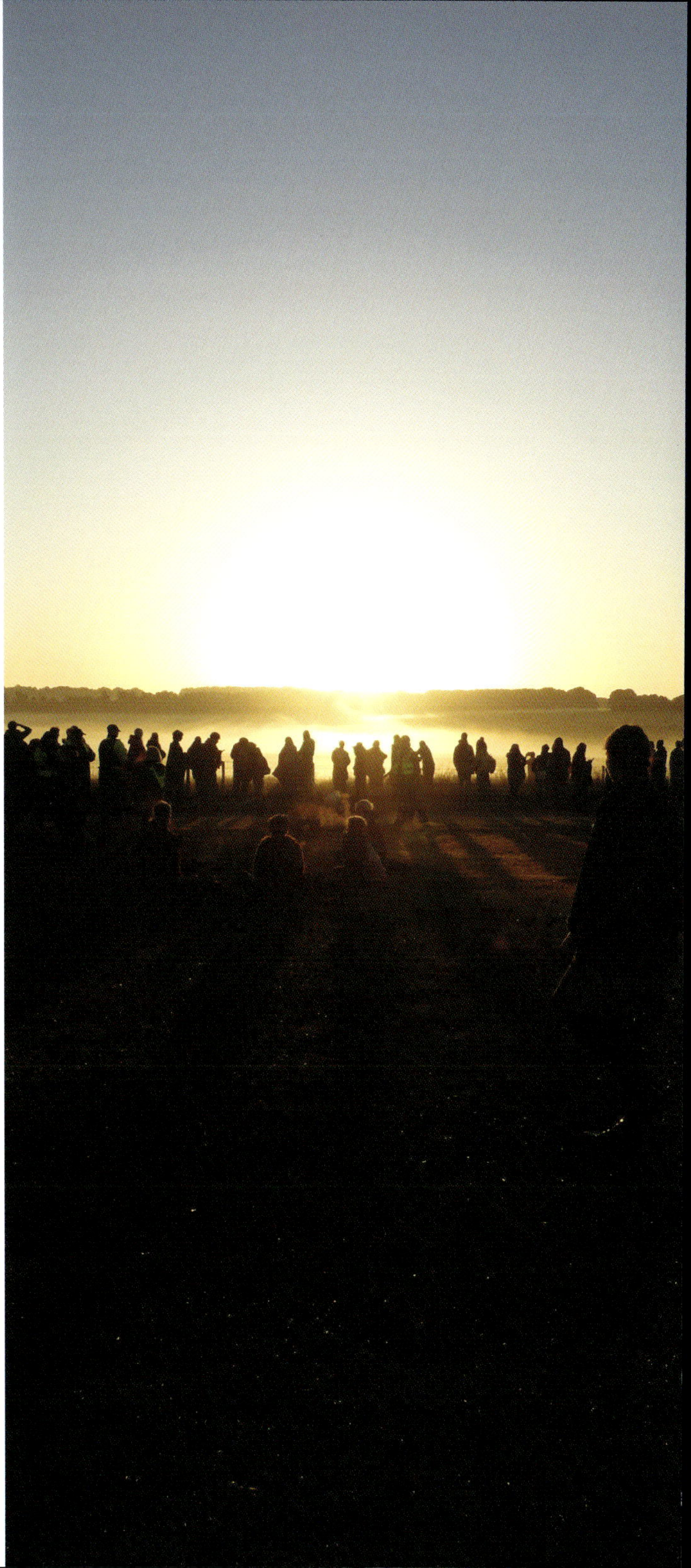

could hear the distant hum of the crowd gathering for the sunset. After a pat-down from security, who also checked I didn't have a sleeping bag or camping equipment with me, I finally made it in.

Inside the enclosure, it was like going into a rave. Everyone was buzzing and waves of noise, of monk-like chanting and drumming, rippled through the crowd, punctuated by raised hands clutching flashing smart phones, as we watched the sun sink beneath the horizon. The stones themselves always amaze me, no matter how many times I've been able to get close to them. It's not just that they're impressively huge, but it's the thought of the people who originally raised the monument, and all the hands that have touched them since, performed rituals around them and done exactly what we were all doing now. The stones are literally soaked in prayer. As I contemplated this, the hairs on the back of my neck began to prickle and a sense of deep time washed over me, of profound timelessness.

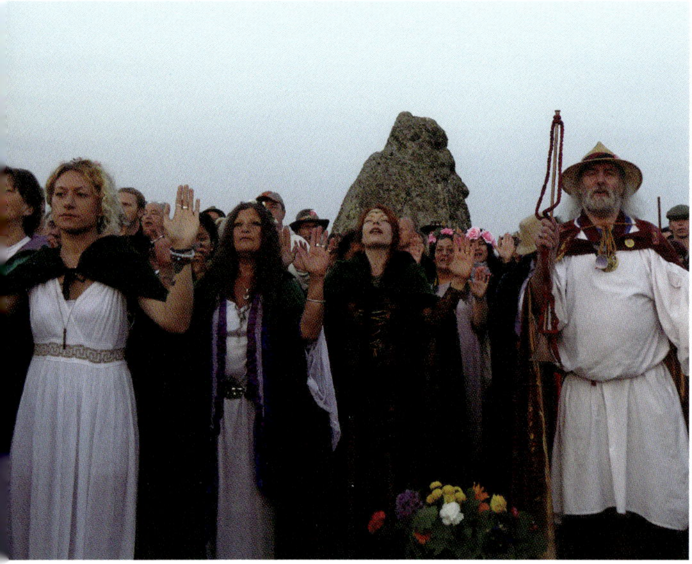

It was all very different to my first visit to Stonehenge. Then, Arthur Pendragon had been campaigning against extortionate carpark charges at the site, which he considered to be an attack on Pagans: in no other faith system would people be made to "pay to pray", as he put it. As a result, he refused to enter the monument grounds, so he and others remained outside the fence that surrounds the enclosure, while those who were not protesting entered.

It felt inharmonious and unsettling at the time; I was exhausted, and I wanted to find inspiration for a painting. A group of people surrounding a fence hadn't been what I was looking for, however well-intentioned they were. Nevertheless, I stayed and watched the sunrise ceremony.

As I wandered off afterwards, I became aware of the graceful silhouette of a lone woman. She wore an incredible dark-red gown that made her look like a Pagan queen of days gone by, perhaps even Mother Earth herself. She agreed to let me take her photograph and told me that she had come all the way from Russia; it was her birthday and her lifelong dream to visit the stones, which made this day doubly significant for her. My disappointment dissolved and I felt privileged to have met perhaps the most authentic pilgrim to have watched the sun rise that day.

Now, the sun continued to sink. When it finally disappeared, the crowd splintered into different groups in the darkness. The main party remained at the centre of the stones, where the energy pulsed like the heartbeat of the complex. Orange-robed Hare Krishnas wandered round the perimeters, their enthusiastic chants of "hare hare" to percussion and bells adding to the atmosphere.

Bathed in moonlight, the stones gleamed purple-blue. As the night deepened, I wandered between fire pits where people gathered. Close to a small stage where dancers were swinging each other round to folk music, I spotted the familiar figure of Arthur Pendragon in conversation with a white-robed man and a tall individual wearing antlers. I wandered over and Arthur greeted me warmly. He explained that "people have gathered for thousands of years for the longest and shortest days". Stonehenge, he said, is "a solar clock that tells you the time of year. Hunter-gatherers, on becoming agricultural farmers, needed to look at the shadows cast to know when to plant. And this was wizardry to the locals; it's been a place of magic ever since."

The antlered man slipped away as I struck up conversation with Arthur's other companion, Rollo Maughfling, who told me that he was "Stonehenge officer for the Council of British Druid Orders, who represent all sections of Druidry throughout the British Isles". He shared his belief that "Nature herself is holy and the divine can be found in Nature, not only in animals but in the stars and galaxies too"; that "everything in Nature is holy".

Feeling inspired, I walked back to the stones, where the Hare Krishnas had assembled a makeshift shrine on wheels, with effigies of gods at the front, which they pushed while dancing and singing and bringing much-needed energy to the waiting crowd. People in beanie hats, or with hoods up and wrapped in blankets, leaned against the stones, some dozing, some praying and meditating, and some simply staring toward the heel stone, which sits outside the circle and marks the rising point of the summer solstice sun.

There was a faint glimmer, which turned into a fiery glow, as a sea of mist rolled across the landscape. The anticipation mounted when the sun threatened to pierce the horizon. Cheers and mounting hysteria greeted the sunrise, along with the thudding of marching drummers, faces painted, followed by a group of Neopagans and Druids. A circle formed and, as Arthur Pendragon stood close by, Rollo led the sunrise ceremony. Prayers were read out, with the crowd echoing the words: "We swear by peace and love to stand, heart to heart and hand to hand, mark in our spirit and hear us now, confirming this our sacred vow."

With the sun risen above the mist, trees and horizon, women in robes and with horns and flowers in their hair chanted, "We share the same home, our beautiful planet Mother Earth." The ceremony ended in awed silence, while those with "Save Stonehenge" placards stood and reflected quietly. Then a girl started to throw herself into yoga poses, while others prayed to the glowing stones. I've never felt more alive; taking the time to honour the cycle of Nature felt like a radical act of defiance in the face of climate change. Here there is hope and Mother Earth is still honoured. It's not too late.

While the crowds dispersed, I made my way past burial mounds dotted across the landscape. Then I checked the map on my phone to find the B&B that I'd booked. It was much further away than I thought, unless I cut through a farm. Dog-tired, I decided to take my chances, climbed the fence and started down the dusty farm track. After a short while, I passed a group of men who smiled and said good morning as they flew their model aeroplanes in the clear blue sky. Now more at ease, I kept on walking, and despite my tiredness I felt like all my senses had been heightened.

I was thinking how great it would be to see a hare, one of my favourite animals, when one shot straight past me, stared at me, then dived into the long grass. I could see its ears poking out of the greenery for some time before it disappeared. To this day I don't know whether I was hallucinating from exhaustion or whether the solstice sun had given me magical powers. To add to this slightly trippy experience, a field of cows hissed at me. I've never seen a hissing cow before or since. Happily, I reached the B&B unscathed.

Before leaving Wiltshire, I decided on impulse to return to Stonehenge, even though the stones would be fenced off from the public. After spending a while in the visitor centre, studying a replica village that showed how the builders of Stonehenge once lived, I jumped on the shuttle bus to the ancient monument. There stood a line of figures in white robes. As soon as I stepped off the bus, they began walking; I couldn't quite believe what I was seeing: it was the London Druid Order who, unbeknown to me, meet the day after the solstice to perform their own ceremony at the stones. The hour was exactly midday and it had happened again: I was in exactly the right place at the right time, and I knew these moments of serendipity had to be some kind of sign from the great unknown that I was on the correct path.

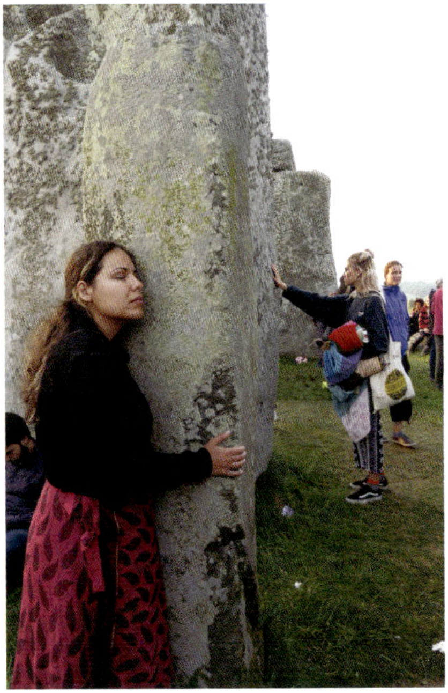

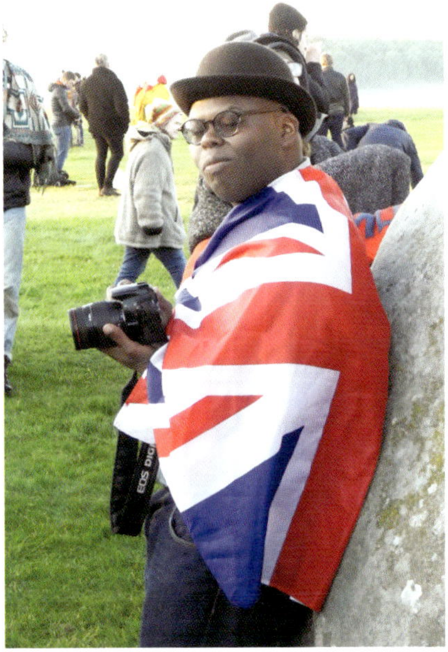

SUMMER SOLSTICE, STONEHENGE

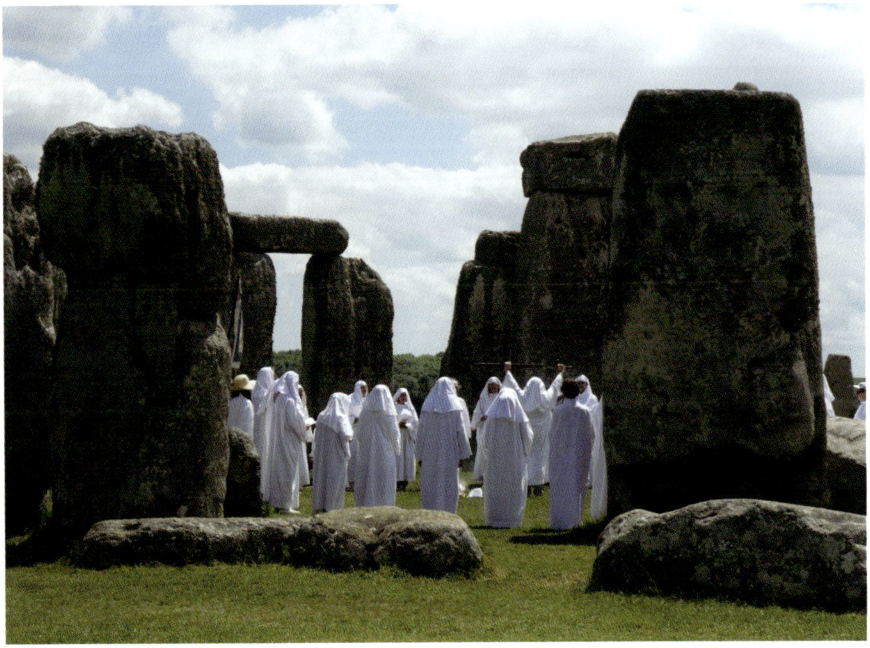

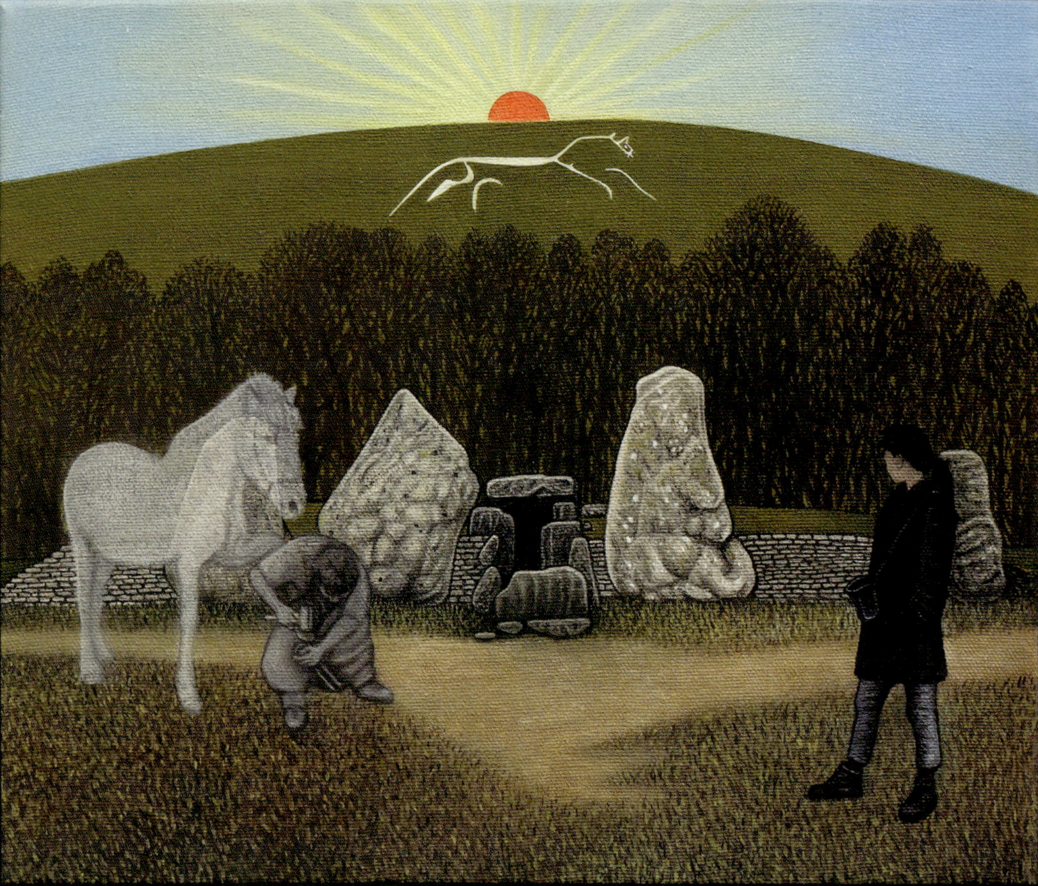

THE VALE OF THE WHITE HORSE

Oil and Chalk from the Uffington White Horse on Canvas, 30cm × 25cm

2022

The Vale of the White Horse

OXFORDSHIRE

JULY VISIT

When standing on top of White Horse Hill, one thing was clear to me: spiritually significant sites such as these choose themselves. The view was breathtaking, and it felt like I was in a holy place, as skylarks soared above me, and next to my feet molehills revealed dug-up pieces of the chalk hidden beneath the surface, which had been sculpted by the melting ice caps during the Ice Age, creating a rippling pattern in the hillside that overlooked the six counties visible from this highest point in Oxfordshire. Directly beneath the hill was a natural mound with a flat top, which resembled some kind of ceremonial stage. Known as Dragon Hill, according to local folklore, this is where the battle of St George and the dragon was said to have taken place.

I was there today to witness the chalking of the Uffington White Horse, a ceremony that has taken place in some shape or form from as early as 1380 BCE, when this mysterious and highly stylized silhouette of a horse was first etched into the hillside. As I approached the figure, its placement seemed slightly peculiar as it faced up toward the sky, instead of appearing on the hillside, where it could have been seen for miles around. Scattered around the hillside were large bags made of a sort of plastic tarpaulin, filled to the top with pieces of chalk collected from the hill and surrounding areas, which was periodically shovelled out before being broken down, to give the Uffington White Horse his brand new shiny white coat. Already, the chalky trenches were full of volunteers and the tapping of multiple hammers, breaking the chalk pieces into dust, resembled the sound of a galloping herd of horses.

I got a hammer too, and added an extra set of hooves to the noise. There was something addictive about the hammering and soon I didn't want to stop. Next to me, a man in an Uffington White Horse T-shirt was hammering away as well, as two young girls proudly worked nearby on the Horse's eye. I picked up a few pieces of chalk and put them in my pocket as a lucky souvenir of the day.

After a little while, I got chatting to Mark, one of volunteers in green National Trust polo shirts, who told me the Horse would have been dug out as trenches by people three thousand years ago, probably using antlers as axes. "In the deepest parts, it's about a metre deep," he said. "They then filled the trenches with chalk and flattened the chalk, to make it a permanent memorial." He explained that over the ages, there used to be what's known as a scouring of the Horse every seven years, but now the National Trust did it every year to make sure the Horse stayed there.

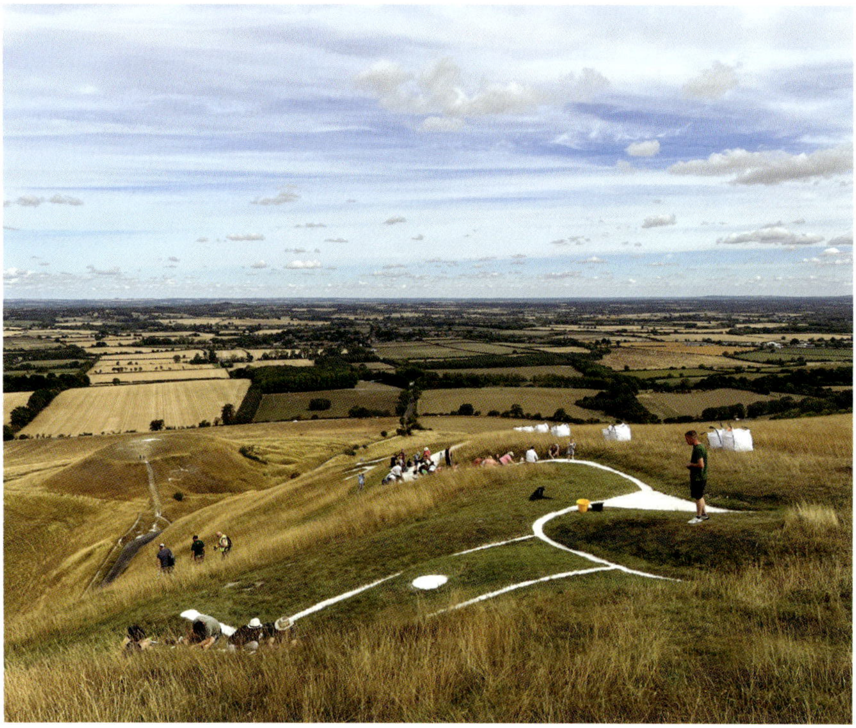

When I asked Mark his thoughts on the monument's origins, he said, "Some people see it as a horse, some people see it as a dragon, some as a dog, but the horse is my favourite. There are a number of theories, such as it was the symbol of the tribe that lived in Uffington Castle, just over the brow of the hill there. My favourite is that it was associated with a sun god. In Celtic mythology, the sun travelled on the back of a horse, or possibly in a chariot pulled by a horse, and the mid-winter sun rises on the tail of the Horse here, and goes over the back and sets over its head." This suggestion made a lot of sense to me, with the figure of the Horse being positioned to face the heavens and not the people in the settlements below.

He also mentioned the local belief about Dragon Hill that, "When St George killed the dragon, some of the blood landed on the hill, burned off the top of the hill, and formed a flat top and now nothing grows there."

Before visiting the site, I'd read in Thomas Hughes's book *The Scouring of the White Horse* that, up until 1857, a festival known as the "Pastime" used to take place here at the time of the summer solstice in honour of the scouring. As well as the scouring, there would have been cheese rolling, wrestling tournaments, competitions to climb a greasy pole, sack racing, pipe-smoking marathons and, of course, much drunkenness. Such activities were believed to "help boost the sun around the bend of the year". When I asked Mark about this, he informed me that in the year Thomas Hughes visited, "Thirty thousand visitors came to scour the Horse, and after that it was banned 'cause they couldn't get rid of them!"

One thing was clear to me: spiritually significant sites such as these choose themselves.

The Vale of the White Horse runs between the ancient Ridgeway trackway and the River Thames across the Cotswolds (once part of Berkshire) in Oxfordshire. My wife's hometown of Faringdon also sits within the Vale, and her primary school uniform featured the symbol of the White Horse in its logo. The Horse appears as well in a mural on a local housing estate, along with the Neolithic chambered long barrow known as Wayland's Smithy. My wife Rose and I had visited the area together on many occasions, not just to see the Horse, but to visit this ancient monument, too.

Wayland's Smithy has been dated to 3600 BCE, and according to the folklore that Rose first learned as a child, it's said that if a traveller's horse were to lose a shoe, the traveller could take the animal to the site and leave it overnight with some money. By daybreak the horse would be shod and the money gone. It's also said that the nearby Uffington White Horse will disappear on occasion (most commonly under the guise of snow), as it makes its way to Wayland's Smithy for some new horseshoes. The legend of the blacksmith, aka "Wayland", derives from an Old Norse legend about a master blacksmith of supernatural skill, who the Anglo-Saxons believed had made the long barrow his home.

One misty day, on our way to Wayland's Smithy and White Horse Hill, Rose and I were driving along an old road surrounded by gnarled trees, when I noticed a silhouette of a man standing in the middle of the road. As we got closer he came fully into view; he had dirty long blond hair, filthy clothes and a huge leather backpack. Suddenly, he put both his hands on the bonnet of the car and snarled at us. His eyes protruded from his head and each of his teeth appeared to have been sharpened to a point. He started walking round the side of the car, as if about to open the door. Rose put her foot down, and got us out of there. We were both terrified – was this a ghost? What the hell had we just seen?

Shaken up, we carried on to the long barrow, and as we approached I recalled the stories that Rose had heard as a child. It was as if they were coming alive, and I imagined Wayland himself shoeing the ghostly hoof of a white horse, while on the hillside above, the Uffington White Horse carried the sun across the sky. The idea was complete: I would paint Rose gazing upon Wayland's Smithy while bringing alive the legends of the Vale of the White Horse that she'd always known. I still had the chalk from the scouring back in my studio, so I decided to mix that into the paint while making my painting.

Another story relating to the Vale that I'd like to share concerns *The Portrait of Sir Henry Unton*, which hangs in the National Portrait Gallery. Ever since my teens I've been obsessed with this painting, which depicts the whole life story of its subject, and it's become a huge inspiration on the way that I compose my own work. During one of my first visits to Faringdon to visit Rose's childhood home, we wandered into the local church, and much to my amazement, there it was a reproduction of my favourite painting on the wall: it turned out that Sir Henry Unton came from a local upper-class family who were patrons of the church and were all buried there. What's also striking about the church is that it's missing its spire, which was toppled during the Civil War. The painting, which dates to around 1596, shows the spire still present and is now the only visual record of what the church would have once looked like. To add more to this serendipitous moment, my ongoing sign of good luck and a symbol for me of being in the right place at the right time appeared again: along the old church pews a whole row of Green Man faces stared out at us from the shadows.

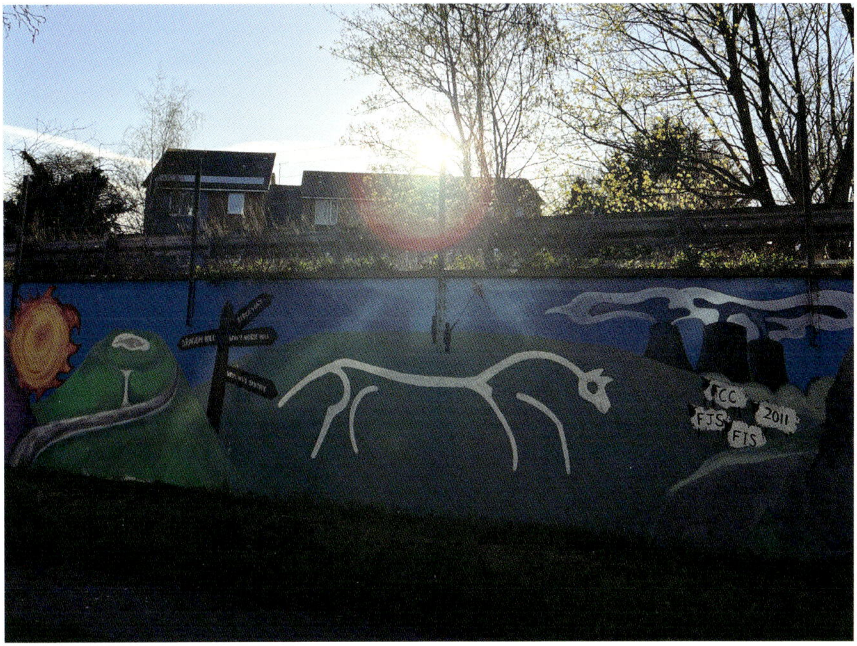
CC
2011
FJS
FIS

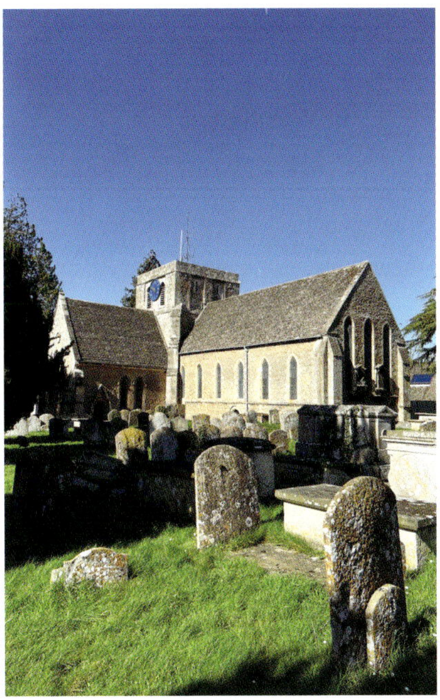

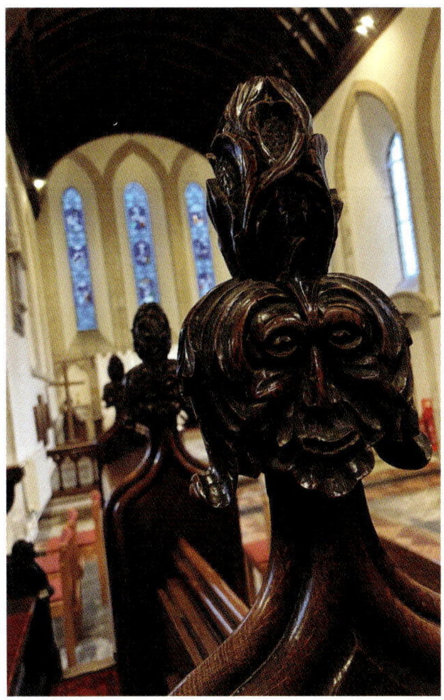

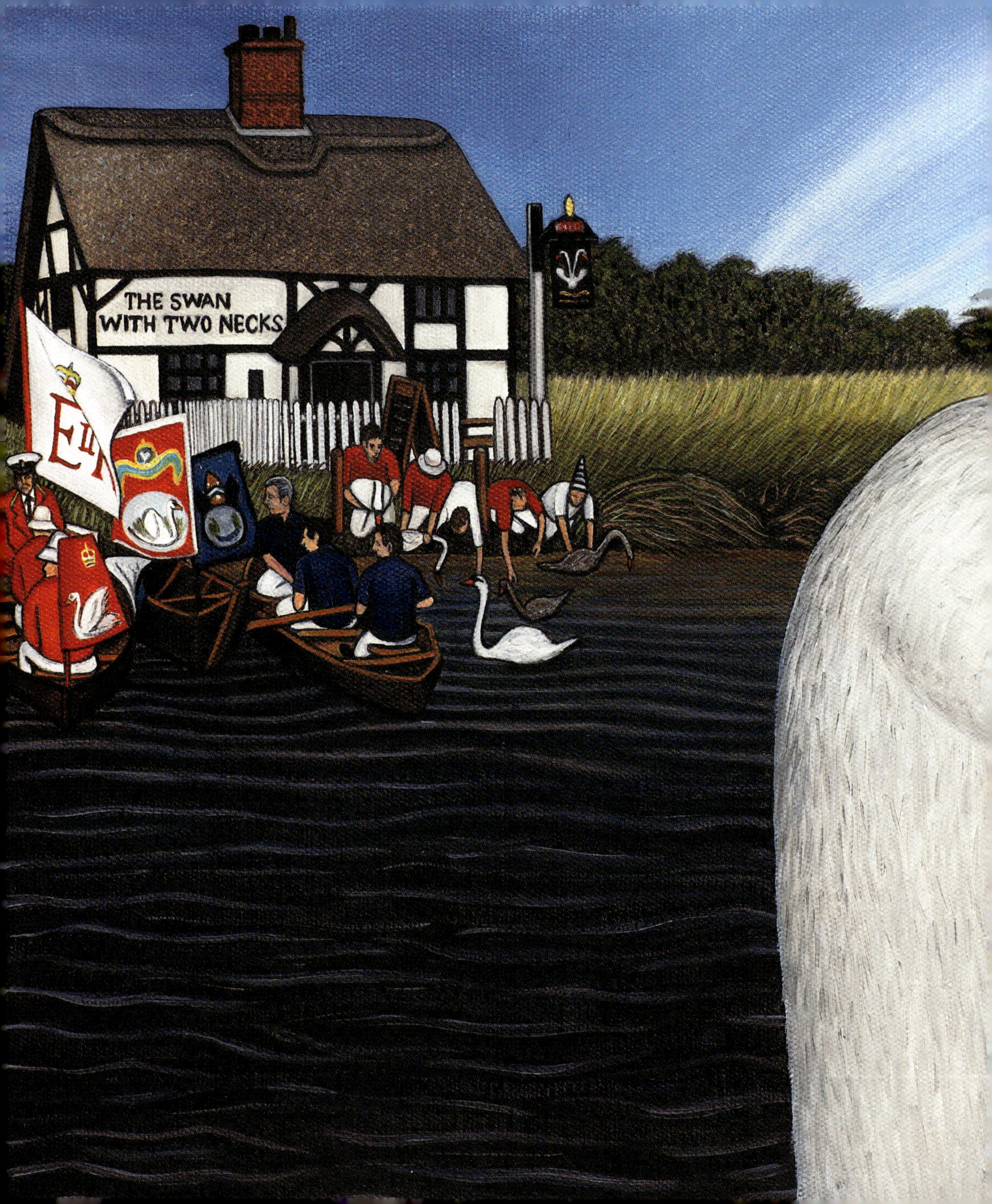
THE SWAN
WITH TWO NECKS

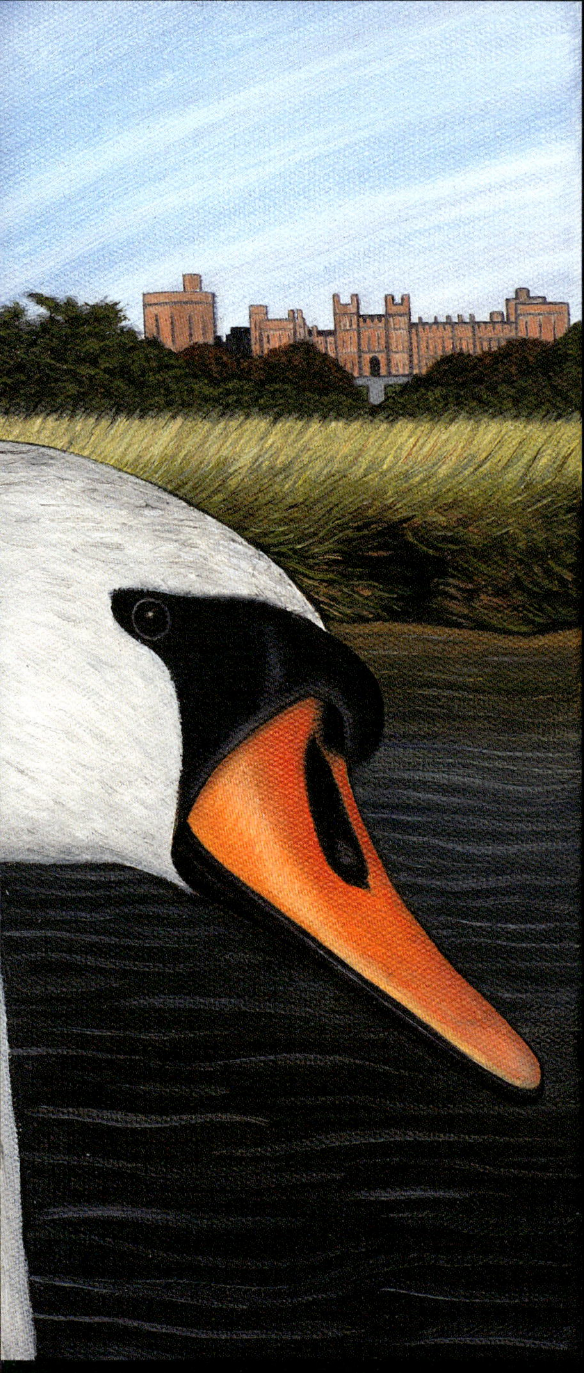

SWAN UPPING

Oil on Canvas, 25cm × 30cm

2018

Swan Upping

OXFORDSHIRE

THIRD WEEK OF JULY

The ancient tradition of Swan Upping begins at Sunbury-on-Thames, where the Royal Swan Marker and his party, along with representatives of the Worshipful Company of Vintners and the Worshipful Company of Dyers, set off in skiffs along the River Thames to Abingdon, on a five-day journey that covers 79 miles (127km). It takes place in the third week of July, when the adult birds are in moult and the cygnets aren't yet able to fly.

During one Swan Upping, I was able to ask the Royal Swan Marker himself, David Barber, about the practice. He explained that it's believed to date back "all the way to the twelfth century. Today swans are no longer eaten and are a protected species, so the purpose of this custom is now the conservation of mute swans and education about their welfare and the habitat they need to survive." The young birds were once a delicacy eaten by the aristocracy and the well-to-do around Christmas time, so Swan Upping was a form of gamekeeping, making sure there was a flourishing swan population and enough birds to eat by those who could claim ownership of them. Today, besides the King, only two Livery Companies, the Vintners and the Dyers, as well as the Ilchester family of Abbotsbury can claim official ownership of swans.

A complicated marking system once indicated who each bird belonged to, while unmarked swans automatically belonged to the Crown. An elaborate symbol known as a "nick" was scratched into each swan's bill, with two nicks for those birds belonging to the Vintners, and one nick for the Dyers, for example. Any cygnets of an already marked swan would be marked with the same symbol and remain under the same ownership as their parents; unless the parent birds belonged to different owners, in which case the ownership of the cygnets would be divided evenly. Nowadays, the nicks have been replaced with leg tags.

Originally, awarding ownership of the birds was one way that the royal family rewarded subjects for their loyalty and support. Now, the tradition is more of an environmental practice, where the swan population is monitored and protected, and any fishing tackle that may have got caught around the birds is removed. In 1985, the swan population on the stretch of the Thames from London to Henley had fallen drastically to just seven breeding pairs, due to lead poisoning, which was the result of the birds swallowing fishing weights. Thanks to the work of the Swan Uppers and other environmentalist groups, the weights were banned and the swan population quickly recovered.

The first time I went to watch the Swan Uppers, I arrived to find nothing much going on. As I stood beneath a large bridge, peering anxiously up and down the glittering river, a passing dog walker spotted my predicament. After a short chat, he informed me the Swan Uppers had set off twenty minutes earlier than usual. As I was on foot, I thought there was probably no way to catch up with them, but I'd do my best all the same.

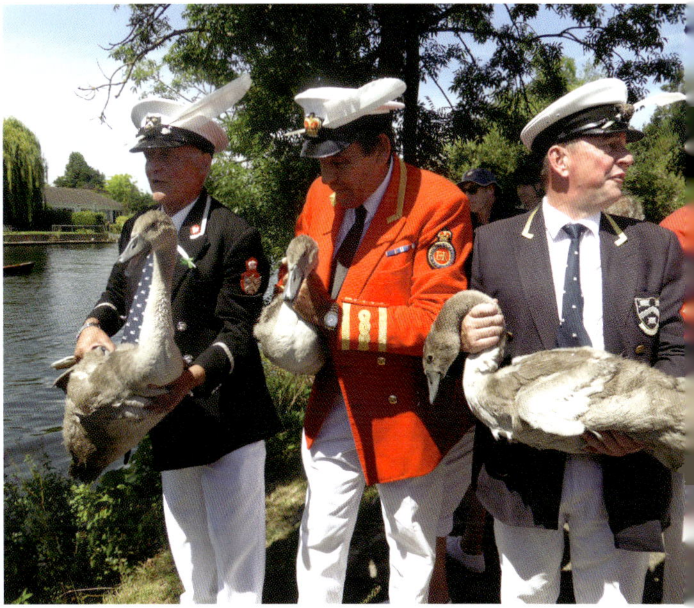

Thanking the dog walker, I walked briskly on, occasionally breaking into a jog, but the path petered out in a dead end. Frustrated, I turned round and noticed a bell. The sign next to it said that a ferryman was available to take passengers across to the other side every fifteen minutes; you just needed to the ring the bell to let him know you were there. It happened to be dead on quarter past the hour, so I gave the bell a ring.

On the opposite riverbank, a man in a polo shirt and shorts clambered into a grey ferryboat and made his way across. Once on board, I told him I was looking for the Swan Uppers, and he said they'd already set off, but that if you look on their website they do say the times are subject to change. Optimistically, he added, "If you're quick they'll be stopping off at various sites and the locks slow them down – you'll be fine catching them." I clambered ashore and jogged past a couple with binoculars, who also informed me that I'd just missed the Uppers as they'd "set off early".

As I hurried along beside the sunlit Thames, past luxury houses and under lush green trees, I found myself enjoying being out in the fresh air, in a new environment. Soon, I spotted a flotilla of skiffs with flags on the water ahead, and photographers gathered on the concrete banks above them: I'd managed to catch up with the Swan Uppers, who had, as predicted, been held up by a lock.

In a boat with the royal standard at its stern, the rowers wore red T-shirts emblazoned with the royal cypher: these, I later learned, were the Crown's men commanded by the Royal Swan Marker, who sported a swan's feather in his hat. In another boat, the rowers wore blue; these were the Dyers, commanded by the Barge Master. The Vintners were dressed all in white and commanded by their own Swan Marker. Now, the smartly dressed crews were taking the opportunity to pass around a hipflask.

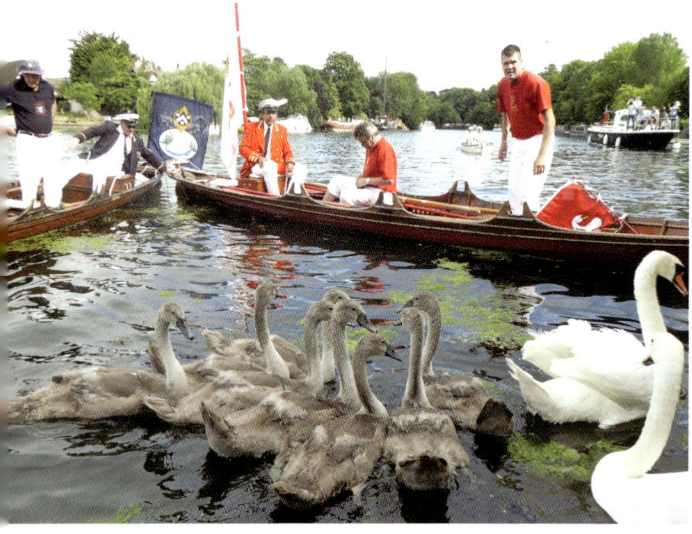

Full of relief, I began to take pictures from the concrete bank, but as I moved to get a better picture I was shouldered out of the way by a clammy man with a beard, who seemed to think I was an intruder of some sort. He then stepped down on to what turned out to be the press boat. When the boats finally made it through the lock, the skiffs were tied to motorboats and off they went. I couldn't believe it, I was back to square one and, once again, started running along the water's edge, trying to catch up with the Uppers.

I carried on the chase and heard someone shout, "ALL UP!" which is the traditional call when a group of swans has been spotted. The skiffs were released from the motorboats and the Uppers surrounded the birds, but my view was obstructed. I was on the wrong side of the river and to add further insult to injury, the press boat had positioned itself next to the Swan Uppers, completely blocking my view. I decided to turn this into an opportunity to hurry on and find the next wedge of swans.

I'd got quite far along before the skiffs caught up with me. And I was in luck: a swan was feeding on the bank with her cygnets. It was a narrow spot, so I got ready to take some photos while the skiffs drew up alongside the birds. A few passing walkers and other Swan Upping enthusiasts appeared alongside me, making the area even more crowded.

We were soon joined by the press boat, whose passengers jumped off nearby. The man who had shunted me out of the way earlier reappeared and my heart sank; he was almost like a bouncer, protecting the party. When I attempted to sneak round him, he pushed me out of the way again. But at that moment the birds were being lifted out the water, so I focused instead on the swan and her cygnets, whose feet were being bound by rope. They were placed in a line and the Swan Uppers then lifted each one up, weighed it and inspected it, ensuring that no fishing wire or any other foreign objects were wrapped around the swans' bodies.

In this case, the mother swan, or pen, had already been marked and was the property of the Worshipful Vintners. The cygnets were then marked, with half belonging to the Vintners and the rest to the Crown. I presumed this must be an unwritten rule, as the father bird, or cob, wasn't around, so it would be impossible to know whether he belonged to the Vintners too. After the tagging had taken place, the birds were released into the water where they swam away gracefully if somewhat flustered.

It was a truly beautiful day and I continued on my way, while the skiffs sailed on up the river. By the time I reached Staines, I could just about see them in the distance. Crowds were waiting and I discovered the Swan Uppers would be stopping for lunch at the aptly named Swan Hotel. I carried on walking along a particularly stunning stretch of the river; the water and the riverside were a vibrant green, glistening in the sun, and birds chirped from the trees. This section of the river was very wide, adding to my sense of relaxation. I thought about how far I had come from my dark days of depression; the uptight city boy was loosening up and I had our wonderful folk culture to thank for that. I could now see a bright future in front of me. I took off my shoes and socks, and sat with my feet dangling in the water. From that moment, something shifted. It was a healing experience; I felt part of Nature.

The day continued in the same vein: I waited to be caught up by the Uppers while hanging around families of swans; I attempted to take some photos and then hurried on to get ahead. This cat and mouse game continued until I found myself deep in the countryside. There were no houses and the reception had gone on my phone, so I couldn't work out where I was. I had no choice but to keep going. I'd walked for hours, I was getting sunburned and the muscles in my legs were aching.

The beauty of the river was enough to keep my spirits up until I reached a town, where I met an elderly lady standing by a bridge. She was holding an old camera, and when I said how far I'd walked, she couldn't believe it. "You're on the outskirts of Windsor!" she said. She told me she came to watch the Swan Upping every year, but that she didn't think they been through the town yet, as they made various stops along the way to speak to groups of school children and corporate parties.

She said she had been photographing the Uppers for as long as she could remember and told me how, as a girl, she had met the artist Stanley Spencer, who was also interested in the event and painted a picture called *Swan Upping at Cookham*. She explained that the traditional pub name the "Swan with Two Necks" was actually a mutation of "the swan with two nicks". I loved this story, as this is what happens in folklore: things evolve and mutate yet remain deeply rooted in past traditions. The idea that you could be drinking today in a pub called the Swan With Two Necks, thinking it referred to some kind of freaky bird that once lived in the area, when it's in fact related to the Swan Upping tradition, really excited me. I knew I'd need to reference it in my painting somehow.

We said goodbye and I carried on walking. My thighs were roaring with pain as I entered the town centre. Locals had gathered near a large group of swans, obviously knowing that this was a good spot to watch the event. I sat and rested after my 18-mile (29km) walk.

The sun was gradually sinking in the sky when the skiffs appeared in the distance. "ALL UP!" came the shout, as the boats approached a family of swans right in front of me. The birds splashed their wings against the water desperately as the Uppers moved in, grabbed them and hauled them up on to the skiffs and bound their feet. I got some perfect shots and turned to photograph the birds still on the bank, but I hadn't realized the press boat had also arrived and from behind me came muffled swearing from the press photographer who'd shoved me earlier.

He complained I was in his way and this time I couldn't hold it in anymore; I told him he had no right over me or anybody else, and that anyone could come and take pictures. People are always interested in documenting our country's traditions and no one has more right than anyone else to be there. It got heated, with neither of us backing down, until one of the Swan Uppers came over and said, "Come on now, let's all calm down." Thankfully, I had all I needed and hobbled my way to Windsor station; despite the dispute, it had been a successful day and I now had a painting in mind.

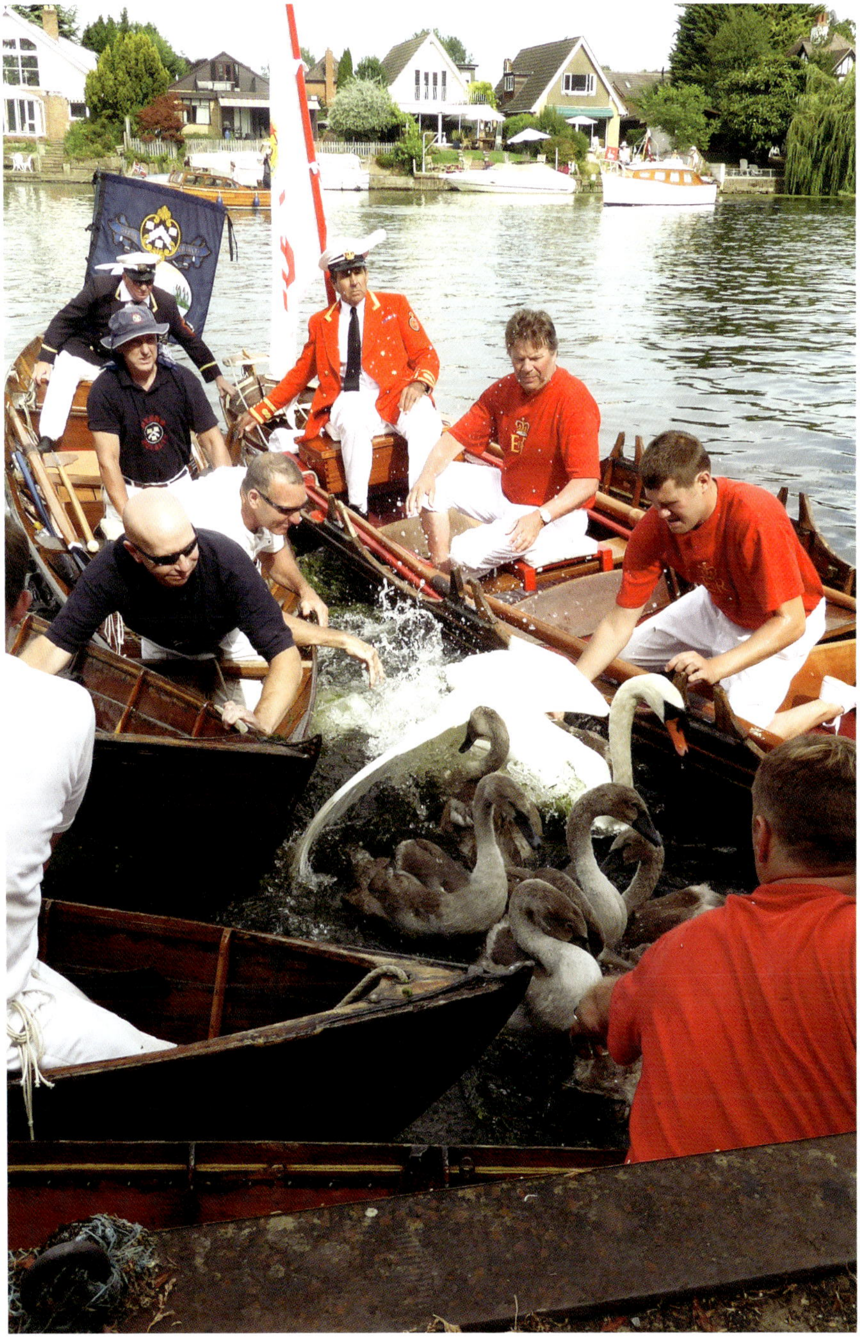

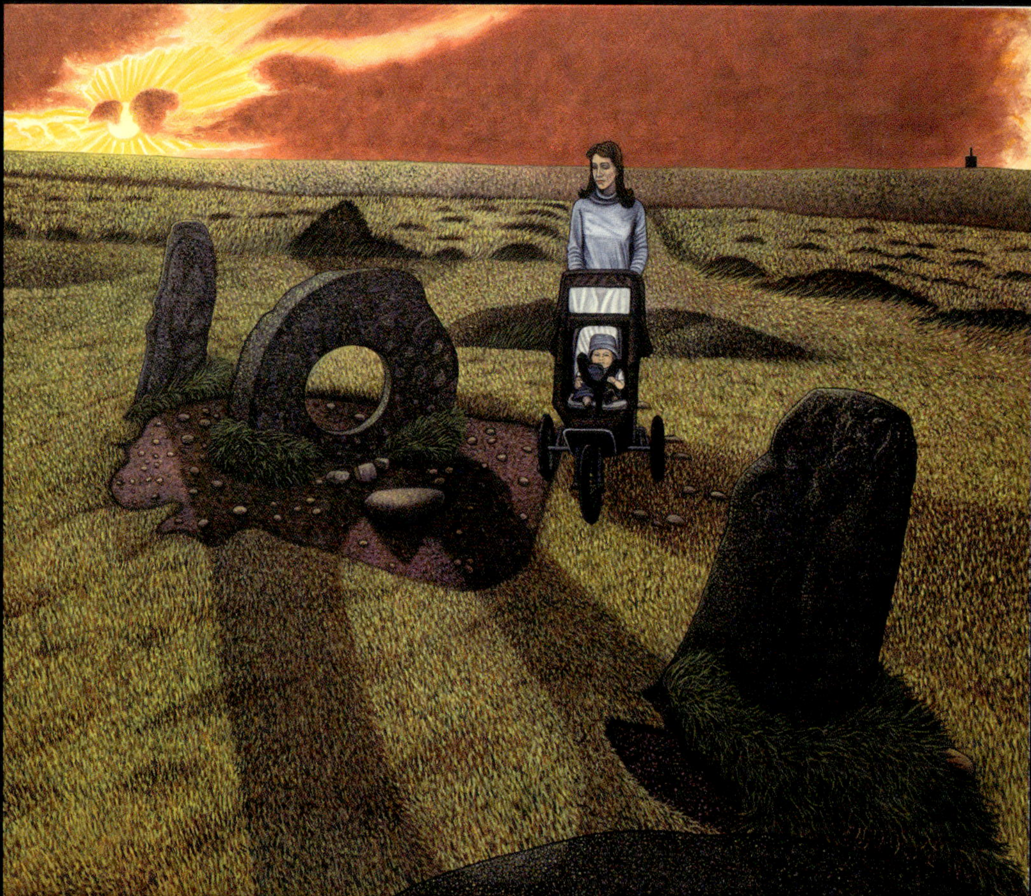

MÊN-AN-TOL

Oil on Canvas, 50cm × 60cm

2022

Mên-an-Tol

CORNWALL

JULY VISIT

I had been invited by my good friend, fellow artist and in fact early influence, David Harrison, to see some of his sculptures in Cornwall, on private land near Penzance. His pieces, which he called his "magic cats", were based on megalithic and spiritually significant sites in the area. After seeing his works, the plan was to explore the ancient surrounding landscape that had been David's initial inspiration.

Our first stop that hot July day was at the mysterious holed stone known as Mên-an-Tol. After walking up a narrow track along hedgerows full of wild flowers and chirping birds, we climbed an old stile, and there in the distance, much smaller than I'd imagined based on what I'd seen in pictures, was Mên-an-Tol: a humble-sized round stone with a near-perfect hole in its centre, flanked on either side by two standing stones of a similar height at about 1m (3ft) tall. There was something incredible about the stones being so small: these weren't monumental monoliths like those at Stonehenge or Avebury, whose sheer size and impressiveness explain their survival. The fact that these small stones had nevertheless somehow still survived for thousands of years in a farmer's field blew my mind. In fact, I credit this moment as being when my standing stone obsession began.

If a woman were to crawl seven times through the hole backward at the time of a full moon, she'd soon become pregnant.

As we reached these Cornish granite mysteries, David immediately crawled through the holed stone with a big grin on his face. "It's good luck to crawl through it!" he said, and told me about the superstitions and local legends associated with Mên-an-Tol, which he'd learned when researching the site for his project. One was that if a woman were to crawl seven times through the hole backward at the time of a full moon, she'd soon become pregnant. Another was that if a child suffering with rickets was passed naked through it nine times, the child would be cured.

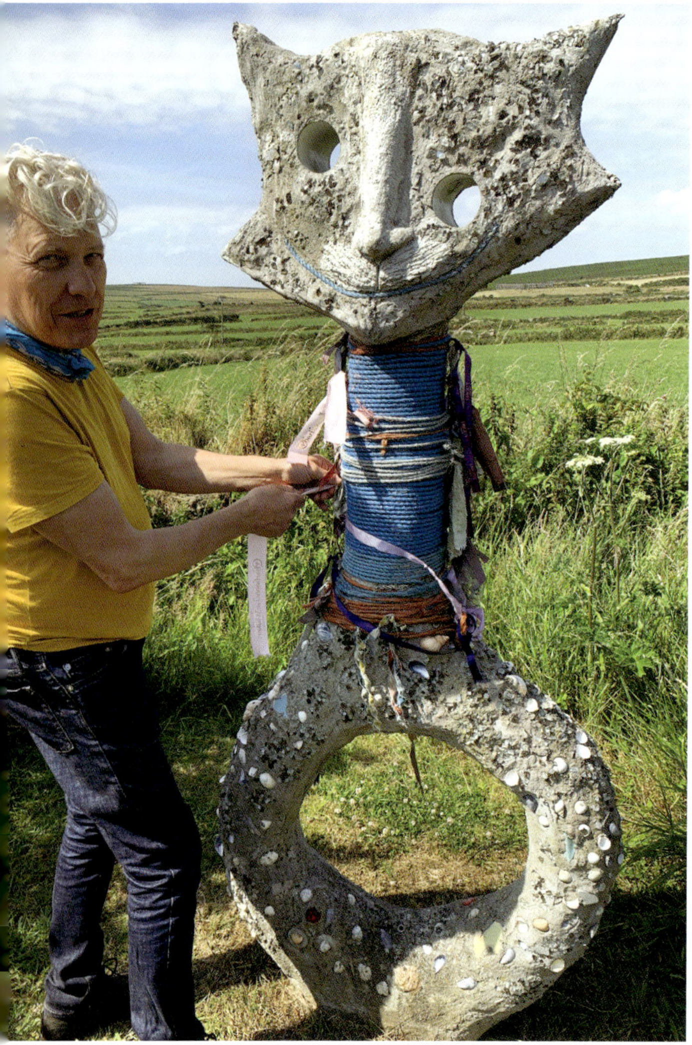

As we stood there, I could see an old chimney of a tin mine in the distance. In the hot sun, the shadows were particularly long, with each blade of grass gleaming in the light. In my mind's eye, I could also see a woman with a pram, who'd heard of the local folklore and had made the journey to see if the magic was real and if her child could be cured. A new painting had revealed itself and after hearing David's stories my initial questions had been answered too: despite their humble size, the stones were still here because the surrounding folklore and superstitions had kept them alive. Their mystery had captivated people's imaginations ever since they were first erected, all those thousands of years ago, a true testament to the enduring power of storytelling.

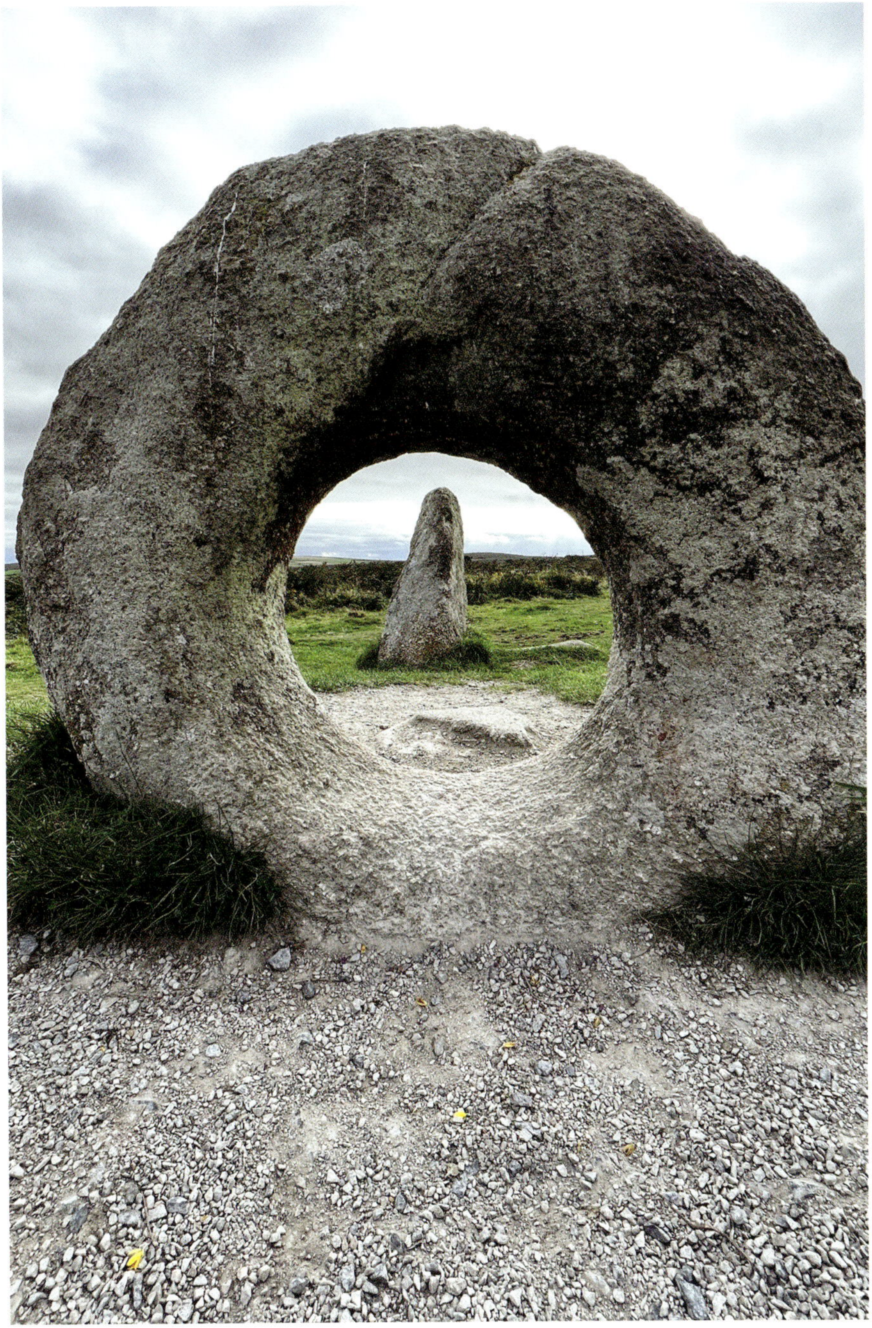

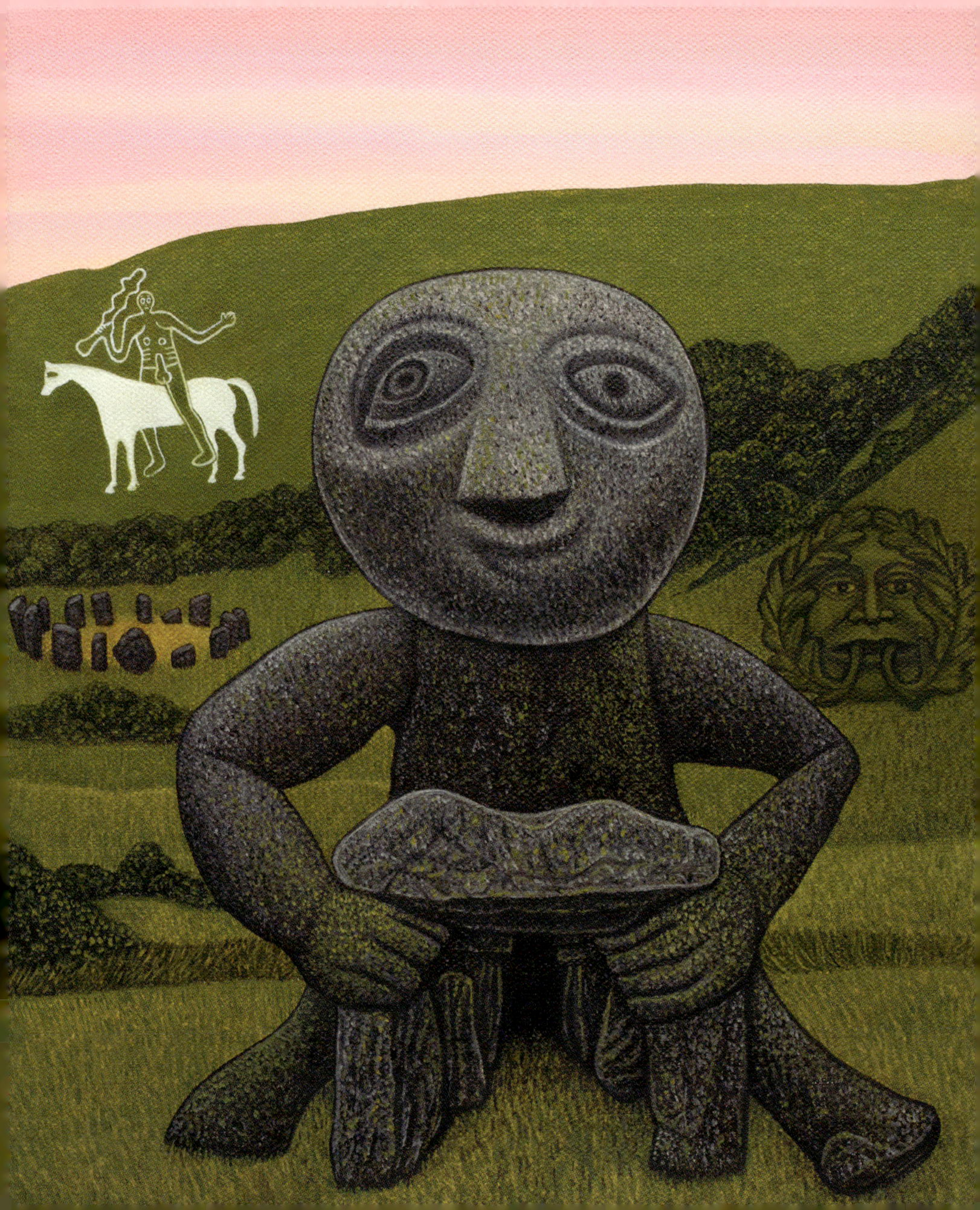

EARTH MOTHER

Oil on Canvas, 30cm × 25cm

2024

Kilpeck Church Sheela Na Gig

HEREFORDSHIRE

JULY VISIT

I travelled to the Church of St Mary and St David in Kilpeck, rural Herefordshire, with my friend and musical collaborator Elspeth Anne, who is a folk artist, to take a look at the remarkably preserved doorway and eighty-nine incredible corbel carvings on the exterior of this Norman church. A corbel juts out from a wall to support the structure above it, and the ones at Kilpeck are particularly special. Here you will find depictions of animal faces, the tree of life, beasts, snakes, dragons, the Green Man, a cartoonish dog and rabbit, and most famously of all, the Kilpeck Sheela Na Gig. A primitive sculpture of a woman, exposing her exaggerated genitalia by pulling them wide open with her hands, this symbol can also be found in other ancient churches, with the highest concentration being in Ireland.

On the church website there is a video in which James Bailey, who is a specialist on Kilpeck and its architecture, explains that the Sheela Na Gig could symbolize lust, because many of the corbels represent the sins of the world, or it could be intended to frighten away the Devil. However, his hunch is that the figure is most likely to be a Celtic fertility symbol and a celebration of life.

Elspeth, who regularly visits the church as part of her singing practice, to benefit from its ancient atmosphere and acoustics, explained what the Sheela Na Gig represents to her: "They're a symbol of fertility, and feminine power, I guess. It's not a depiction of a man

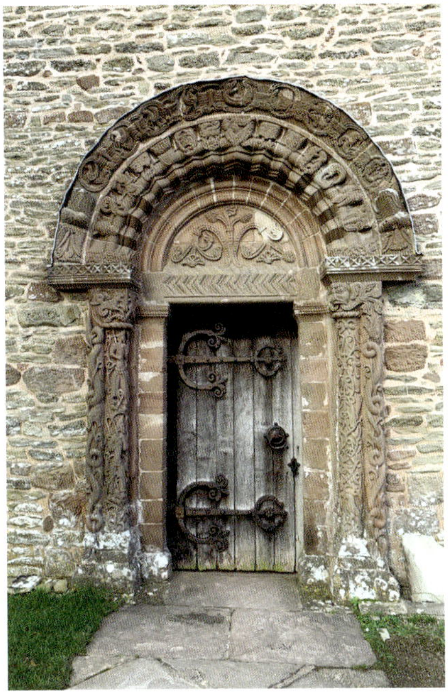

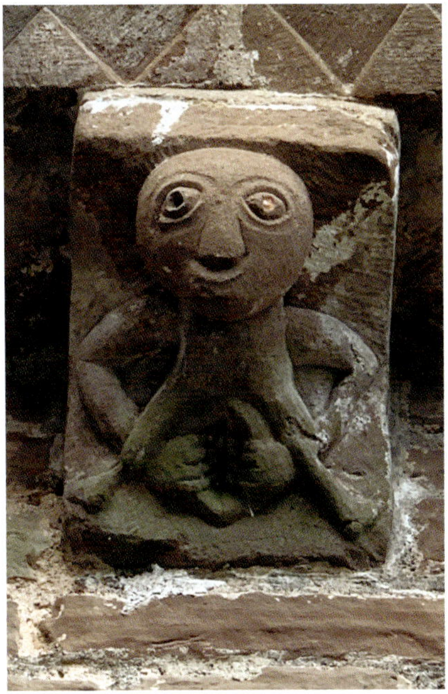

KILPECK CHURCH
SHEELA NA GIG

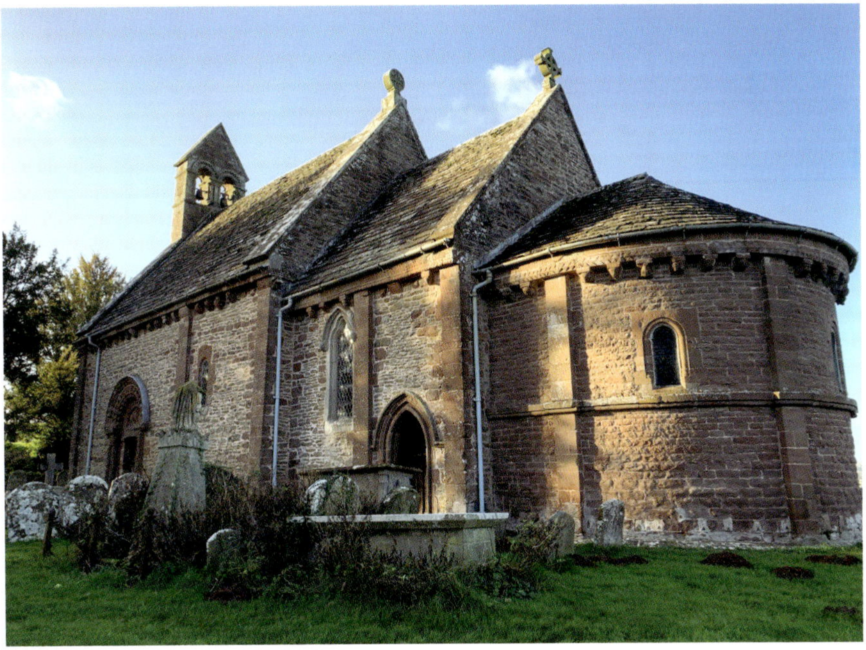

and a woman, and of him touching her; it's not trying to make her beautiful. She's quite raw-looking and she's touching her genitals herself, not some bloke. She's a bit in your face, just showing you who she is, no shyness about it." I took from this that Elspeth sees her as an unashamedly feminine and feminist symbol, who can inspire women to be proud of who they are, without the need to conform to the pressures of the male gaze. The fact that she sits so well preserved on a church, an establishment that has historically demonized and repressed the liberation of women, adds to the feeling of triumphant female empowerment.

The more I've found out about Sheela Na Gigs, and when coming across incredible examples like this one, I can't help but see them as representing some kind of ancient mother goddess, a Mother Earth who unites us by reminding us that we all come from the same place: Mother Nature herself. I'd wondered for a long time how to incorporate her into one of my paintings and it wasn't until I visited West Kennet Long Barrow, near Avebury, that an idea came to me.

When entering that chambered tomb, it felt like I was journeying into the centre of the earth. As my eyes adjusted to the darkness, I wandered through to the back of the chamber, where I found two women chanting as they lit candles and placed them neatly upon the natural shelves formed within the stones. As I stood and watched, caught up in this otherworldly sight, they lay flowers on the ground and began slowly walking out toward the light of the entrance, when they noticed me and smiled warmly.

I asked them what they were doing, and in reply they described the long barrow to me as "the womb of the Mother Goddess" and said that the "bones of our ancestors were given back to the earth, and placed in here over five thousand years ago". They informed me that they were part of a Goddess tradition and had travelled up from Glastonbury. After hearing their thoughts, I couldn't help but think of the Sheela Na Gig of Kilpeck and how both of these ancient symbols and sites could both be representing the same thing, Mother Earth.

Interestingly, both date back to transitional moments in British history, with long barrows first appearing around 3650 BCE when we were switching from being hunter-gatherers to farmers, and the Sheela Na Gig of Kilpeck being carved not long after the Norman invasion of 1066 CE, when the stone masons combined local beliefs with the new ideas brought with them from cultures across the world. This mishmash of ideas is such a British thing, as our nation has been sculpted by the repeated coming and going and movements of peoples to and from these isles, creating new hybrid cultural ideas. With all of this in mind, I envisioned a "Sheela Na Long Barrow", a hybrid of both versions of the Mother Goddess – Mother

Nature and Earth Mother (as I would later name the painting). I then decided to place more masculine symbols in the background to show that these all came from the same place, and in this very British tradition, I mongrelized the Dorset hill figure of the Cerne Abbas Giant with the Westbury White Horse, placing him on the back of the chalk horse and riding across the hills. I also included the Drombeg Stone Circle of County Cork, as a nod to my own part-Irish heritage and to suggest how travelling ideas have shaped these lands, and to acknowledge that the Sheela Na Gig herself is often found in Ireland. Finally, I included the Green Man as the male companion to the Earth Mother, who also keeps the Sheela Na Gig company on Kilpeck Church itself.

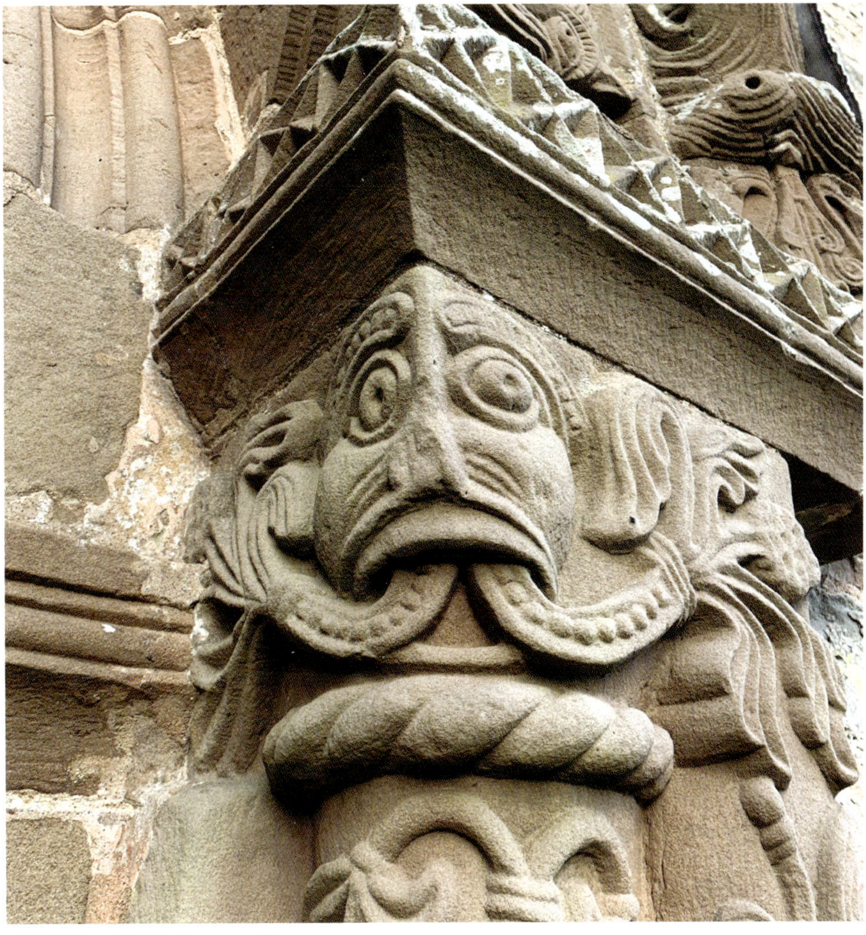

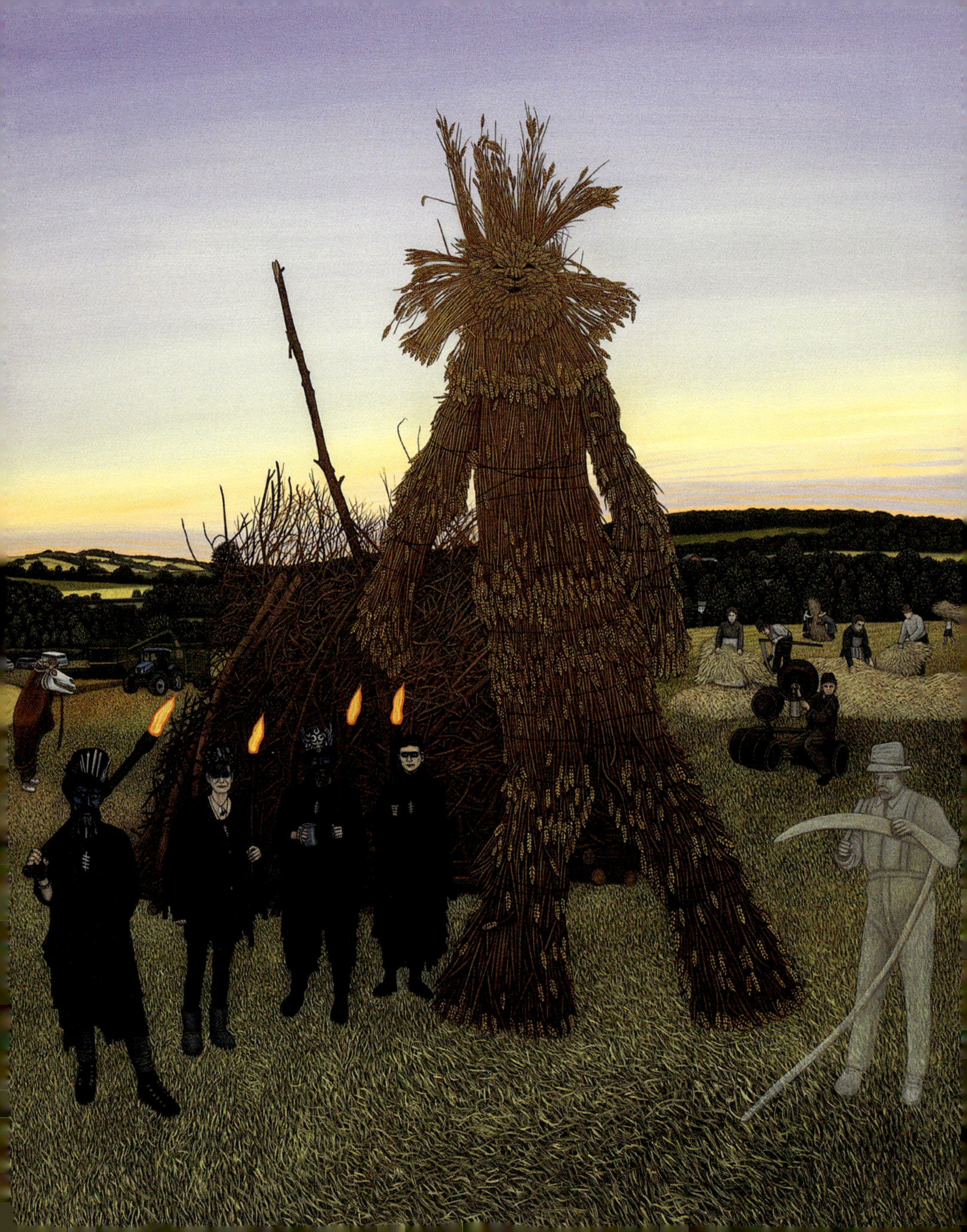

JOHN BARLEYCORN MUST DIE

Oil on Canvas, 100cm × 80cm

2023

Lughnasadh Folk Festival

HEREFORDSHIRE

AUGUST 1

It was Lughnasadh, the Gaelic festival marking the beginning of the harvest, and I found myself in Herefordshire, this time in the company of the Blackthorn Ritualistic Folk morris side, who'd created a contemporary festival to mark this ancient harvest celebration. It'd been a particularly hot and dry summer and as soon as I entered the scorched field, I was struck by the hard work and detail that had gone into organizing the festival. A huge handmade banner welcomed me with the words "Lughnasadh Folk Festival" next to the Blackthorn logo: a graphic horizontal line with diagonal lines crossing through it, symbolizing the blackthorn in the ancient Celtic Ogham alphabet. There were long, thin, black, blue and white flags flapping in the breeze, rows of tents, a stage with haystacks for seats and market stalls selling handcrafted items. Last but not least, a huge standing effigy made of wheatsheaves and representing the mythical John Barleycorn, part man and part crop, loomed over the whole area. A large pyre stood behind him, where I presumed he would later be burned as a harvest offering.

The legend of this uncanny figure is immortalized in the song "John Barleycorn", which tells the story of the cultivation of barley for whisky and beer, and the various stages of harvesting, reaping and malting. It ends with the eventual sacrifice of John Barleycorn to Mother Earth, to give thanks and to ensure that his crop will be reborn the following year. In some versions of the song, he is celebrated as a saviour who gives us courage, and in others he seeks revenge through intoxication and hangovers. John Barleycorn reminds us, just like the Green Man does, that Nature is alive and mustn't be taken for granted; that we must replenish the land we take from, or there will be consequences. As I stood looking at this beautifully crafted effigy, I imagined the fields around me coming alive with spectres of the past in old-fashioned dress, cultivating beer and whisky, and wielding sickles. I knew for certain that these spectres and John Barleycorn would feature within my painting, alongside this contemporary group of morris dancers, the Blackthorn Ritualistic Folk.

As mentioned, the idea that we are all part of an unbroken lineage of ritual is always present in my mind, and the deeper you get into this stuff, the more the idea of needing to trace everything back to Pagan times to give it authenticity seems to become completely irrelevant. All of these practices are interconnected and part of something much larger than ourselves, something profoundly human through which we try to make sense of our existence, of who we are, where we are, and where we're going. So whenever I witness a new ritual such as this festival, which has one foot firmly rooted in the past and one

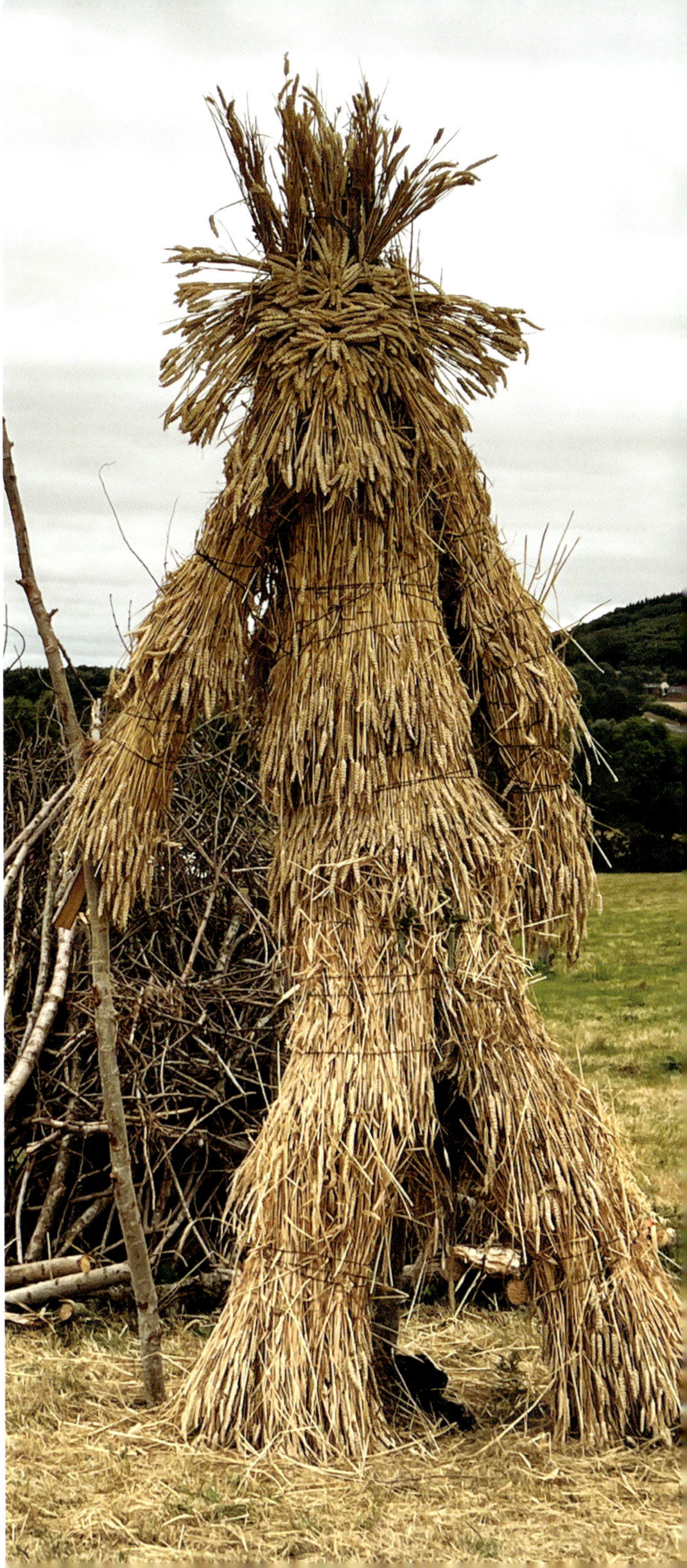

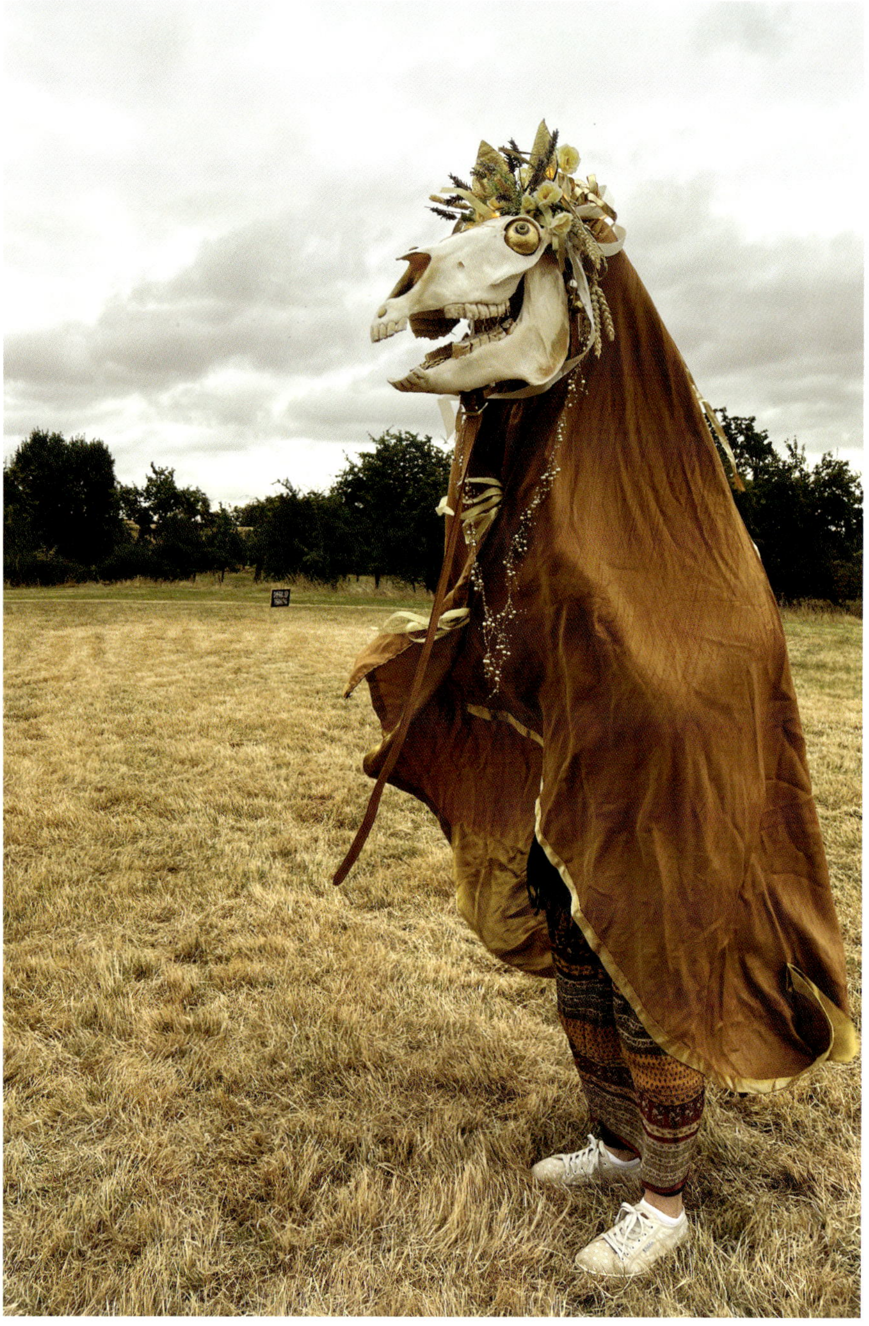

foot striding into the future, it feels no different to a folk custom that's been going on for centuries: it all comes from the same place, that very human need for ritual, to celebrate being alive, to build communities, to plug into Nature, the cosmos and the great unknown.

To me, Blackthorn Ritualistic Folk represent one of the finest examples of a pioneering new approach to contemporary folk culture. Like Boss Morris (see page 268), they demonstrate the innately human need for ritual and reconnection with Nature, the strength of which can be measured by the large crowds and young audiences that these new morris sides attract. During my dark days of depression I was so far removed from all this – from Nature, the seasons, the feeling of being part of something larger than myself. You could say I was urbanized; I had no sense of purpose, I was stuck inside my own head, and constantly ruminating about things that were out of my control. Once I came out the other side, it was as if I was mirroring the patterns of the seasons that these ritual practices acknowledge and celebrate: I had passed through the darkness of my own internal winter and reached spring. It was if I had come back to life and had been given a second chance. After speaking to members of Blackthorn, I found their community had helped them in similar ways. Clarky, an extremely charismatic member of the group who acts as a kind of compère/master of ceremonies, later told me, "Blackthorn lifted me from a very dark period in my life; the bond and the brotherhood is something I've never felt in my life before."

After musical performances and various forms of entertainment throughout the day, with the horse skulls of Mari Lwyds (see page 231) and other sinister-looking creatures wandering about, torches were lit and the Blackthorn Ritualistic Folk gathered on the yellow grass. Their costumes were dark, and their faces painted blue and black to represent the colours of the blackthorn berry, a plant I was told has long been associated with witches. Their clothes were covered in tassels in the same colours, resembling raven plumage. They started by performing a collection of beautiful haunting songs.

My friend Elspeth Anne (who has since left Blackthorn) blew the crowd away with her haunting rendition of "When I was a Young Girl". When I spoke to her afterward, she explained how the group had helped her make the decision to return from Berlin to her native town of Hereford. "It was folk-related and looked interesting and dark," she said, "and it gave me an impression that things were happening in Hereford, that there was some kind of scene to go back to, which was encouraging."

After the singing, the group danced. In this part of the country, on the borderlands of Wales, the most common style of dancing is "border morris", in which everything has a dark edge: instead of waving hankies, they bang together sticks and there's a general heavy metal/goth vibe. Although not as old as Cotswold morris, in some ways border morris seems more ancient and there's a sense of it being a magical ancient rite of passage. I felt this particularly while witnessing one of Blackthorn's elaborate rituals, blurring the boundaries between performance art, Neopaganism and traditional morris dancing. For this reason, I'd place them in the new "progressive morris" tradition, aka "prog morris", and I'm fascinated by the way they're inspiring a new generation to engage with their regional culture and not to feel they need to leave their native area to find like-minded people.

Later that evening, I asked Jamie, one of the Blackthorn founders, why he thought it was important to create new festivals such as this, which were rooted in the past. He replied, "It's about reminding people of what we used to celebrate and to be focused on protecting the land and looking after it."

Sarah, another founding member, added, "I think we've lost touch with the old ways; we've gone too far the other way and people are starting to realize that, and that the environment should be at the forefront of everyone's minds."

In the darkness, flaming torches were lit as smoke machines blew a mist across the horizon, and the song "John Barleycorn" was sung by all to the banging of drums as everyone danced together in a grand finale. It felt remarkably spiritual as the crowd lost themselves in this moment of selflessness and danced freely. The Mari Lwyds swayed among them, bagpipes struck up, bells were rung, and everybody clapped in time to the beat. It felt as if we were walking in the steps of those ancestors who once sang "John Barleycorn" while harvesting their fields centuries ago, and again I could feel their spectres around me. The song ended and the crowd cheered. The original plan had been to burn the effigy of John Barleycorn now, but due to this freakishly dry summer, a result of global warming, John Barleycorn couldn't be sacrificed for the fear that the fire would spread and set light to the surrounding fields and woodland.

I thought of my painting and now I could see it clearly: John Barleycorn standing intact in the field, surrounded by the ghosts of the past undertaking their harvest duties, while a Mari Lwyd lingers like some kind of grim reaper among modern farmers who are still awaiting John Barleycorn's fall. Yet the Blackthorn Ritualistic Folk stand with torches in hand, refraining from lighting the effigy in an act of defiance against climate change, and in this way representing the reconnection to Nature that seasonal rituals cultivate within us as human beings.

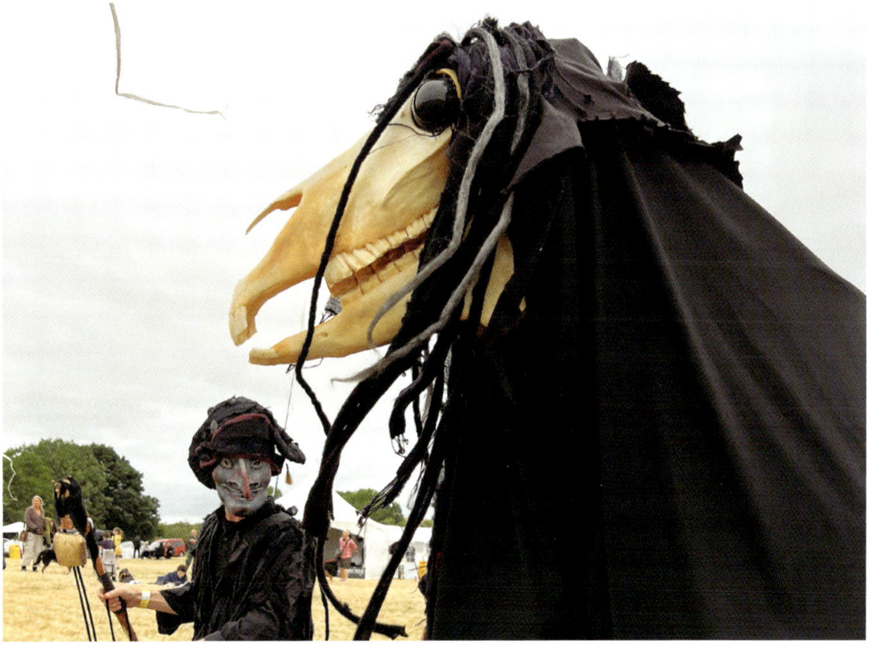

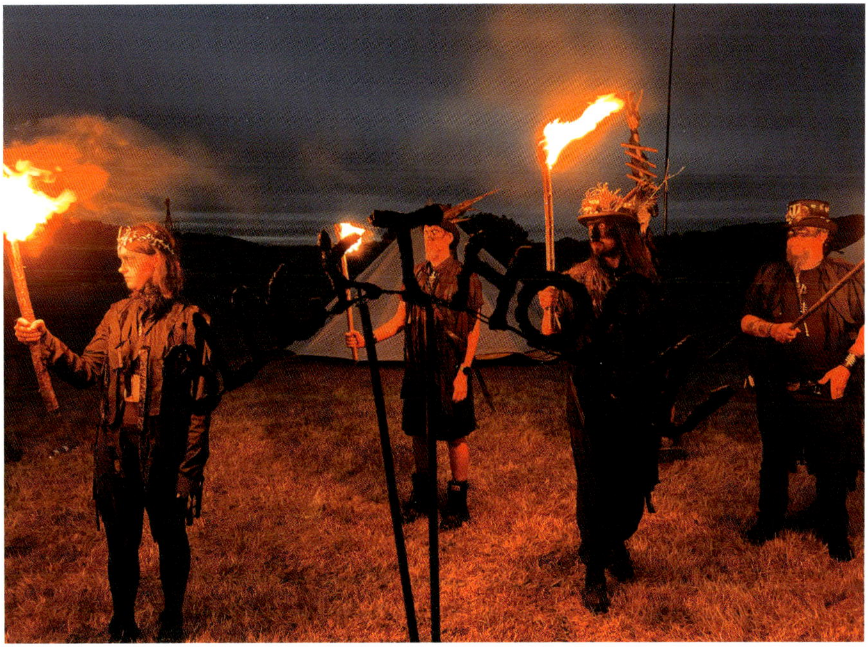

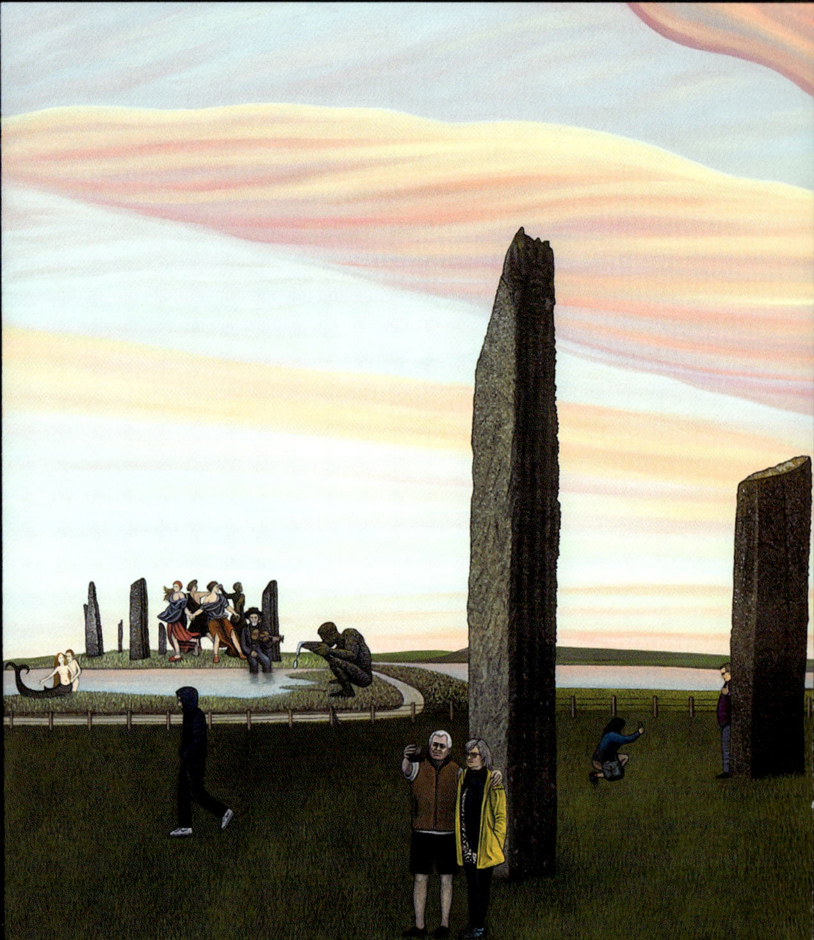

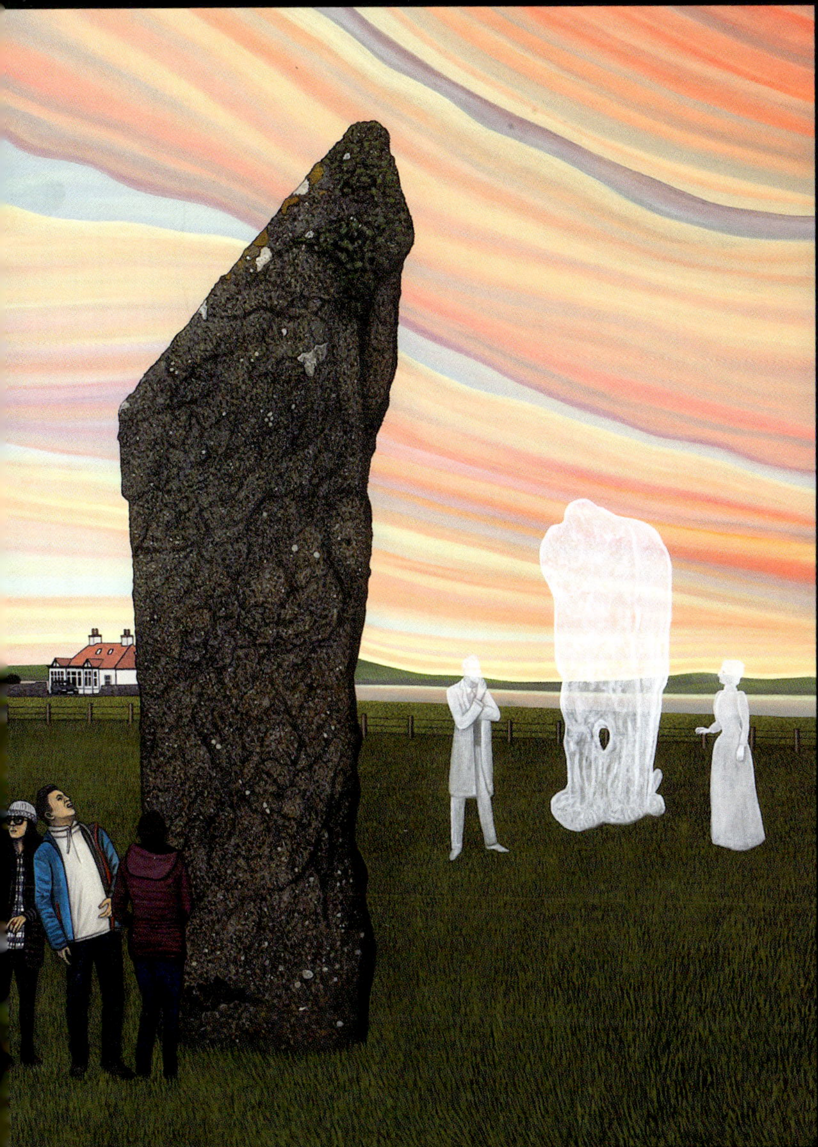

ORKNEY

Oil on Canvas,
100cm × 150cm

2022

The Stones of Stenness and Brodgar

ORKNEY

AUGUST VISIT

I arrived in Orkney by ferry late at night, on the eve of my thirty-sixth birthday in early August. This was to be something of a soul-searching trip, as I wasn't quite sure what I was doing there; all I knew was that I had been drawn by photographs of the remarkable megaliths I'd seen in Julian Cope's iconic book *The Modern Antiquarian*. I had also learned in a BBC documentary that Orkney was once the Neolithic capital of Britain where the cult of standing stones first began, before spreading across the rest of Britain and Ireland.

When I arrived at my hotel in the town of Kirkwall, it was already past midnight, and finding no one at reception, I kipped on a sofa in the hotel lobby before finally being discovered by a member of staff and given the key to my room. In the morning, I was desperate to get out to see the stones, but when I caught a glimpse of myself in the mirror, I couldn't believe how tired I looked. The last few months had been taken up with my *Ritual Britain* exhibition in the Crypt Gallery at St Pancras New Church, which had gone far better than I could ever have possibly imagined (see page 275). It had been a collaboration with the Museum of British Folklore and had attracted thousands of visitors and a lot of media attention. However, while it'd marked one of the most exciting times of my life, it had wiped me out, both mentally and physically. Now, it felt like I was once again heading out into the great unknown, not quite sure which direction my work would be taking me next. All I knew was I'd learned to follow my instinct, which had led me here.

After investigating the town, and discovering a remarkable Norman Green Man carving in St Magnus Cathedral, which made me feel like I was exactly where I should be, I jumped on a bus. While I peered out at the wind-beaten landscape, I imagined Neolithic tribes dragging gigantic stones and building the first monuments. But on arriving at the Maeshowe visitor centre to see the chambered cairn, I was devastated to discover that, following the Covid pandemic, all of the chambered tombs of Orkney were still closed.

After a moment or two, I pulled myself together and headed on foot to the equally magnificent Standing Stones of Stenness. Here, three huge stones had stood like brooding giants since 3100 BCE. The sense of openness, time and space in the landscape was overwhelming; it was an incredibly meditative environment, and it wouldn't have surprised me if this was where the pioneers of building stone circles first dreamed up the idea.

As I approached the Stones of Stenness, I was immediately struck by their size: they were enormous and remarkably thin, and I couldn't help but speculate how the hell these had been erected using simple tools all those thousands of years ago. They also felt powerful, demanding immediate respect. This may explain why so many tales have sprung up around the stones, as folklore is often a way of explaining the inexplicable.

At the time of my visit, the sky was a flat grey, which meant no shadows were visible. Instead, tourists clustered around the stones, with some taking pictures on phones while others seemed to be enjoying a quiet moment with the stones by themselves. I began taking pictures of these contemporary pilgrims, and straight away started to envision a painting. It would be a wide horizontal composition, capturing the spaciousness of the landscape, with the Stones of Stenness in the foreground and these same people assembled around them; now I just needed to fill in the rest. When painting folk customs, there's nearly always a central figure in the ritual to approach and ask about a custom's origins and the local beliefs, but here it was just me and the stones, so I'd brought along some books to give me some insights.

Beyond the stones and closer to the shoreline stood a low, white cottage with a sign saying "Odin House". In my Orkney guidebook, I read that a monolith known as the Odin Stone had stood near there, but was unfortunately destroyed in 1814 by a tenant farmer who resented people trespassing on his land. Until then, the stone had been used in engagement ceremonies, when couples used to hold hands through a hole in it. Magical rituals were also performed, in which people made oaths, promises and took the "Vow of Odin". Today, the house stands close to the spot of the now destroyed monolith and acts as a lone surviving reference to it.

In my mind's eye, I could imagine a couple getting engaged and the stone still standing, and I decided these elements would be making their way into my composition, along with Odin House, as a sort of spectral representation of the destroyed monolith. It felt magical to be wandering through this ancient landscape while the vision for my next painting revealed itself to me.

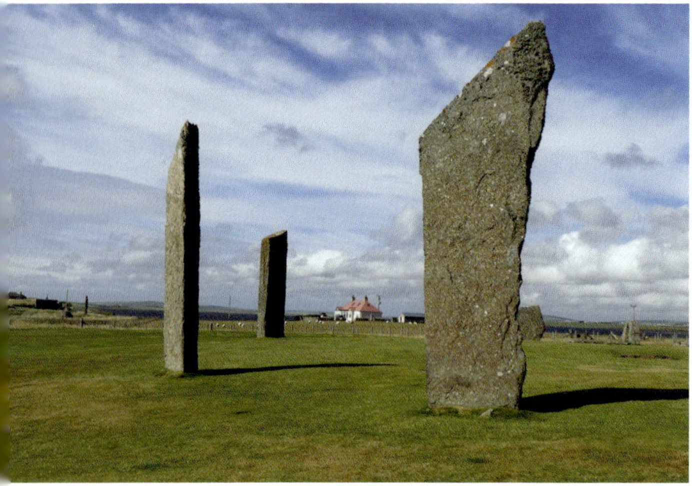

On leaving the Stones of Stenness and making my way to the narrow bridge that leads onto the Ness of Brodgar, I passed the Watch Stone, a monolith that's said to come alive every year at midnight at Hogmanay (New Year's Eve) to take its annual drink from the loch.

According to local author Tom Muir's *Orkney Folk Tales*, there are many traditional Orcadian beliefs connected with magical sea beings, including the Finfolk, mermen and mermaids, and the selkies, a type of hybrid human–seal that can transform themselves into full human form. Tales about these mythological creatures described how they seduced real humans and lured them from land into the sea. Now, visions of them appeared to me as I scribbled in my sketchbook.

I wandered on toward the Ring of Brodgar, one of the largest stone circles in Britain, dating from about 2500 to 2000 BCE. On my way there, I passed the Ness of Brodgar, where a major archaeological dig was taking place, unearthing buildings in a giant complex dating to about 3300 BCE, roughly the same time as the Stones of Stenness. Here, I met a tall archaeologist with a ponytail, who told me that the structures in the complex didn't look residential. He also said that the twenty-seven stones that survived today of the original sixty within the Ring of

Brodgar came from all over Orkney, suggesting that different tribal communities may have come together to build these monuments. I loved the idea that, like folk customs, the building of monuments strengthened community bonds and brought people together.

I asked him whether he knew any folk tales connected to the Ring of Brodgar and he told me one that I've heard in other forms at other standing stone sites across the UK: that a party of giants and a fiddler once gathered at the site where the stones now stand, and as the revellers danced through the night, they lost track of time. When the sun rose on the holy Sabbath, the unfortunate group were turned to stone as a punishment by God.

When I reached the Ring of Brodgar, I stood and gazed in absolute awe at the incredible structure, built from stones that had been brought here from all over the Orkney islands, and I imagined the giants dancing to the fiddler's tune, and then the unfortunate moment when they were all turned into stone. My composition complete (well, almost), I turned and headed back through the incredible landscape of Neolithic monuments. The grey sky had shifted and clouds swirled and danced – as the giants had once done – in a spectacular sunset, while seals (or maybe selkies) dived into the water of the loch as the stones watched on from the land where they have stood vigil for over five thousand years.

This was proving to be a life-changing walk. Not only did I have my painting in mind, but I'd also learned about the fantastical tales associated with ancient monuments, and I'd started imagining what other great stories could be told about similar sites across the UK – a new series of paintings had been born.

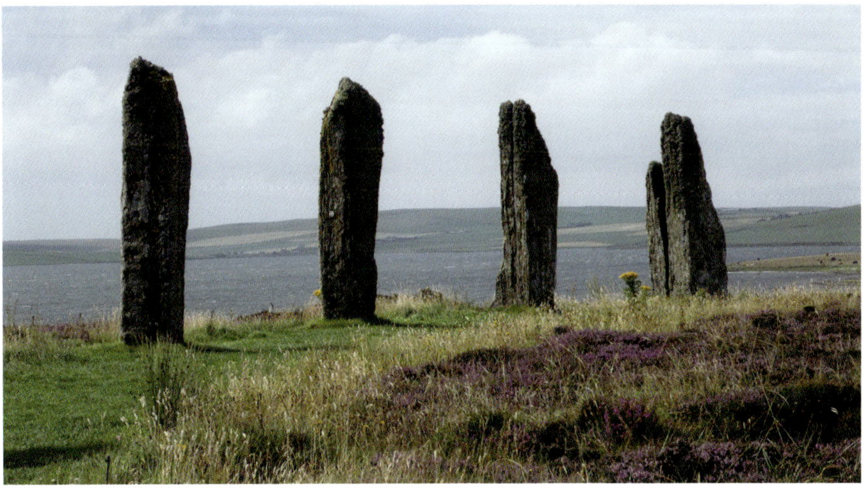

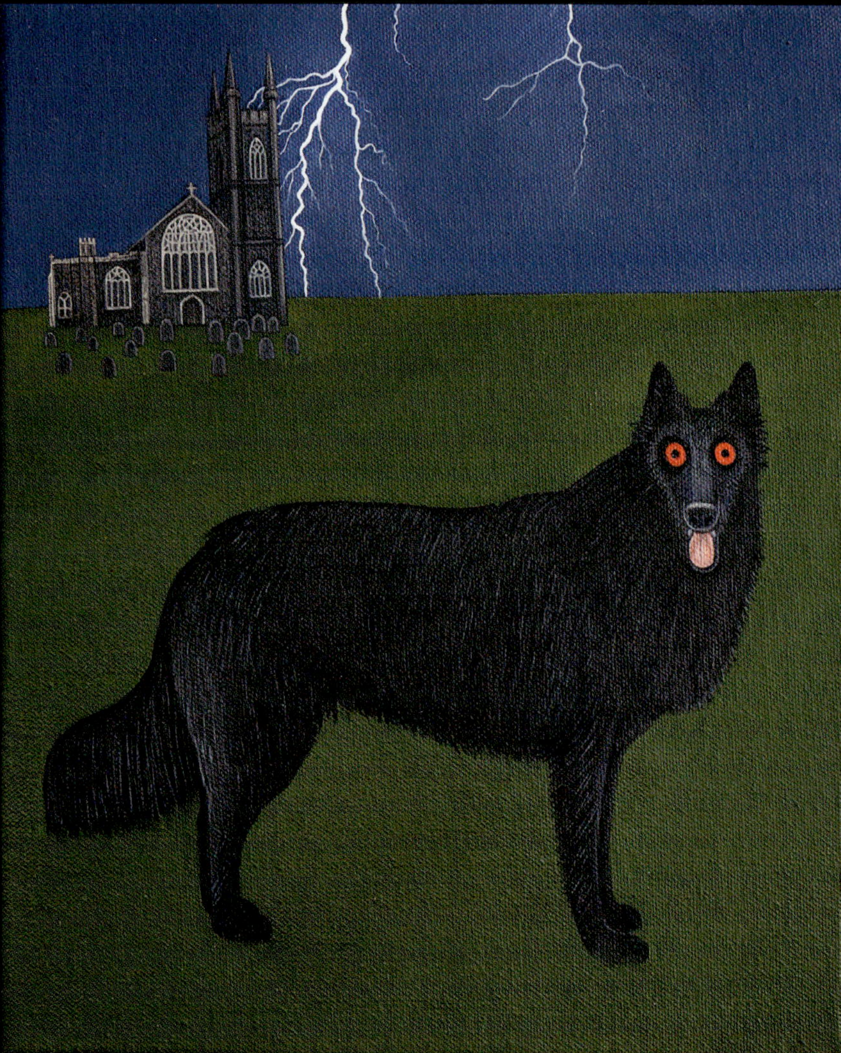

THE BLACK SHUCK

Oil on Canvas, 30cm × 25cm

2023

The Black Shuck

SUFFOLK

FIRST WEEKEND IN AUGUST

I have long heard tales of ferocious black dogs in British folklore, with the most famous of all being that of Black Shuck in Bungay, Suffolk. Here, a new festival has recently been created to celebrate the mysterious and harrowing events that took place on August 4, 1577. I had been invited to Bungay by one of the festival founders, my fellow artist Stuart Pearson Wright, to take part in an exhibition that would run alongside the festival, with the theme being of course Black Shuck, as well as Suffolk folklore in general.

When I arrived, I went straight to meet Stuart at St Mary's Church, where the original story is said to have taken place. I asked him about the origins of the new festival, and he explained that it was based on an account written by Rev. Abraham Fleming in 1577. While Fleming hadn't been present himself, according to his account, terrified parishioners had taken shelter in St Mary's Church during a particularly violent thunderstorm. Many of them were praying when suddenly there was a loud noise, and a huge black dog burst into the church. It ran up and down the aisles in a frenzy, and killed two people in prayer. Then it attacked a third person who survived, but was left in a state described bizarrely as resembling a "leather draw purse, pulled tight". Stuart concluded, "After that attack, Black Shuck, who's more commonly known as the black dog in Bungay, headed off to a town called Blythburgh about 17 miles away and is said to have killed more people. He also left some claw marks in the door of the church, and then disappeared."

Stories of sinister black dogs have been reported all around Britain and according to Stuart, the legend of Black Shuck was still very much alive and kicking here in East Anglia. In most accounts, the dog is described as being the size of an ox, with shaggy black hair. Stuart noted, "The word 'Shuck' could relate to an old English word, *shucka*, or something along those lines, which means shaggy or hairy. The etymology of the name 'Shuck' could also mean the Devil, and Abraham Flemings puts forward the possibility that the Shuck is the Devil or in such a likeness. It's also said in descriptions that he has glowing red eyes." Stuart added that in one of the accounts, Old Shuck is associated with Norse mythology and said to be one of Odin's black hounds which had escaped and roamed the area ever since.

Unlike most of my work, my painting of Old Shuck was made prior to my visit, based on folktales about the beast. The idea of a mysterious black dog pursuing victims had particularly resonated with me, as the animal has often been used as a metaphor for depression, famously by Winston Churchill. It seems there is a psychological edge to the legend of the Shuck.

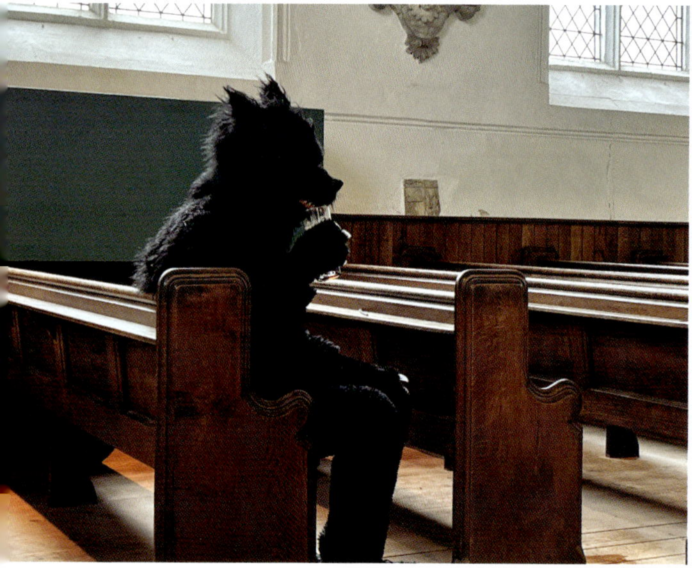

Stuart appeared to share some of my sentiments and explained, "Black Shuck is sometimes thought about in the context of mental health, so one of the things we're doing in the festival is to invite people to write down their personal demons on a card and then we burn those cards; so in a sense we're encouraging people to rid themselves of their personal demons."

Interestingly, he explained what the legend of the black dog represented to him on a personal level: "Perhaps it's partly a connection with Nature, but it's also a connection with the mammalian essence within us, which human culture has in a way sort of squashed, and I like to think that by thinking about Shuck, it's possible for us to connect with our pre-human mammalian self; for me, that's at the heart of what I might loosely describe as Shuckism."

I loved hearing Stuart's thoughts, and particularly the idea of connecting to our pre-human selves. I'd come across the idea of reconnecting with Nature and our pre-Christian selves many times, but the idea of going one step further and reconnecting with the pre-human self was something that I had not heard articulated so clearly until now. Yet it made total sense, especially if you take into consideration the amount of animal guising found in so many folk customs.

When it came to the festival, as in the original story, the weather was terrible with torrential rain, so the main parade ended up being moved into a local hall. During the parade, a huge effigy of Black Shuck was placed on a large "bonfire" that used lights and smoke to mimic flames, while children danced and chanted,

Children of Bungay, pray your hardest tonight –
Something is coming that feels far from right.
Rumbles of thunder, flashes of lightning,
Red eyes in long grass, watching you, frightening.
Here comes the hound to chase you from bed,
The scratching, the snarling, turn around and you're dead!

There was also a wide array of other events, such as a comical "In Discussion with the Black Dog", where Black Shuck boasted about his lack of remorse for the murders he'd committed in 1577, and philosophically accused the host and the human species as a whole of having "forgotten what you are". Then there were theatrical musical performances in the church itself, with a huge effigy of the black dog being paraded around the church pews, before Black Shuck himself, or at least a man in a shaggy dog suit, with red eyes and snarling jaws, ran through the aisles, clambering over the church pews and terrifying the spectators as the folklore enthusiast and comedian Stewart Lee (who has family connections to this part of the world) played the character of Abraham Flemings and read out his original account with some funny additions, before being dramatically devoured by the black dog. The whole festival felt completely unlike anything I'd ever experienced before, a refreshing contemporary take on an ancient tale.

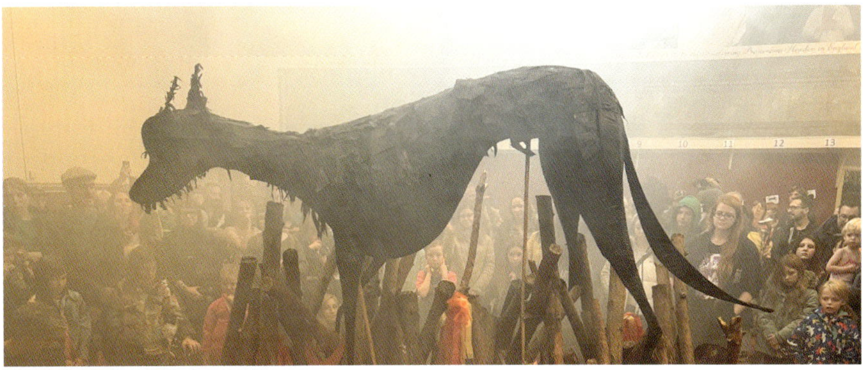

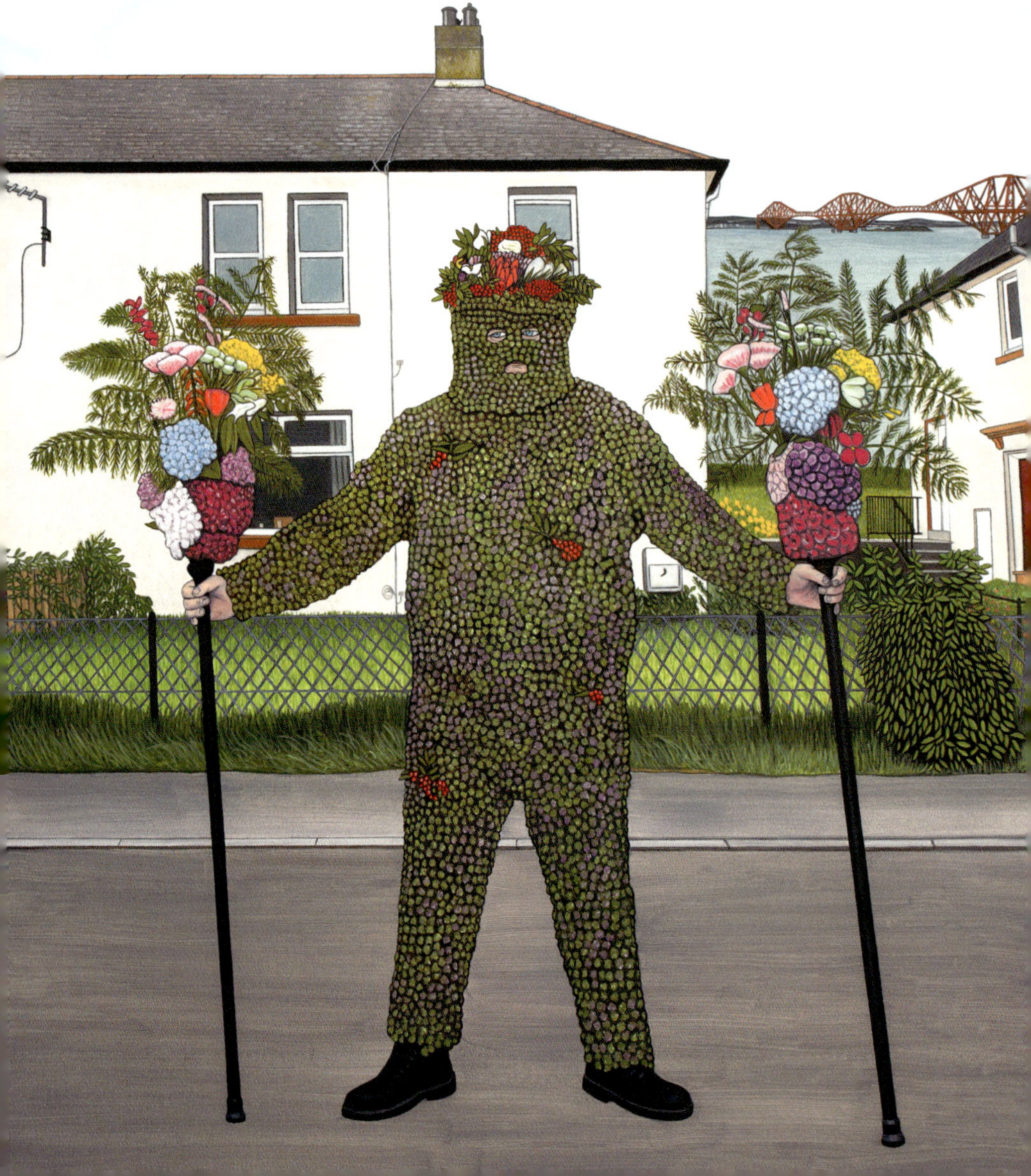

THE BURRYMAN

Oil on Canvas, 80cm × 70cm

2018

The Burryman

NEAR EDINBURGH

SECOND FRIDAY IN AUGUST

Of all the traditions I've come across, perhaps the most creatively inspiring has been that of the Burryman of South Queensferry, who has given rise to a number of my paintings, sculptures and even a song.

I will never forget the first time I arrived in South Queensferry and saw the famous Forth Bridge with its crisscross structure of red-painted steel spanning the Firth of Forth. The view was so vast that I felt a peacefulness come over me and immediately fell in love with the place. I've since been back many times and in those years when I haven't been able to make it, I've felt distracted and agitated, like I'm missing out.

That first evening, I watched from my B&B window as the horizon lit up pink and orange in the setting sun, while drunken teenagers wandered about laughing, followed by the sound of smashing glass and running footsteps. As I was sitting there, the folklorist Doc Rowe rang to find out where I was staying. He invited me to the private ceremony for the dressing of the Burryman, which would take place the next morning at the Stag's Head Hotel, just up the street from where I was staying. I felt honoured; Doc had again opened doors for me in ways that could have potentially taken me years to manage.

The next morning, I woke early and went straight to the Stag's Head, where I was made very welcome. There was the smell of sizzling bacon as, laughing in thick Scottish accents, people queued near the bar to help themselves to the complimentary bacon butties. In a back room, the first thing I noticed were sheets of newspaper with sticky green burrs laid out neatly across them. Burrs come from burdock, those bristly seeds that stick to your clothes (and dog) when you're out on country walks. Apparently they were the inspiration for the invention of Velcro. These seeds are what give the "Burryman" his name, as he is literally covered from head to toe in them. The second thing I noticed was that the sheets of burrs were spread out across a dance floor with disco lights.

I was introduced to the man who was about to become the Burryman for the eighth time. He seemed focused like an athlete before a race; I could see in his eyes that this was a serious undertaking, a self-sacrifice of sorts, and no joke. After a brief chat, he made his way to the disco floor where a party of people, including Doc Rowe, began to dress him. Doc was perhaps the first man who wasn't from Scotland to take part in the dressing.

The first step involved the Burryman putting on a long-sleeve black top and matching leggings, which were then sewn together at the waist. A balaclava was also sewn on to his outfit, while his footwear consisted of a pair of sturdy boots. His eyes, his mouth and his hands would be the only areas of his body not to be covered in burrs. Watching him being dressed highlighted the discomfort the Burryman was about to endure.

The sheets of burrs were pressed onto his body, beginning with his legs and working upward, with any missing patches being filled in by hand. Once covered, his legs would have to remain slightly apart. When the dressers reached his upper body, two people stood next to him who were the perfect height for him to lean on their shoulders, so his arms could also be covered. His arms would have to remain in a raised position all day, as if he were to lower them, they'd get stuck to his sides. To help keep his arms supported, the Burryman holds two upside-down rakes covered in flowers.

There was something unnerving about his balaclava being covered, like watching a regular man becoming a hybrid part-plant, part-man; as if he were leaving behind his human form and taking on a new identity, which of course he was: he was being transformed into the Burryman, who was to become the scapegoat of the town, taking away all the bad luck.

When I got an opportunity to speak to the Burryman in his costume, he shared the stories he'd been told about the custom's origins. "It dates back nine hundred years," he said. "With this being a fishing village, at times of a poor harvest the Burryman would go about as a scapegoat to take away the evil spirits and the fishing would return." Today, in exchange for a lucky burr to bring them good fortune throughout the year, the locals feed him whisky through a straw to ease the burden of his pain. One of the Burryman's dressers, the Scottish storyteller Erin Farley described the tradition's appeal as a "combination of the community that surrounds it". Erin added, "It's hard to describe exactly what it is that it does – it's very human and very local to South Queensferry, but also universal." She confirmed its herring fishing origins, describing it as a "plant-based, surf and turf tradition".

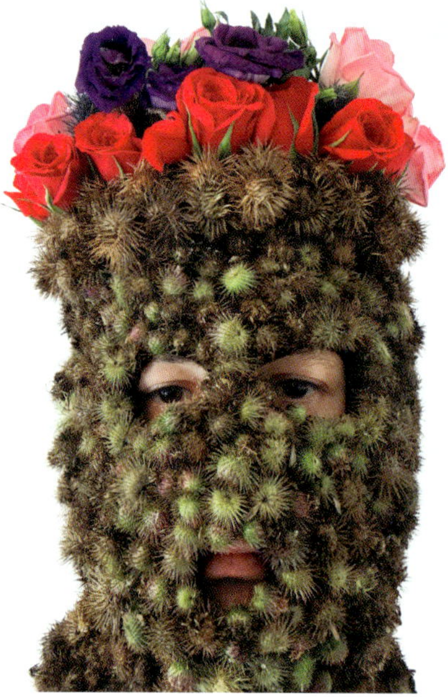

SELF-PORTRAIT AS THE BURRYMAN

Plastic flowers, burdock seeds picked from Hampstead Heath and balaclava worn by the artist, 36cm × 23cm

2020

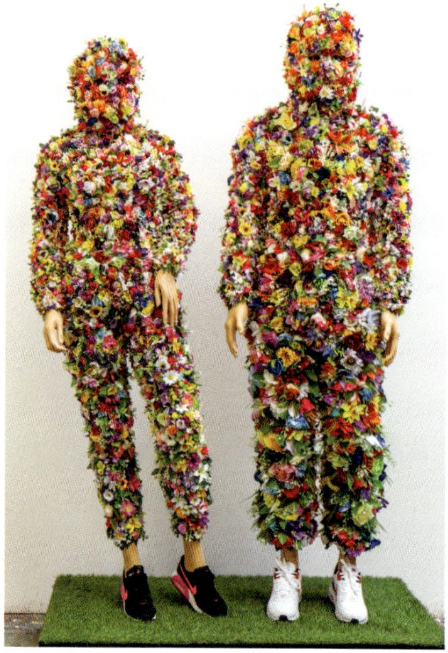

MAN MADE NATURE

Synthetic flowers, sports trainers on plastic mannequins and artificial grass, 196cm × 122cm × 61cm

2022

Doc Rowe shared his thoughts, telling me, "There were once Burrymans all over the east coast of Scotland in fishing communities. When the fishing was bad, they took one of their own and dragged him through the streets in a net and they would throw anything at him, herring bones and burrs; he was a scapegoat and next time the hauls were great." He said when he first came to the event in the sixties, the main story was that, "King Malcolm was hiding from the English, and accidentally got covered in burrs and thought this is great, and then patched up his whole body in burrs and escaped", highlighting how the stories of folk traditions such as the Burryman come and go.

The final task of the dressing was to put the Burryman's hat on his head and secure it in place with burrs. The hat was a bowler with a brim covered in burrs and with flowers beautifully arranged on top.

Once dressed, the Burryman was ready to begin his gruelling 9-mile (14.5km) hike through the streets of South Queensferry. The local press were waiting outside to get a shot of him appearing from the Stag's Head, accompanied by the two kilted attendants who would help to support his arms and remain by his side throughout the day. The cameras started clicking, the ritual began, and the bell ringer leading the procession started to shout repeatedly, "Hip hip hooray, it's the Burryman's day", all the while ringing his bell.

The Burryman and his party set off toward a housing estate, where locals appeared from their homes in fluffy slippers and dressing gowns, armed with trays of whisky. The sight of the Burryman in front of the pebbledashed houses seemed to make perfect sense, despite it being so surreal. Both the Burryman and the houses looked as if they belonged to South Queensferry; texturally they worked together perfectly. I knew I had to paint this, and the scene of the Burryman standing in front of a pebbledashed house, with the Firth and Forth Bridge stretching into the distance, has since become one of my most popular paintings.

The juxtaposition of the manmade with the natural burrs, and the fact that Velcro is a synthetic version of a burr, reminded me that all things have their origins in Nature, even though some may now seem far removed from it. This later inspired me to make a sculpture called *Man Made Nature*, in which I covered two life-sized mannequins with synthetic flowers, gluing them to the same sort of undergarments that the Burryman wears: a balaclava, long-sleeve top and long johns. As he wandered through the streets of South Queensferry, the Burryman made me very aware that we are part of Nature and not above it.

The photographers were still following the Burryman and trying to order him where to stand, but he was having none of it. Instead, he politely supped whisky through a straw as burrs were picked from his body, much to the delight of the locals. I imagine they were not necessarily superstitious people, but when it came to the Burryman, they responded to him intuitively; I got the sense that this belief ran deep, tapping into an ancestral consciousness of a time when rituals such as this were part of everyday life for people all over Britain.

The chink of coins being dropped into cups could be heard as volunteers collected money from the laughing crowds. The Burryman was offered more whisky than he could possibly drink, so it was shared among his party. To my surprise, I was handed a plastic cup with "Paddington Bear" printed on the front, and given regular top-ups throughout the day. As we continued through grey streets pulsating with life and character, more and more locals come out to perform their personal rituals of offering the Burryman a sip of whisky in exchange for a lucky burr, while terrified infants burst into tears and dogs barked behind windows with children's illustrations of the Burryman stuck to the glass. Some houses were decorated with elaborate displays in their front yards, often with imagery from children's films. This, I was told by a man and his daughter whose front lawn was covered in *Shrek* decorations, was connected to "the Ferry Fair that's happening over the weekend, where a kind of pageant is held and a queen is elected".

We walked on from the housing estate to blocks of flats, then to other streets. Besides the whisky, there were other kinds of offerings, such as songs and poetry. At the end of a cul-de-sac, a top-hatted elderly gentleman read a poem for the Burryman, while his wife, glowing with pride, passed round drinks. The next time I came, there was no man in a top hat, just the woman, who read a poem with equal delight but tears in her eyes. I still get a lump in my throat thinking about that moment.

We pressed on, fuelled with warmth from the alcohol. Our stops were becoming less residential, and more pub-based and boozy. With a large crowd now following the Burryman, we passed through a funfair on the riverfront, where a girl's braids got tangled in the Burryman's burrs and he danced tipsily from side to side. After a while, we passed right beneath the Forth Bridge; and the final stretch was now upon us. The bagpipes started to play and emotions were running high; it'd been a long day, we were all staggering slightly, and I could feel the hairs standing up all over my body. A tingle of anxiety came over me that this would soon all be over. There was one more pub stop, where the Burryman leaned on the bar, seeming euphoric but exhausted. It's the hardest bit of an act of endurance, the end. Keeping it together while knowing that it'll all soon be over.

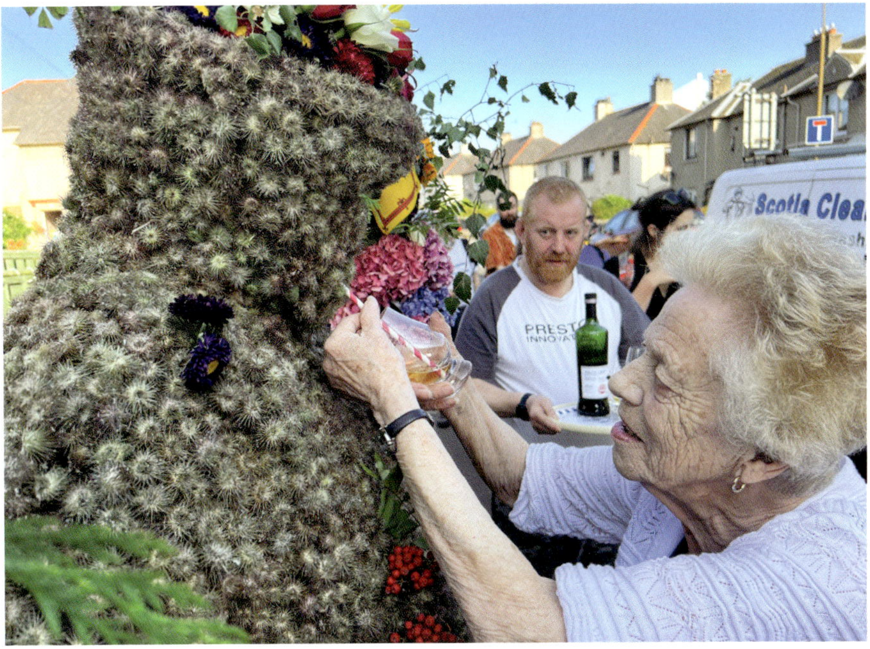
Scotia Clea
PRESTO
INNOVAT

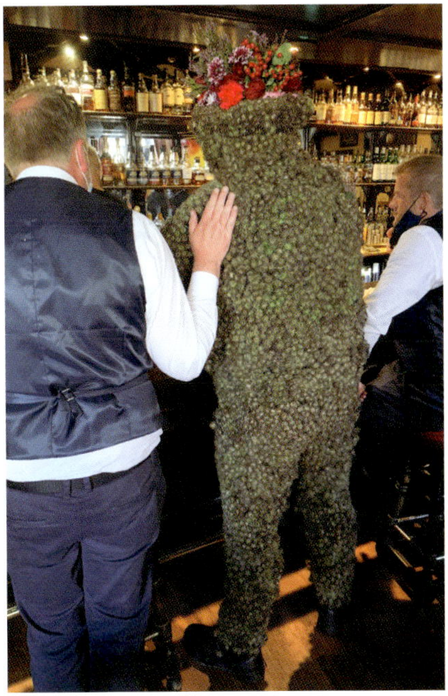

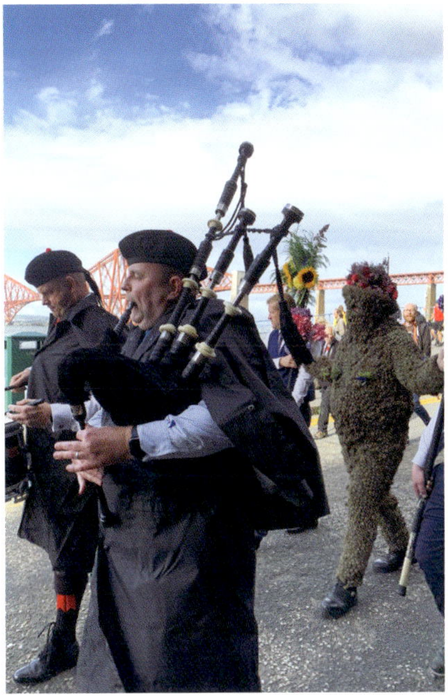

For me, the act of following the Burryman was like a form of walking meditation: you lose yourself in the moment, your everyday problems dissolve and you give yourself over to the force of the Burryman. I found it incredibly cathartic and natural: it makes so much sense at the time and nothing else matters, as if an ancient feeling that has been switched off within our DNA has been turned back on. To give ourselves over to a force that represents something greater than ourselves feels like harking back to times of Nature worship, superstition and magical thinking. I was completely lost in the moment. It's a somewhat addictive feeling. Like I say, the anxiety is that you never want it to end.

When we were nearly back at the Stag's Head, a group photo was taken at a spot where the Forth Bridge could be seen in all its splendour. Then we headed through the pub doors and back to the dance floor where the day had begun. We were all drunk but fully present. The Burryman's kilted companions used scissors to get his mask off as quickly as possible; they peeled it back, steam came out like a boiled kettle and the scratched, red face of the man inside appeared; it was like a rebirth and as if a different man had emerged from the one who went it in. It'd clearly been a transformative experience not just for him, but for all of us who'd spent the day following him.

I discovered that at the end of the ceremony, it's a great honour to be gifted the hat to look after for the next twelve months. When I've been back over the years, I've seen tears roll down the cheeks of the recipient from a sense of honour that's touching to witness. In 2020, I was lucky enough to be gifted the actual mask worn by the Burryman, which I turned into a sculpture by recreating the hat with artificial flowers.

Admittedly, my memory of my first visit is hazy from this point on, but I do remember sticking around for a bit and then waking up on the train at King's Cross in London at around midnight, with a pocket full of burrs and unopened cans of beer at my feet.

Hangover aside, I can only imagine the intense discomfort the Burryman must have felt for days if not weeks afterwards. I myself have picked burrs on Hampstead Heath and made my own mask to use in a video for a song I wrote about the Burryman; my face felt itchy for days afterwards and I only had it on for about ten minutes. The idea of endurance really interests me as an artist; firstly, as the detailed way I paint can feel like an act of endurance and, secondly, when I was actually painting the Burryman I was working in a tiny studio with no ventilation, so I had to keep my feet cool in an ice bucket as we were in the middle of a heatwave. The enigmatic Burryman teaches us about self-sacrifice, endurance and much more; he brings the past into the present and reconnects us with the natural world.

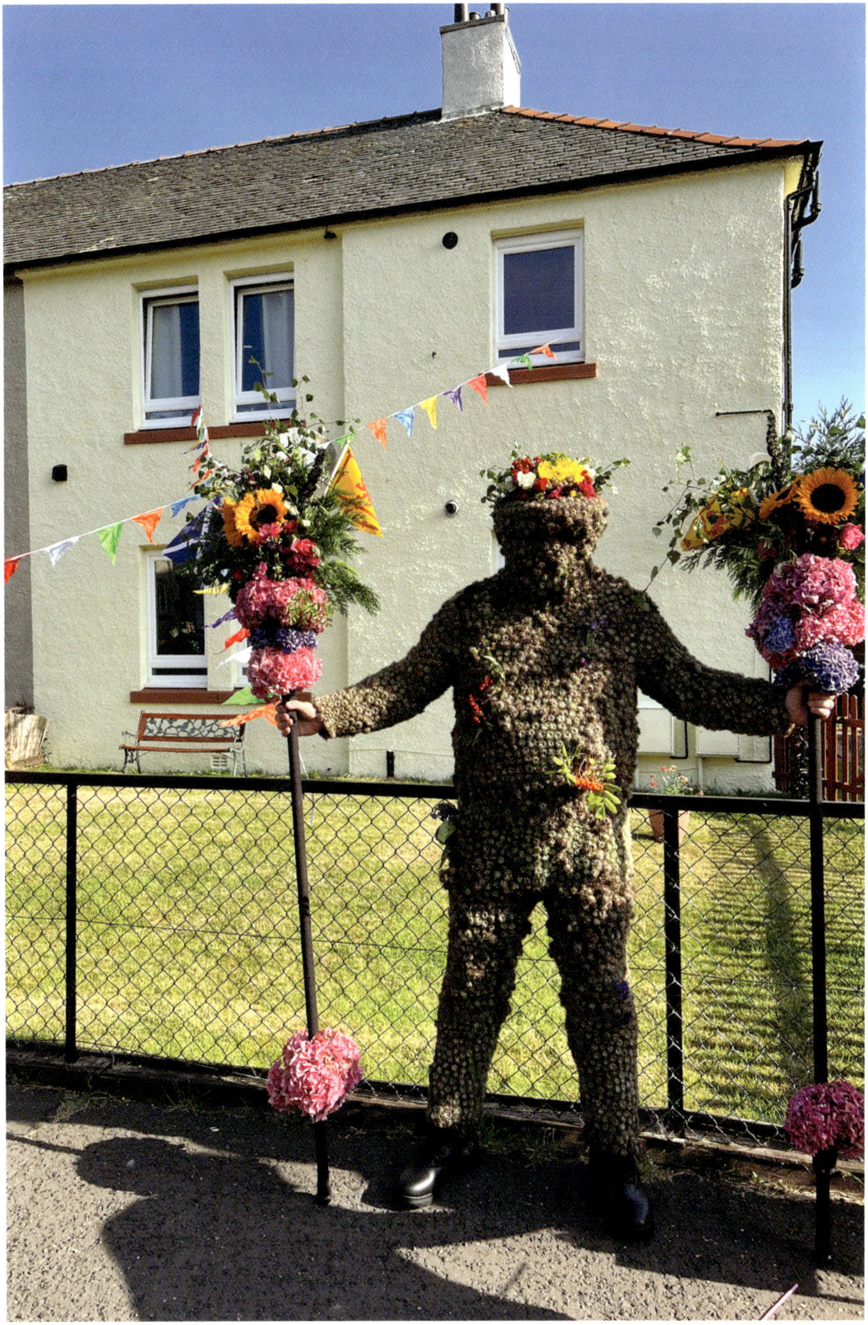

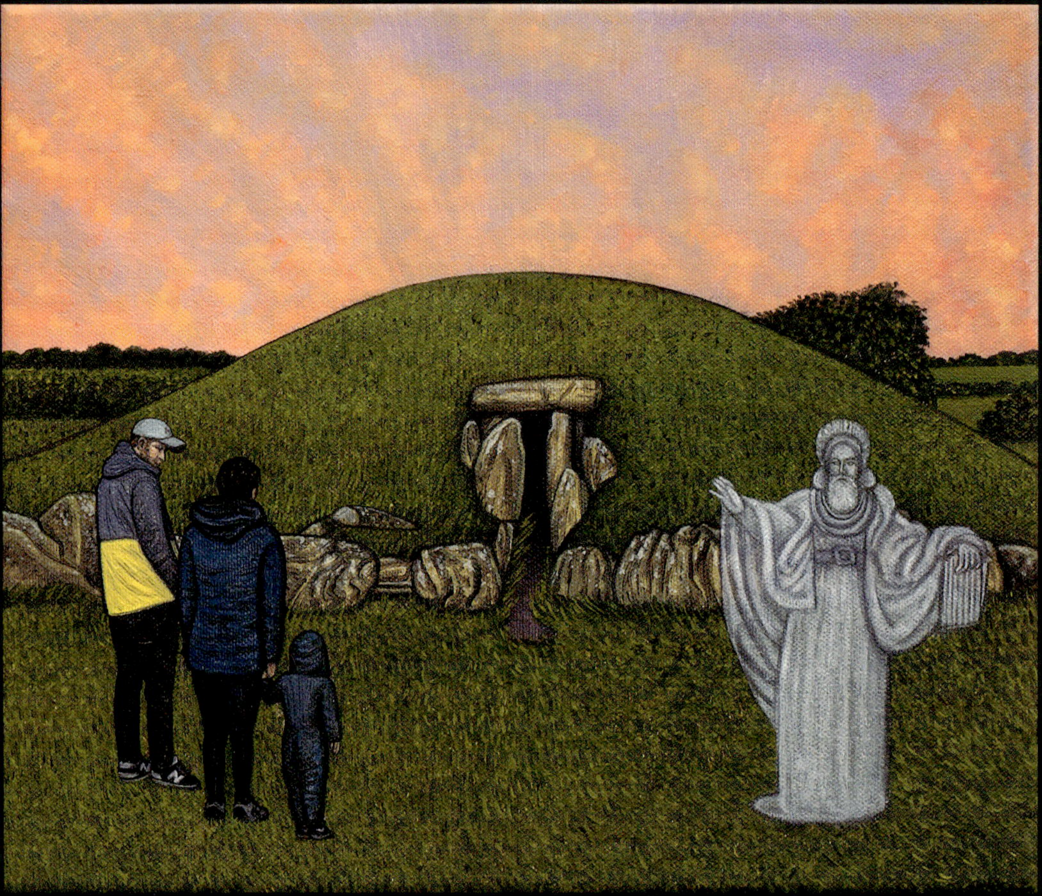

BRYN CELLI DDU CHAMBERED TOMB

Bryn Celli Ddu

GWYNEDD
AUGUST VISIT

On a drizzly weekday in August, Rose and I wandered down the path that led to a Neolithic burial chamber built to align with the rising sun of the summer solstice. The five-thousand-year-old Bryn Celli Ddu, whose name means the "Mound in the Dark Grove" in English, is one of the most famous ancient landmarks on the Isle of Anglesey, off the coast of North Wales. It was first properly explored in 1865, and then excavated in 1928 to 1929. Today, we arrived to find a family holding hands beside the monument in what seemed to be a private moment of shared grief, while children played on the top of the grass-covered mound and two or three people waited to go inside.

Bryn Celli Ddu is what's known as a passage tomb, in which the burial chamber is accessed through a narrow passageway, and the chamber and the passage are covered in soil, creating a small hill in the landscape. When we entered the mound, I could imagine the sun perfectly aligning with the entrance and the spectacle of the chamber inside being illuminated by the dawn rays of the summer solstice – how in days gone by it must have made you feel like you'd entered some kind of portal into the spirit world.

Rose and I made our way along the passageway, with its walls of rock slabs, into the main stone chamber. At the back of the tomb, there was a small shrine consisting of shells, pebbles, buttons and even a small plastic dinosaur wedged into one of the gaps between the stones. As my eyes adjusted to the darkness, a sense of timelessness arose within me, and I could imagine the original people who used this monument to lay their dead to rest, and an immediate feeling of connection with our distant ancestors came over me. I thought of the poet Maya Angelou's quote: "I come as one, but I stand as ten thousand".

I'd been particularly interested in visiting Anglesey after learning of its significance during the Roman conquest. By the year 50 CE the Romans had pretty much eliminated Druidic culture from Britain and all the Druidic strongholds had fallen except the one in Anglesey; and it was here the Druids made their last stand in about 60 or 61 CE. Before defeating Boudica, Queen of the Iceni, Suetonius Paulinus, the governor of Britannia, turned his attention to the Druids of Anglesey. The Roman historian Tacitus describes the scene in his *Annals*:

> ***On the shore stood the opposing army with its densest array of armed warriors. Between the ranks dashed women, attired in black like the Furies with their hair dishevelled, waving burning brands. All around them were Druids lifting their hands to heaven and pouring forth dreadful imprecations. Our soldiers were so petrified by the unfamiliar sight that as if their limbs were paralysed, they stood motionless, exposed to wounds. Until at last, urged by their general not to quail before a troop of frenzied women, they bore the standards onward, smote down all resistance, and wrapped the foe in the flames of his own brands.***

Tacitus goes on to say that the army then established an occupying garrison among the defeated population of the island.

When I first read this account of conquest and colonization by the Roman Empire, it made me think of the horrors committed during the years of the British Empire: how the people in these lands were once the oppressed, and what a shame it was that they themselves had to become the oppressors. I couldn't help but wonder whether if more people were aware of the complicated story of Britain – of its history of being both the oppressed and the oppressor – they would behave the way they do toward other cultures today. With this in mind, a vision for a composition came to me, as I imagined a ghost-like figure of a fallen Druid carrying the weight of the history of Anglesey and hovering beside a modern family, who were gazing upon Bryn Celli Ddu. For me, part of this incredible structure's power and awe lies in the fact that it has not only survived all this time, but it has borne witness to thousands of years of history.

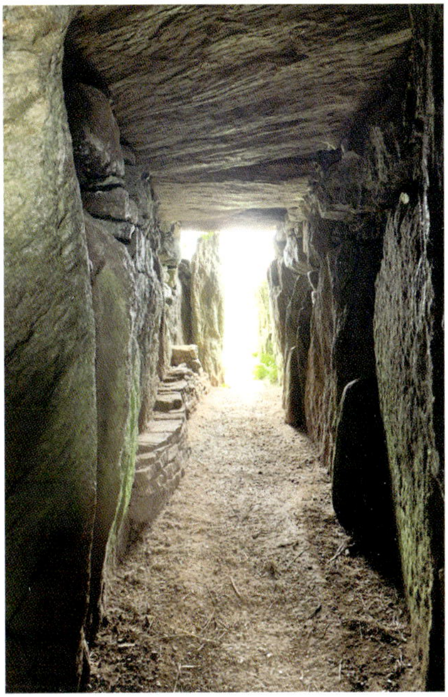

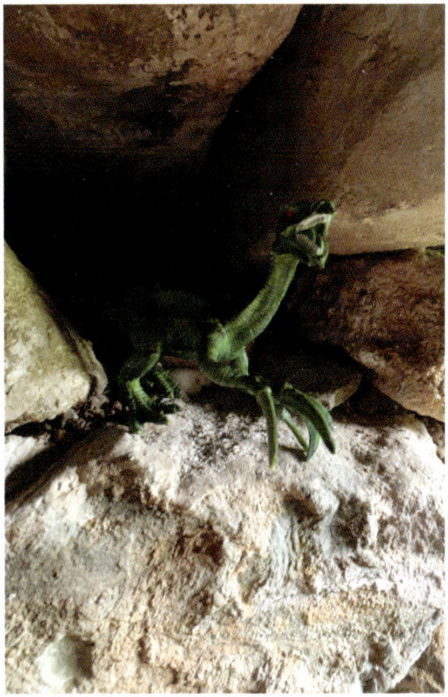

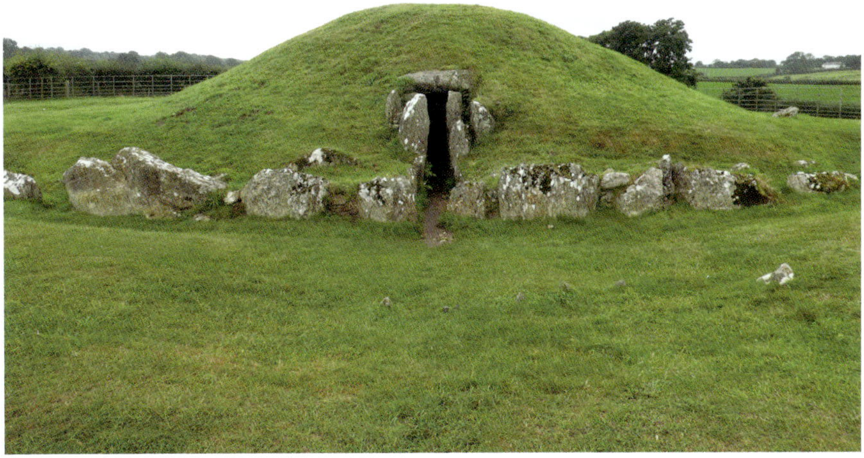

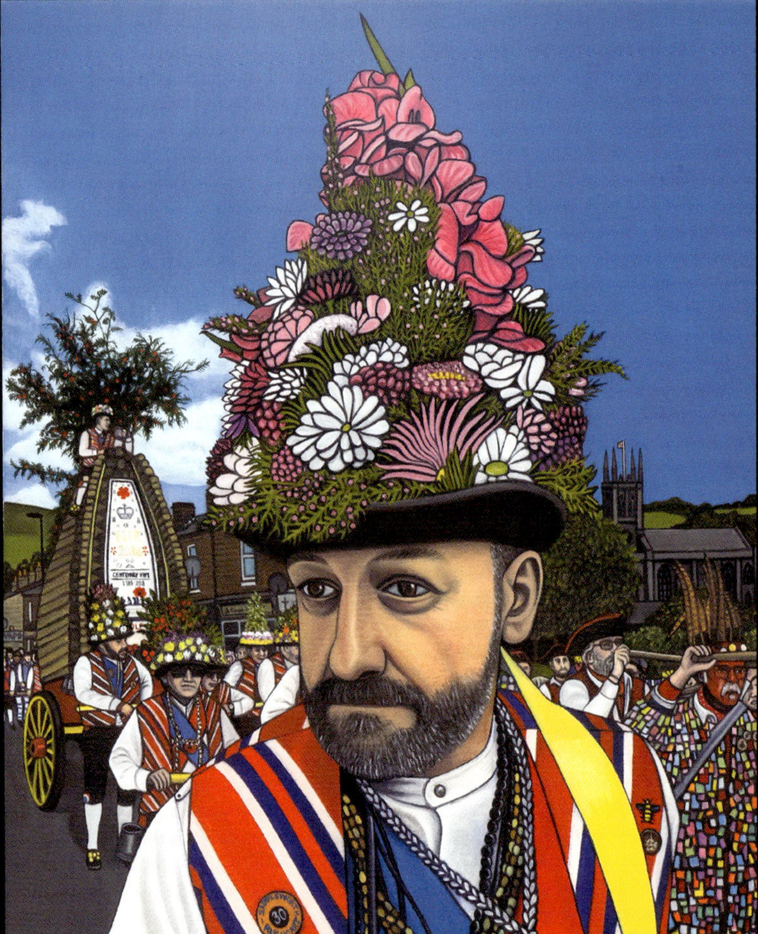

THE SADDLEWORTH RUSHCART

Oil on Canvas, 40.5cm × 30cm

The Saddleworth Rushcart

GREATER MANCHESTER
SECOND WEEKEND AFTER AUGUST 12

On the morning of the Saddleworth Rushcart, the tinkling of bells can be heard all around. For on this special weekend, morris sides from up and down the country flock to the parish of Saddleworth to take up the honour of pulling the famous Saddleworth Rushcart. A towering construction is built from layers of rushes, a type of reed, which are tied together and piled up on a large cart. Long ropes are tied to the cart's handles, enabling scores of morris men to pull the cart, acting both as its accelerator and, for those behind, as its brakes. To add to the magic, a man known as the "Jockey" sits on top of the Rushcart, from where he throws down sweets to children.

On the morning of the ceremony, I headed to the starting point in the village of Uppermill, the Commercial pub (or "Commie") where the Rushcart stood at the back. The whole pub sounded like it was chiming with thousands of bells. I love the sound of morris bells, they have a twinkly magic to them that's heart-warming, whimsical and welcoming, although not to the evil spirits they're said to deter. A large group of men in multicoloured flower-covered hats, wearing striped red waistcoats and pulled-up white socks with garters, were standing outside the pub or busy attending to the Rushcart. These were the Saddleworth Morris Men responsible for the festival, who were preparing to begin the day's proceedings.

I noticed a man on a walkie-talkie who seemed to be at the heart of the organization. His serious expression suggested he was carrying a lot of responsibility for making such an elaborate and potentially dangerous event run smoothly. How much it mattered to him on a personal level was also apparent and I knew straight away that he would be the central figure in my painting. Later that day, I had a good chat with him and learned his name was Dave Biggs, aka "Biggsy", the Squire of the Saddleworth Morris Men, which meant he was a captain of sorts.

He shared the origin story of the custom that he had become familiar with since first joining the side at the age of nine, with this now being his thirty-sixth Rushcart. He told me, "During the late 1800s, early 1900s, there would have been lots of rushcarts in this area. They would build their own, but we just have this one now. Originally, it was to take rushes to the church, which is just up the road, to spread them on to the earth floor and keep the parishioners warm in the winter. It started from that and then built up to more and more elaborate carts. Then it built up into a holiday. This weekend is the old Saddleworth Mill Wakes, the second weekend after the twelfth of August. It's a coincidence that it's a bank holiday; that's when the mill wakes [the workers' holidays] were and that's when they'd have all their fun."

With all the preparations in place, the Saddleworth Morris Men disappeared round the back of the pub, while the public remained on the road, chatting animatedly alongside horse-masked figures, dancers dressed as fools and the guest morris sides, some of whom were already tipsy and holding tankards of beer. I decided to stay where I was as I knew I could get some good pictures. The woman next to me, who I presume had some kind of connection to the Saddleworth Morris Men, added to the sense of the day's significance when she turned to me and said, "You should make sure you're here next year, as what you're seeing today will be the last time it will be men only. Women will be allowed to pull the cart from next year on."

The men then appeared from the side of the pub, wearing serious expressions and pulling the cart behind them. When it had stopped in the middle of the road, all of the Saddleworth Morris Men (which happens to be the largest side I've ever seen) began to skip ceremonially with their bells ringing in unison. After their dance the Jockey climbed up a ladder to sit astride the top. Also attached to the top of the cart were some upright branches, making it look as if Jockey were perching in a tree like a goblin. He laughed nervously, and lowered a kettle on a length of string, which his fellow morris dancers filled to the brim with alcohol,

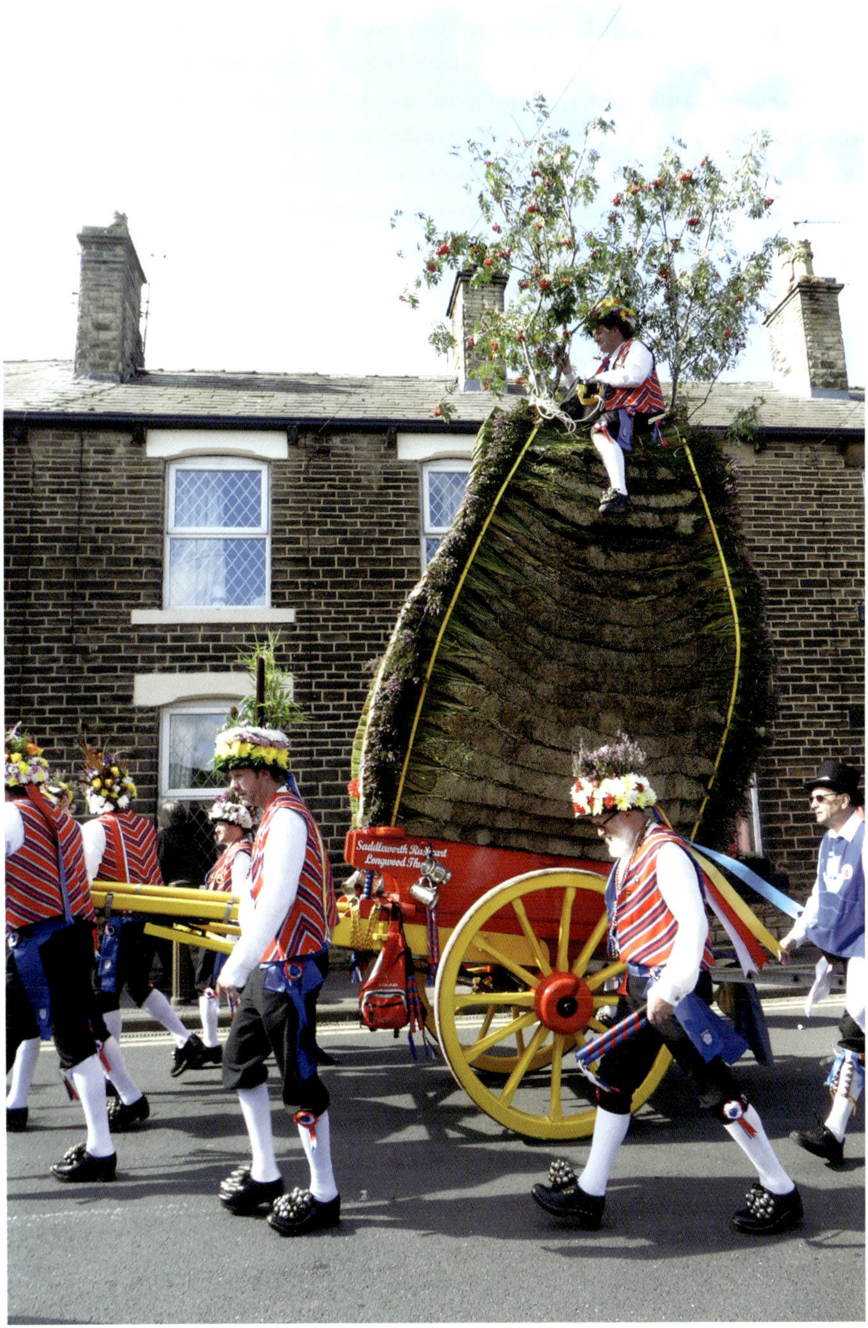

before he hauled it back up to top up his tankard. The kettle meant he could keep himself well watered throughout the day, perhaps easing the discomfort of being dragged around the villages of Saddleworth.

Once the Jockey was in place, the morris dancers took up their positions on the ropes attached to the cart and began to pull, with Dave shouting orders from the front to make sure no one was in danger. They processed down the road among the traffic, with the Jockey seated high above passing double-decker buses. He was dragged through some trees and I couldn't believe he didn't fall off. He clung on for dear life and then lay down low to make sure he wasn't taken out by a telephone wire.

There was shouting when the procession was about to hit a sharp bend, while men at the front lifted their arms in attempt to take more weight and to stop the cart rolling so fast. We passed a line of terraced houses that looked as if they'd been mined straight out of the surrounding Pennines. An old mill chimney rose up; the weight of the industry that was once common here can still be felt in the landscape of Saddleworth.

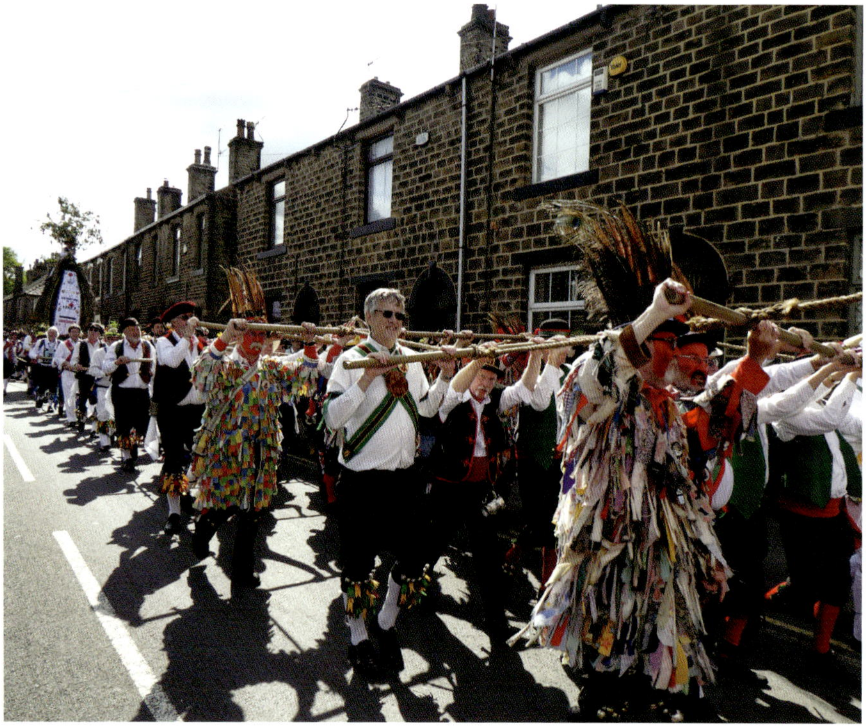

We passed under a high viaduct and stopped at various locations, where different morris sides danced. The Saddleworth men took their turn and awarded a waistcoat to a new member, who was now officially part of this large and ever-growing side. The kettle was lowered, refilled and we were off again. As the day went on, the heat intensified, sweat ran down the faces of the half-drunk morris men, and even the bells sounded like they were struggling to tinkle. A man fainted in drunken exhaustion and the Rushcart stopped until medical care could arrive, so everyone piled into a pub to squeeze in a quick drink. It turned out that the man was all right and refusing to leave, but he was overruled and taken away. The cart pressed on through residential streets as smiling children followed in the hope of catching the sweets that the Jockey continued to throw. The atmosphere was infectious and I felt like I was in a fairy tale, quite literally.

As the first day came to an end, the town erupted like a university campus, but instead of rowdy students it was tankards, bells, fools, beasts and morris men; I headed back to my B&B on the edge of the town, where I had dinner in a nearby pub and got chatting to locals, while more and more morris men kept arriving until the early hours, staggering and slurring their words. Eventually, even the barman fell asleep and a local took over the bar and started pouring the drinks.

At breakfast the next day, the B&B owner came out looking rather distressed. She approached the table next to mine where a group of morris dancers from Essex were sitting and said loudly to a man in the corner, "You'll have to pay for the mattress!" The group started laughing, and the man denied any knowledge before claiming that the woman's dog must have gone in there and "pissed on it, as it certainly wasn't me". The whole table roared with laughter, and as far as I know he never paid for a replacement.

Later that morning, I headed back to the starting point, the Commie pub, which was already full of bells and tankards. This was the more traditional day, where the Rushcart would be taken to St Chad's Church in the village, and rushes would be symbolically strewn across the church floor to honour the original tradition.

Today, there were different morris sides in attendance, including the Bacup Coconutters who blacken their faces, which I was told was to "honour to the coal miners who first started the tradition, who would have permanently black faces from working down the mines and would perform the dance in their lunchbreaks". The Joint Morris Organisations (JMO), who are very much part of the Saddleworth Ruschart community, and even elect the JMO Squire at St Chad's at the end of the day, have since banned the use of blackface at any of their events due to its racist connotations and potential to cause harm and exclude.

Other sides such as the Red Leicester Morris Men changed the colour of their face paint long ago to red, and appear like cockerels with multicoloured plumage as they attach multiple tassels to their clothes. Their appearance is striking and as soon as I saw them pulling the cart, and remembering that women would also soon be part of the ceremony, I felt they represented the sort of forward-thinking discussions and changes that have been occurring within the world of British folklore since the pandemic. I have included one of the Red Leicester side pulling the cart within my composition for this reason.

Today, when the Rushcart set off, it headed up a steep hill, while the expressions of the men pulling the cart suggested that it was a much tougher stretch of road than the previous day. Of course, this could also have had something to do with the collective hangover kicking in. The South Pennines could be seen in all their glory as the spire of St Chad's appeared in the distance. The Rushcart was then led down a slope to the churchyard in a scene with a Werner Herzog-like quality, reminding me of his film *Fitzcarraldo* where a steamship is dragged through the Amazon so an opera can be performed. This was obviously a very English version where a hundred morris men dragged a huge Rushcart with a Jockey on top across the South Pennines to cover a church floor with rushes.

I use the word "magic" a lot when describing folk traditions, but "fairy tale" is much more appropriate for the Saddleworth Rushcart. In the end, this was one of the strongest inspirations behind my final composition, as I wanted to capture the fairy tale-like quality of the day and the labour-intensive task of delivering the rushes to the church in such an elaborate way. At the centre, the expression of the Saddleworth Squire, Dave, reflects the collective importance of the event to the people who hold it dear to their hearts.

I also love the idea of ceremony itself and how something so simple, such as transporting rushes to a church, inspired neighbouring villages to compete to outdo each other; and how this grew and grew into such a dreamlike event, with each generation adding a little bit on top, quite literally. It's a metaphor for how we function generationally as a society: we all take something a little bit further, collectively evolving through time. It also got me smiling to myself about the more recent tradition of boy racers who try to outdo each other by elaborately modifying their cars: what might that tradition look like in five hundred years' time?

When we arrived at the church, the Jockey climbed down a metal ladder placed against the Rushcart. On reaching the ground, he walked in a comical wide-legged manner, as I'm sure his thighs were red raw by this point. Everyone cheered and then headed inside for the church service where the rushes were to be strewn across the floor.

During the service I found it hard to concentrate as I was transfixed by beautiful handcrafted banners hanging from the balconies; these were all the banners that have decorated the Rushcart over the years, with a different member of the Saddleworth Rushcart Morris Men being elected to create one every year since 1975, when the side revived the tradition. Each told a story and reflected the events and popular culture of the year they were made. As the service concluded, the Saddleworth Morris Men trooped out to the churchyard and performed some incredible dances that reflected the milling and weaving industry of the surrounding area. As they impersonated the movements of the millers and weavers, they highlighted the ways in which folk traditions not only connect us to Nature but also to our ancestors and the hard lives of industry that sustained them and helped shape the world as we know it today.

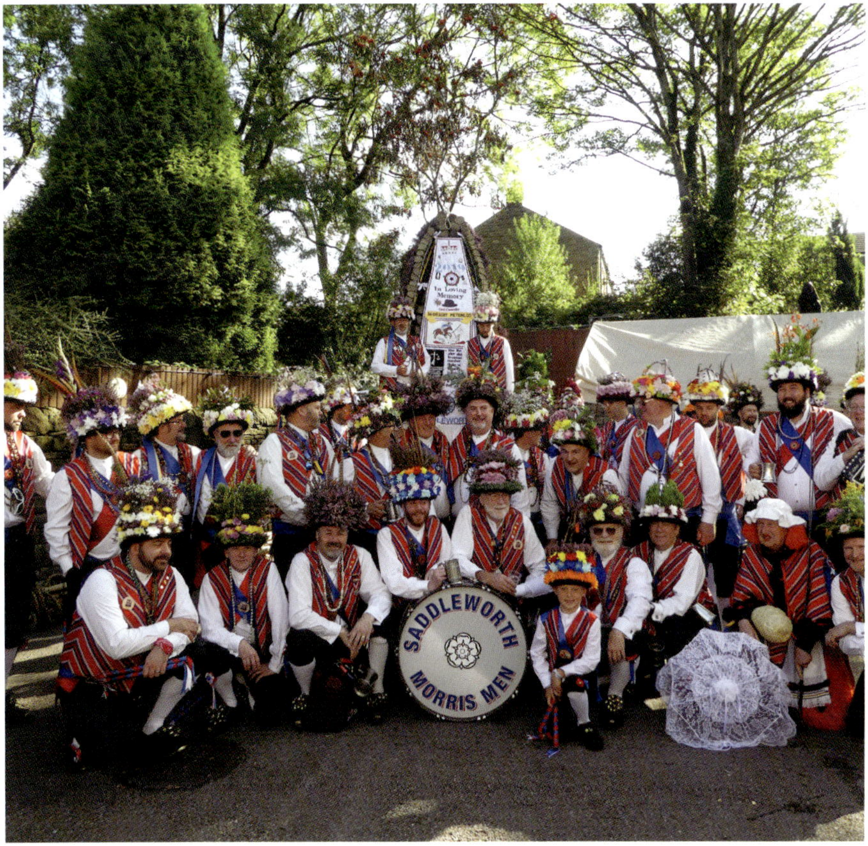

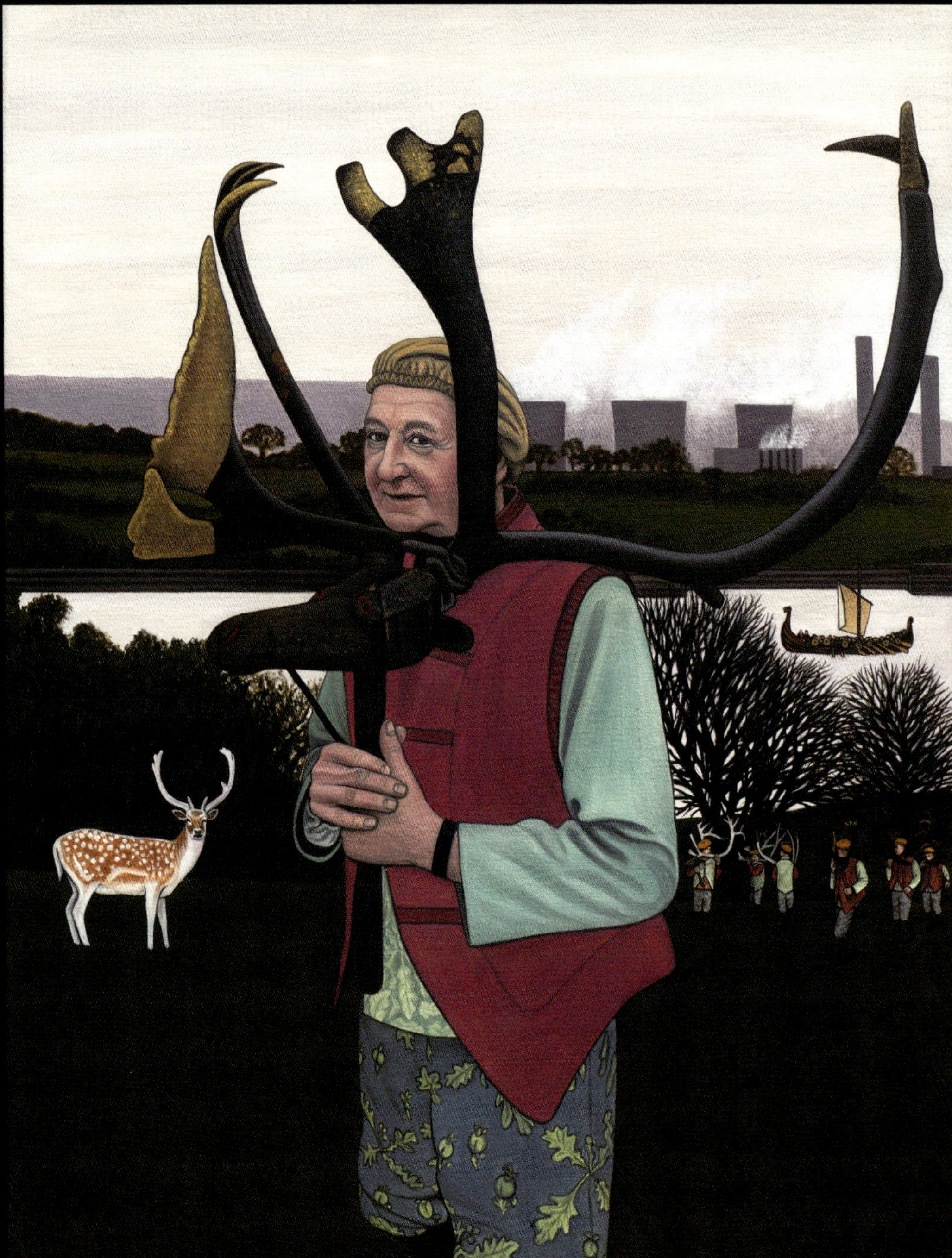

THE ABBOTS BROMLEY HORN DANCE

Oil on Canvas, 65cm × 50cm

2018

The Abbots Bromley Horn Dance

STAFFORDSHIRE

MONDAY FOLLOWING THE FIRST SUNDAY AFTER SEPTEMBER 4

The Abbots Bromley Horn dance is held each September in the village of Abbots Bromley, Staffordshire and is believed by many to be the oldest folk dance still taking place in Britain today. I was fascinated by the story about the dance's origins and wondered whether the dancers themselves and the locals believed it to be true.

On the day of the dance, I was drawn to a striking man who seemed to be one of the leading dancers, and knew instantly that he would be the ideal figure to base my painting around. It turned out that the man, Jeff Bradbury, had taken part in the Horn Dance for over forty years and after I'd attended twice, he told me about what he understood to be its origins: "It's a Pagan ritual supposed to be for a good harvest. The little white horn was carbon-dated to a thousand years [ago] at Keele University and that's as far as they could take it back." This tallied with what I'd read about the custom, the general consensus being that the horns had originally travelled over from Scandinavia with the Vikings. Unlike most traditions, where there's no evidence to support their speculative origins, in this instance one of the horns had been dropped and a small fragment broke off, which was sent for carbon-dating. Remarkably, it dated to 1065, a year before the Norman Conquest, and was discovered to come from a reindeer extinct in Britain by that time, lending credibility to the local belief.

On my first visit, I caught the train to the town of Rugeley, where I hoped to get a bus or taxi to Abbots Bromley itself. Soon I realized I had no choice but to walk there, a distance of roughly 4.5 miles (7km); which would normally be fine, but I'd just inherited some boots with a troubadour vibe about them from my dad, and I'd put them on purely for aesthetic reasons. I'd only gone a short way down the narrow country lanes when I was already regretting it, diving into thorny bushes whenever vans and lorries rumbled past. The tight leather boots started to rub at my ankles and I knew this wasn't going to be a very pleasant walk. I kept going despite the discomfort and reached a huge reservoir with some equally huge cooling towers. The water rocked calmly, with small waves slapping against the concrete banks. Silhouetted in the distance was a rowing boat and people with fishing rods, and I imagined the Viking ship bringing the original horns with them from Scandinavia. The vision for my painting had already begun to unfold.

When I finally reached the outskirts of Abbots Bromley, I checked in to where I was staying, took off my boots and built some makeshift ankle supports with socks, which seemed to do the trick and stopped the rubbing. After a rest, I wandered into the village and found a local pub where the walls were covered with paintings and historic photos of the Horn Dance. Despite hearing a local say "Scotland's that way", referring to my green tweed jacket I can only assume, I was excited to see images of the dancers of the past staring back at me. I got chatting over a pint to some locals and met a couple of the dancers themselves, who were very friendly.

They warned me to be careful on my way back to my B&B, as it was getting dark and there were no street lights; but having had a few drinks, my judgement was perhaps a bit impaired and I stayed longer than I should have. They weren't lying: the streets were pitch black. I couldn't even see my hand in front of me. It was terrifying, especially when the occasional car came past. I made it through the dark using the torch on my phone – the relief!

When I returned the following year, I stayed in the centre of the village and had promised myself an early night, but as I was walking back I heard the sounds of what sounded like an army of violins. I followed the sound and ended up in another pub, the Bagot Arms, where

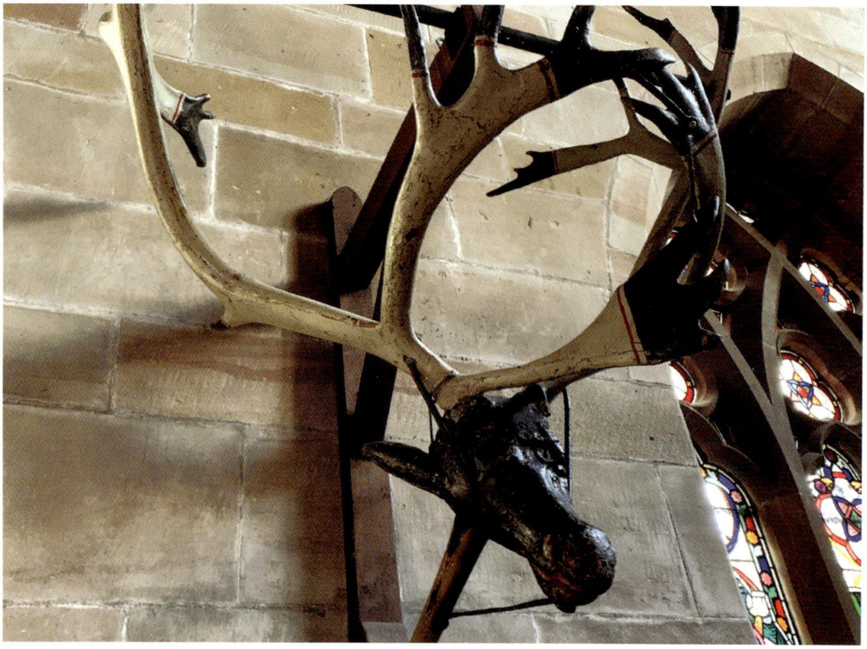

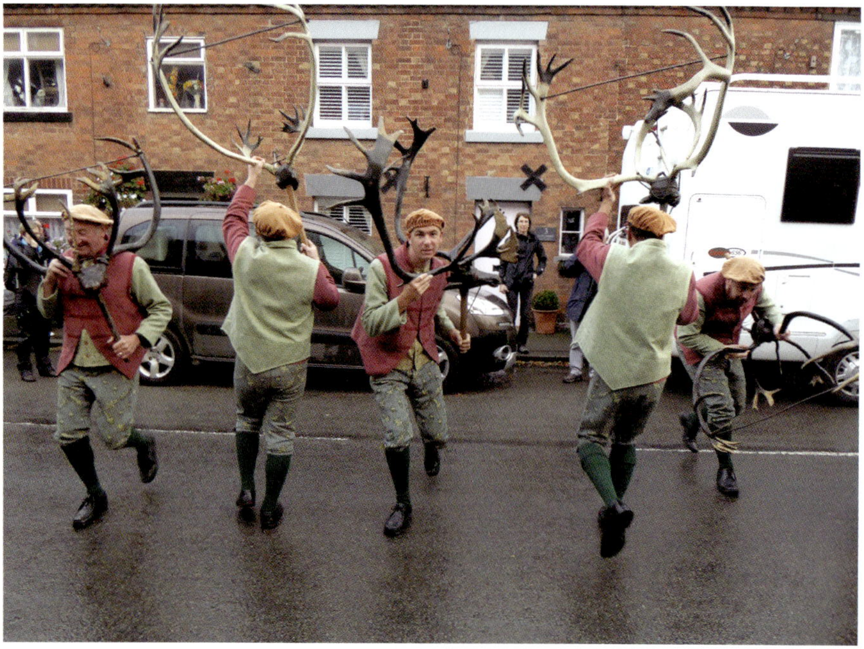

to my amazement there was a room full of fiddle players. The dancers and their entourage were also there and a great time was had by all – perhaps too great a time. I was invited round for a bacon butty in the morning and to help collect the pig's bladder from the local butcher's that would be used by the fool. I never quite made it, regrettably ... But I did make the church service on time, where everyone laughed and someone said, "Your bacon butty's gone cold."

The ceremony traditionally started at 8am in the church, which felt like a bizarre setting when the dance has such a Pagan, pre-Christian feel to it. Despite this, the dance is embraced by the church and the six sets of antlers, the horns, are kept on the church walls all year round and blessed on the morning of the dance.

The deeper I get into my journey exploring British folk customs, the less important the romance of their Pagan origins becomes. In fact, you start to realize that it's all just one hybrid continuum from the dawn of mankind. The ceremonies and rituals themselves evolve, stop, start and are changed beyond recognition from what the earliest people would have done to celebrate the wheel of the year. But it's the fact that people are marking these significant times, responding with their own creativity informed by their own regional cultures, that has kept my fascination burning. The traditions are a reflection of the people and times of the participants, not historical re-enactments. Folklore is about contemporary culture and always has been. This was confirmed to me in Abbots Bromley by one of the accompanying musicians, who explained that this was a "ritual dance done not necessarily for the purpose of entertainment", but "for agricultural purposes, ensuring a good harvest and, as it benefited the farmers, they plied the dancers with food and drink – and that's what you see today, food and drink and people dancing. Obviously the reasons have changed, but the essence of it is still there, it's living history."

After the service, the six horn dancers, or "Deer-men", and their party emerged from the church. Three of the dancers were holding white sets of antlers and three held black sets, perhaps representing winter and spring, a kind of dancing of the seasons, the rhythm of the wheel of the year. The suggestion of these opposing forces of Nature was further heightened by their outfits, as one half of the troupe wore green shirts with a maroon waistcoat, while the other half wore maroon shirts with green waistcoats. All the dancers wore pulled-up green socks and stylish oak-patterned trousers, which I would love to own a pair of myself.

There was also a fool who resembled a medieval jester in motley, whose earthy orange and brown outfit matched the colours of early autumn. He held a pig's bladder tied to a stick, and one of the Deer-men later told me, "If a woman is hit with the bladder, she'll become pregnant within a month."

Further emphasizing the element of fertility, Maid Marion played a part in the proceedings. She was performed by a man in drag, who wore a long blue dress with yellow trim, and held two pieces of wood. One was a long straight piece of timber, while in the other hand, she had a sort of ladle with a hole at the end, so the pieces could be slotted together. Later, the person playing Maid Marion explained to me, while holding up the piece with the hole, "This is to represent a female, this is to represent a male; like I say, it's a fertility dance so you can sort of work out what they're for."

Then there was the traditional figure of the hobby horse, dressed in a maroon cape with a wooden horse's head poking out. There was also an archer, played by a boy who repeatedly shot at the hobby horse during the day. And there were also young children playing the triangle, who may become horn dancers themselves one day. Last but not least, two accordionists with bushy white beards brought the much needed music to the dance. The tune they played was immediately familiar to me as "The Wearing of the Green", an old Irish song that had puzzlingly replaced the original Abbots Bromley Horn Dance tune. You can still find the original played online by various contemporary folk groups; it's truly entrancing.

The dance itself was quite primal. In parts, it was as if the dancers were impersonating rutting deer and embodying the feral, testosterone-charged character of a stag locking horns with other stags in an attempt to win a mate. In other parts, the movements were reminiscent of the cycle of the seasons, where the three black-horned dancers broke away from the three white-horned dancers to form separate circles before re-joining in one large circle.

The dance is very male, apart from the Maid Marion character. However, at each stop there was also an opportunity for spectators to take part and have a go with the antlers. When I spoke to a young woman who I noticed joining in a few of the dances, she told me her grandfather had taken part in the Horn Dance for about seventy-two years. He'd had six daughters, but as girls weren't allowed to take part at all back then, "they would be called Sid and Ernie for the day, and would tuck their hair under their hats and take part as triangle players". She also told me that the beautiful badge-covered hat that she was wearing once belonged to her grandfather and it had been kept at the church for years after his death, before being lost. When it was found again, her mum had it for a while and then she'd inherited it. She said she was wearing it to feel close to her grandfather on the day of the dance, and when the Deer-men first saw her wearing it "they all burst into tears" and said it felt as if her grandfather were there with them again.

I couldn't resist the opportunity to hold a pair of the antlers too; it's a remarkable feeling, as though a museum cabinet has been opened and an ancient item of great significance has been thrust into your hands. It's both unnerving and exciting: you can imagine all the generations that have held them. I had that familiar feeling of time dissolving. It's a feeling that seems to be at the heart of all of the traditions that I've visited, but with these horns of living history, the feeling was particularly strong. As intrusive thoughts of accidentally dropping them kept making their way to the forefront of my mind, I passed the antlers back with great care.

During the day, the procession passed through housing estates, farms, bungalows and local businesses. Some had incorporated the horns into their logos and signs. One stop that particularly etched itself into my mind was at a farm overlooking the reservoir. As I watched the dancers, the Viking ship appeared in my mind again, reinforcing that part of my painting's composition. Then an elderly man, who was sitting in a plastic chair next to his

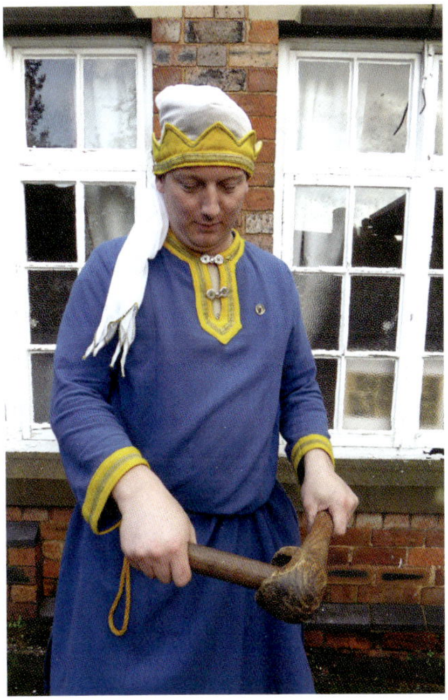

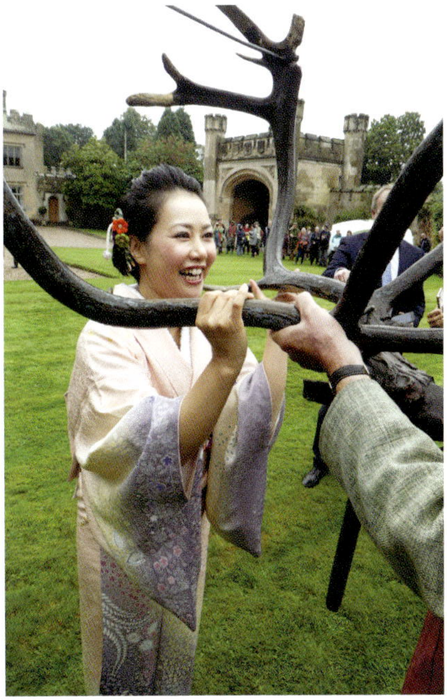

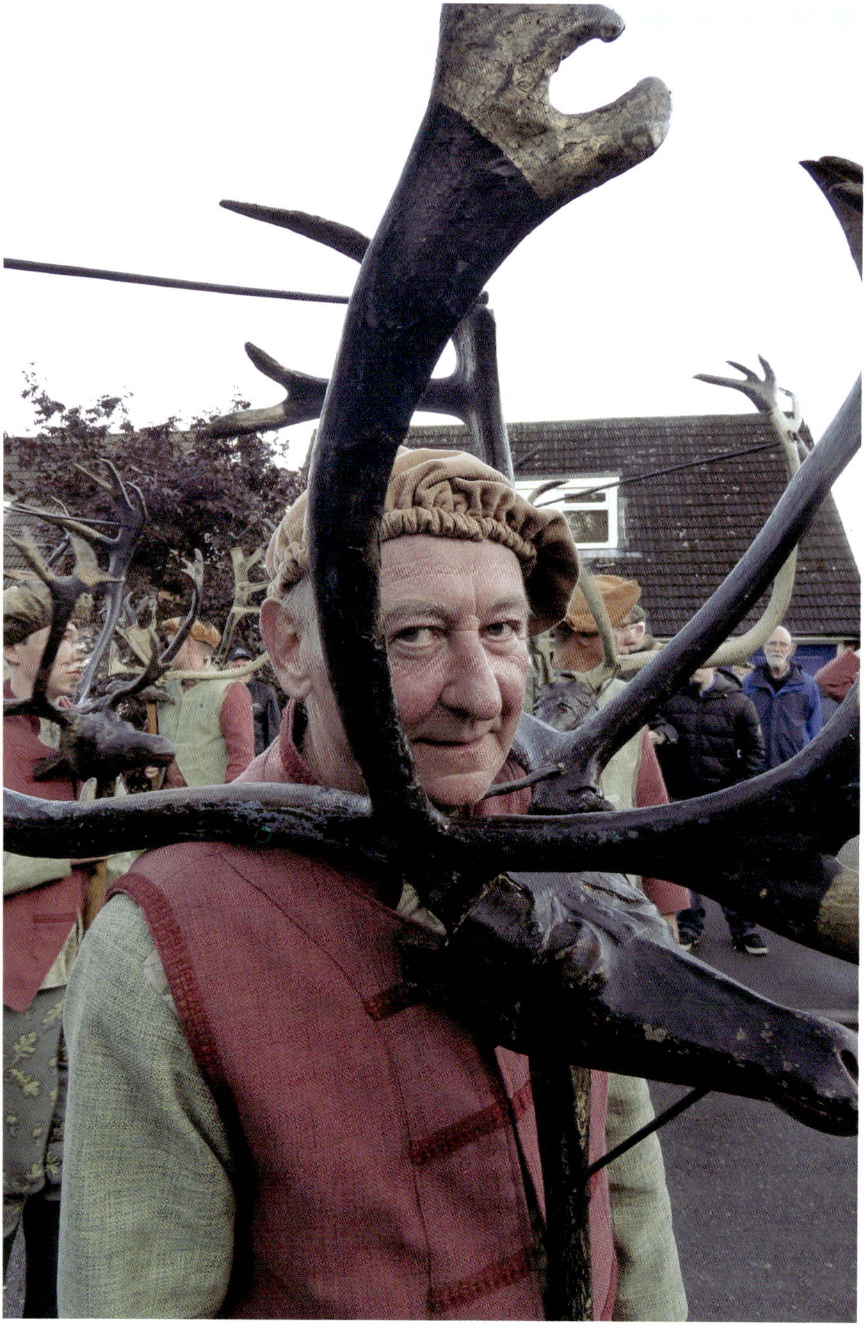

wife, announced that they were emigrating to Australia. Emotional speeches were made, glasses raised and a gift presented to the man, who was a retired Deer-man. The act of honouring the past generations is always apparent wherever I go and never fails to move me.

We moved on as heavy drizzle began to fall, illuminated by bright sunlight, and the dancers jumped into a van. Luckily for me, as I'd got to know them at the pub the evening before, I was invited into the van with open arms. While the dancers and their friends sat in the back on hay bales, passing round hip flasks, one of the musicians explained, "Back in the day, pre-motor vehicles, the dance took a week, as they had to walk everywhere." The van then shunted forward and everyone laughed and cheered as we pulled off with the door still open for ventilation. Looking out, I recognized some of the country lanes that I'd walked down in agony the day before.

The next stop was somewhere I most certainly didn't expect, a stately home, which I later found out belonged to an aristocratic family with long-established connections to the area, the Bagots, the name of the pub where I'd later come across the fiddle players. It turned out that the Bagots have supported the Horn Dance for generations by offering them a lunchtime spread in exchange for a private performance.

Separated from the surrounding area by a large wall, the stately home's grounds were like a stage. Before we jumped out of the van, I was passed a paper ticket that meant I was allowed to enter. We passed underneath a large stone arch, where I noticed the carved face of a Green Man peering down, as the dancers processed through to an awaiting audience of well-dressed people in crisply ironed shirts and floral dresses. On the other side of the wall, outside the grounds, ordinary folk had gathered to catch a glimpse of the performance, too. It's unusual to be reminded of such a class divide during a folk custom.

Among the smartly dressed "ticketed" crowd on whose side I was currently standing, I noticed a woman in a traditional kimono. She and her husband were guests from Japan and I watched as a member of the Bagot family introduced them to the Deer-men, explaining that the dancers were "similar to the Samurai in your culture". The comparison seemed somewhat amusing to the dancers, who tried to keep straight faces.

As the performance began I got chatting to a white-haired gentleman who was interested in why I was taking pictures. I explained I was an artist and curious about the custom's origins. He shared the story he had always known, which was that it was to do with "land rights, and that people were granted access to private land as a reward for good deeds and were presented with horns that they carried through the village to ensure they were recognized and not prosecuted as trespassers when hunting in Needwood Forest". The antlers also helped them in the hunt, as they could use them to mimic the deer. He cautiously added that he didn't know if there was any truth to this, but that was what he'd always been led to believe.

A deer, a Viking ship, dancers in the distance mimicking deer. My thoughts were racing and the composition kept unfolding vividly within my mind as the day progressed. I now knew that my painting would include the reservoir and cooling towers I had encountered, the ship bringing over the horns, the deer and of course the Deer-men in action, with Jeff holding a set of antlers as the central figure. (Little did I know that this was soon to become a poignant piece, demonstrating the fleeting nature of life, with the cooling towers since being demolished and Jeff sadly passing away after the painting's completion.)

Once my vision for my painting was complete, I could relax and enjoy the hypnotic Horn Dance. After a few more stops, including a replenishing hog roast where you could smell the sweet apple source and crispy pork from the street outside, we were back in the centre of the village where the locals had gathered and the dancers seemed to become both more energized and unwound. They could see I was in it for the long haul and were now posing for pictures for me in a way they hadn't done until then. The Deer-men kept dancing until sundown, on into dusk, before returning the horns to the church, where they were blessed by the vicar and hung back on the wall. The ritual was complete and the fertility of the land ensured for another year.

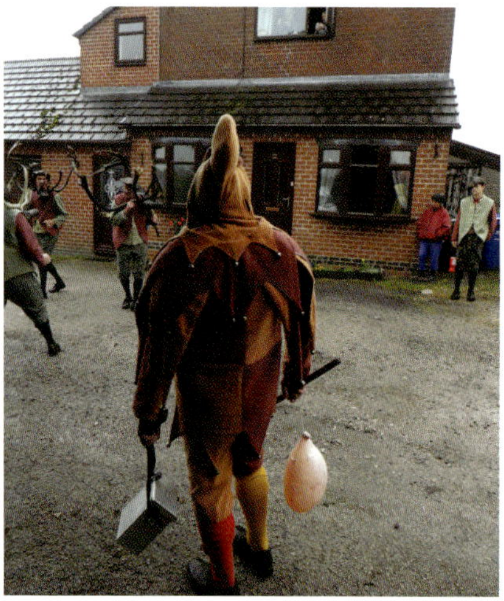

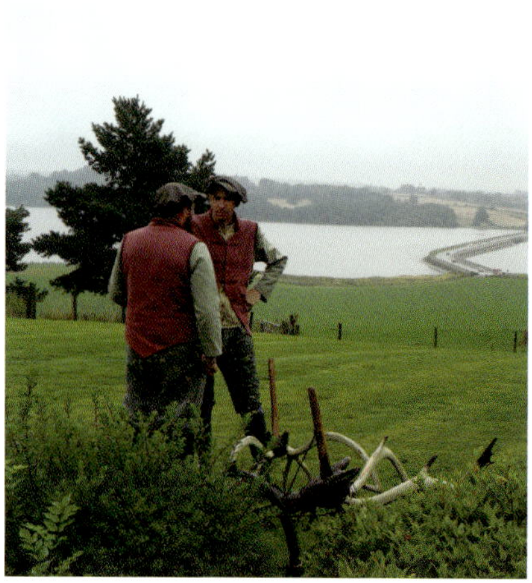

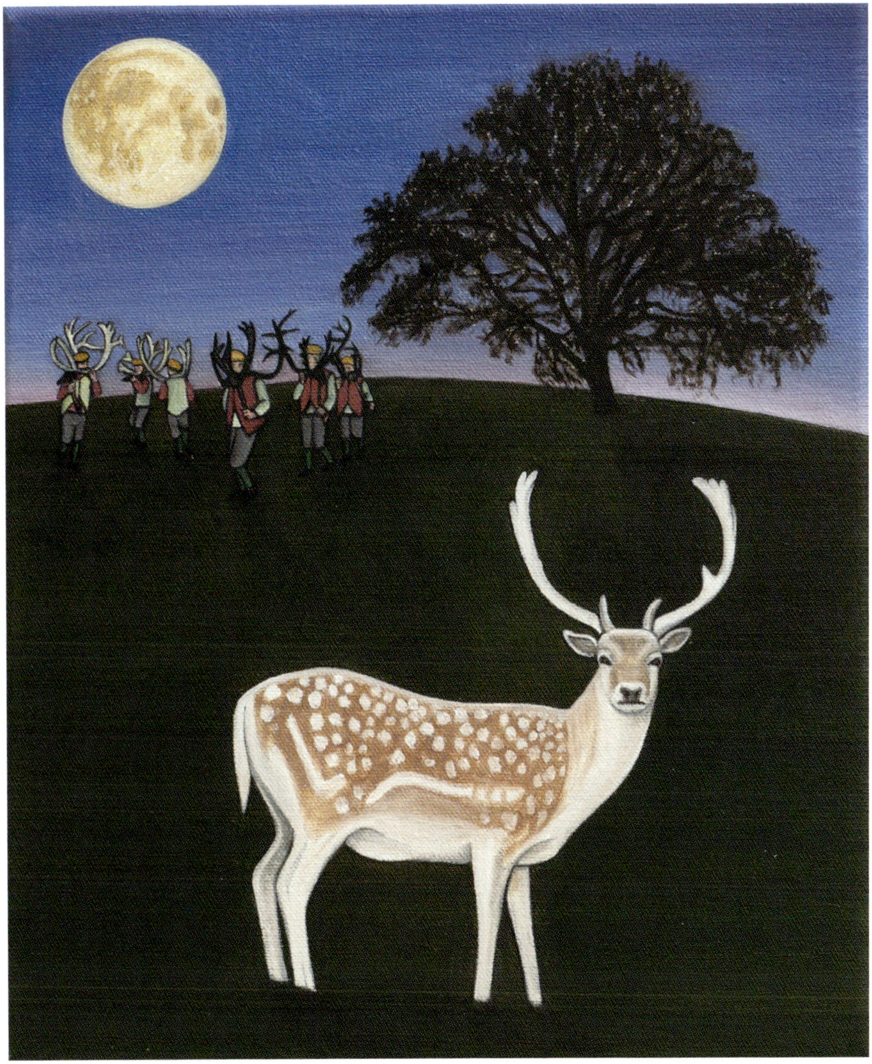

HORN DANCE AT HUNTERS MOON

Oil on Canvas, 30cm × 25cm

2018

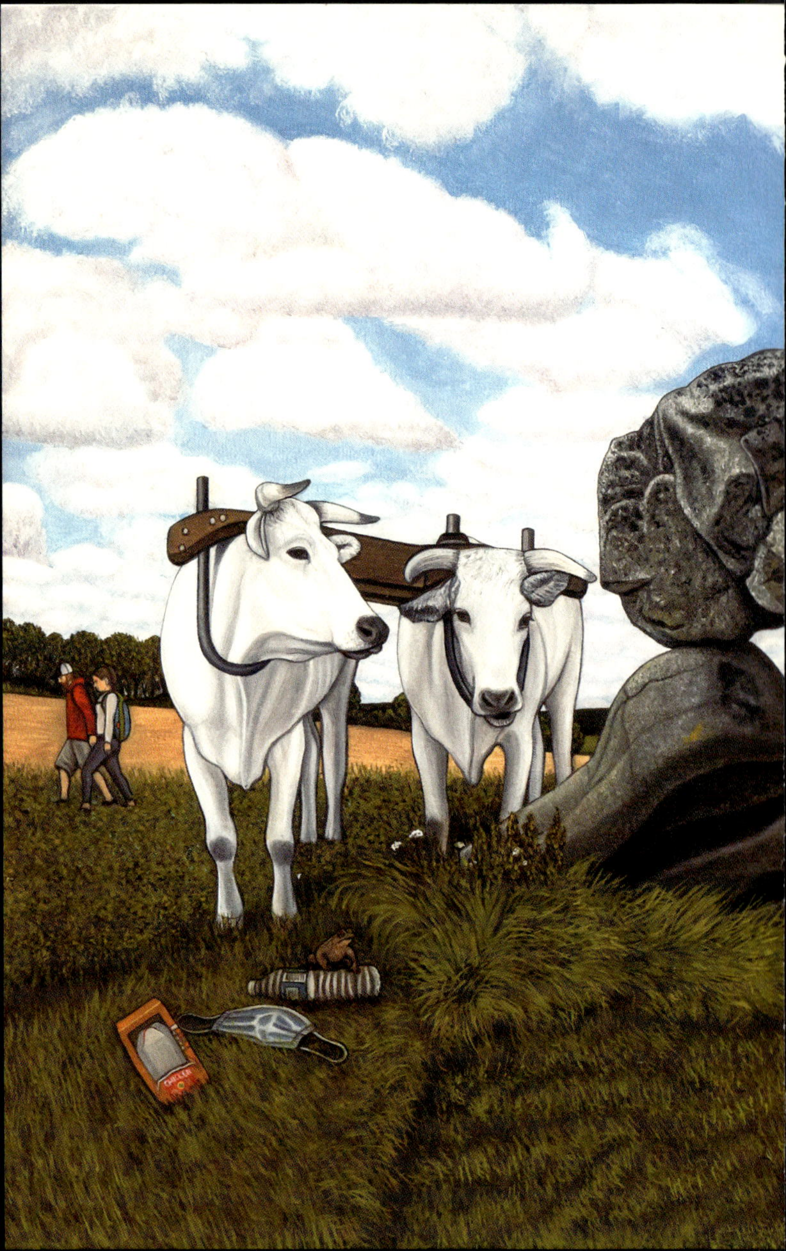

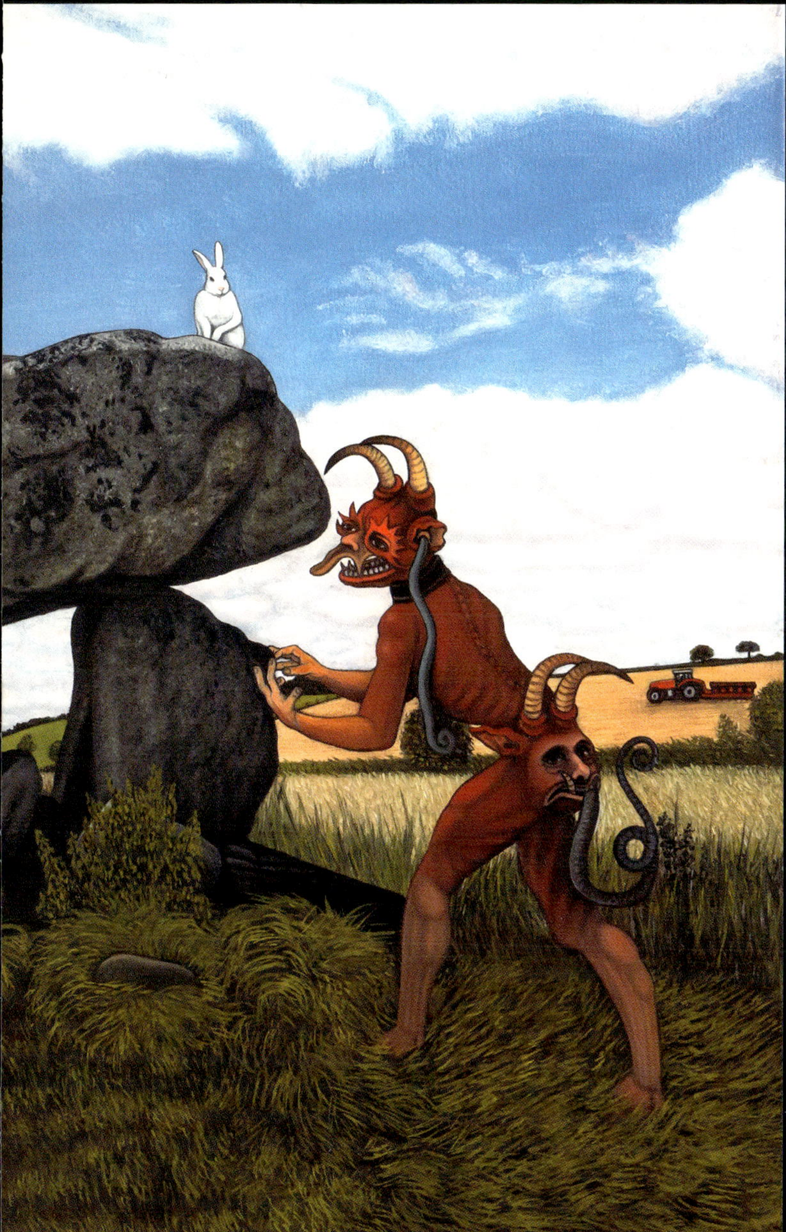

THE DEVIL'S DEN

Oil on Canvas, 45cm × 60cm

2021

The Devil's Den

WILTSHIRE

SEPTEMBER VISIT

Fyfield Down lies not far from Avebury, close to the ancient pilgrims' trail of the Ridgeway, and is the site of what is known in local folklore as the Devil's Den. I had first read about this site in the zine *Weird Walk*, which describes itself as "journal of wanderings and wonderings", and which has undoubtedly inspired a recent rise in interest in the megalithic sites of Britain. Now, I was walking along the long main road in the baking September sun while cars whizzed past, heading toward Marlborough from Avebury, when I got slightly lost and ended up clambering over a fence into a field. Despite barbed wire snagging on my trousers, I made it over in one piece and shortly afterwards found myself in front of the remains of a prehistoric burial chamber known as a dolmen, which in this instance consisted of two upright megaliths and a huge capstone.

I'd brought along my copy of *Weird Walk* as part of my research, and turned to the piece about the Devil's Den. As I sat upon a natural groove within the dolmen itself, I soaked in the folklore, mythology and ancient atmosphere that the stones themselves generated. Then I read about the hollows on the capstone and how legend has it that pouring water into these cavities at midnight will summon a demon who'll drink them dry by sunrise. While I wasn't sure if I believed in demons, I was definitely starting to feel a bit creeped out, sitting there all alone in a burial chamber. I could almost imagine demonic eyes watching me from the bushes and trees.

There were other stories about the dolmen, too, such as how it was said to be impossible to remove the capstone; the story went that on one occasion, people had tried to pull it down by harnessing together twelve oxen, but the harness immediately fell to bits. A similar tale had it that the Devil himself would arrive with a team of white oxen at midnight and try to pull it down, encouraged and advised by a white rabbit with flaming red eyes, which sat on top of the dolmen.

While today there wasn't a demonic rabbit in sight, I noticed the whirr of a tractor harvesting a field nearby and then the sound of approaching voices. I stood up to see a young couple striding toward the dolmen, and decided to walk a bit further away and get a view of the whole site. When the couple reached the stones they climbed through the dolmen's portal and took photos, before sitting on the edge and eating their sandwiches. They didn't stay long and when I went back I found some bread crusts around the foot of the monument. I sat back down and continued to read.

This time, the tale was about a fire-breathing toad said to dwell in the portal itself. Apparently, local children once believed that circling the monument seven times would provide them with a report on their behaviour: while a good child need expect nothing in particular on the seventh lap, a bad child would be greeted by the vile toad and its flaming spittle.

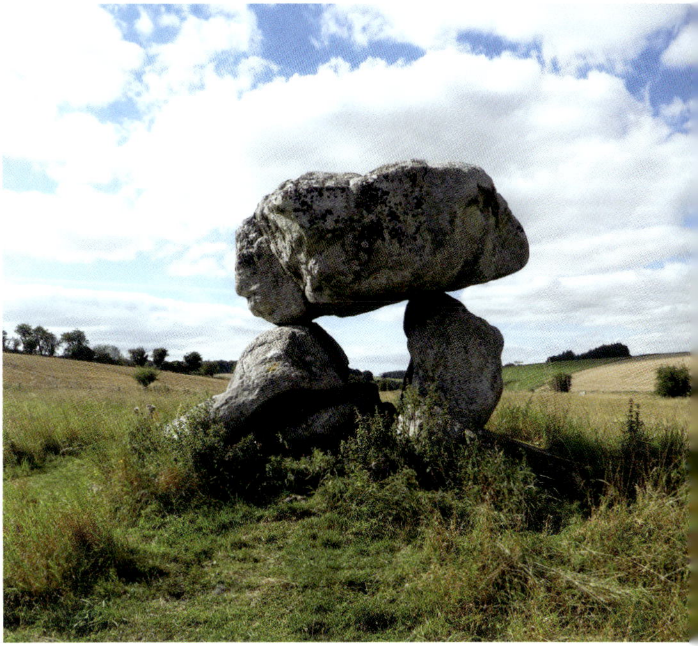

Maybe it was just because I'd read these tales but something about the site did make me feel uneasy. I took a few photos and videos but felt some kind of presence watching me; I didn't want to stick around long. As I got up once more and gazed upon the dolmen in its full glory, I imagined Satan himself, under the command of the small white rabbit on top, as the fire-breathing toad circled beneath, and behind the dolmen the white oxen prepared to attempt to pull off the capstone. I looked at the bread crusts and the evidence that people had been here. This was in between the Covid lockdowns and I thought about how people had started engaging with not only their local landscapes but also their regional cultures, and how this young couple may not have even made it out here at all if it wasn't for the pandemic. To symbolize this, I added an abandoned Covid mask and some litter to the crusts, while the couple walked off in the distance, the tractor hummed and a face in the bushes watched over me, adding to my sense of unease.

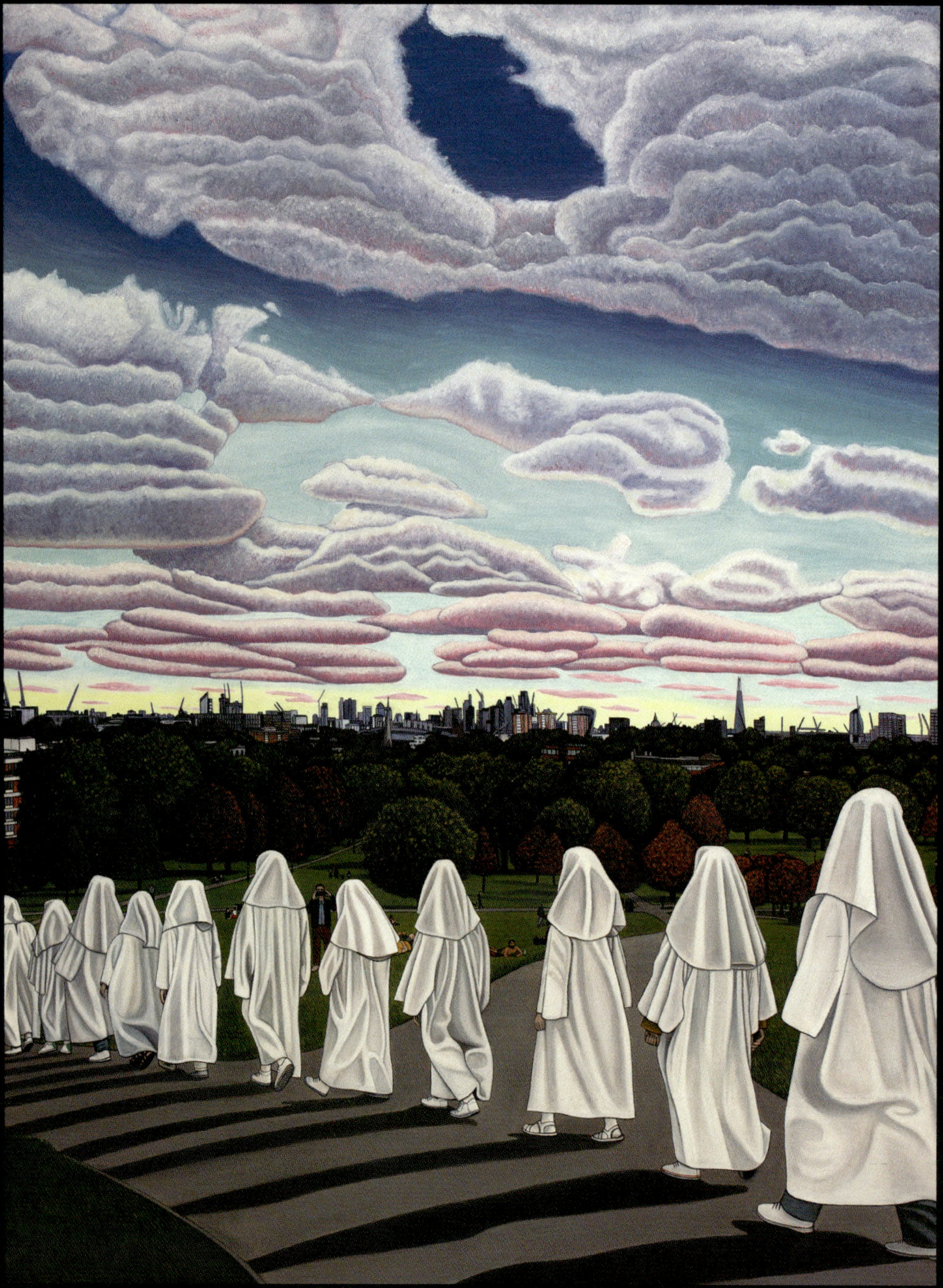

THE AUTUMN EQUINOX

Oil on Canvas, 110cm × 82.5cm

2018

Autumn Equinox, Primrose Hill

LONDON

SEPTEMBER 22 OR 23 (NORTHERN HEMISPHERE)

As I entered the park gates, a shimmering group of white figures was gathering further up the hill, one of the highest points in London. When I got closer, I could see their bags had been neatly stacked against a plane tree, while a woman in small, round glasses, her eyes enlarged by the lenses, was passing out neatly folded robes from plastic containers on fold-out tables. Six or seven people were already dressed in robes and white hoods, while some of the women had flowery garlands on their heads. One woman was wearing a golden cape and a metal crown, and a man held a flag decorated with a pair of scales, representing balance.

We had arrived at the autumn equinox, like the spring equinox a time of year when day and night are of equal length. Now the long dark nights of winter were looming, when the days would get shorter and nights longer until the winter solstice marked the darkest night.

Once more people were dressed, a line began to form, with a man holding a sword at the front. A bare-chested man with his hair in a bun ran over and asked what was happening. I heard someone explain that this was a very significant day for the Druid Order, who were marking their 300th birthday with the ceremony on Primrose Hill. Someone else claimed that William Blake would have been there on that day in 1717 as a founding member, though in reality he wasn't born until 1757. According to the Druid Order's website, Blake was its Chief Druid from 1799 to 1827.

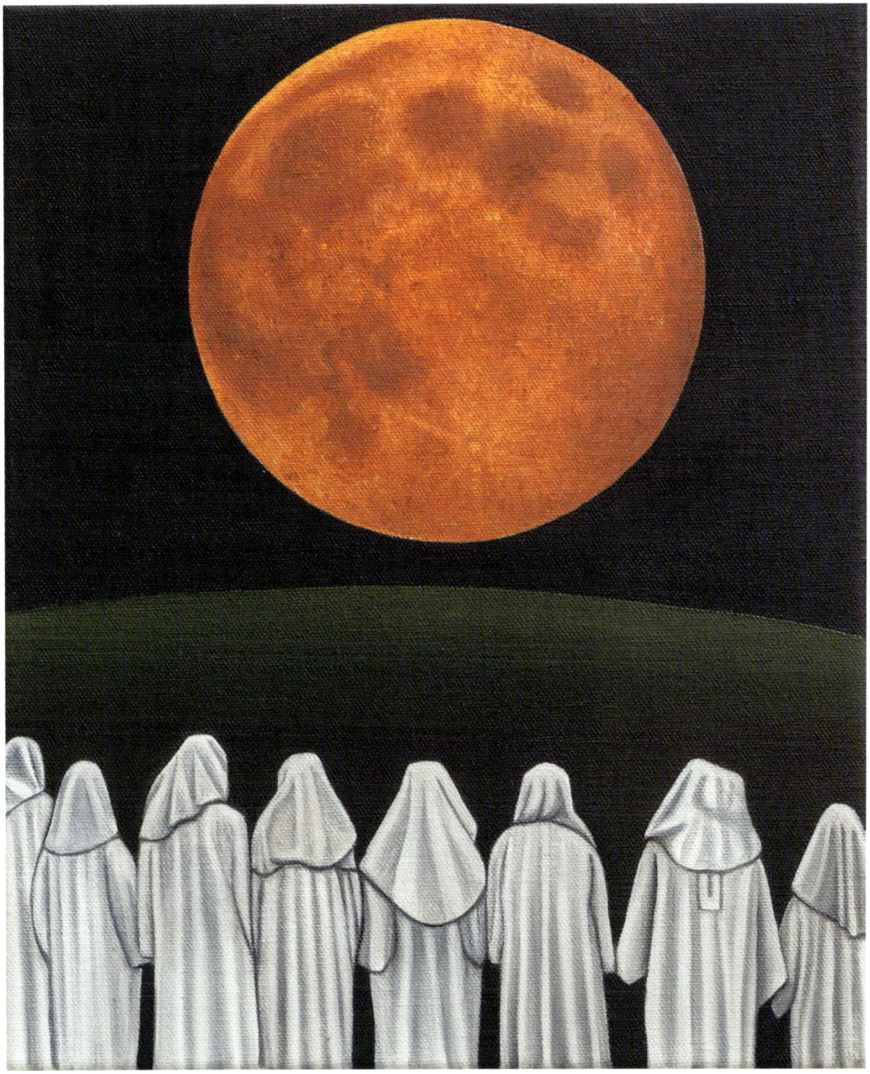

AUTUMN EQUINOX,
PRIMROSE HILL

HARVEST MOON

Oil on Canvas, 30cm × 25cm

2018

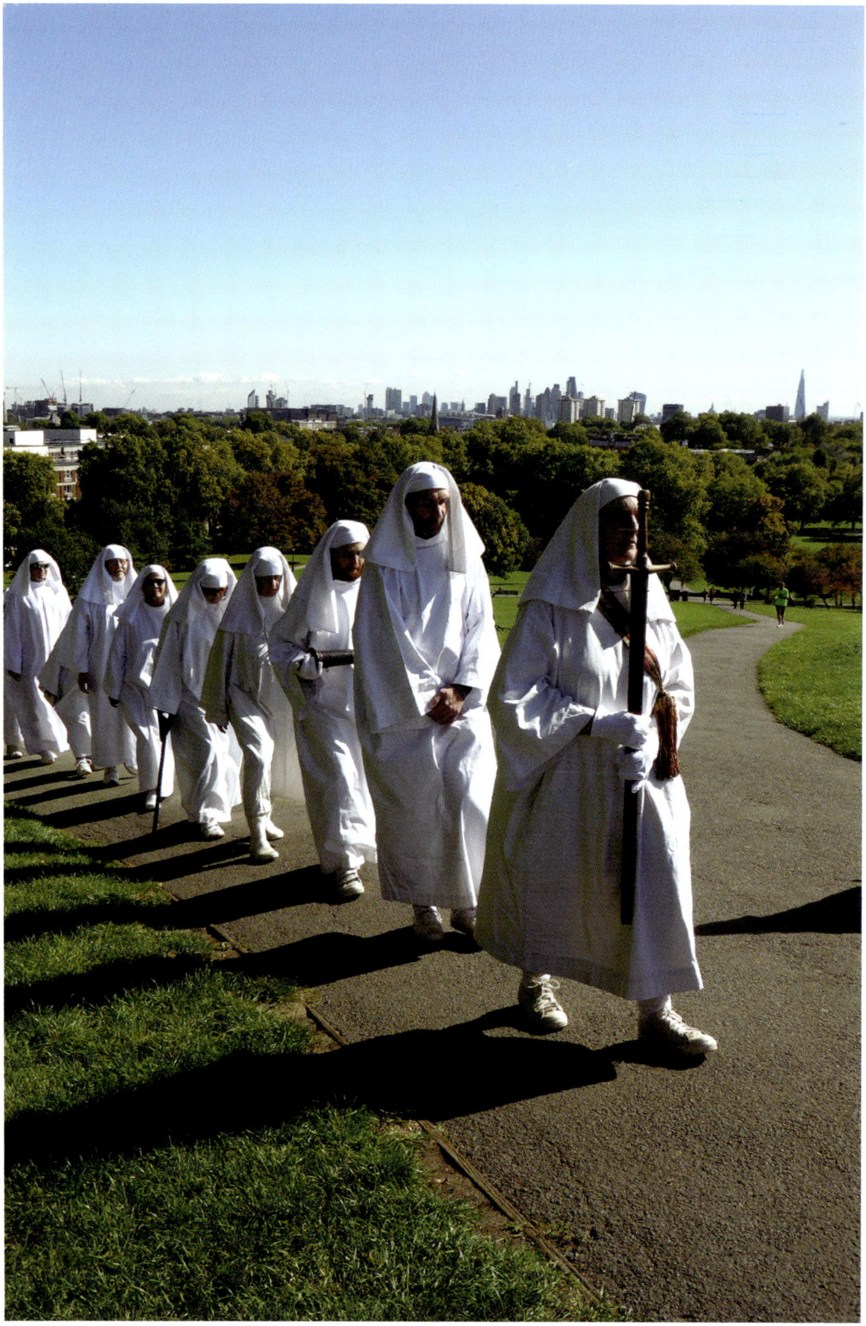

Photographers were now beginning to arrive and jostle with one another to find the best spot. I was getting more assertive about taking photos at these events, as it's important to document them properly for future generations, so I stood my ground and continued to photograph and chat with the participants. These sorts of experience are part of what's helped me find my confidence again after my breakdown.

The leaves overhead danced green and gold in the breeze as the Druids adjusted their hoods and got ready to begin. Against a skyline of buildings poking out from the sea of trees and among the distant roar of the city, they walked in complete silence, with a dignified peacefulness that was meditative to watch. The sight of white gowns against a modern cityscape never ceases to inspire me: I could feel three hundred years of history flashing into a single moment as we assembled on the summit of Primrose Hill.

While the Druids were forming a circle I spotted a plaque; the inscription read:

I have conversed with the Spiritual Sun,
I saw him on Primrose Hill
– William Blake

It sent a shiver down my spine. William Blake seems to have followed me (or me, him) my whole life. My dad lives a few minutes' walk from Bunhill Fields where Blake was buried, and his gravestone intrigued me as a boy. Later, I worked in a shop on Carnaby Street where I would sit on the steps of "William Blake House", the block of flats built on the site of Blake's childhood home, where he first had a vision of God at the age of seven. On Primrose Hill, I'd been inspired to paint a self-portrait during a dark period in my life that led to my accidental discovery of the Druids on Tower Hill and the beginning of a whole new chapter. Now, I was here again on the Order's 300th birthday, and Blake was believed to have attended a ceremony here. Isn't life magical sometimes? The signs were everywhere, and I didn't need to be a man of faith to know that I was once more in exactly the right place at the right time.

I wandered back to the circle, which was surrounded by people taking pictures on their phones and barking dogs, confused about what was happening. A trumpet was blown, a sword pulled from its scabbard and ancient rites read. The crowned woman, representing Mother Earth, entered the circle with a drinking horn, while two female attendants with garlands in their hair and baskets of fruit and flowers carried her cape behind her, followed by the sword bearer, holding the sword in front of his face.

She approached the head of the Druid Order, the Chief Druid, handed him the "Horn of Plenty" and said, "I bring this offering as a symbol of hope, of Earth's life stream." The Chief Druid responded by taking a drink from the horn, holding it up to the sky and announcing, "In this symbol recognize the emblem of the eternal." Then he poured the contents of the horn symbolically on the ground, and said, "Recognize the blessing on your land for ever." The flowers and fruit were also placed on the ground as an offering. I watched one of the Druids take a picture of the offerings in a contemporary act of Nature worship. This, I knew, would make an interesting painting in its own right, which I did paint later but changing the landscape to a rising sun. "The fruit of the fields is the gift of the eternal," declared the Chief Druid, before a dog comically wandered into the circle and urinated up his staff.

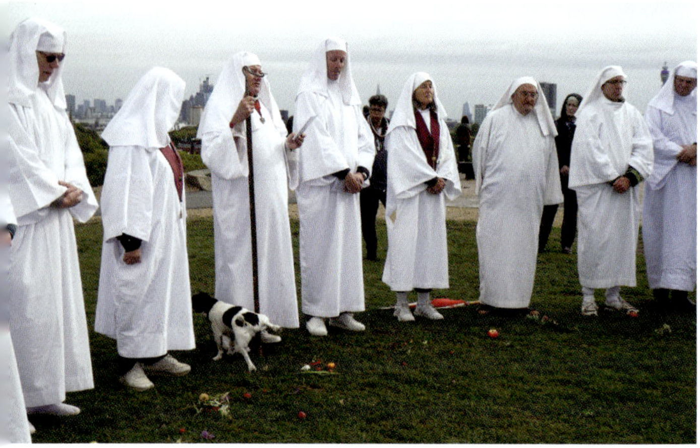

As the ceremony concluded, four Druids entered the circle and announced between them, "May there be peace in the orient, peace in the oxidant, peace in the north, peace in the south, peace throughout the whole world." Another orderly line was formed and the Druids wandered back down the hill in silence, as tall glass buildings gleamed in the distance. At that moment, I looked up at the sky and noticed a ring of clouds; I had just got back from Rome where I'd visited the Pantheon, the Roman temple with a circular opening in its roof. Immediately, I got the same feeling I'd had when gazing up at that, but here I was in an open temple, Nature's temple, and this became the basis of my painting of the Druid Order's autumn equinox 300th anniversary.

On a later visit to the ceremony, I was invited to take part and donned a cloak and walked in line as a flag bearer. It was such a surreal experience: I felt like I'd stepped into my own painting, like a form of time travel. Although I enjoyed the experience, in the future I'll probably remain on the outside looking in, but as far as beliefs go, theirs is one that I can definitely subscribe to. A Druid friend summed it up perfectly for me: "Druids don't believe in anything; it's not about belief, it's not about dogma. It's not about discriminating against other belief systems, it's about deriving the best out of everything."

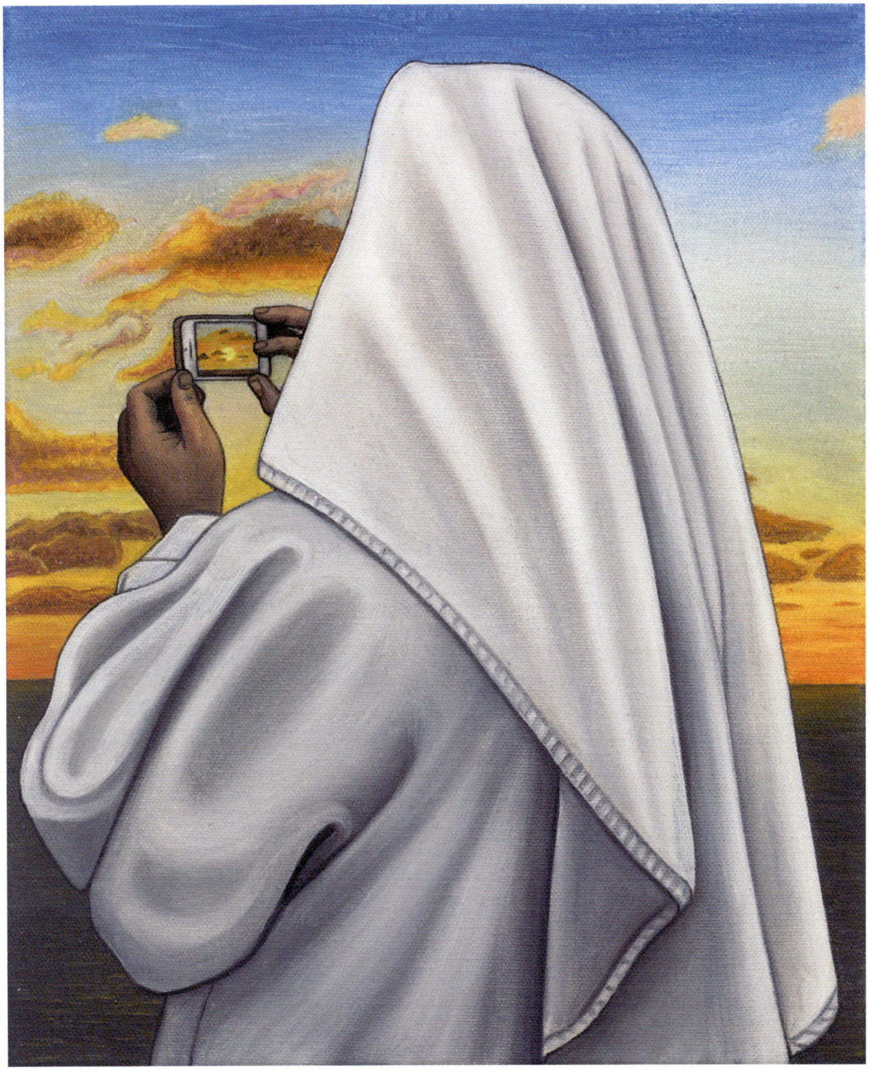

AUTUMN EQUINOX,
PRIMROSE HILL

NATURE WORSHIP

Oil on Canvas, 30cm × 25cm

2018

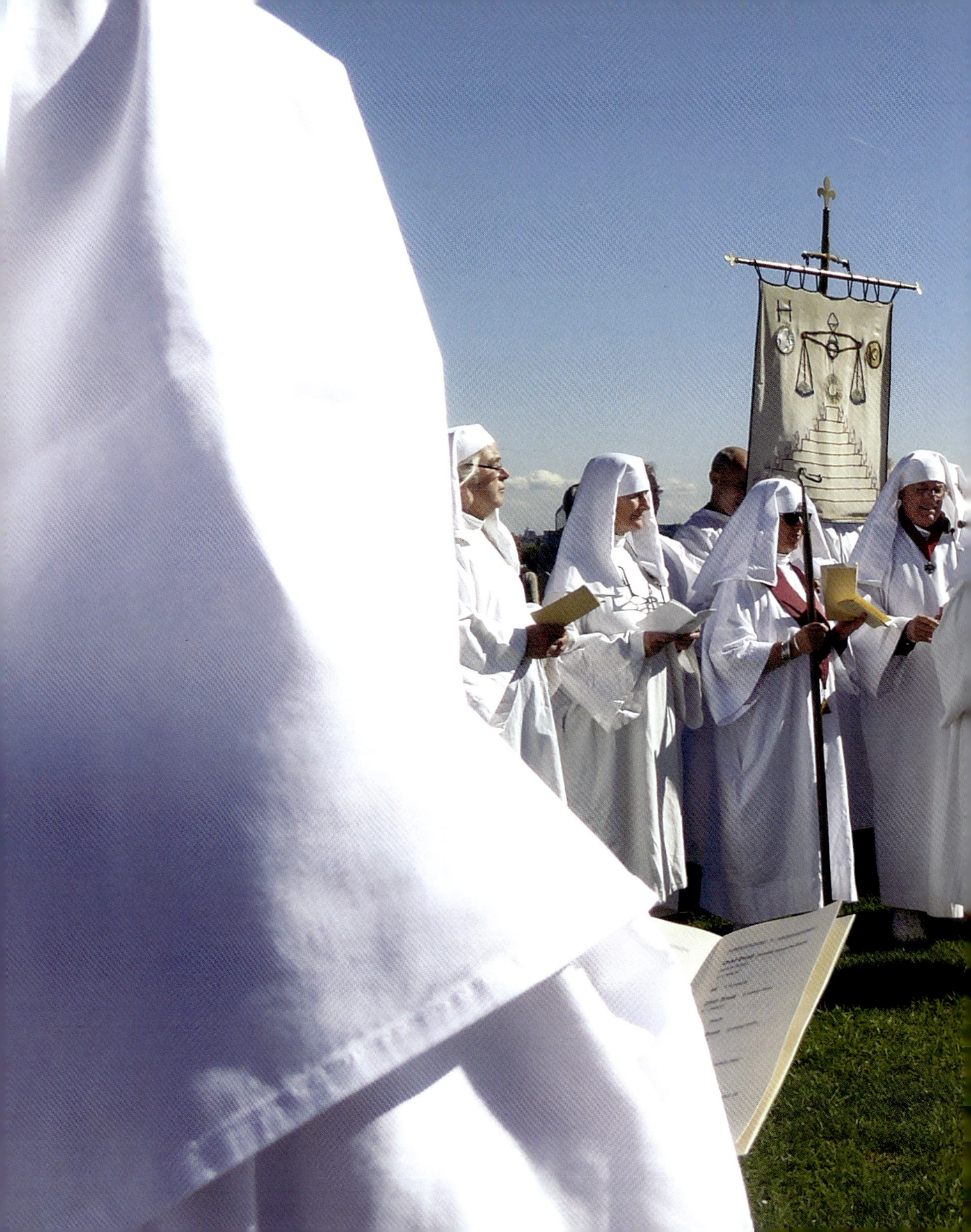

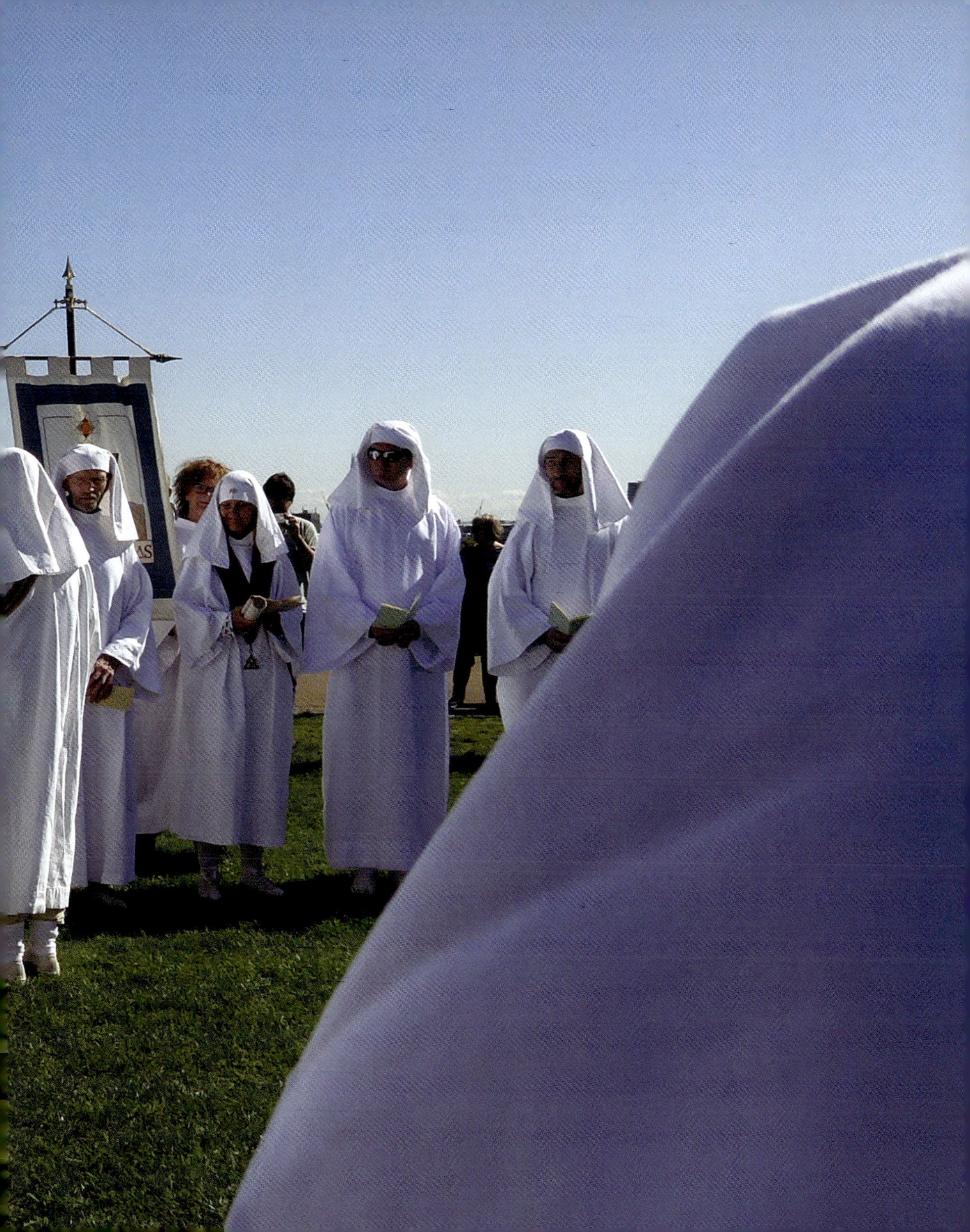

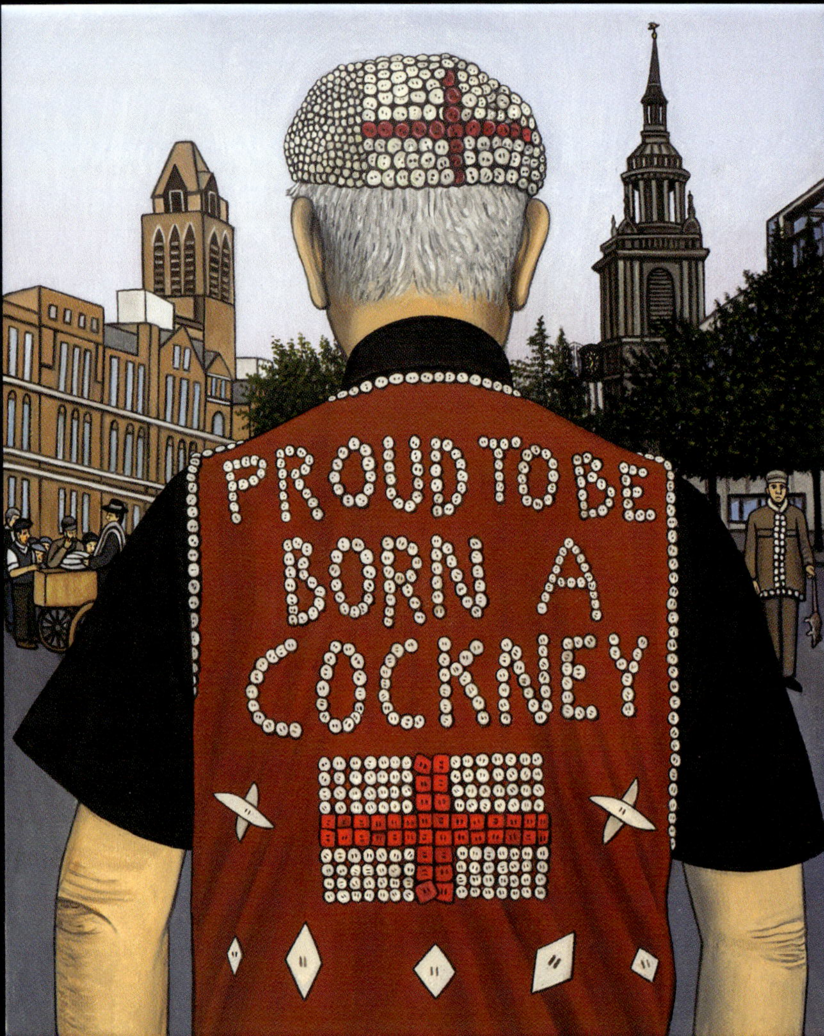

THE PEARLY KING

Oil on Canvas, 30cm × 25cm

Pearly Kings and Queens Harvest Festival

CITY OF LONDON
LATE SEPTEMBER

Many think that the London lore, about being born within the sound of the Bow bells making you an official Cockney, refers to Bow in East London, when in fact it refers to the Church of St Mary-le-Bow in Cheapside, whose bells could be heard as far as Lambeth in the days pre-motor car. Perhaps with the rise of the quieter electric car the perimeter of those born Cockneys will again expand. Nearby, at Guildhall Yard in the City of London, a harvest festival was about to begin with a procession to the historic church, where a service would be held in honour of both the harvest and the original Pearly King, Henry Croft.

I arrived at Guildhall Yard to the sound of a large fairground organ piping old Cockney tunes under a bright September sky. Pearly Kings and Queens were already wandering around, posing for selfies and talking to the general public who'd come along for the spectacle. A Pearly pug was being tugged around on a lead by the Pearly Queen of Greenwich and there was a morris dancing side with a member who resembled the punk icon Sid Vicious; I loved the idea of two very British traditions, punk and morris dancing, merging in this way. There were also some Chelsea pensioners in their smart red coats and black caps on one side of the square, while on the other, a man stood with a huge Saint Bernard dog that was attached to a dog cart with harvest offerings inside, including bread, cans of beans and vegetables.

As I watched the scene, two men resembling characters out of *Oliver Twist* arrived in a truck with "Nobby Clark & Son" written on a plaque above the windscreen. Nearby, the Pearly King of Smithfield was holding his Union Jack-lined jacket open, posing for the crowd; he brought my grandfather to mind, who used to work at the meat market and was fluent in Cockney rhyming slang. A little further along, another Pearly King wore a waistcoat with the words "Proud to be Born a Cockney" stitched on in buttons. Bingo! I thought. Until that moment I hadn't been sure what the centre piece for my painting would be, but I'd found it now.

I continued to wander around and chat to the Pearly Kings and Queens, one of whom kindly invited me to put on his jacket so I could feel its weight. I couldn't believe how heavy it felt on my shoulders and I can't imagine what wearing a whole suit must feel like, especially for the day. I was also amazed to meet a family of Italian Pearlies who had come over specifically for the festival; the tradition is spreading overseas!

It was nice to see the new generations come through as well, the Pearly Princesses and Princes. I spotted the Pearly King and Prince of Finsbury at the edge of the square, standing next to a wonderful old couple who were draped in British flags and dressed in red, white and blue. I'd met this Pearly King and his son before, at other events. Today, John Walters was wearing a button-covered cap over a pair of sunglasses and had Pearly patterns of lucky horse shoes on his tie. He recognized me and we got chatting.

When I asked John about Henry Croft and the origins of the tradition, he told me, "The history of the Pearly Kings started in 1875 in St Pancras: our founder who was thirteen years old when he came out of the workhouse there. That's where he was born and the same place he died in 1931. The Parish got him employment as a rubbish sorter in the Barnaby depot and he then became a road sweeper for Charlton Street market and the market at St Pancras; he was amazed by the costermongers, who sold vegetables on the streets of London, and how they helped the poor out and their colleagues out if they couldn't raise any money."

He continued, "The costermongers used to have seven buttons up the sides of their trousers or round the piping of their waistcoat, so Henry Croft decided was to sew a load of old buttons on an old suit that he had, a pair of moleskin trousers. And he got the

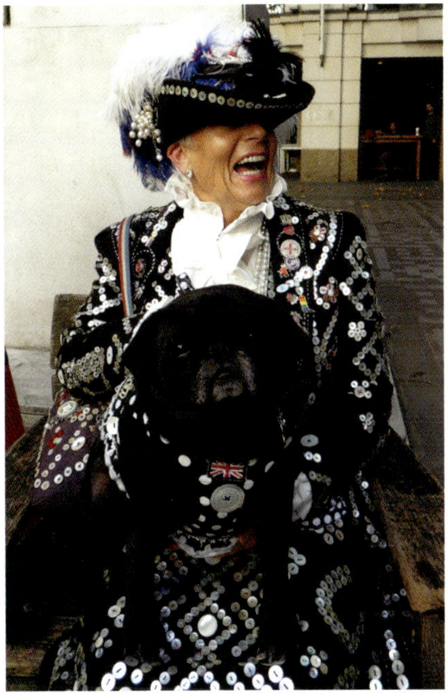

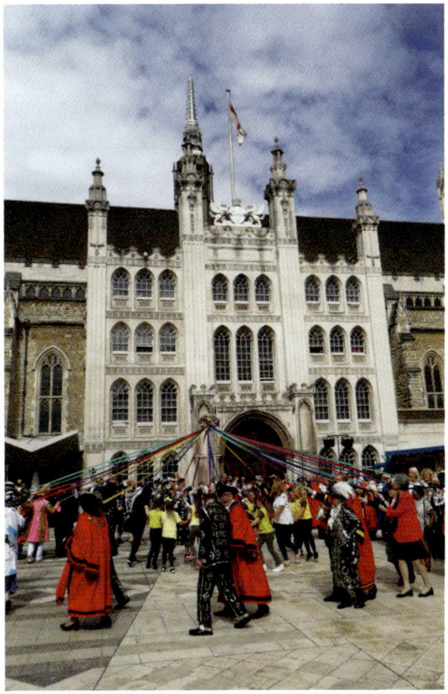

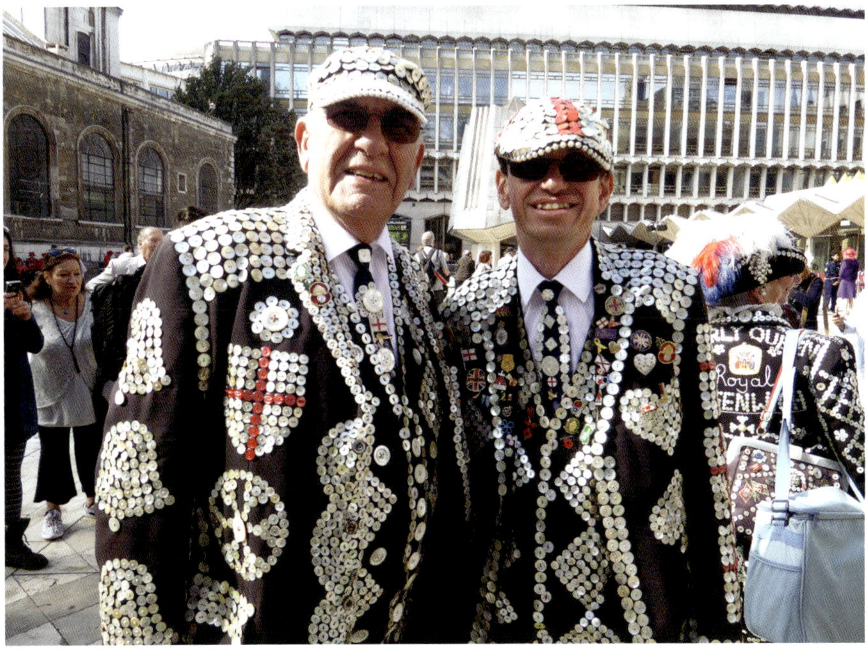

costermongers together and they sewed more buttons on their working clothes, and then they became the London Pearly Kings and Queens."

By now the whole of Guildhall Yard was crowded with all sorts of Pearlies, some dressed in so many shiny white buttons that their suits appeared to glow, while others had symbols on their clothes such as cart wheels, which seemed to be a reoccurring motif. Another had the St George flag sewn in buttons on his lapels. When I got talking to him, he explained, "The first Pearly, Henry Croft, was a rat catcher, a street collector. He saw the way all the market traders looked after each other in times of need, and he wanted to do something to help where he was born in the orphanage, so he came out one day in a suit of buttons, 'cause the old market traders used to wear the buttons across their pockets and down their trousers. Then everyone wanted him to collect money for their own charities, so he asked all his friends from the markets; then it grew and grew and soon there was a Pearly family for each London Borough." He then said he'd better make his way over to the row of chairs that had been put out for those involved in the ceremony, which was about to start.

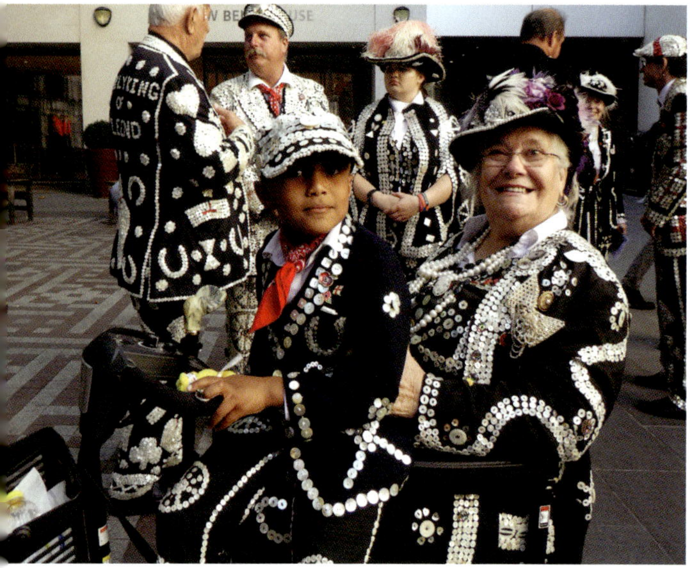

While I'd been talking to the Pearly Kings and Queens, metal railings had been placed around the square. Now on the crowd's side of them, I made my way to the front to get a good view. A maypole had been put up in the centre of the square and a woman's voice echoed through the PA system in a thick London accent, announcing that the Sheriff of the City of London would arrive soon to give the welcoming address. Some of the metal railings were parted and a classic London black cab made its way through, which the Sheriff stepped out of. Rather disappointingly, he was in a plain black suit when in my imagination he should have been in a ten-gallon hat, straight out of a Western. Amusingly, when he made his speech he actually did have an American accent. He said that the first drink he ever had in a London pub was in the Pearly King, which has now sadly gone.

His speech was followed by a few words from a couple of the borough mayors, followed by maypole dancing which was led by an energetic lady in multicoloured clothes and her immaculate white poodle. Then the Pearlies sang "Maybe it's because I'm a Londoner", after which a drumming band played and there was morris dancing, where the character who resembled Sid Vicious banged his sticks and stomped about energetically.

It was now time for the main procession. All sorts of dignitaries in red coats and pointy hats assembled alongside the Pearlies, before a marching band in military attire kicked off proceedings. Collectively, the buttons of the Queens, Kings, Princesses and Princes made a magical tinkling sound as they walked out of the square and set off down the road. Everyone followed the procession through the streets, passing black cabs and red buses whose laughing passengers looked on in pure joy and took pictures. It soon became apparent that the Pearlies represent the best of humanity and spread happiness wherever they go. Spending all their spare time collecting money for charities, they are the unofficial working-class royal family of London and it was emotional to watch the Pearly King of Bow himself being pushed along in a wheelchair to St Mary-le-Bow Church in Cheapside. There was a patriotic atmosphere: not of oppression, empire and conquest, but of kindness, charity and selflessness, a form of patriotism that I could get behind.

The sounds of the city floated beneath the band's tunes; you could hear the clatter of scaffolding poles being assembled, roaring motors and machinery. As we reached the church some bagpipe players appeared, it started raining and the Pearly Queen of Greenwich and her pearly pug took shelter beneath a Union Jack umbrella, while a man in a beret at the front of the band swung a ceremonial staff and the Bow bells rang out. A double-decker idled patiently as the procession came to a standstill in front of St Mary-Le-Bow, whose spire was once destroyed in a tornado in 1091, and then again in the Great Fire of 1666. Finally, everyone made their way inside for the service, with one of the Pearlies carrying a huge harvest loaf.

There's something about the story of Henry Croft that says a lot about the kind of Londoners I used to meet as a boy, when I'd visit my grandad and his friends: they didn't have much financially and did hard manual jobs, but they were rich in character and incredibly generous people with an infectious zest for life. The Pearlies connected to me on that level, too, and the idea of my painting was to celebrate the kind, hardworking and charitable spirit of people of the city, the true Cockneys, in which I would use the story of Henry Croft to symbolize the true spirt of the working-class Londoner.

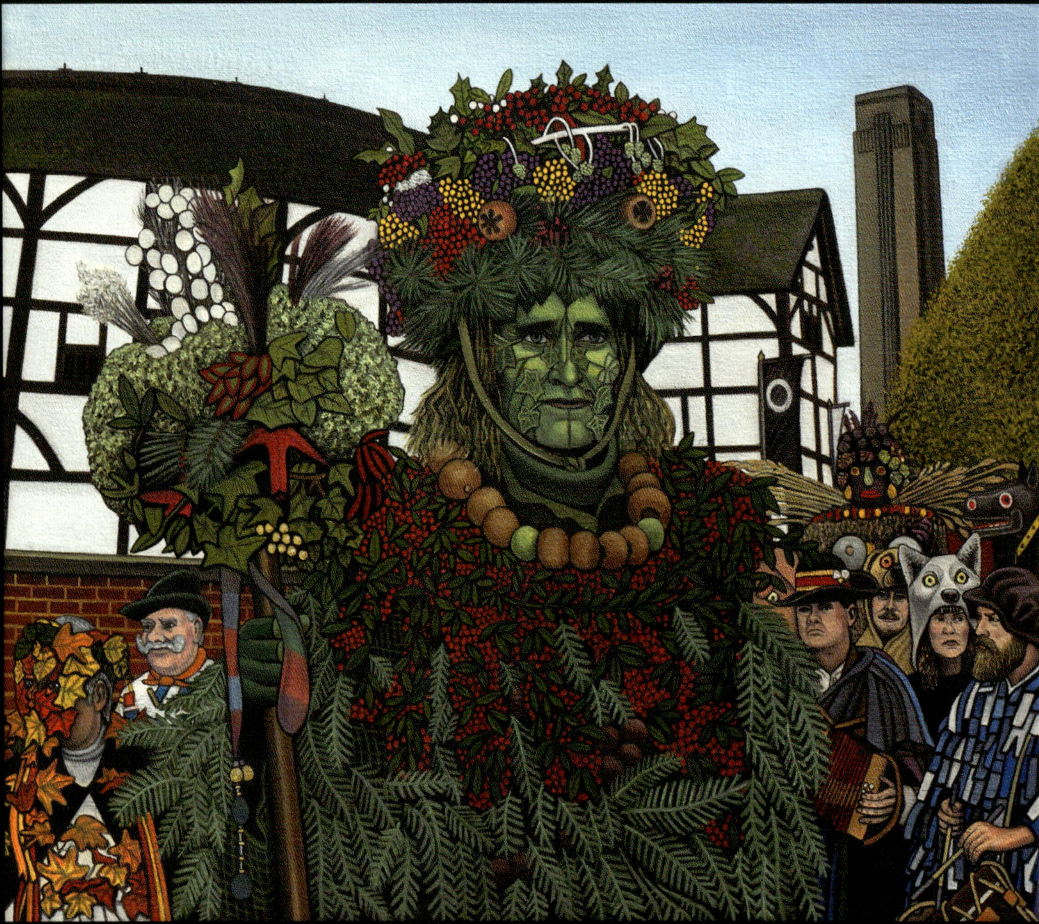

THE GREENMAN OF BANKSIDE AND OCTOBER PLENTY

Oil on Canvas, 46cm × 40cm

2019

The Green Man of Bankside and October Plenty

SOUTHWARK, LONDON

SUNDAY IN LATE OCTOBER

It was a beautiful bright day in October on the Thames. As I stood outside the Globe theatre, a woman approached. She was dressed in medieval attire and ringing a bell, and followed by various figures including a Green Man, a large corn effigy representing the Corn Queene on a cart and an array of musicians and people wearing animal masks, parading along the riverfront. Today was the October Plenty festival, when this procession and various plays relating to harvest time were to be performed here and in London's famous Borough Market.

I was there to paint London's very own Green Man, a figure that has played a part in my life from my childhood right up until today and has not only inspired some of my paintings but also sculptural works. My grandfather was fascinated by the Green Man and carved his face on the end of walking sticks. He claimed he'd seen him in the woods and would take me and my siblings and cousins looking for him. He even had a friend who claimed to have a photo of him. To me, the Green Man was real, scary and magical all at the same time, and as I've got older, whenever I see the motif it's always felt like some kind of sign. My journey into British folklore has been guided in good measure by my grandfather's interest in this mythological figure.

This was one reason why the idea of London's own Green Man of Bankside particularly appealed to me. At the October Plenty festival, he appeared in his guise of the "Berryman" and his costume reflected the natural bounty found at this time of year. With its autumn berries and beautifully crafted foliage, it screamed "paint me", so here I was now, standing in front of this figure surrounded by other traditional harvest characters, and a painting had already begun forming in my mind.

The October festival itself was started by Sonia Ritter of the "Lions part" theatre company, whose actors are involved in the festival and have associations with Shakespeare's Globe theatre. My friend the folklorist Doc Rowe told me he was in Sonia's front room when the idea for the festival first came about, some thirty years ago; however, when he went to the first one, he happened to be in a newsagent when someone asked the man behind the counter about the event, and the man replied, "It's been going ever since Pagan times, it's hundreds of years old." The story is funny but it also highlights that while folklore events such as these often seem uncanny and weird, yet there's also a familiarity about them that makes complete sense. This familiarity seems to tap into a kind of ancestral memory deep within our DNA, which is ready to awaken whenever called upon by festivals and folkloric characters such as those associated with the wheel of the year.

Today, a large crowd had formed in front of the Globe and a piece of street theatre was taking place (naturally, what with the participants being Shakespearean actors), which included a very medieval-looking hobby horse whose jockey wore a large-brimmed hat with a long feather, which nearly fell off when he jumped over children who'd volunteered for the privilege. The performance ended with a harvest song sung so beautifully that you could have heard a pin drop in the awestruck crowd.

After some morris dancing accompanied by a wooden horse mascot known as a "hooden horse" (see page 196), which snapped its jaws at the crowd, the procession was ready to begin in earnest. A jolly song was played by accomplished musicians, the bell began to ring, and a man in a long coat with a clipboard and pen, who was clearly in charge of crowd safety, shouted, "Make room, make room, to the market!"

Off we set, with the eerie figure of the Corn Queene appearing to glide along Bankside. A group of people dressed as sheep made baa sounds and a tail formed of spectators. The

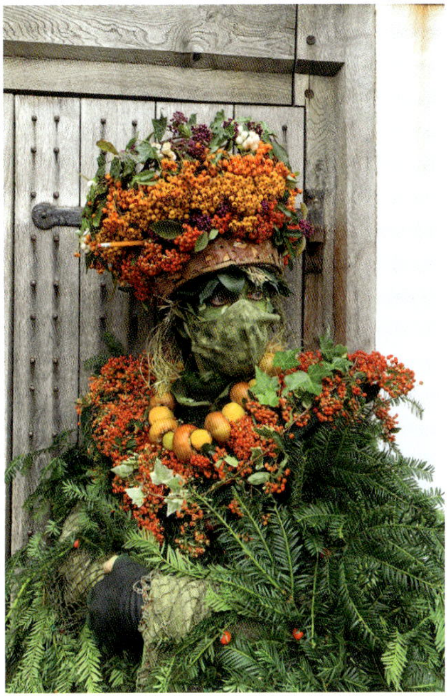

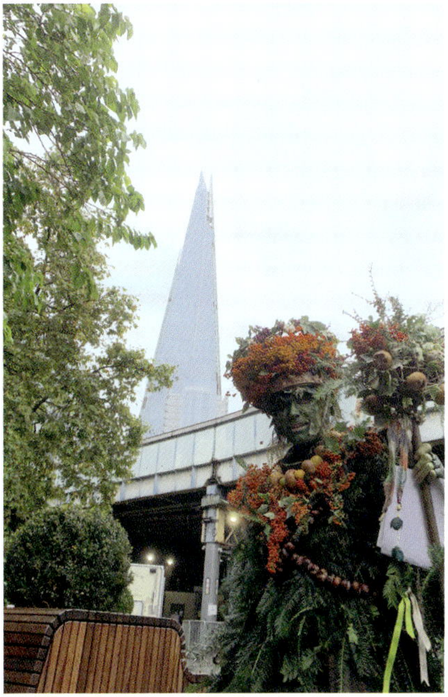

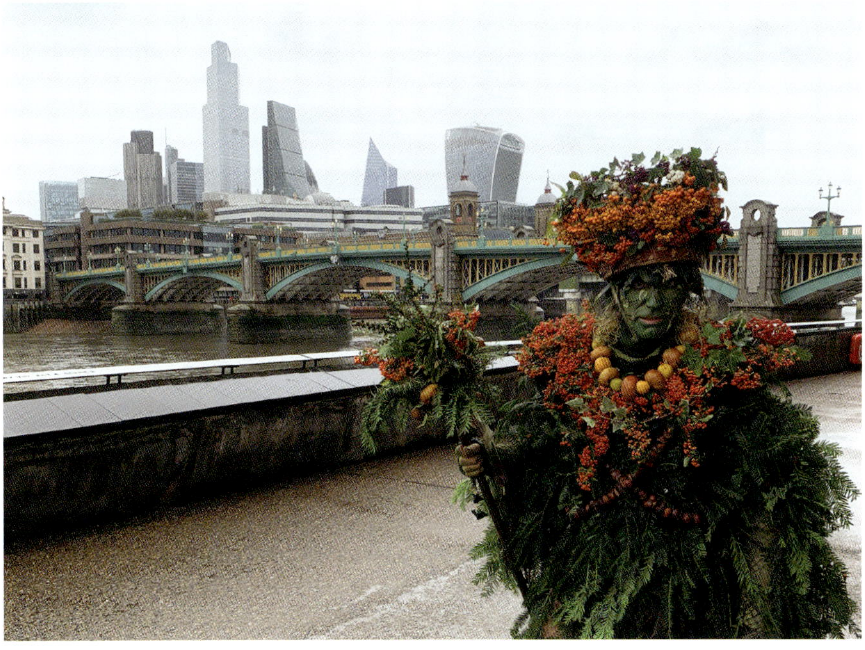

Green Man led the way, dancing arm in arm with members of the public, the sky was bright blue, the air cold and crisp, and the atmosphere one of pure joy. We passed a Pizza Express from where the tops of lorries and buses could be seen peeking over Southwark Bridge and when we processed beneath the bridge's dark arches, people shouted gleefully to create echoes. The Walkie-Talkie building loomed in the distance on the other side; then we passed the Old Anchor pub, once a favourite for smugglers and river pirates and fittingly the site of the inn where Shakespearian actors might once have refreshed themselves after performances, and from where the Shard now dominated the skyline.

Then we went under a railway bridge where another collective racket was made, which quietened down by the time we passed the old Clink Prison, perhaps named for the sound made by inmates dragging a ball and chain. These leg irons were attached to the ankles of prisoners with certain privileges who were permitted to wander the streets. We were now getting close to our destination of Borough Market, where more plays would be performed and the Corn Queene effigy dismantled.

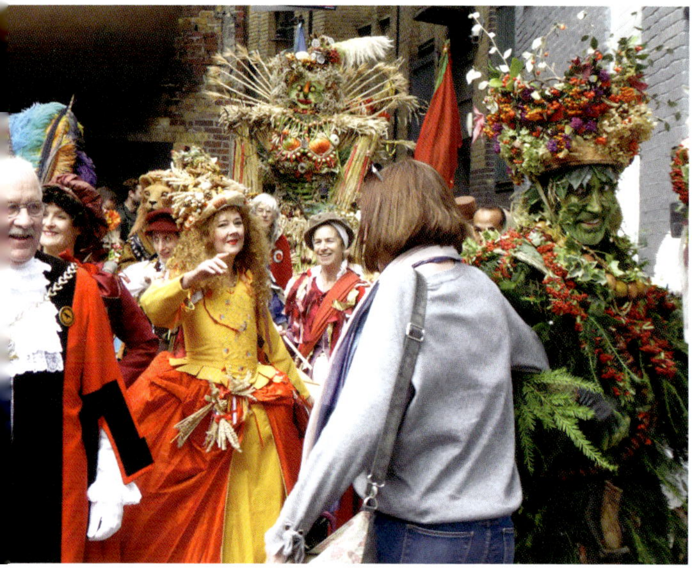

We entered the narrow passageways of the market, where among the sizzling meats, strong-smelling cheeses and mulled wine, stall holders and their customers looked on in a mixture of amazement and confusion. In the market, the Corn Queene was set down next to a small stage, while the Green Man wandered about and talked to the crowd.

The Green Man of Bankside, aka David Risley, is someone who I've got to know well in the course of my folkloric adventures. During the pandemic, when the October Plenty festival couldn't go ahead, I was asked to help make a digital online version of the event, for which I had the privilege of walking through a desolate London with David and filming him as he followed the processional route and relived it in his memory. We got to go into an empty Globe theatre, where David walked in costume across the famous stage as the rain poured down. It's an image that lives vividly in my memory, and I turned it into a short film called *Awaken the Harvest Within*.

David and I have had many discussions about the Green Man. Although the name is said to have been coined in the 1930s by the amateur folklorist Lady Raglan, who used it to refer to the foliate heads in churches, the description of a "Green Man" covered in leaves and foliage, taking part in calendar customs such as parades and pageantry, can be found going back to the sixteenth century. This processional figure, also known as the "Whiffler", would lead parades and clear space through the crowds, and like a Wild Man would carry a club, which was sometimes laced with fireworks.

For me the Green Man is an archetype that runs deep within the human psyche and can be traced right back to ancient cultures, to green deities associated with resurrection and life, such as the ancient Egyptian god Osiris, described in the Pyramid Texts at Saqqara as the "Great Green". There is something about the symbolism of leaves sprouting from a human body or face that speaks to human beings of all backgrounds and cultures about our connection to Nature, and taps into our ancestral memory – a phenomenon that Carl Jung described as "synchronicity" and Alan Moore as "idea space".

On one occasion, I asked him his thoughts on the figure's origins, and he replied, "The Green Man's sort of a strange figure, isn't he? He's sort of a mythical character from prehistory, claimed by the Pagans, but when you walk across the country or the city, you'll find four to six Green Man pubs; there's even got a Green Man pub in the basement of Harrods. Then, of course, you see these great state occasions going on in Westminster Abbey, and there overseeing it is the Green Man on the medieval facade, which is quite astonishing really.

"So I don't really know what the Green Man's all about; some say he's a sort of medieval thing, a foliate head that you very often see in churches and cathedrals. People used to think in terms of the cathedrals and abbeys: maybe the masons were thumbing their noses at the Church. The Green Man bosses that you see now are very often tucked away very high up, and you can't quite make out what they are, so they may not have been approved of."

I asked David what the Green Man meant to him on a personal level. He explained, "For over thirty years, I've been the Green Man of Bankside. I've made this costume over a hundred times. I feel very privileged, as people come at you with all sorts of viewpoints – some people are blown away, and some people revere this character. I've been asked to bless people's weddings; he's a very reverential figure, an earthbound god as opposed to the ethereal gods and goddesses, and you have to respect that people revere this character. There are people that see an earth god in this character." This was very much what my grandfather saw in the Green Man and made it all the more puzzling when I first found the figure lurking in the corners of churches and cathedrals.

When I asked David what the Green Man represents today, he told me, "I think people are looking for some sort of grounding in environmental concerns and that may mean making a lot of sacrifices; we've got to a point where we're flying too close to the sun, really, and the Green Man can help us find the ground again, before our wings get burned."

There was definitely a grounding earthiness to the October Plenty festival. As the day progressed, much cider was drunk and everyone clapped wildly and cheered the actors during their performances. The iconic moment came when the Corn Queene was "stripped" and dismantled, and the pieces of corn and winter fruits that the effigy is made from were tossed out to the crowd. An apple hit me right on the head, as desperate arms in all directions tried to catch the airborne produce and children shouted, "Me, me, please, me!" I was surprised by the sudden hysteria that'd been whipped up. Perhaps this would have been further heightened in times past, when the audience may have relied on the food being thrown to them. Once the Corn Queene had been pretty much dismantled, there was an auction in which the melons that had been used for the breasts were sold off, much to the amusement of the crowd.

Afterwards, I spoke to the actor who'd been played the part of the goddess Iris throughout the day. She explained the meaning of the effigy and festival as a whole, telling me, "It's essentially a harvest festival: you used to see the kind of Corn Queene that we have in English villages in past centuries, and villages would make effigies from corn and parade them round. There are also corn dolly traditions where the last sheaf cut would be made into a corn dolly and perhaps buried or burned."

As the day concluded, the Green Man of Bankside and some other members of the Lions part theatre troupe invited me to join them for one final stop, a trip to Crossbones Graveyard, where their friend John Constable, aka John Crow, would be waiting for them. We left the market and passed a large old painted advertising sign that read "Take Courage", then crossed busy Southwark Street and walked on toward Redcross Way. Ahead of us, a crowd had already gathered, at the front of which stood a man with white hair and bright blue eyes that seemed to radiate warmth and enthusiasm.

Seeing us, the man strummed his guitar and burst into song: "The Green Man is come, the Green Man is come, to bless our garden, with flowers and trees, with flowers and trees, for future children ..." John Constable, aka John Crow, is no ordinary man. He'd been campaigning to honour the paupers buried within Crossbones, who were interred in unmarked and unconsecrated graves. In many instances, they were medieval prostitutes licensed by the Bishop of Winchester to work in the brothels of the Liberty of the Clink, which lay outside the law of the City of London. It was now the custom for the Green Man to come and honour those described as the "outcast dead" every year.

Crossbones was now a special place where ribbons had been tied all around the metal fence outside in remembrance, and there was even a shrine to the Green Man inside. It was a fitting place for the day to end, with the enigmatic figure of the Green Man blessing a garden that welcomes all faiths and none, which honours the outcast and downtrodden, and whose guardians have defied property developers in order to keep this small piece of green space within the city thriving; a garden steeped in legend, mystery and magic, much like the Green Man himself.

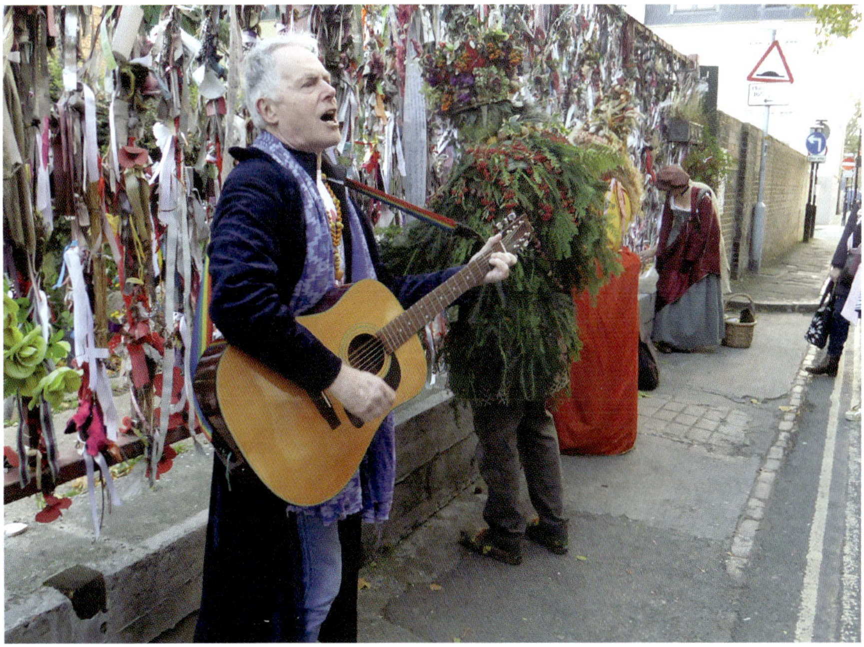

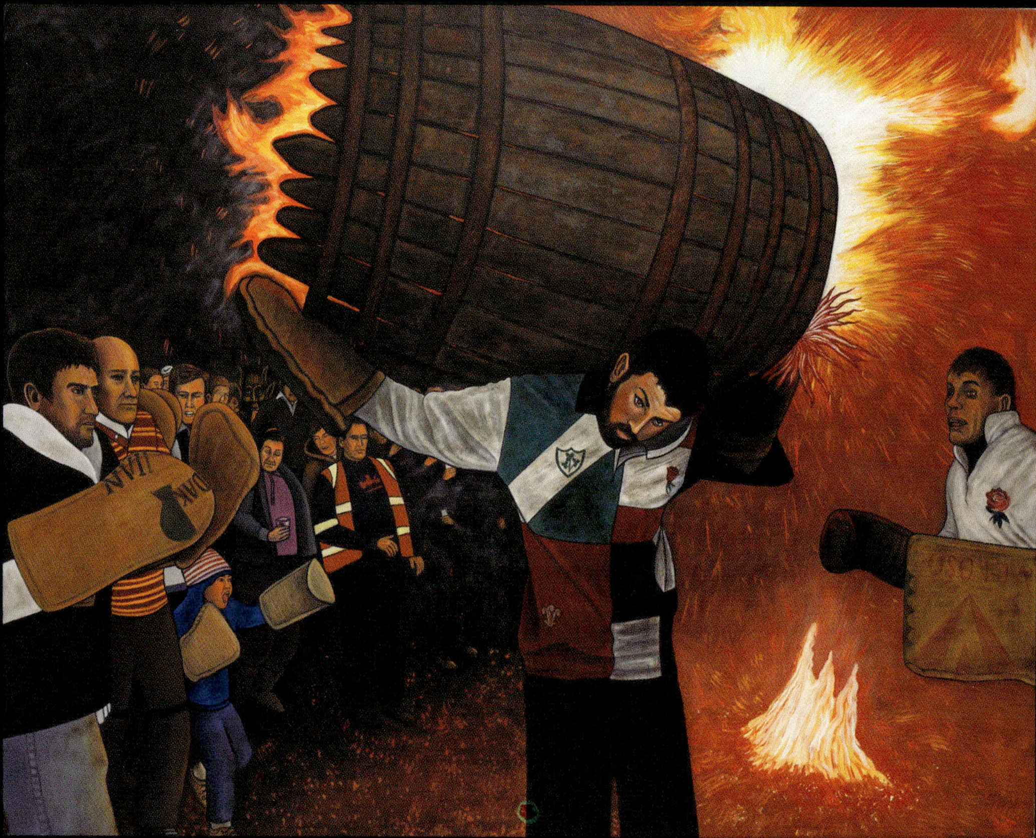

THE FLAMING TAR BARRELS OF OTTERY ST MARY

Oil on Canvas, 65cm × 80cm

2020

The Flaming Tar Barrels of Ottery St Mary

DEVON
NOVEMBER 5

I arrived in Ottery St Mary to find an apocalyptic atmosphere pulsating through town. The Boots Pharmacy was already boarded up, with large sheets of plywood hammered over the windows, and "Open 9–5" crudely scribbled over the battened-down doors. At the butcher's, a man up a ladder was banging nails into boards, while catering vans were starting to line up along the street just beyond the town square.

I went into a pub just as everyone else seemed to be rushing out the door and there was a loud "bang, bang, bang" like a gun going off. It shook me up, but turned out to be the sound of what are known locally as "rock cannons" being fired; these handheld devices are blasted throughout the day, even at four in the morning to wake up the townsfolk. Everyone headed back into the pub, where I noticed a group of men with necks like tree trunks, dressed in rugby shirts that had been burned and blackened by last year's fires. On further inspection, I realized the men were actually wearing multiple layers, which made them look even wider and more muscular, almost like bulls ready to run into the ring; which in some ways they were, only they were getting ready to run with flaming tar barrels instead.

Over a pint, I learned that the children's barrels event would start at 4pm, so I had a bit of time to kill and headed to the nearby Church of St Mary's, on a raised spot close to the town centre. When I went inside, I soon found a Green Man with golden leaves coming out of his eyes, nose and mouth; I had spent some time with the Green Man of Bankside recently and it seemed like the Green Man was making himself known to me more and more often as I journeyed around Britain.

Next, I wandered up the hill to a street of predominately terraced houses where people were gathering around a man kneeling in the middle of the road. He was squirting some kind of flammable liquid from a large metal tin straight into a tar-lined barrel, while a man in white England rugby shirt watched over the proceedings with an authority that suggested he had run with many a barrel in his time. Other men with T-shirts that read "Tar Barrel Committee" were standing close by, as if waiting for orders.

A group of children hovered next to the men, some looking terrified and close to tears, while others smiled nervously. While the adults laughed and joked, the children were mostly silent. All of them were wearing gloves resembling oven mitts made of sack cloth.

Once the first barrel was rolled and reached full flame, the black smoke forced the children to squint, cover their eyes and recoil. Behind them, their excited parents started encouraging them; the future of this tradition lies on their young shoulders, after all. The nervous energy increased and all of a sudden a boy in a red hoodie set off, clutching the burning barrel. I felt like I was witnessing a rite of passage; as if the children were entering a new phase in their lives that meant their parents would look at them in a new light.

The children started to take turns to sprint with a burning barrel before passing it on to the next runner. Soon, some had singed hair and holes burned in their clothes, and one child even threw his glove on the ground when it was engulfed in flames. A cheering woman who I guessed to be the mother of one of them noticed me looking worried and said, "They'll all be at school tomorrow showing off their battle scars."

I was particularly struck by a young girl in a pink hoodie, who was struggling to work up the nerve to grab one of burning barrels. The crowd kept encouraging her, and then, out of nowhere, she took a barrel from a boy, lifted it onto her shoulders and ran triumphantly through the streets, her mother cheering with delight. The girl was elated, and ran straight back to join the queue to run again. Her inner fear beaten, she'd become one of the long line of barrel runners of Ottery St Marys.

Another child to catch my attention was extremely confident. He kept running further and faster than the rest, even screaming "Get out of my way!" at times. While it'd been difficult to get any good photos as the crowd was so tightly packed, I got a great shot of the boy with his arms stretched out and his mouth wide open, as if embodying the willingness of the next generation to undertake this rite of passage and ensure the tradition's survival. He would be going into my painting, I decided; the first piece of the jigsaw in place, the rest still unknown.

As the barrels burned until they broke completely apart, tiny sparks drifted across the crowd. The sun got lower and our shadows grew longer until an appropriately fiery sunset

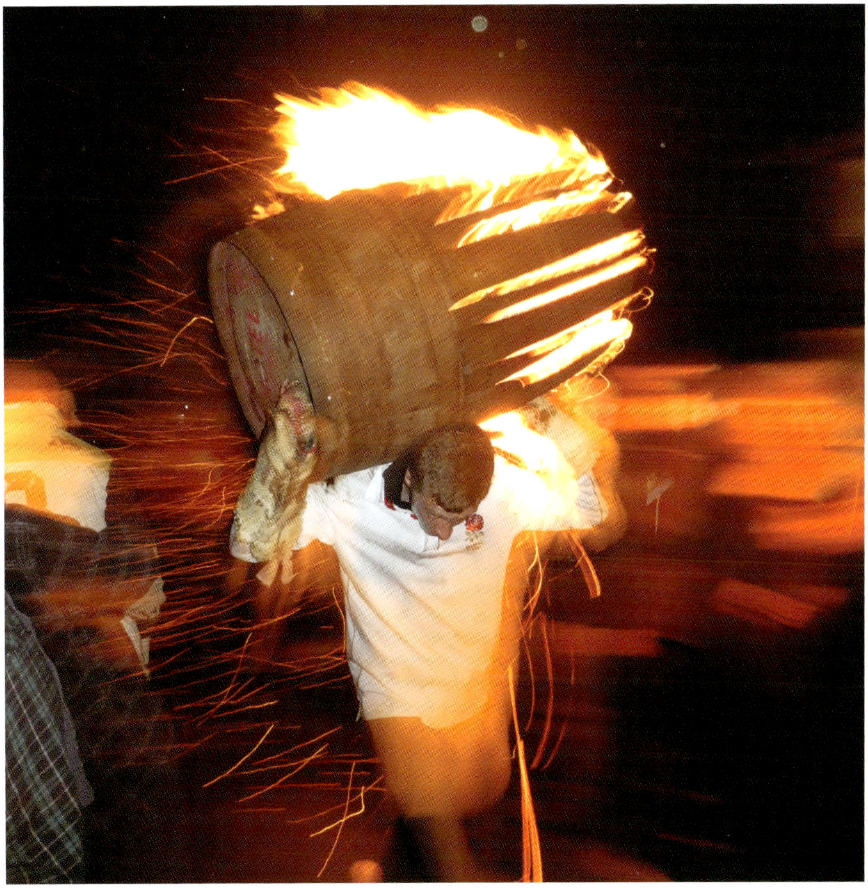

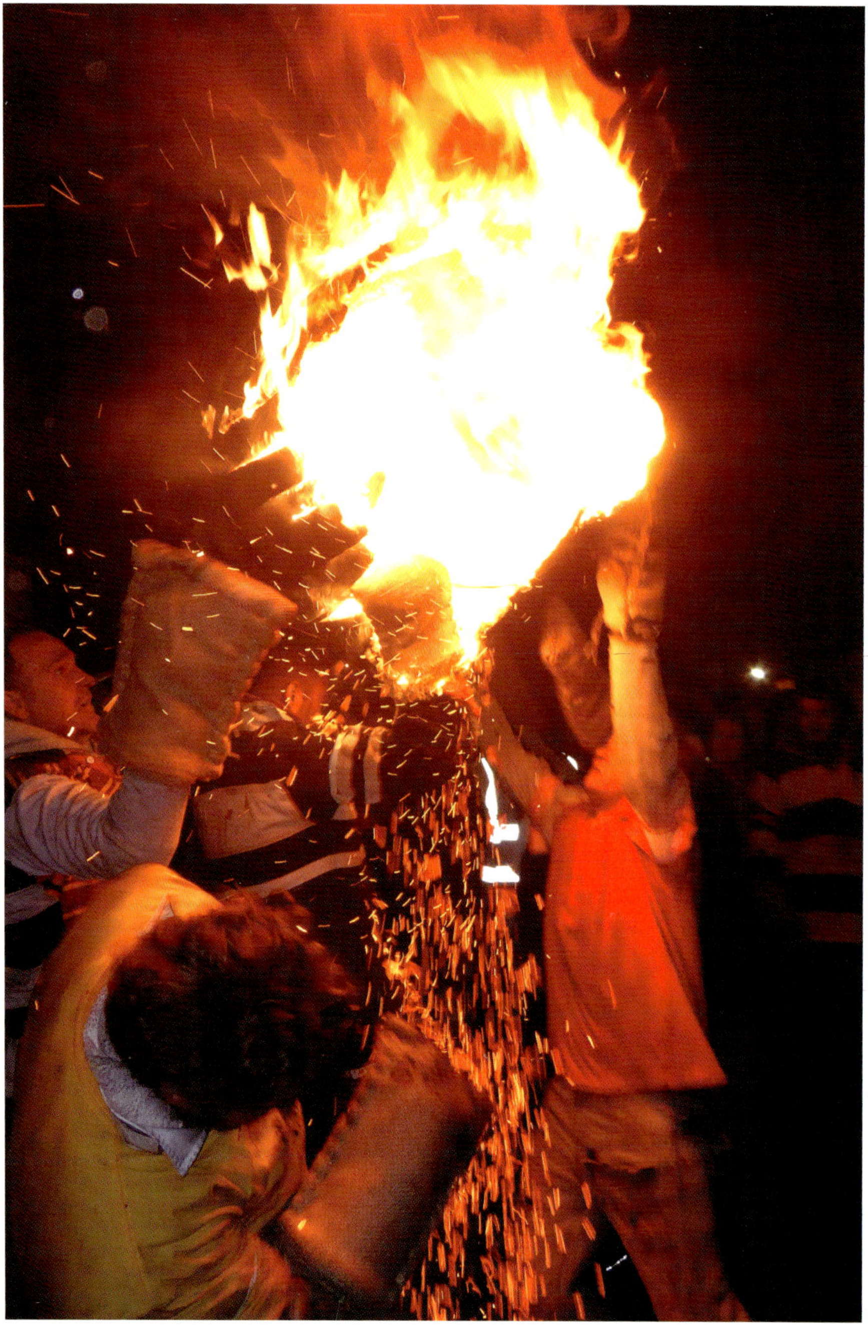

lit up the horizon. It was soon dark and the adults began to take over. The barrels got larger and the danger greater, while the flaming tar filled the streets with a dramatic glow and the runners and the crowd were lit up like a Caravaggio painting. I realized at that moment that I'd need to create a scene full of drama if I were to depict the tradition accurately.

Under a bright moon, the air was full of the smells of burning wood, tar, singed hair and burned clothes, along with the aromas of hot dog stands, frying onions and sizzling beef burgers. Huge barrels were now being carried by testosterone-filled young men, some of whom started showing off by rocking the barrels up and down as they ran, making sparks fly and their hair literally go up in flames.

I spotted the man in the England rugby shirt from earlier and went to talk with him. When I asked him when he first started running with the barrels, he said, "When I was seven year old, good fun; like with these kids there doing us all proud and hopefully they'll carry this on as long as we have. It keeps the town together: all the youngsters want to do what their parents have done, and keep the tradition going in the same format." I asked him about the local beliefs and stories surrounding the tradition, and he replied, "It goes way back. It's Pagan, an ancient tradition. There used to be fire festivals all over the country and there's only a few left now. There's records going right back before the Gunpowder Plot, fumigation rites and things like that, warding off evil spirits."

I kept following the barrel runners, getting braver myself and closer to them. The heat of the barrel is something else: your skin stings and you can feel your hair being scorched. Occasionally, when I found myself on the wrong side of the barrel, where the open flame roars out, it was as if my face had blistered and my eyebrows burned off. After all this boisterous activity, I made my way over to watch the women's barrels, where the atmosphere was the polar opposite: there was a supportiveness and a respect for danger that seemed lost on the men.

Although it was a long evening, starting at four and going right through until midnight, it was another of those traditions that I couldn't get enough of. As I ran alongside the barrel, nothing else mattered: my senses were on full alert, ready to duck out the way of danger at any moment; I felt primal and it felt great. Forgetting the problems and concerns of everyday life is both therapeutic and liberating, a meditative practice in its own right.

I took lots of pictures to capture the excitement – the sparks like fireflies, the screams of concern among the barrel runners and the part-terrified, part-enthralled spectators. The soot on your face, the searing heat; that's what I wanted to capture in my painting. I also loved the idea of the ritual being to cleanse the town of evil spirits and could imagine lurking demons being forced to run and hide as the barrels made their way through the packed streets.

Soon, it was time for the barrel simply known as "Midnight". My instinct proved right and there, at the centre, was the man in the white rugby shirt, part of a group getting ready to hoist this giant into the air. It's an honour to hold the Midnight and there was an added layer of emotion, as this was the first time for some of the younger men, who were about to become elders of the tradition. Watching the barrel being rolled as flammable liquids were pumped inside was reminiscent of the mouth of hell, and people scrunched up their faces in pain as the smoke hit their eyes. It roared with a life of its own as it was hoisted up.

The heat was like an inferno; I got too close, and this time I was sure my eyebrows were gone; I felt for them: they were still there but definitely singed. Suddenly, a drunken teenager ran and smacked the back of the barrel; a barrel runner squared up and gave him a jab to the face: "You could've fucking killed someone!" he yelled.

We were now in the town square, spilling over with people; the press of bodies was unbearable, as if we were being crushed, although whenever the barrel came near, space somehow appeared, as everyone legged it, diving against the buildings and out of the way. The barrel kept burning, bits falling off, and getting more and more treacherous to carry. With burning pieces hitting the heads and scorching the hair of the runners, it was run literally into the ground, just a flaming ball with only a few parts of its wooden structure still intact. Until *crash*, it fell apart. Bagpipes played, the barrel runners formed a circle and sang arm in arm around the remains of the flaming Midnight barrel; more flammable liquid was pumped on, there was one last giant burst of flame and a huge cheer erupted across the town square.

The crowds began to disperse amidst the sounds of crunching rubbish beneath our feet. Buildings were black with soot; discarded food trays were lying everywhere, crushed into the pavement; it felt dystopian, a primitive madness in the air. I headed back to my B&B, passing the illuminated church where I'd spotted the Green Man. In my room, I looked in the mirror: I was literally covered in soot, the collar of my jacket was seared, and bits of my hair were blackened and burned. "Never again," I said to myself, "until next year."

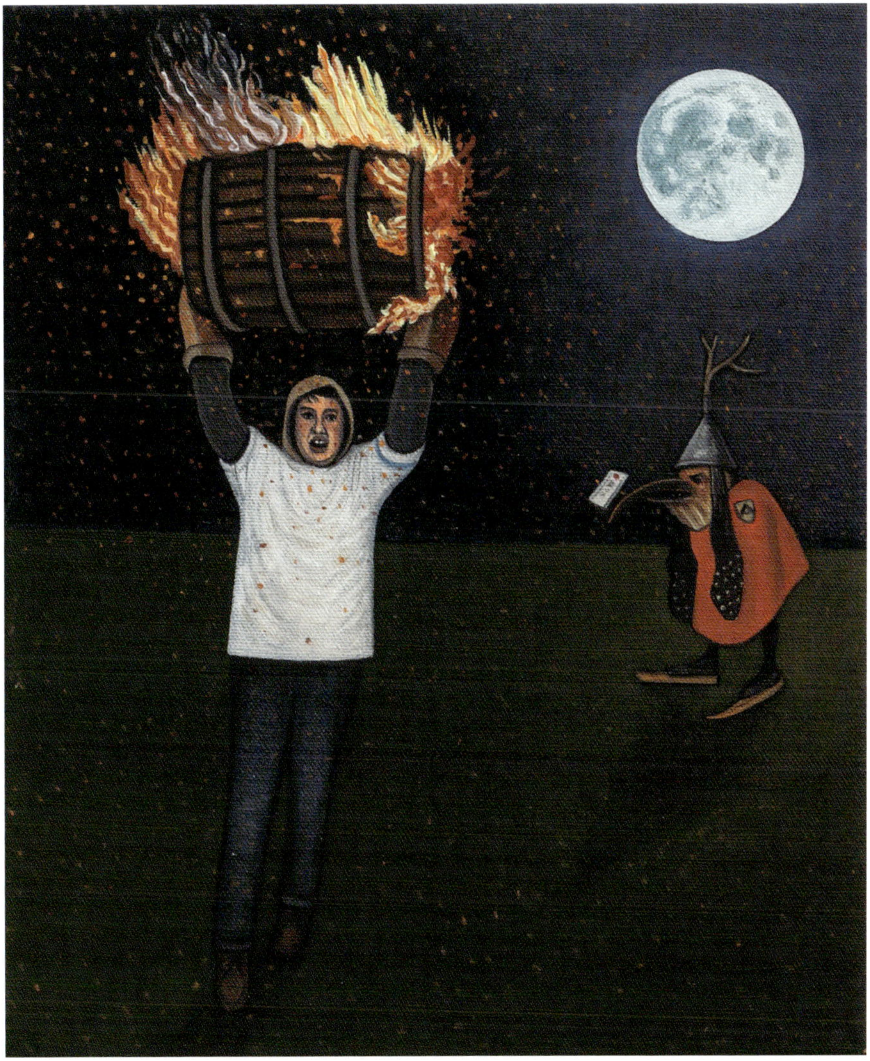

MOURNERS MOON

Oil on Canvas, 30cm × 25cm

2019

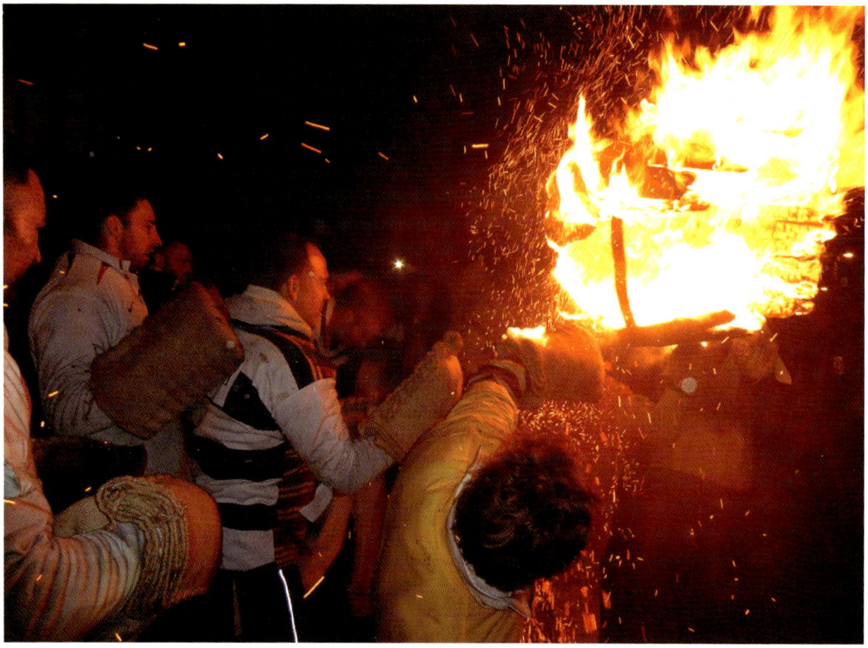

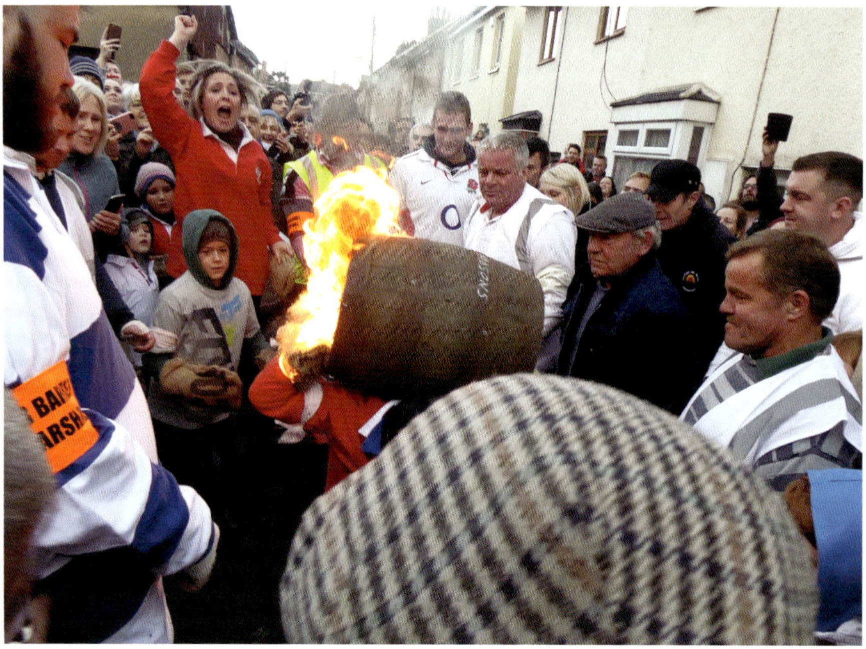

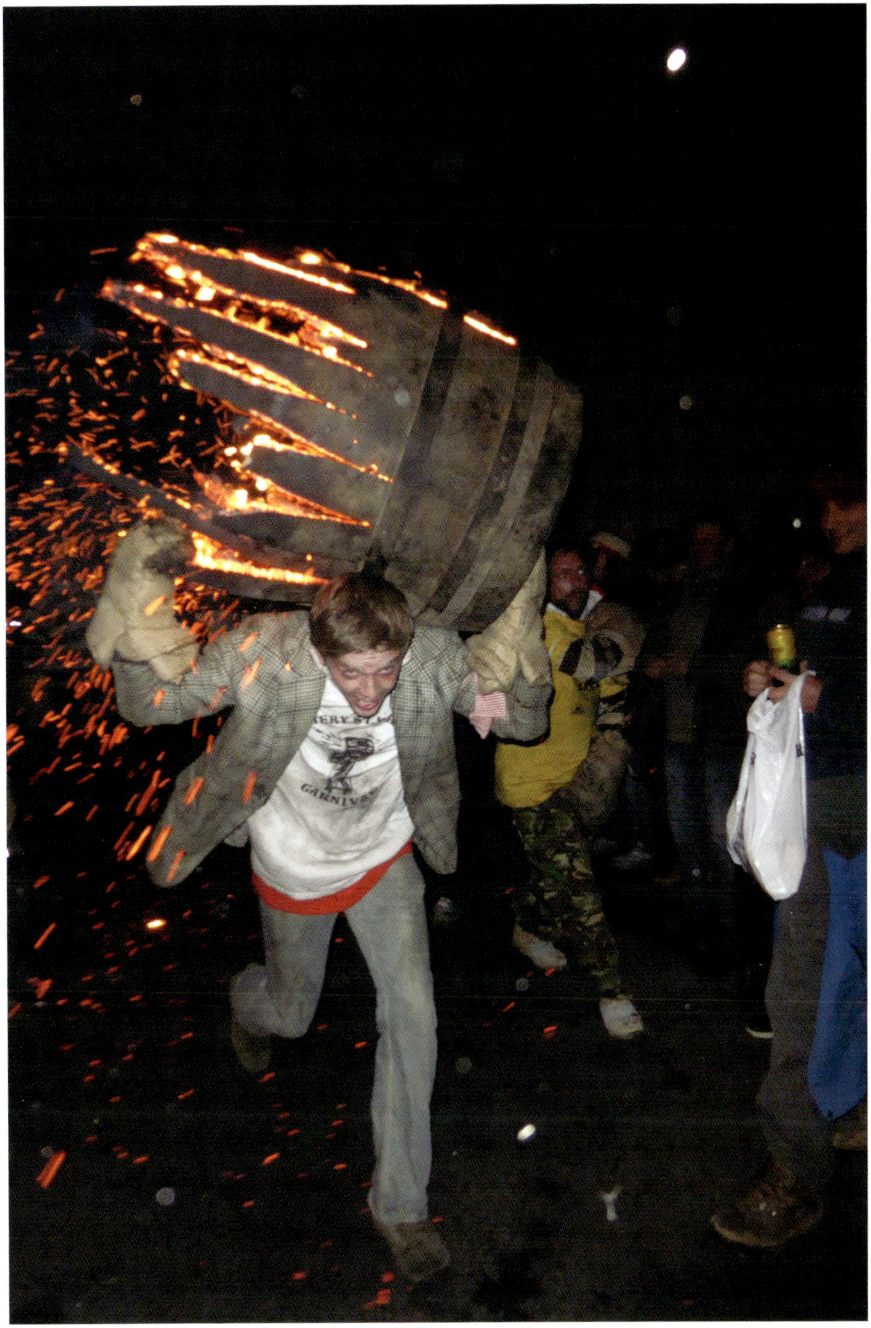

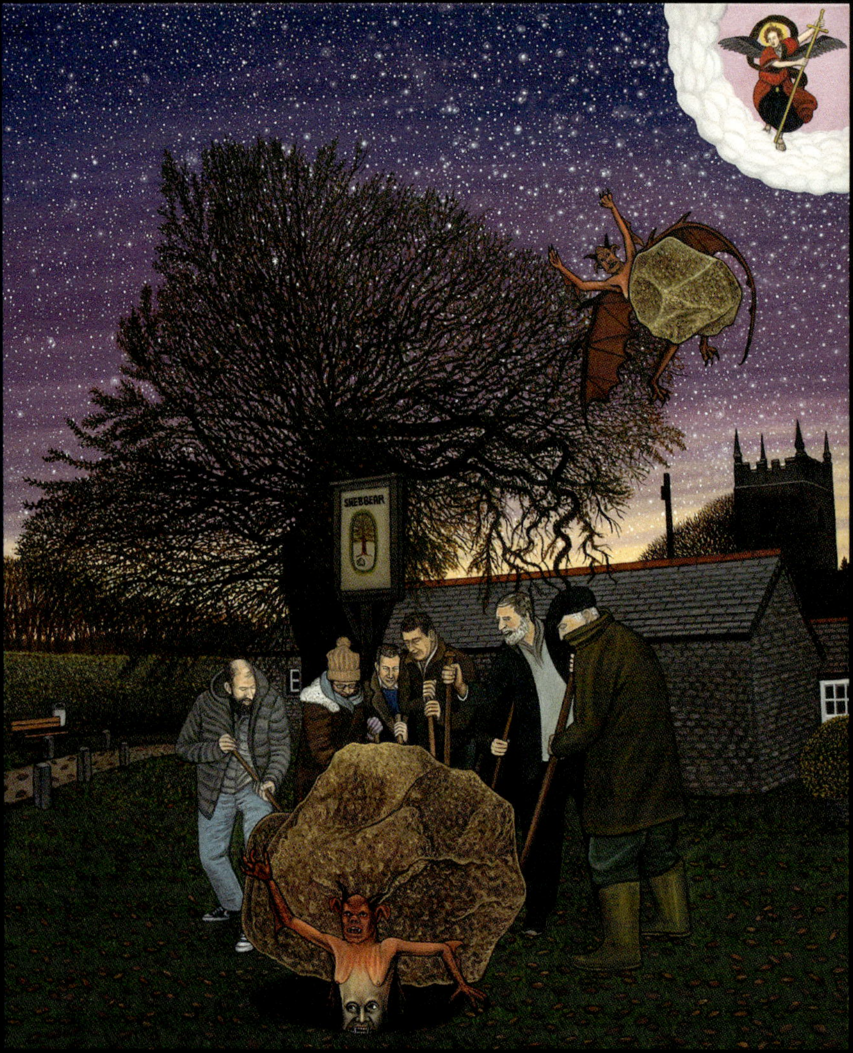

TURNING THE DEVIL'S STONE

Oil on Canvas, 60cm × 45cm

2024

Turning the Devil's Stone

DEVON
NOVEMBER 5

I'd arranged to meet the vicar at the Devil's Stone itself, and wandered over the wet grass to where the huge rock squatted beneath an ancient oak in the village square. Nearby, a tall figure was hovering, wrapped up in a scarf, gloves and coat: the vicar, a softly spoken man named Martin Warren who had kindly offered to speak to me about the origins of the strange tradition. He shared the story he had been told on becoming the vicar of Shebbear over twenty years ago.

"We don't do bonfires here, Guy Fawkes and all the rest of it," he explained. "Instead, we turn the Stone on the fifth of November. The bell-ringers of St Michael's ring the bells beforehand to scare off the Devil. Then they come out and turn the Stone with crowbars." He pointed at the ground and continued, "You can see the dent from where it was last year. The story's based on the Book of Revelation, which describes a war in heaven between St Michael and the Devil. The legend is that when the Devil was ejected from heaven, a stone was hurled after him, trapping him here."

When I asked the vicar about the Stone itself, he said, "The Stone is probably a glacial erratic; it doesn't belong here and presumably arrived during the Ice Age. So the story's an attempt to explain why it's there." There is so much creativity born out of "not knowing" in folklore; whether it's local folk tales, costumes or, in my case, artworks, it's a never-ending goldmine of inspiration.

I've long heard stories of churches being built on the sites of standing stones, but the Reverend Martin wasn't convinced that was the case in this instance. Instead, he explained, most of the churches dedicated to St Michael were built on hilltops, which connect them with the idea of heavenly battles. Then he led me into the church and showed me an old grave decorated with a skull that had greenery growing out of its eye sockets, which he agreed was a type of Green Man. He added, "The fact that there's all the foliage coming out of it speaks of fertility. So it's going right back into pre-Christian times, but was adopted and seen as a symbol of God's life of creation." He also showed me a beautifully preserved Norman doorway, carved with stylized animal heads "to scare away evil spirits", and explained that a church would have stood on the site all the way back to the Saxon era; that the Devil's Stone was probably connected to the collection of taxes in the Shebbear Hundred, where it would been a central point. As I looked around, he apologized and said he had to head off to prepare the speech he would be giving later.

I wandered back out to find that a gazebo had been raised outside the Devil's Stone Inn, where preparations were in full swing. A big crowd was expected and when I popped into the pub, a local who'd made himself comfortable at the bar explained, "We got new owners: the past ones fell out of love with both the pub and the tradition, but this lot have fully embraced it; they got it right, there'll be a hog roast later too." Then he added, "Be careful in here, it's haunted you know; I've seen things myself: there's a bit by the bar where you can feel the temperature drop, it's gets so cold. This is actually one of the most haunted pubs in the country."

He was surprised I'd travelled down from London. "You come all this way to see a stone flipped!" he laughed with a gappy grin. "You know it takes a year for the Devil to burrow down and escape, so they have to flip it to keep him trapped down there? Well, that's the story anyway."

My kind and helpful hosts in the village had mentioned me to a local historian, Ron Ackland, who said he was happy to talk to me, so after leaving the pub I crossed the square to his house, where he welcomed me in. He already had a selection of photos laid out on the table and explained proudly, "I did it for twenty years and my dad did it for forty." He added, "All my family were bell-ringers and the bell-ringers do it."

When I asked him how long the tradition went back, he broke into laughter and said, "No one knows why we do it", before becoming serious again and saying, "They call it the Devil's Stone now, but before the war it was just known as Shebbear Stone. It's been going on for ever. During the war they missed a turning and things in the war were going bad, so some of the boys went out and flipped it one night, and the war changed. There was another time when a rat ran out from under the stone when they were turning it, and people thought that was the Devil himself." When I asked him where he thought the Stone came from, he said, "I always like to think it's a meteorite; it's a bit of this, it's a bit of that. It's not like slate or granite, it's just an amalgamation of all sorts of things."

As we were talking, there was the most stunning sunset, the sky glowing like fire, with soft, purple clouds drifting across the horizon as the sun slowly sank into the Torridge Valley. When he saw me out, Ron, now aged eighty-eight, said he'd be watching from indoors. There was a buzz now around the pub, a bar had been set up in the gazebo and the hog roast van had arrived; queues were forming for food and drink, so I decided to wait inside for the turning to begin.

It soon fell dark and the scary-looking devil on the pub sign was illuminated spookily by lights. Children were playing wildly around the Stone itself, leaping over each other and getting rougher in their play. The fact that no parents intervened suggested this always happened, almost like it too was part of the tradition. A woman with dark-red hair and a fleece zipped right

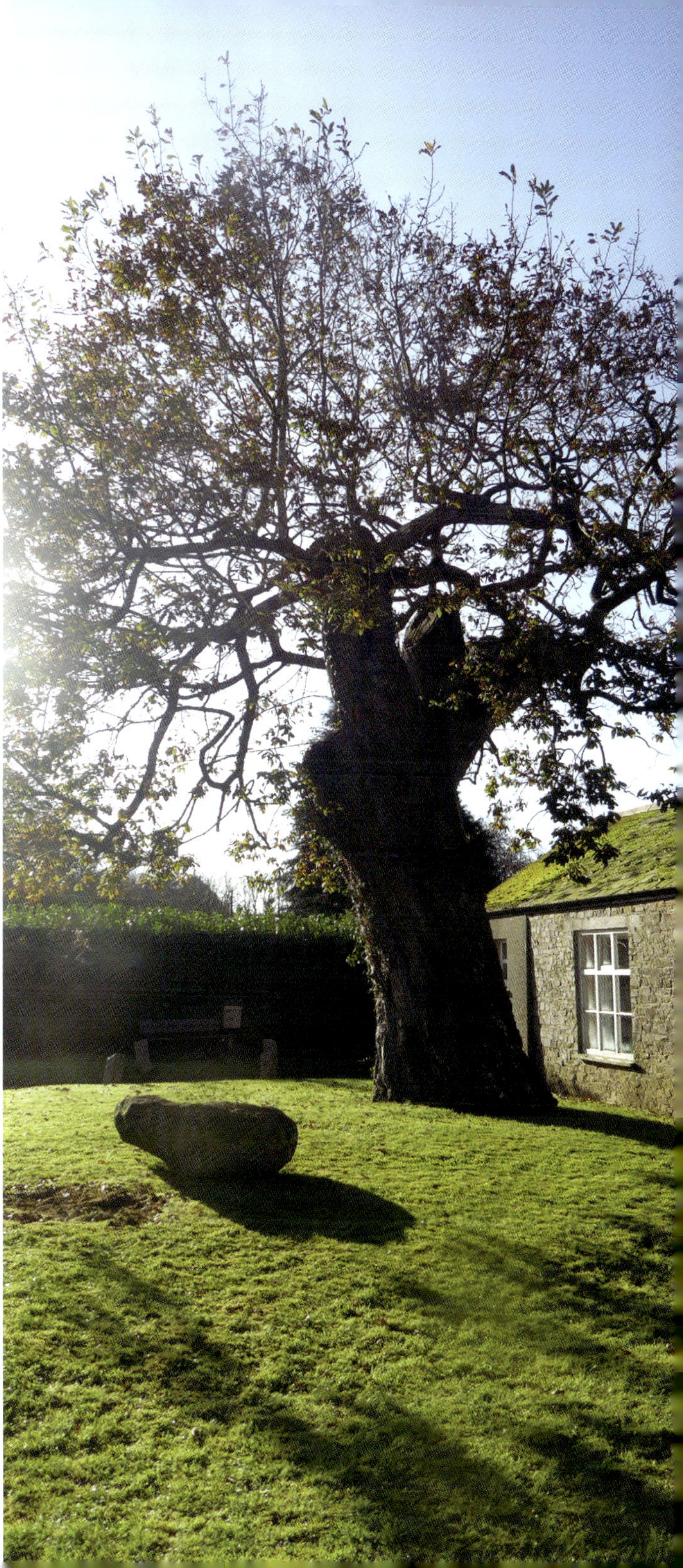

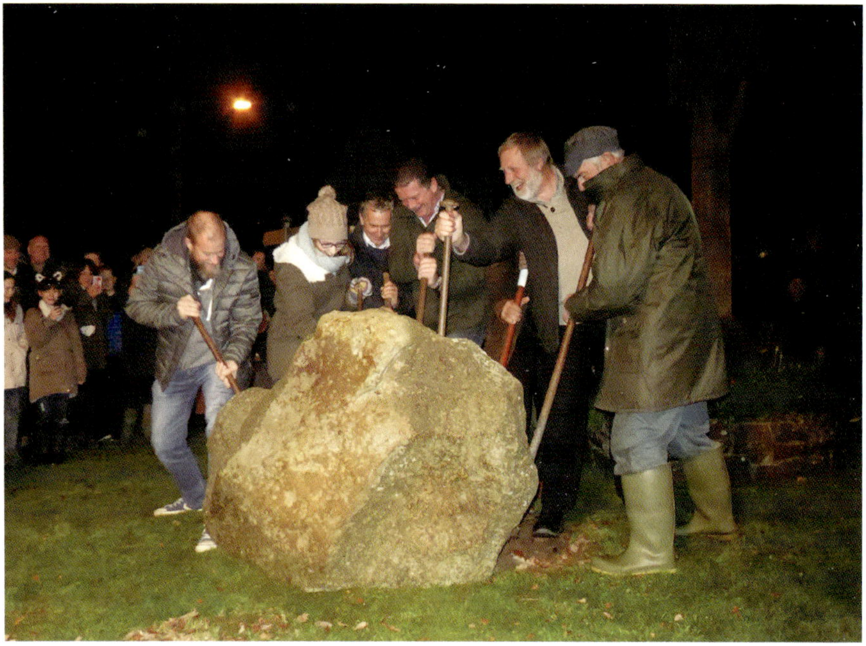

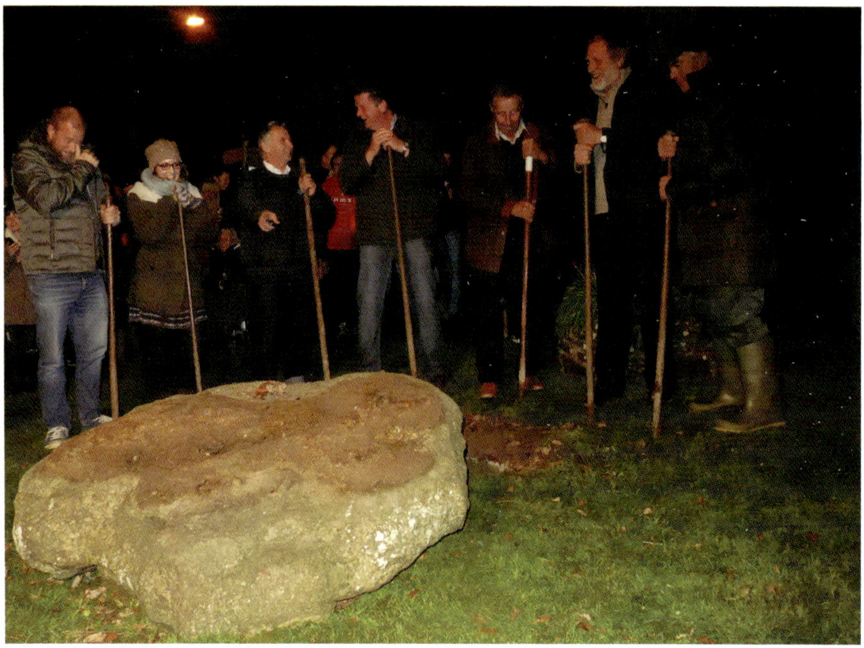

up to her chin told me in a rich Devonshire accent, "I've been witnessing this since I was three years old, and I'm now nearly fifty-one." When I asked her about the children, she explained, "When we were younger, if you were jumping over the Stone and if you caught your hand or your foot, it was always told that the Devil had caught your leg." Suddenly, the bells started pealing and the children's excitement grew. She continued, "You could guarantee you'd always end up with a cut on your hand or something wherever you landed, and that's surprising as it's grass."

The ringing of the bells ebbed away into the night air. As the bell-ringers who were to flip the stone appeared alongside the vicar, the children parted ways and everyone took their position under the street lights that lit up the ground where the Stone lay. In a loud voice, the vicar declared, "So we come a-fresh this year to turn the Stone once more, to declare the Devil does not have the last word, to stand upon the rock, upon the stone of faith." Then he called upon Shebbear's bell-ringers to begin their task and the chant rose, "Turn the stone, turn the stone, turn the stone ..."

As the seven bell-ringers pushed their crowbars beneath the rock, and started to jack it into an upright position, I could imagine them alone, no crowds, just like that time during the war – a group of superstitious people flipping a stone in the black of night. I could visualize a cloud opening, St Michael ejecting the Devil from heaven as he falls underneath a large stone; perhaps he's accidentally crossed paths with a passing meteorite. He passes distant stars, galaxies and planets, before hitting the ground and disappearing beneath the black earth. My composition was forming it in my mind's eye: the Devil just breaking through the surface as the Stone reaches its most vertical point, a boy shouts, "Hurry up" – just before it falls, crushing the Devil back down beneath the earth. The crowd cheered, the tradition upheld. Everyone disappeared back into the Devil's Stone Inn, as local bands played and the drink flowed freely. My work was done.

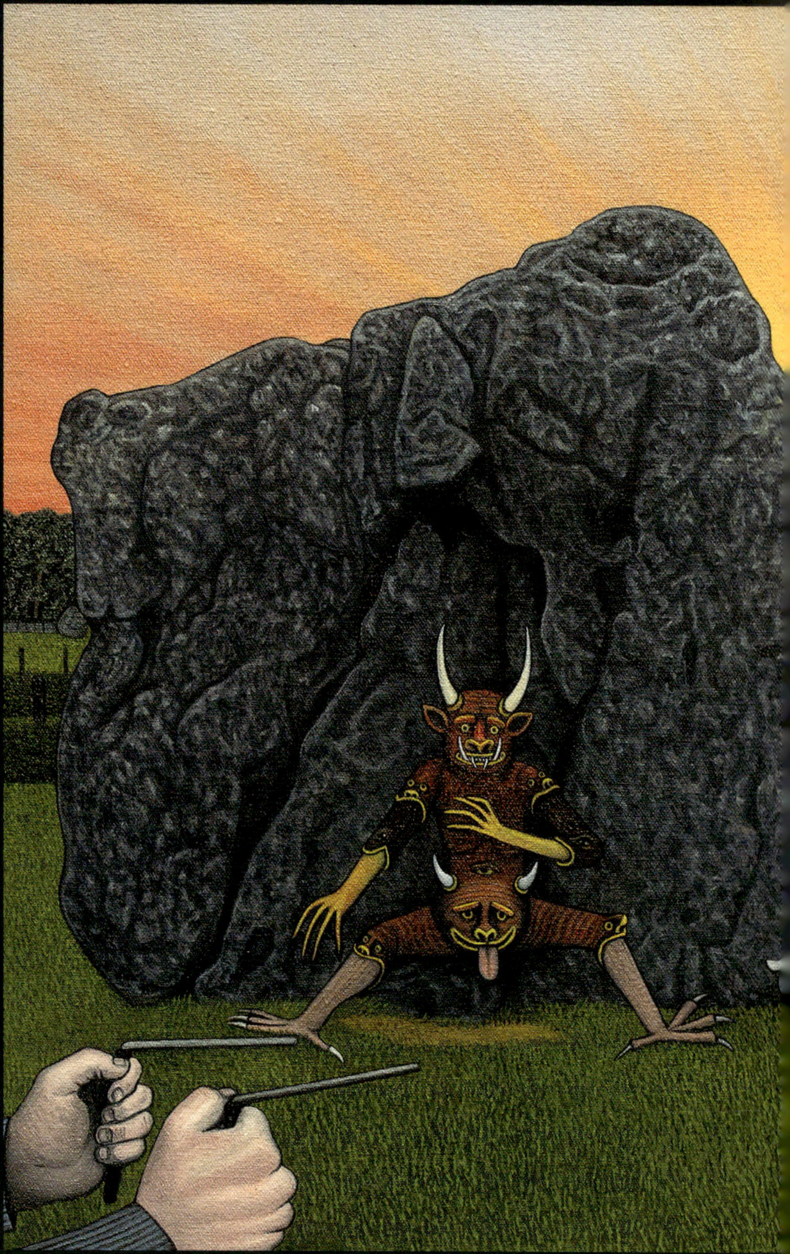

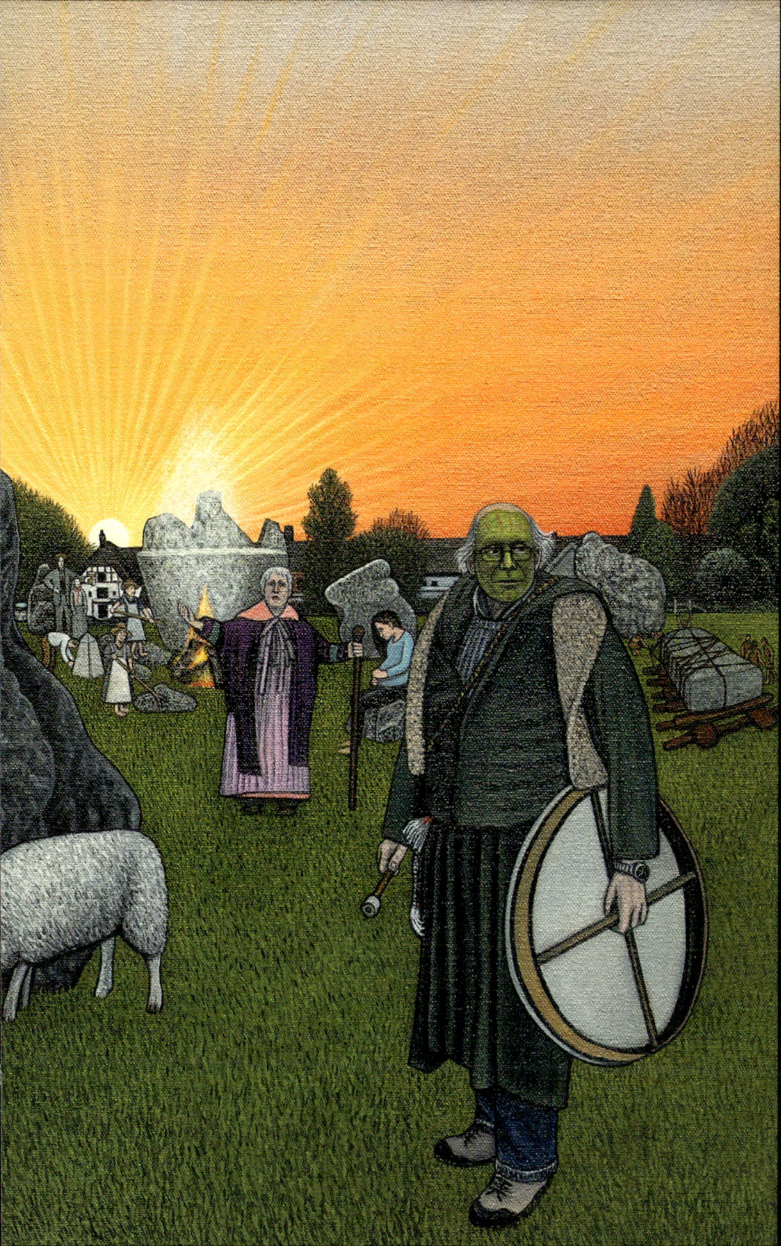

THE RISEN SON AT AVEBURY

Oil on Canvas, 45cm × 60cm

2024

Avebury

WILTSHIRE
NOVEMBER VISIT

It was a dull day in early November, when I went to Avebury to make a film about the stones there. It's a place where I've spent a lot of time over the years; there are few other settings where I feel more relaxed and completely in the moment than wandering around this epic Neolithic complex, which consists of a huge stone circle enclosing two smaller stone circles to the north and south, and with all the stones being surrounded by a gigantic henge, formed of a ditch and bank, with four causewayed entrances. At the southeastern entrance, two parallel lines of stones create what's known as West Kennet Avenue. Nearby are West Kennet Long Barrow, the sacred Swallow Head spring, and the giant artificial chalk mound of Silbury Hill.

What makes the village of Avebury even more special is that it lies partly within the stone circle itself, and includes the Red Lion pub, which has the bragging rights of being the only drinking establishment in the world to be situated within an ancient monument like this one. It was here that I was sitting at the bar when I got talking to man called Dennis, who happened to be a practising Wiccan. I told him about my art and that I was hoping to make a painting and film about Avebury. As we sat talking, his eyes widened.

"All my life I've been a conduit, I've connected people," he told me and explained that he was going to introduce me to someone called Gordon Rimes, who was a Wiccan high priest and would be the ideal person for me to film. We finished our drinks and wandered over the road, with glimpses of the stones all around us, to an old cottage where Dennis knocked on the door. A man with a long, white pony tail, bright eyes, red cheeks and a wide grin answered. When Dennis explained who I was, Gordon invited me back the following day for a tour of the stones.

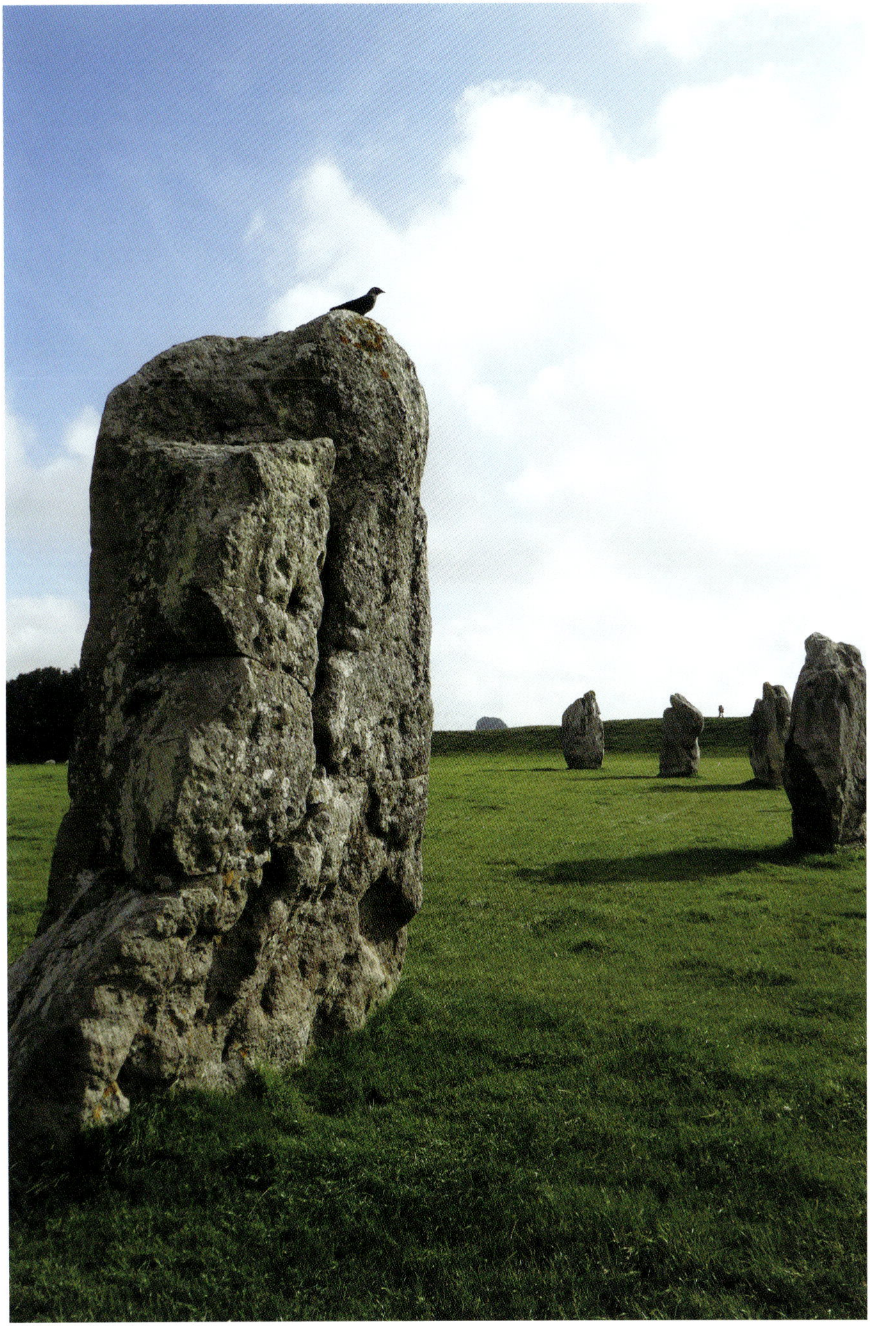

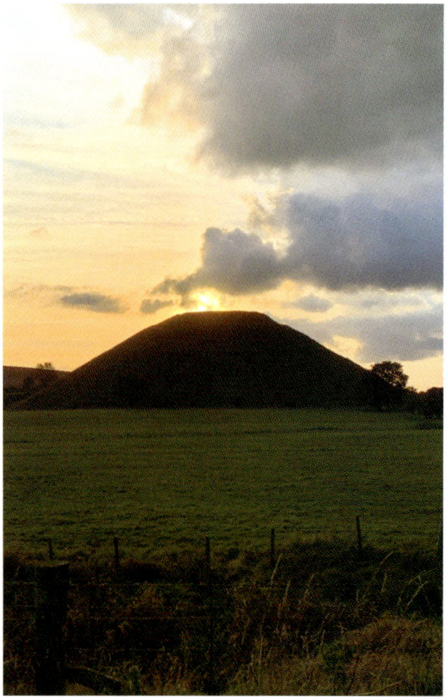

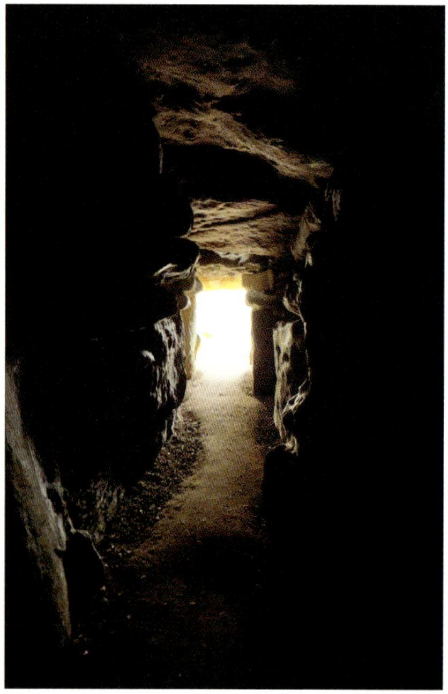

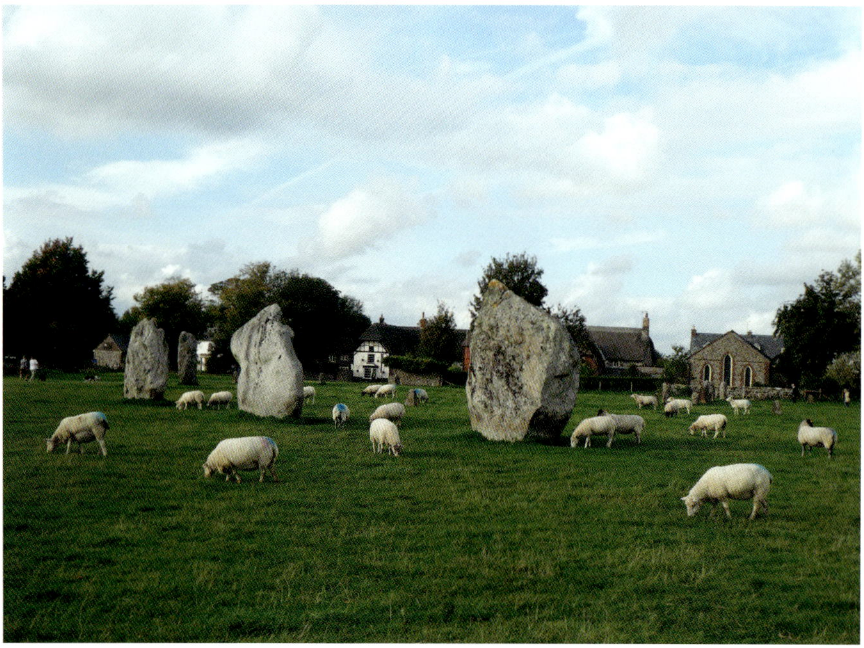

As agreed, I returned at noon the next day, to find Gordon standing in his doorway, holding a tall staff and signing for a package. Past the noise of cars, tractors and trucks from the road that runs directly through the centre of the circle, he led me over to the mossy grey stones, which came in all shapes and sizes, from the relatively thin and modest to the immense, towering twice as tall as us; resembling conscious beings, with each having its own distinct personality.

I asked Gordon if he'd be happy for me to record him and when he said yes, I started to film him on my phone; I've found that people are used to phones, whereas they sometimes behave differently if you put a video camera in their face. When I asked Gordon what it was like to live inside a stone circle, he said, "I find it OK. Some people struggle as obviously there's a lot of energy going on. The Michael and Mary ley lines cross the site and there's also the energy of some people who come here, who don't realize they're affecting things: they leave crystals stuck in the stones and make other crazy offerings."

We began to wander among the stones in the inner southern circle. The huge bank and deep trench that surrounded the whole area resembled the stands of a stadium, where perhaps the ancients once watched their priestly class perform rituals within the circle. I asked Gordon what exactly would have taken place within the stone circle in its heyday and he explained that he believed the circle we were standing in related to the sun, while the other circle was related to the cycles of the moon, as did the outer circle, forming a sort of planetary calendar. I asked whether rituals took place here and he firmly believed they did.

He then excitedly took me over to a thumb-shaped stone taller than both of us and pointed his staff in the opposite direction toward a concrete plinth. "There was once an obelisk in the middle there that was five metres high," he said, then turned back to the stone next to us. "On the morning of Beltane, the fertility festival on the first of May, the shadow of that obelisk would have hit this stone." He pointed to a large slit in the centre of the rock, which had a small bulge poking out directly above it. "Everything that the female vulva has," he noted, and the stone's markings were certainly reminiscent of what he was saying.

He continued, "You can see how smooth this side of the stone is and how worn and weathered the other side is. Now, Mr Keiller [the archaeologist who restored Avebury in the 1930s] put the stones back up as part of preserving the site, but some of the other stones are more worn on both sides than this one is. So some people think it'd been down longer on the ground than the others, and that it was probably knocked down by the Druids when the Romans arrived, because the Druids didn't want the Romans to know that this was a fertility circle, important for the fertility of their people."

We walked on and I asked Gordon about a small chapel located nearly in the middle of the stone circle. With a smile, he told me, "Back in the 1700s we had a very zealous vicar, who encouraged the locals to break the stones, and there are some who say this chapel's built with the obelisk from the centre, though it's very difficult to say whether it actually is. It was what's known as a Five Mile Chapel, built when there was a split within the Church and nonconformist ministers weren't allowed to preach within five miles of their original parish. This one's more than five miles from places like Marlborough and Devizes."

I wondered whether the Church had a problem with the stones because of their Pagan origins. In reply, Gordon pointed to the stub of a stone in the distance. "There's a little bit of stone over there that, legend has it, is the remains of the Ring Stone used by the villagers for handfastings. Because weddings were a relatively new thing, the Church decided they needed to register instead, so the vicar had that stone taken away. But for ten years, they had no children in the village, and the villagers said we want our stone back. Now, obviously they'd broken up most of the stone, but the vicar brought a piece back, and after that the villagers would go to church and get married, and then handfast over the stone, and they had children again." He also told me about a more recent legend: "Legend says that if you're trying to get pregnant, your chances will be greatly improved if you sit on the Ring Stone at dawn ..."

Later that day, Gordon introduced me to a kind-natured Dutchman called Henk who also lived within the stone circle and was soon to become the Archdruid of Avebury. Henk told me about the Beltane Stone, which sits much further out in the field. "Quite a few children here in Avebury have been conceived on that stone," he said with a smile. "It's shaped in several ways so you can do different positions, and it's just far enough away so people won't see you busy on it at dusk!"

I spent a lot of time with Gordon that day and could almost write a whole book about his fascinating theories, but here are just a couple of his tour's highlights, such as when we passed a seat-like stone known as the Devil's Chair, which according to Gordon is actually the "Goddess Chair, now demonized by the Christians". We then walked up the bank surrounding the circle and continued along the ridge, passing beneath some huge copper beech trees that looked straight out of a fairy tale, with limb-like roots that appeared to twist and flow down the steep slope. Hundreds of ribbons and strips of cloth known as a clooties had been tied to their branches as offerings. According to Gordon, this was where the author J.R.R. Tolkien got his inspiration for the Ents in *The Lord of the Rings*.

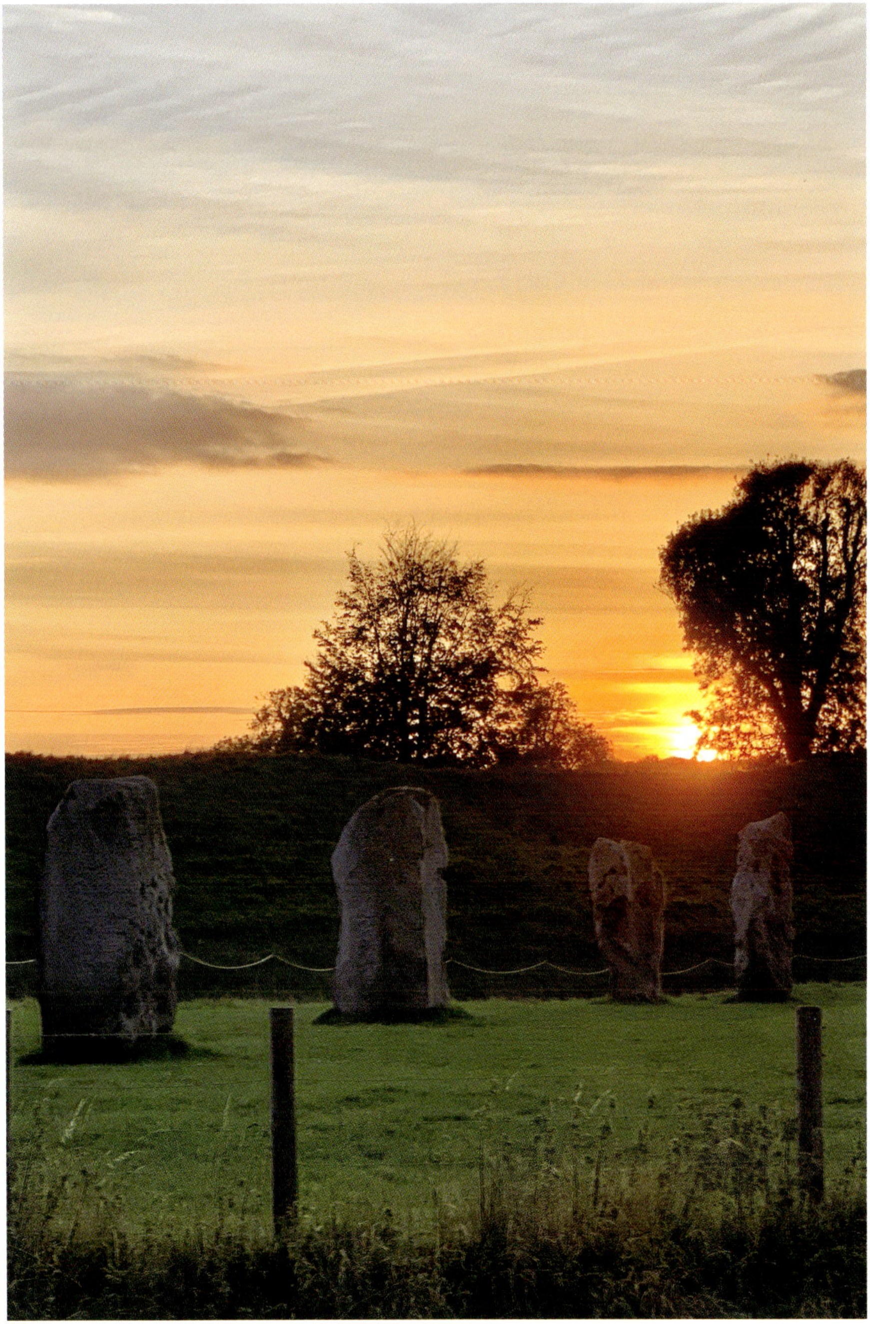

We crossed the road and entered a gate into the next section of the circle, where sheep were gently grazing. Here, he showed me a stone that lay flat on the ground and explained why he believed the powers that be that owned the land were reluctant to re-erect it: "'Cause if you stand it up on its end, it's a penis with two testicles; think they'd rather leave it laying on the ground," he laughed.

We walked on past the "lady's broken heart stone", where Gordon told me brides-to-be would, before a hand-fasting, psychologically throw their past relationships at the stone. We crossed another road and passed through a gate, where I became reacquainted with the first stone I'd ever seen in Avebury, the aptly named Swindon Stone next to the road to Swindon. It was impressively large, at least 4m (13ft) high, and looked like a diamond standing on one point, as if it'd been dropped from a great height and stuck in the ground.

Gordon pointed out some examples of stones that had been broken up during the 1700s. He told me a bit more about Alexander Keiller, too, saying, "Older folks may remember him as the Marmalade King, as in Keiller's marmalade. He was a local aristocrat, and liked fast cars and fast women. He was also an amateur archaeologist, quite a good one actually. If he hadn't done what he did in the 1930s and put the stones back up, I think this would be a little housing estate right now. We'd have lost this circle. He made it significant again." Gordon pointed at some concrete posts: "Here the stones couldn't be retrieved, so Mr Keiller put the markers in to mark where they were."

Tour concluded, we headed to the pub and Gordon pointed his staff toward one of the pub's upstairs windows. "There's a story about the Avebury Giant [Frederick Kempster] who used to live in the pub and was tall enough to put a pint through the upstairs windows." When we entered the Red Lion, Gordon drew my attention to a table that was in fact an old well with glass top over it. He informed me, "They found a skeleton in that well, and the ghost of Florrie, as she's known, is supposed to haunt the pub. There's various stories about how she ended up down there; one is that her husband went off to war, and she thought he'd died so she married somebody else. Then he came back and she threw herself down the well. The other is he found out what she'd been up to and he threw her down the well himself."

Over a pint, Gordon told me how he'd recently celebrated Samhain, the Celtic festival that is the precursor to Halloween. He explained the ceremony was far too sacred to be photographed or filmed, but invited me back the following May Day to witness the Beltane celebrations then. In them, he said, women and men played kiss-chase into the early hours of the morning to celebrate the return of summer. When I returned the following year,

I watched as Gordon and others erected a maypole within the stone circle, where they danced, sang and welcomed the rising sun. They gave thanks for the replenished fertility of the land, and Gordon gleefully revved up the crowd by shouting, "Hip, hip, hooray, first of May, outside shagging starts today!" During this visit, Gordon also took me to the nearby All Saints' Church in the parish of Alton Priors, where there is trap door which, when lifted, reveals the remnants of the ancient stone circle that originally stood on site.

Whenever I reflect upon my time in Avebury with Gordon, I'm very grateful for the way he brought so many vivid pictures alive in my mind and was so generous with his time. It was fascinating to get a glimpse into the world of the Wiccans and Druids and their contemporary magical practices, superstitions and beliefs. Before I left Avebury once more, I stood on the outer edges of the circle, from where I could see not only the stones but the houses of Gordon and Henk, the Five Mile Chapel and the Red Lion pub. I imagined the Avebury giant passing a pint through the pub's top window, as poor Florrie is thrown down the well by her furious husband; while the original builders erect the stones and the Druids pull down the Vulva Stone in a panic to hide their fertility rites from the Romans; as the Marmalade King attempts to restore the circle to its former glory and undo the damage of the zealous vicar and villagers of the 1700s. It was all happening at once in my mind's eye, like it always does, as the spectres of Avebury gathered together among the modern-day Wiccans, Druids, tourists and ramblers, bringing to life the composition of my next painting.

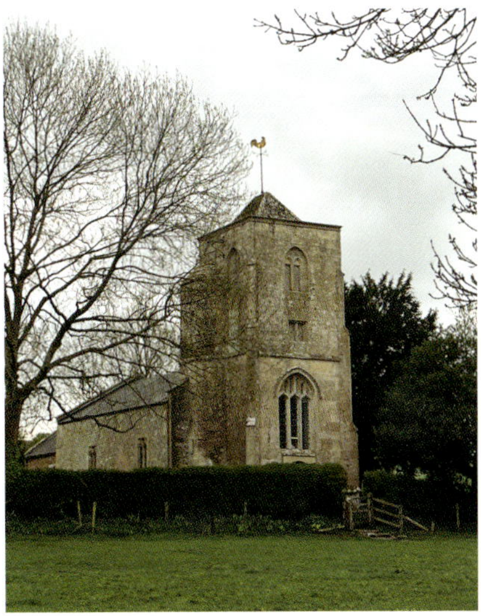

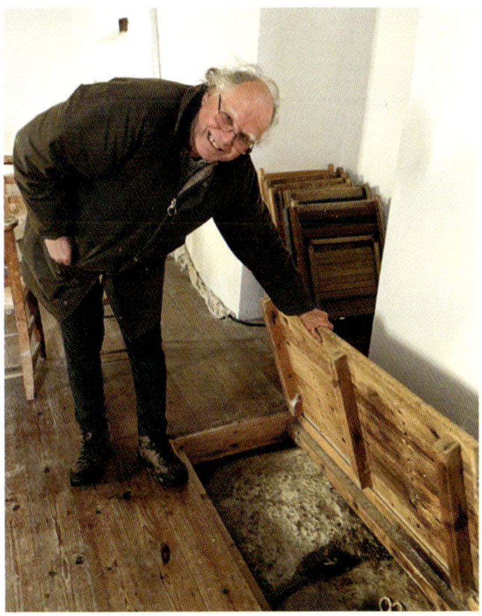

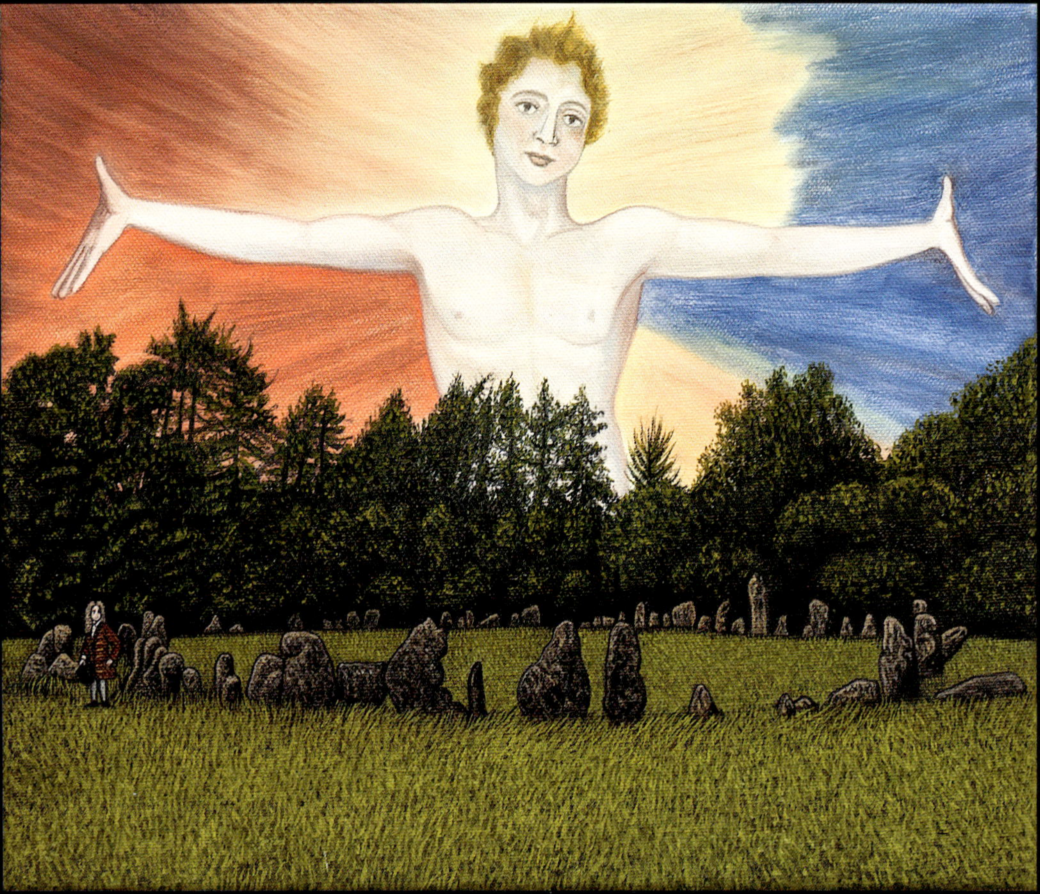

THE ROLLRIGHT STONES

The Rollright Stones

OXFORDSHIRE

DECEMBER VISIT

My wife Rose and I were in Oxfordshire, close to the Warwickshire border, where we parked at the side of the road and walked through a small area of woodland to the field in which the Rollright Stones stand. While the stones themselves are relatively modest in size, they form an impressive circle, known as the King's Men.

As I wandered around, I discovered that each stone seemed to have its own character, their surfaces having been interestingly weathered over the years. While the road nearby hummed with traffic under the bright December sun, I went back to the information board. Here I learned that the King's Men is a ceremonial stone circle thought to date from the late Neolithic period, *c.* 2500 BCE, and that it gets its name from a local legend about a witch who'd turned a king and his army into stone. The stones were said to be uncountable. On the other side of the lane stood the solitary King Stone, and a short distance away there was the Whispering Knights dolmen, said to be formed from treacherous knights who'd conspired against the king.

As always, I loved the story that had helped to keep this great mystery alive, but today it was not folklore that had drawn me to the stones, but the work of the eighteenth-century antiquarian William Stukeley, which I had recently been studying. He'd had a life-changing experience in which he was struck by the notion that stone circles such as the Rollrights were ancient temples built by the Druids. This inspired him to document the ancient monuments of Britain obsessively and create an incredible body of illustrations that have since proved vital in the maintenance and restoration of many of our ancient sites. Stukeley's ideas were later to influence William Blake's own thinking on the Druids, and Blake is even claimed by the Druid Order as one of their Chosen Chiefs.

Although Stukeley was right in dating the stones to pre-Roman times, the Kings Men are actually more than two thousand years older than the Druids, and the Whispering Knights dolmen is a thousand years older still. Nevertheless, this lineage fascinated me. As I've mentioned, William Blake has been a huge inspiration to me and more recently so too has Stukeley. As I stood there thinking about William Stukeley's epiphany, which would later inspire William Blake and then later myself, I felt part of a lineage, a custodian of something – as if I had been passed a baton that connected me and the work I was destined to do today with the minds of past eras, who had laid down the groundwork that allowed me to do what I was doing. I also recalled how the names of both William Stukeley and William Blake had been read out by London's Druid Order at Tower Hill on the day of my own epiphany, which made it all feel even more powerful and meant to be.

From the edge of the field, I photographed the circle and imagined William Stukeley dressed in Georgian attire and having his Druidic epiphany, while William Blake's *Albion* (believed to be a self-portrait) rose up into the sky, awakening from his sleep as a new vision of Britain is revealed.

Then I walked over to a sculpture nearby, woven from willow, one of several that have been installed over the years at the Rollrights to reference the local folklore of fairies and witches. Just as Rose and I were leaving, a group of modern witches arrived and began to scatter flower petals on the ground within the circle, preparing for a magical ritual of some kind and proving that the traditions live on to this day in this ancient site.

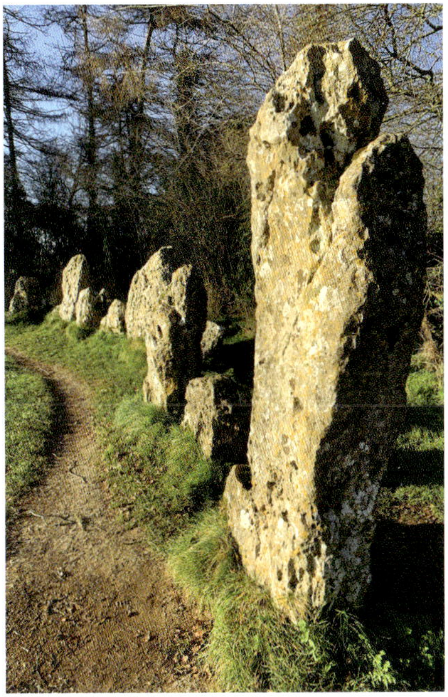

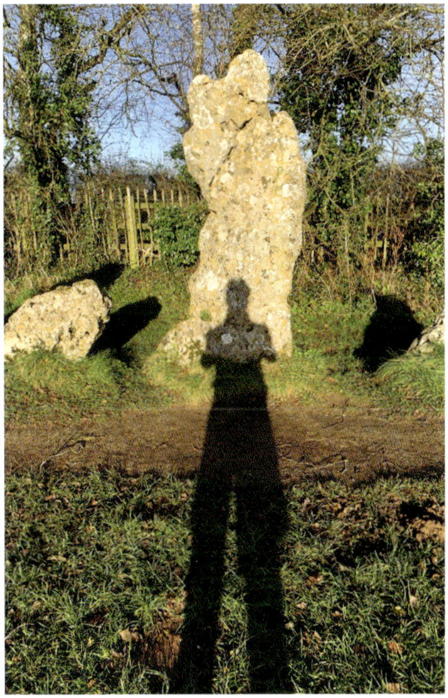

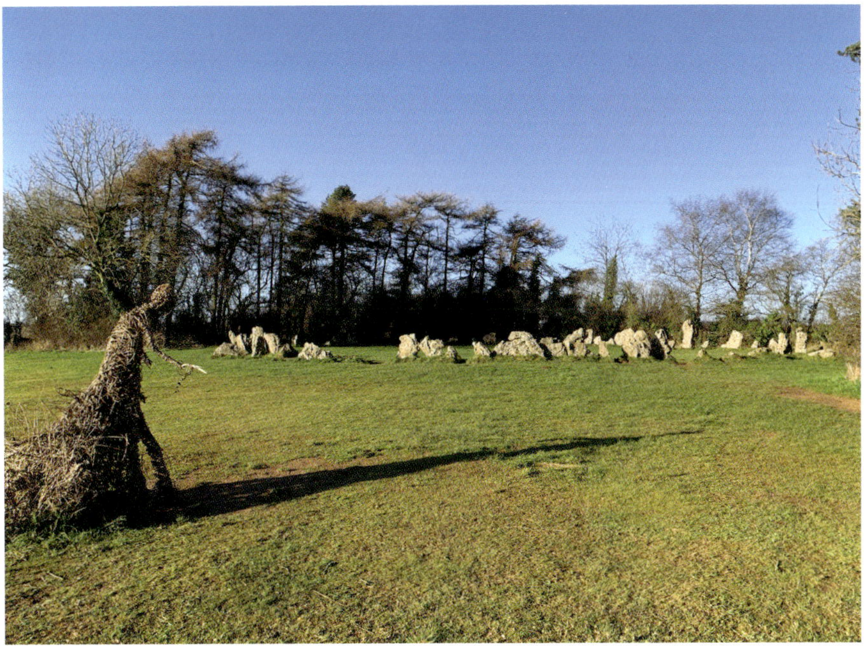

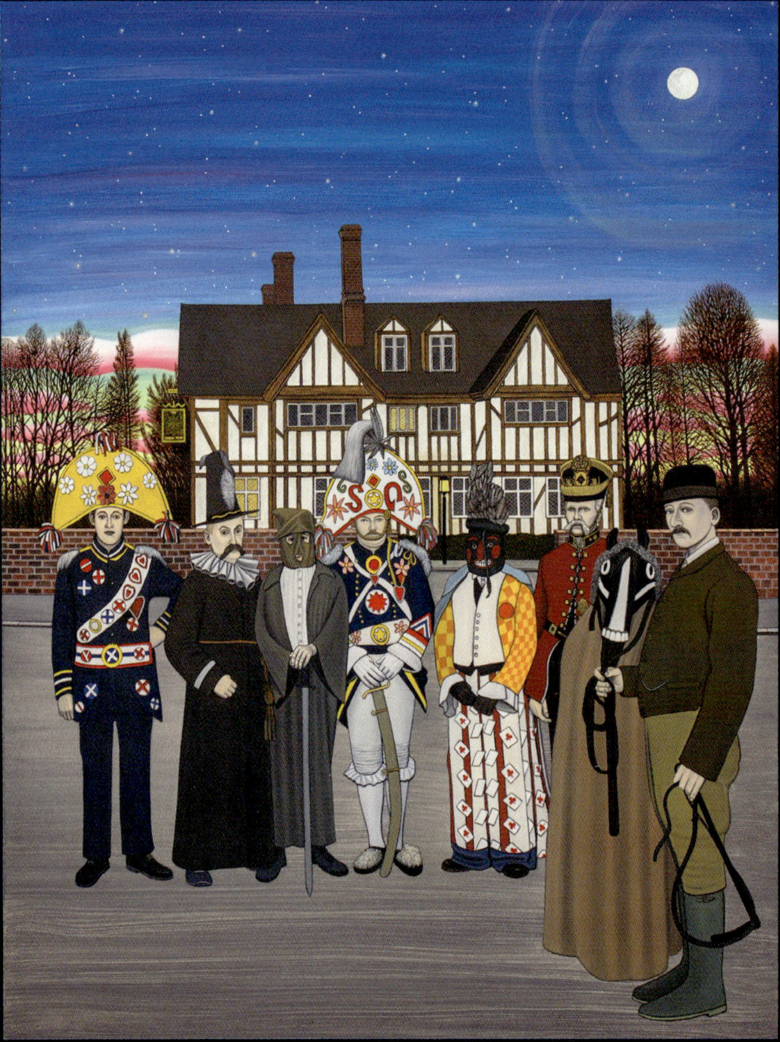

THE MUMMERS PLAY

Oil on Canvas, 130cm × 100cm

2021

Mumming, Hoodening and Folk Drama

KENT
CHRISTMAS TIME

All across Britain around Christmas time, folk plays with themes relating to death, resurrection and the cyclical nature of the seasons are performed by amateur actors known as mummers. As with the tradition of the Welsh Mari Lwyd (see page 231), it's generally accepted that the tradition of mummers was started, or at least kept alive, by farmhands and labourers who invented ways to beg for beer money and food during the tough months of winter, when work was scarce, so it's yet another example of the creativity of poverty.

Over the years, I've seen various mummers' plays, and I've even made a painting of mummers based on a photo taken in 1920 of the Alderley Mummers (with permission, from the private collection of Mary Houseman). I usually only work from my own pictures but something about this image embodied the core nature of mumming to me and the range of characters that appear in the plays. After investigating the photo with the help of a specialist on the troupe, I found out that the Alderley Mummers were all members of the

Barber family who were based in Brynlow Farm, tenanted land on the Alderley Park estate belonging to the Stanley family. From the early nineteenth century until 1937, when the estate was broken up and sold, four generations of the Barber family performed in front of six different Lord Stanleys as part of their Christmas-time celebrations. It would have been typical of mummers to go where the money is, although they'd also go from house to house, and pub to pub to entertain the everyday folk, which is where I've usually seen them.

In particular, I've watched the Wantage Mummers perform on Boxing Day in my wife Rose's hometown of Faringdon. There, one of the actors once told me, "Mumming plays are pretty much all the same: they fight, someone is killed, they get better; they fight, someone is killed, they get better; somebody asks for money and everybody goes home." He explained he doesn't buy into the plays having Pagan origins, saying, "The most important character in a mummers' play is usually the Doctor, because basically it's all about the incompetence of doctors, and this is from three hundred years ago, when they possibly killed more people than they do now."

For an online version of the Twelfth Night celebrations during lockdown, I had the pleasure of filming the mumming play performed by the Lions part on Bankside in London, with the Green Man of Bankside also making an appearance.

From what I've seen, besides the Doctor, the most common characters appear to be St George or Robin Hood, a knight called the Beau Slasher, a Groom and his horse, a Molly (who's usually a man in drag with a broom), and a Fool. There's also nearly always a Beelzebub/Devil figure who makes a satirical speech at the end about the political issues of the day. As the Wantage mummer confirmed, the general gist of the plays often consists of a sword fight in which the hero is killed and then resurrected by the Doctor, or an attempt to seduce the Molly, who turns her suitors down for the Fool; sometimes both these storylines combine in the same play. There are also themes relating to the legend of Robin Hood, the noble outlaw who steals from the rich and gives to the poor. It's worth noting, too, that other types of mumming plays are staged throughout the year which I've yet to research, such as "Pace Egg" plays at Easter in northern England and the practice of "Souling" at Halloween.

In Kent, there's a particular version of mumming known as "hoodening", in which a similar type of play is performed, but it's very specific to the region. One December, I had the good fortune to spend some time with Ben Jones, a leading member of the St Nicholas-at-Wade Hoodeners, who owns a number of "hooden horses", which are literally wooden horses' heads with snapping jaws. Ben's home village of St Nicholas-at-Wade is situated in East Kent where the tradition of hoodening was born, before spreading to other parts of the county.

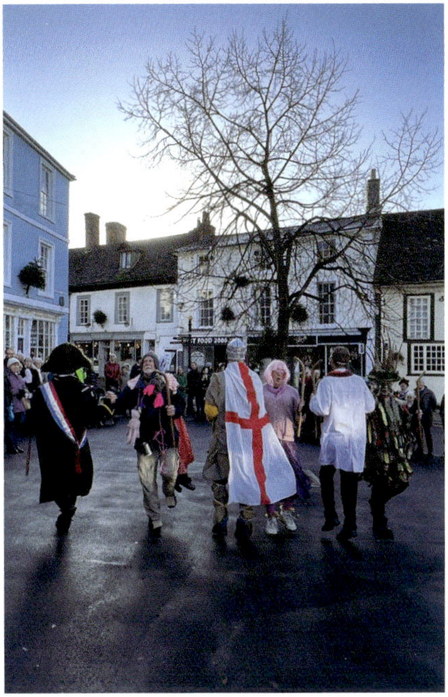

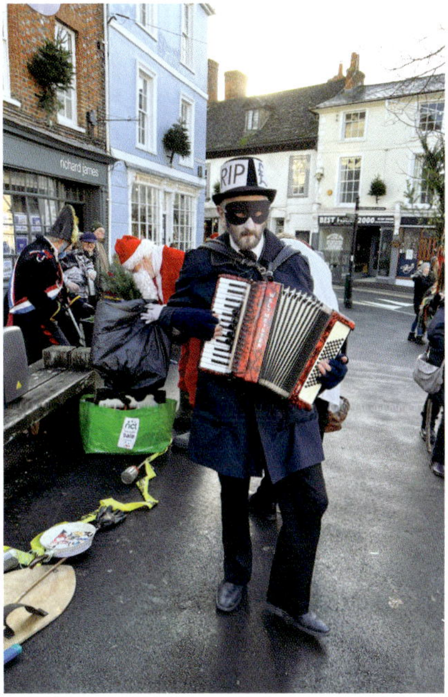
richard james
RIP

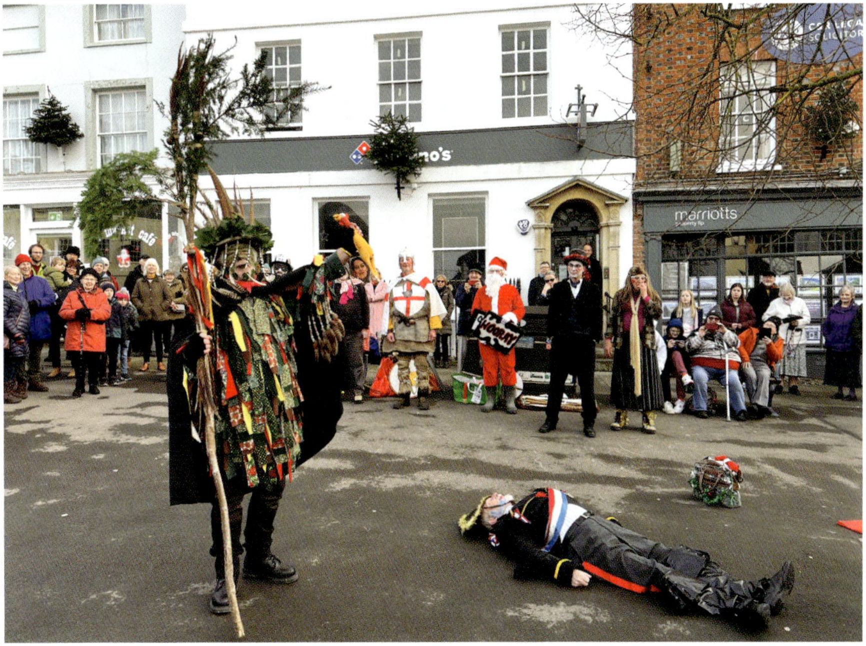
marriotts

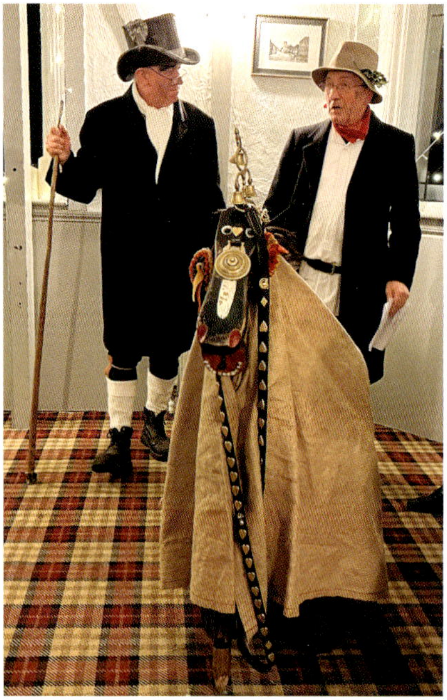

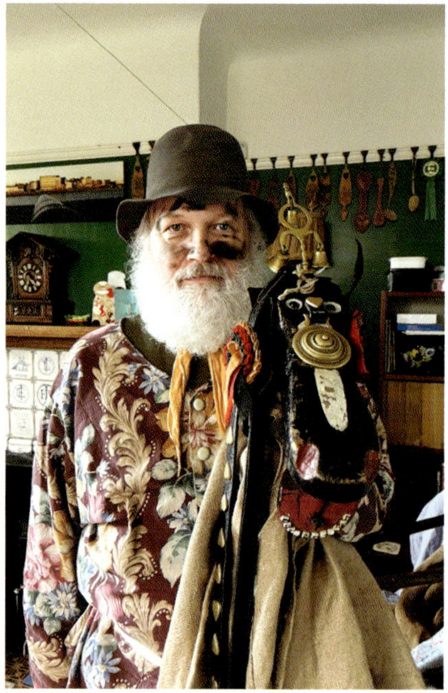

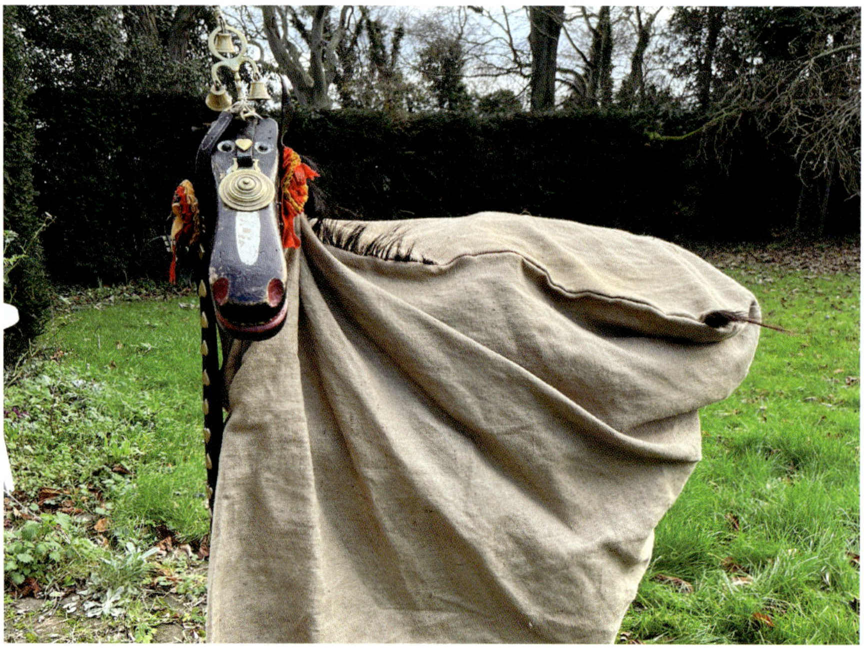

When I visited Ben at home, he brought out his collection of hooden horses to show me. He was very tender with them, like they were living creatures, members of the family. He described what it was like to step beneath one of his beloved beasts: "When you go under the horse, you do feel like a horse; you don't respond to people like a human wearing a costume. It's hard to explain, but it's liberating in a way. You can throw off the trappings of so-called civilized life and enter a simpler realm, closer to Nature, I guess. And it also allows you to do the sort of things that you couldn't do as a human!"

He then carried two of his hooden horses over his shoulder to the garden, where he introduced me to them. The first, Satan, was "a heavy beast" with a particularly menacing look. Its jaws snapped loudly, a bell rang on the top of its head, its ears flopped forward and it appeared ready to bite. Ben disappeared beneath the sack cloth draping beneath the mask so that just his lower legs could still be seen; then he impersonated the horse snapping its jaws ferociously at me. It was fascinating to watch him embody the spirt of the animal and I knew that Satan would need to appear in my painting.

Ben put Satan safely down and introduced me to another hooden horse, Dobbin, who looked much more friendly and endearing, with both his eyes sitting at the front of his wooden face, with upright ears and a gentler jaw. Fortunately it would be Dobbin, not Satan, who'd be coming out with us later to do the hoodening rounds and take part in the play I was going to watch. Before then, we had a few hours to spare, so Ben took me to the village church and showed me two perfectly preserved Green Men from Norman times, including one of the finest examples of a "Green King" in the county, which had a crowned foliate head.

The evening of hoodening began in the village hall, where the play started with the hoodeners entering through a side door. The characters included Dobbin who, in Ben's words, plays "the poor old horse exhausted by the hard labour forced upon him"; the Wagoner "who carries a whip and ensures order is kept"; and a Molly, "an evolution of Maid Marian from Robin Hood themed plays". There was also Sam the Farm Labourer, "who's lazy, nasty, unwashed and always on his phone", and a boy who tries to ride the horse – "he's young and excitable and a bit of a show-off". And there was a second figure in drag, who was a lot younger than the Molly and wearing a blonde wig and tight flowery dress. Last but not least, there was a character called George the Musician, who wore a stunning leaf-and-flower patterned homemade suit made out of curtain fabric and who played the fiddle throughout the evening.

The Molly entered first and announced, "The hoodeners are here!" Then in came the rest of the troupe, who began performing the play while Dobbin snapped his jaws at the front. There were all sorts of jokes, some of which were full of sexual innuendo, as well as mocking the local council – the bin strikes, the busy roads and the new housing schemes. Mention was made too of the success of the crops and the recent death of the Queen. The play seemed a bit sketchy at times and almost on the brink of falling apart, but that seemed part of the fun as the room laughed warmly whenever lines were forgotten.

The younger man in drag fed Dobbin grass, but the horse got wind and made a mess on the floor, so it was fed some beer to settle its stomach. Then Dobbin started to kick out and accidentally killed the farm boy, who now lay dead. There followed a moving toast to "absent friends", those who had died over the past year, which everyone joined in. The farm boy was then resurrected by the younger Molly figure declaring her love for him. Apparently a different character can be resurrected every year and once the hooden horse himself performed the scene. Songs were sung and the strange play came to an end. From the village hall, we moved on to various pubs where locals were waiting eagerly and the hoodeners performed in exchange for money (now for charity) and beer through the night.

It was fascinating to see how the play was highly likely to have evolved from mummers' plays into something very specific to St Nicholas-and-Wade, which had in turn inspired the surrounding area and help re-popularize the practice of hoodening. With folk traditions, I'm always excited to see the impact of regional cultures on universal practices such as "animal guising" in ways that make them unique; they represent to me the never-ending creativity and uniqueness of the human spirit.

With this in mind, I decided to take a symbol of the area, Saint Nicholas's Church, where the two Green Men dwelled (which I've coincidentally seen merged with Father Christmas, aka St Nicholas, in mummers' plays; and a Wiccan priest at Avebury stone circle once told me that "Father Christmas is the Green Man"), and then placed Satan, aka Ben Jones in his animal guise, at the front. The name Satan also appealed to me, as I've heard from many that the horned gods of pre-Christian times were demonized and turned into the devils we know today, in an attempt by the Church to convert Pagan worshippers to Christianity. It's a story I hear often and you can find an incredible depiction of the Celtic horned god Cernunnos, who would have fallen victim to such treatment, on the Gundestrup Cauldron dating from between 200 BCE and 300 CE.

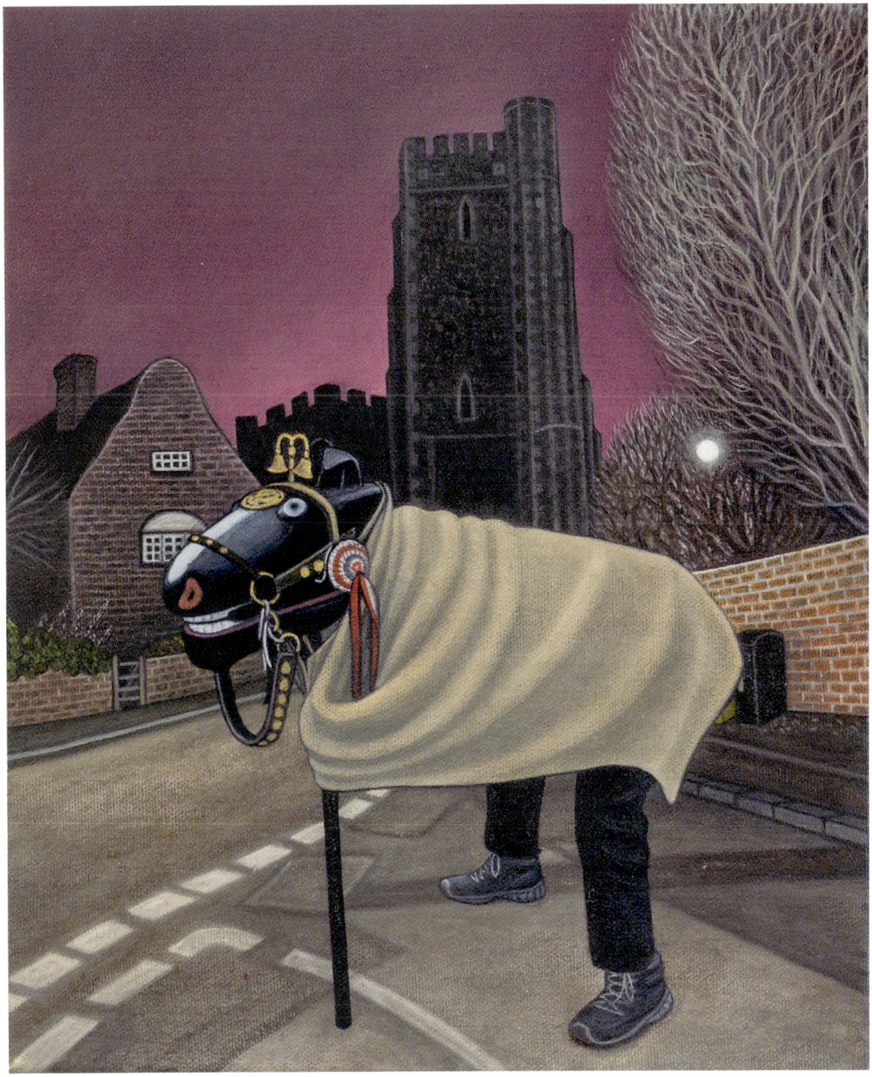

THE HOODEN HORSE

Oil on Canvas, 30cm × 25cm

2023

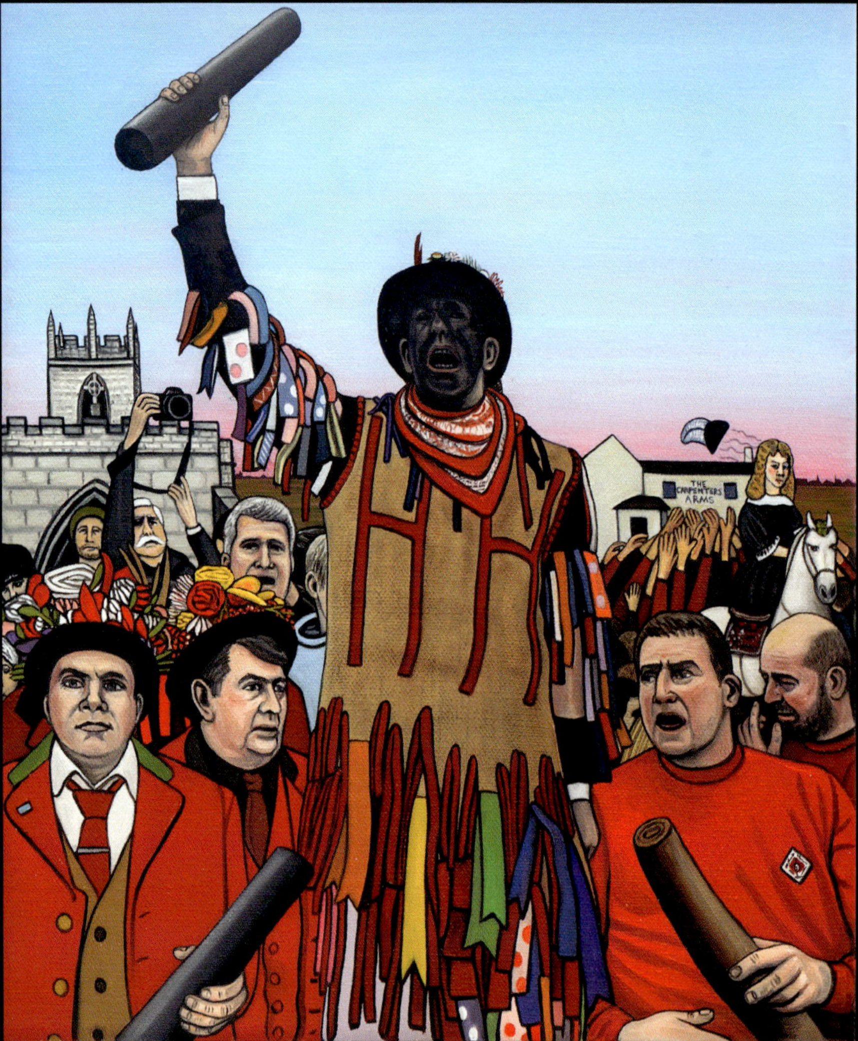

HAXEY HOOD

Haxey Hood

NORTH LINCOLNSHIRE

JANUARY 6

The "Hood", as it's often referred to locally, is a game that takes place annually in Haxey, North Lincolnshire and consists of a long leather-like tube that is fought over in a mass scrum between the men of the town of Haxey and their rivals from neighbouring Westwoodside, with the aim being to get the "Hood" to your local "goalpost".

When I visited in 2019, there had been local outrage during the lead-up to the game, as all the traditional goalpost sites for Haxey, consisting of three pubs – the Kings Arms, the Duke William and the Loco – would be out of bounds for the first time, mainly due to a property developer who was trying to turn them into luxury flats and threatening the very existence of the custom. Ahead of my visit I wasn't quite sure what to expect, having heard reports that the game may not even happen this year.

After checking into my Airbnb, I stopped off at a café and, over the sizzling frying pans, overheard some locals discuss the fact that a new goalpost had been decided upon for Haxey: this year, it was to be the Butter Cross monument, which happened to be quite close to where I was staying. I was extremely relieved and knew that my long journey north would be worth it, after all. I also overheard that the Carpenters Arms, which was the traditional goalpost for Westwoodside, was to host the customary singing. So I decided to take a stroll down there to see what was going on.

On the way, I walked past the vast green that separates the two towns, where the game was to be played tomorrow, overlooked by the huge concrete water tower that dominated the skyline. As I've mentioned before, it's always a good idea to visit the local pub the night before a custom like this takes place. It's fantastic to meet people in this context and I've made some great friends this way, too. Folk customs, for me, are a celebration of being alive: they bring out the best in people.

That night in the Carpenters Arms, I learned more about the local beliefs surrounding the custom. A man at the bar, clutching a pint and wearing a red jumper that signified some kind of involvement with the Hood, was particularly clued up on the tradition, and explained in his Lincolnshire dialect: "It's believed to have begun in the fourteenth century, when a landowner named Lady De Mowbray was out riding and a sudden gust of wind blew off her silk hood. Thirteen farm labourers rushed to retrieve the hood, which was now being blown left, right 'n' centre across Lady De Mowbray's land. After a wild goose chase, one of the farm labourers finally managed to catch it. Being a shy man, instead of handing the hood back to the lady himself, he got another of the workers to do it for him. Lady De Mowbray thanked the man who returned it and said that he had 'acted like a Lord, whereas the worker who actually caught it was a fool'. She found it all so funny that she then donated thirteen acres of land, on the condition that this 'wild hood chase' would be re-enacted each and every year, and it's been taking place ever since."

I also managed to have a chat with a man called Dale Smith, who would be playing the Fool the following morning. He told me, ""I do believe there probably was a Lady De Mowbray, but I also think it was a midwinter festival. The Lady De Mowbray part makes for quite a romantic sort of story, but then there was a John De Mowbray, so there would've been a Lady De Mowbray and they owned this manor, so who knows?"

The following morning, after some homemade pork scratchings and local ale courtesy of the Carpenters Arms, songs such as "The Farmer's Boy" were sung. Dale, now dressed as the Fool in a feathered hat and multicoloured rags, was "smudged" with black soot across his face, which I later learned symbolized the "smoking of the Fool" that would happen later. This was followed by a procession through town where more songs were sung, hip flasks were passed round, pubs visited, and the Fool was hoisted up on the shoulders of a group of men in red jumpers, who carried him through the crowd and placed him on an ancient mounting block known as the Mowbray Stone, which stands outside the local church and was where he would deliver his speech.

It was an incredibly emotional moment, with tears pouring down the cheeks of thickset men in rugby shirts, as this was the last year Dan would playing the Fool, having decided to step down after twenty-five years of service to the Hood. Holding back the tears himself, he shouted, "Now this game is seven hundred years old, so let's respect the game, and long may it live on!" As his speech unfolded, he was indeed bizarrely ritually smoked when some damp straw was set on fire behind him. He said, laughing, "As you can see, things are

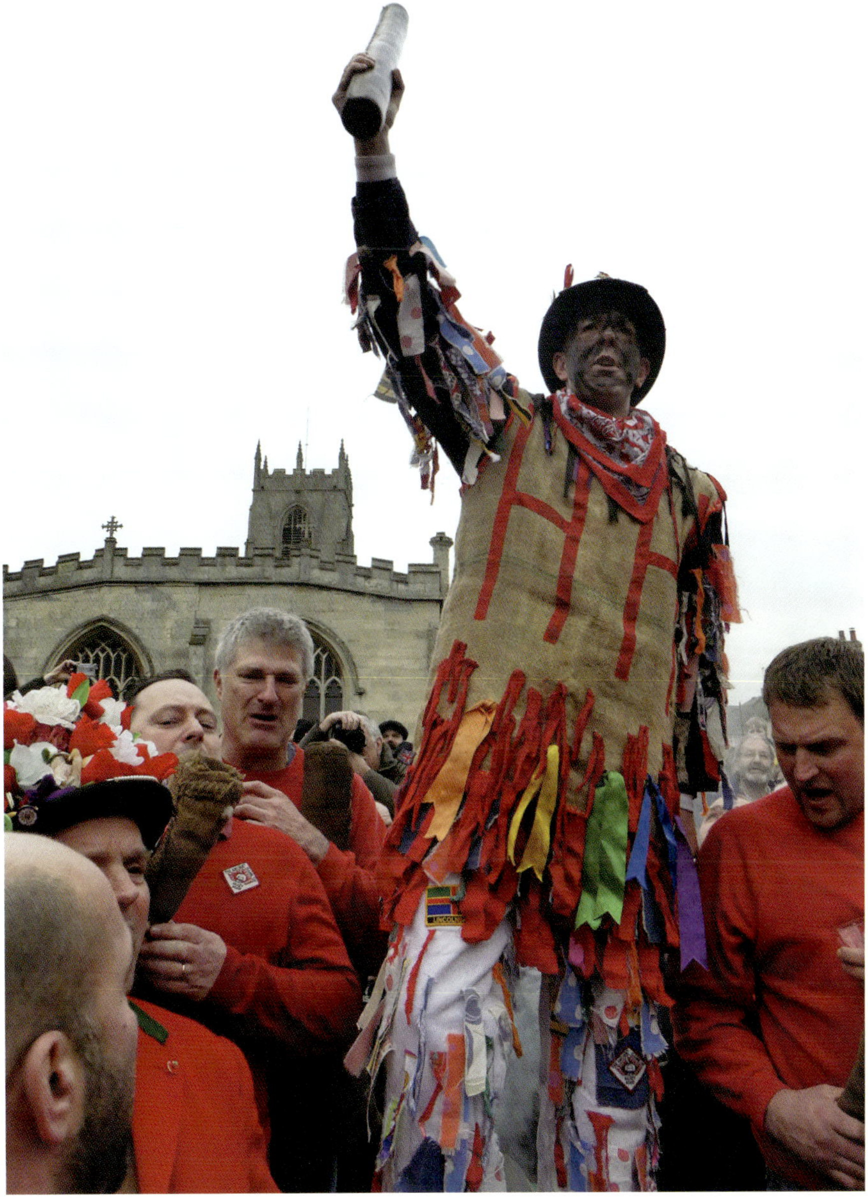

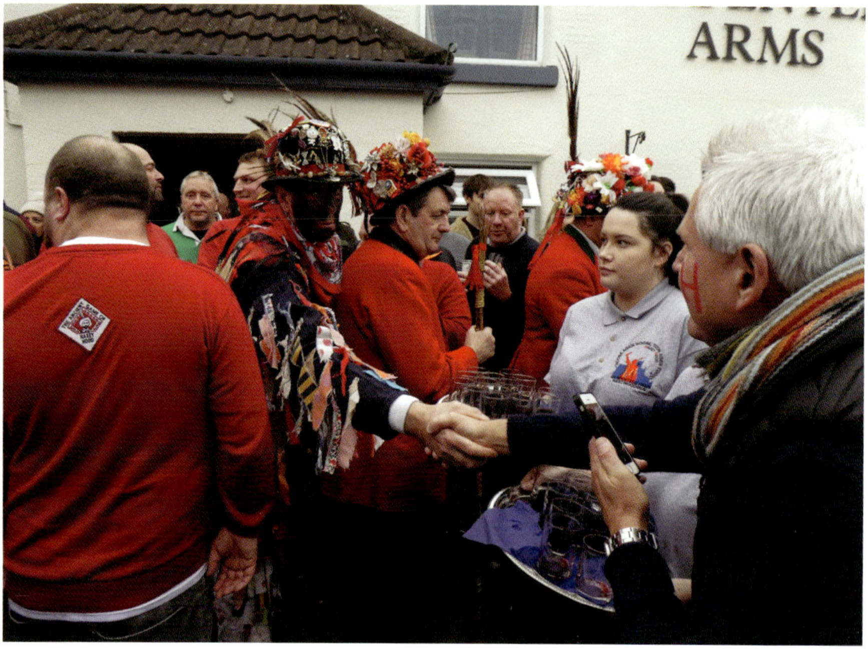
ARMS

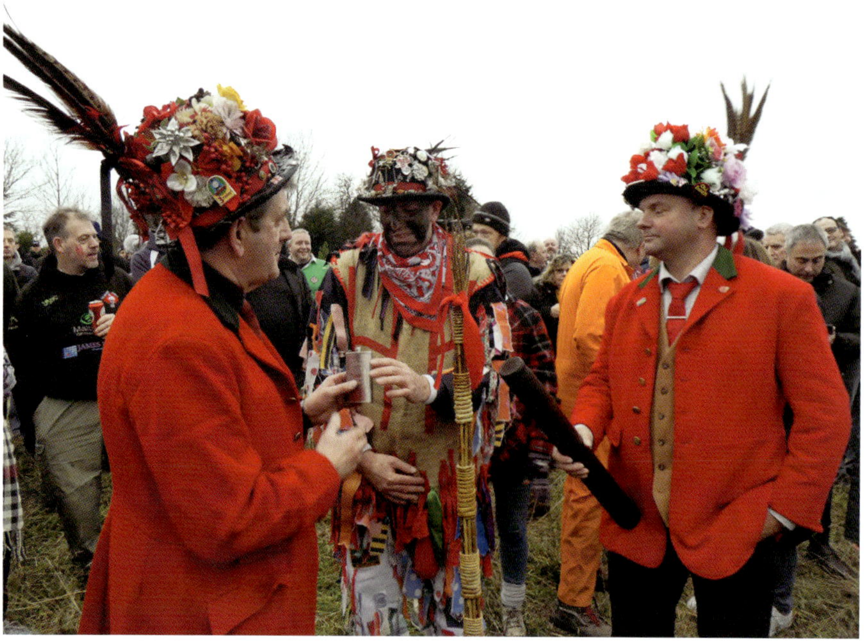

starting to warm up, so it's time for the game to begin ..." Then, with more smoke filling the air, and struggling to keep his emotions in check, he declared, "This is the last time that I'm going to say this, so it's house against house, town against town; if a man meets a man, knock him down but don't hurt him." Even as an outsider, the scene brought a lump to my throat.

I caught up with Dale as we reached the field where the game would begin and he told me about his own history with the Hood: "I lived in Westwoodside, one mile away from this field, so I walked across it as a five-year-old. The world was a lot different then. Then there's pictures of me in about 1977, when I was ten years old, stood behind the Fool, watching that Fool as there're kids now that are stood behind me."

Standing alongside the Fool were two other key characters in the game, both wearing red hunting jackets and garland-covered hats: the Lord of the Hood and the Chief Boggan. With them were ten other men in red jerseys who were known as the Boggans, one of whom I'd met in the pub.

When I spoke to the Lord of the Hood, he explained he was carrying his "wand of office, made of thirteen willow withies bound and tied with thirteen others tied thirteen times round". Unfortunately I didn't have time to ask what the symbolism of thirteen meant before the game was due to begin, but presumed it related to the story of the thirteen farm labourers chasing the hood.

To start things off, the Lord of the Hood threw a series of what were known as Sack Hoods out into the crowd, so children could get involved and to act as a kind of test run for the main game. Once these had all been dispersed and retrieved, it was time to throw the leather Sway Hood used for main game. Everyone crowded round and one of the Boggans burst into tears when the Lord of the Hood announced, "Today, its gonna be up to Dale, who's done this job for twenty-five years." He gave him a hug and passed Dale the Hood. For the very last time, Dale shouted, "House against house, town against town; if a man meets a man, knock him down but don't hurt him!"

The Hood was launched and the game erupted. "Shitting hell!" I heard, as a huge swarm of men locked together; this is known locally as the "sway" and looks like the largest rugby scrum you've ever seen, as the two sides (dressed in plain clothes so you can't differentiate between them) shout and chant the names of their towns repeatedly, forcing each other back and forth in the direction of their own goalposts. Occasionally, some of them would fall and yell in panic from the very bottom of the scrum. Then the Boggans, who act as referees, shouted, "Get em up!" and everyone started helping each other up and it all began again.

The day continued like this and it made me feel like I was back at school, playing rugby, which I hated and would do my best to avoid. On top of that, I'd probably got a bit carried away in the Carpenters Arms the night before, and standing in a muddy, cold field with a hangover soon started to lose its appeal. Then the sway unexpectedly came straight for me and I got taken down, the crowd crushing me beneath it. Again, I felt like I was back in school, when someone would shout "Bundle!" and everyone would dive on top of each other. My leg got crushed and I had a slight limp for the rest of the day. On two counts now I was not having the best time. And whenever I got too close to the edge of the sway to take pictures, I could feel hands on my back pushing me into the centre.

It started to get dark and I grew confused about what was going on. A large crowd had gathered and when I reached it, I was shocked to see that someone was lying on the ground with a broken leg. I assumed the game had been stopped and hung around to see if the man was OK. A concerned man yelled at people to step back, but he seemed to take a particular dislike to me and screamed right in my face, "Fuck off!" Then I noticed a group of drunk teenagers vomiting on the side of the road. That was it, I thought to myself, there won't be a winner this year. I was about to set off back down the hill to my Airbnb, when I heard that the game had continued after all – and the men of Westwoodside had reached the Carpenters Arms, winning the game. I'd missed the shot I wanted to get on camera, of the sway entering the pub and the winners declared, but while I was gutted I'd also learned that neither broken bones nor property development could stop the ancient game of the Haxey Hood.

Although I hadn't enjoyed the latter half of the game, I absolutely loved the experience, the legend of Lady De Mowbray, the emotion of it being Dale's final year as Fool, the singing in the pubs, meeting the locals, and all the ritualistic activity that surrounded the game. I felt inspired and headed back into town the next morning to get some crowd-free shots of the church to use for the composition of my painting.

The scene of the Boggans in tears, while Dale delivered his final speech, would have to be in the painting, too. It represented the strong sense of identity and community that the game instilled in the town, and how important it was to people. It was like something out of a religious painting: a drama unfolding around something significant, but which, unless you were educated about it, you couldn't quite understand. The moment of Dale's speech was as significant as any religious event to people in this town: their long-serving Fool was stepping down.

I also had to capture the Lady De Mowbray story. While watching the game I'd imagined her galloping across her ancestral lands and her hood flying off, with the sway spotting her and making a run for it; so that would feature in my painting, too. And I was struck by the huge concrete water tower, which I felt gave the scene a sense of modernity, so I photographed that as well, before making my way once more to the Carpenters Arms to see the Hood, now displayed proudly behind the bar, and to celebrate Westwoodside's victory – until the following year, where the sway would again compete for it and try to steer it home.

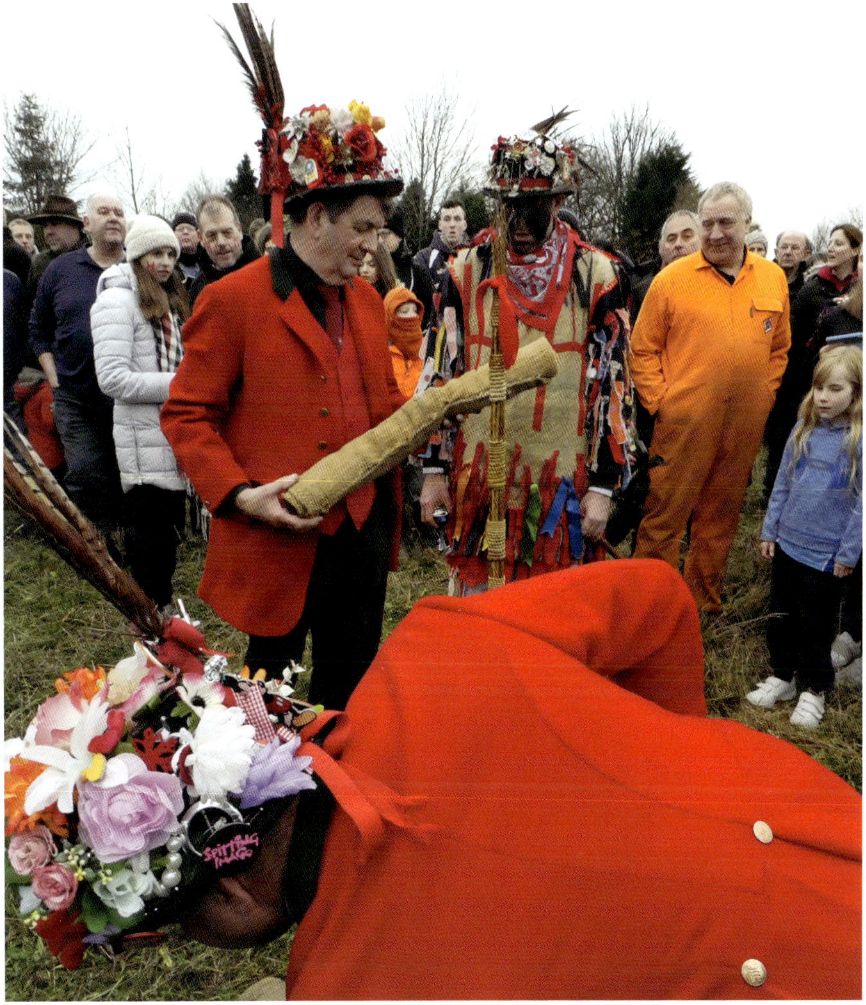

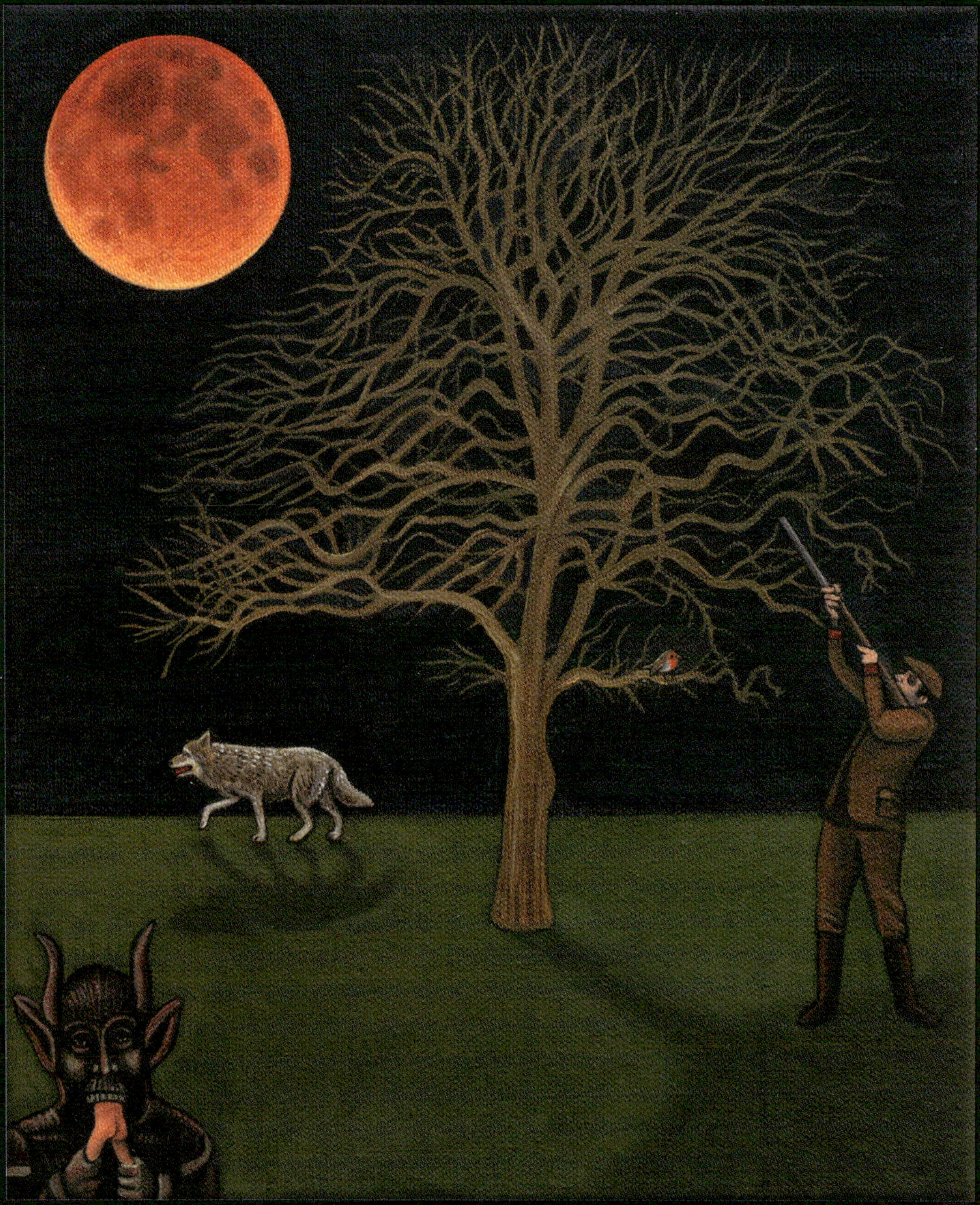

WASSAIL AT WOLF BLOOD MOON

Oil on Canvas, 30cm × 25cm

2019

Wassailing

CIDER-PRODUCING REGIONS

TWELFTH NIGHT: JANUARY 6 (OR TRADITIONAL JANUARY 17)

My first-ever experience of a wassail was in the village of Tarring, East Sussex, in the beer garden of the Vine pub. When my friend Anton and I arrived, we found a Green Man-like figure standing by the bar; he was painted entirely green, including his skin, beard and hat. There were also morris dancers draped in multicoloured tassels of fabric. A procession began on the street outside, as the Green Man and morris dancers led the way jingling, with a group of mummers skipping along behind. The Molly looked particularly happy to be strutting along in fishnet stockings and high heels. Drums and multiple flaming torches accompanied the procession through the dark village streets.

After a while, the Green Man led the crowds round back to the beer garden at the back of the pub, where everybody assembled around an apple tree and one of the morris men, a relatively young man, began to take charge of the ceremony. Holding a large flaming torch, he proclaimed, "All of the birds and all of the insects will come to the tree, they will clean it and cleanse it of evil spirits and ensure a bountiful harvest." He then began a chant and the crowd joined in, repeating each line throughout:

Here stands the jolly good old apple tree,
Stand fast roots, bear well top,
Every little bough bear an apple now,
Every little twig bear an apple big,
Hats full, caps full, three-quarter sacks full!

The crowd then cheered, banged drums and made lots of noise while flares were fired over the trees. People started to pass round a wassail bowl containing cider, drink from it and chant the word "Wassail". The atmosphere was haunting but romantic, with the flaming torches illuminating the crowd as they passed round the cider in the medieval-looking goblet, amid guns being fired and talk of cleansing the trees of evil spirits.

Soon after, I found myself at yet another wassail. This time it was part of the Mari Lwyd festival in Chepstow, where the wassail took place at the foot of the castle (see page 231). As the trees were blessed, groups of Mari Lwyds stood snapping their jaws menacingly at pieces of toast that had been strung up from the apple trees. A similar ceremony to the one in Tarring was performed and cider was poured on the roots of the trees as an offering, while everyone shouted the word "Wassail". A song was sung that I'd later find out was the Gloucestershire Wassail song, which made sense with Chepstow being right on the border, albeit on the Welsh side. These were some of the verses that stood out to me the most:

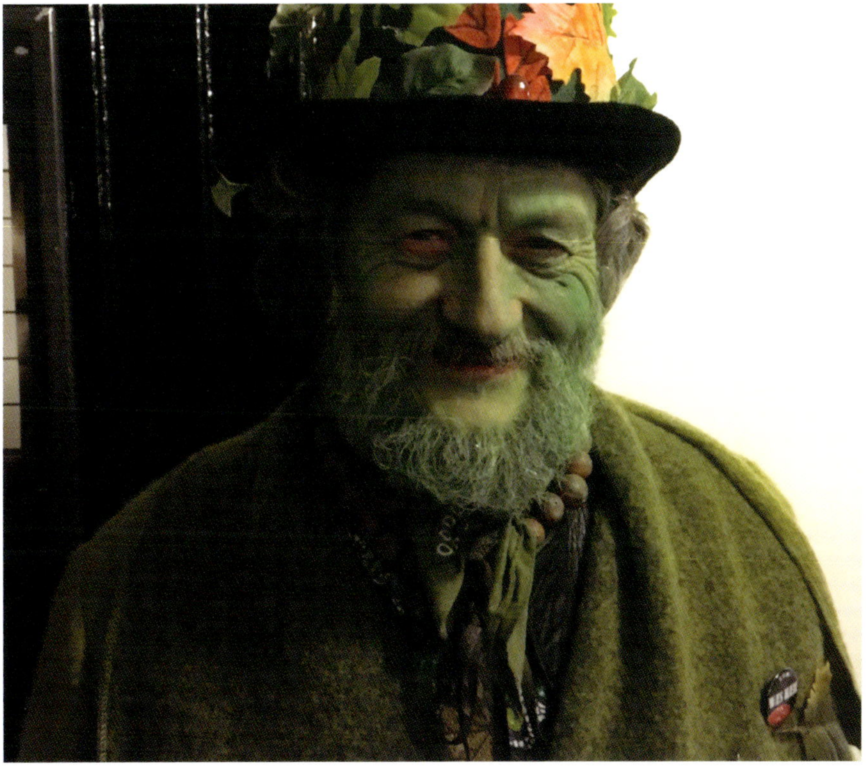

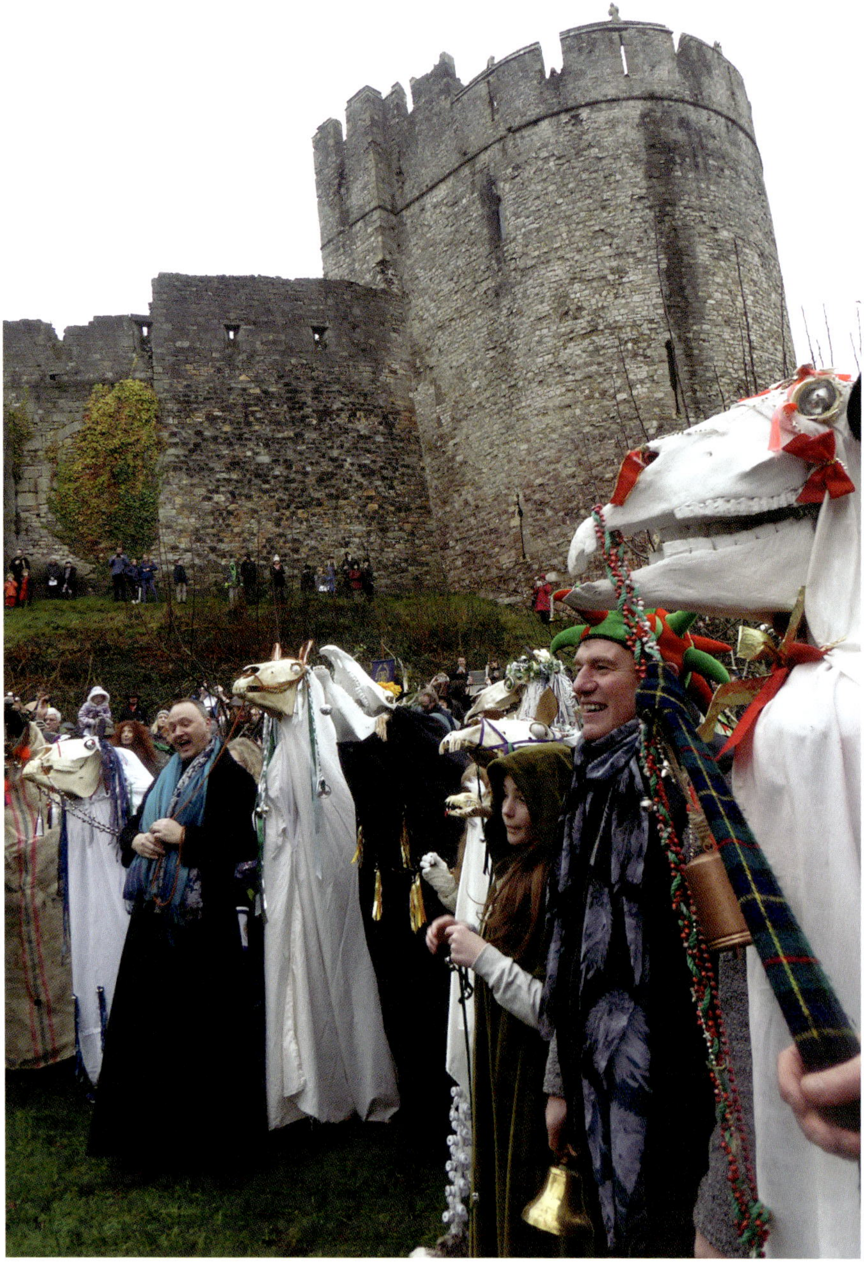

Here's to our horse, and to his right ear,
God send our master a Happy New Year:
A Happy New Year as e'er he did see,
With my wassailing bowl I drink to thee.

So here is to Cherry and to his right cheek
Pray God send our master a good piece of beef,
And a good piece of beef that may we all see
With the wassailing bowl, we'll drink to thee.

Here's to our mare, and to her right eye,
God send our mistress a good Christmas pie;
A good Christmas pie as e'er I did see,
With my wassailing bowl I drink to thee.

Having experienced two wassailing ceremonies in quick succession, I was fascinated to learn more, so afterwards I approached a morris dancer with peacock feathers standing tall in his hat, who was holding a copper megaphone and leading the ceremony. When I asked him about its origins, he told me that wassailing "is an ancient practice, early medieval, probably older, that predominantly takes place in cider-drinking regions. It was also known as howling, where people gather to pour cider on to the roots of apple trees, and tie slices of toast to the branches to attract animals such as robins and insects to purify the trees. And songs are sang and loud noises are made, where guns are fired over the tops of the trees to scare away any lingering evil winter spirits that could interfere with the blessing of the orchard and a bountiful harvest for the coming year."

Later in a pub, a local man clinked glasses with me and informed me that "the wassailing bowl that is passed round at the end was also where the idea of making a 'toast' came from about a thousand years ago." He added speculatively: "This could also explain the toast hanging on the trees."

Wassails are growing increasingly popular. I recently attended a wassail arranged by Blackthorn Ritualistic Folk, in which a spectacular procession, led through an apple tree orchard by a bagpipe player, included an array of Mari Lwyds (see page 231), the apple tree man and the most recent manifestation of the mysterious Dorset Ooser, who I will talk more about in the next chapter.

It took me a while to form an idea around painting a wassail, as I found it to be such a widely practised ritual that it was difficult to choose one particular community to depict. In the end, it was a story about the full moon that would be the inspiration for my painting *Wassail at Wolf Blood Moon*. I was painting a series of works titled *Moonlore*, exploring the folklore and superstitions surrounding the twelve full moons of the year, in which I linked seasonal customs to the full moon that rose around the same time. Interestingly, when I was researching January's full moon, I found out that it was once known as the "Wolf Moon", due to the howling cries of hungry wolves that could be heard at night throughout the tough months of midwinter, when prey was at its most scarce. The last wolf in Britain was said to have been killed in Scotland by Sir Ewan Cameron in 1680. However, there were tales of wolf sightings right up until 1888, and as I mentioned, the custom of wassailing is sometimes referred to as "howling", due to the noises being made to move on the evil spirits. So this connection was greatly inspiring. To add to my inspiration it also happened to be a super blood moon that year, where a lunar eclipse, in which the Earth blocks the solar rays of the sun, causes a red shadow to be cast on the surface of the moon, giving it an eerie red glow.

With all these elements in my mind, I had my composition, in which I would include the super blood moon, a farmer shooting over the top of an apple tree, while a lingering hungry wolf stalks behind, and an evil spirit stands in the bottom corner, about to be scared away by the ritual "howling". I find wassailing to be a fascinating practice; as with many of the customs through which people once tried to influence Nature and the outcome of the harvest, it represents a way in which people took control of their lives. They couldn't know for sure what the future would bring or if the crops would grow, but through performing rituals they could empower themselves with the optimism and positive mindset needed to make it through the tough months of winter – when life was hard and the approaching abundant days of spring were their much-needed light at the end of the tunnel – and this, to me, is a type of magical practice in itself.

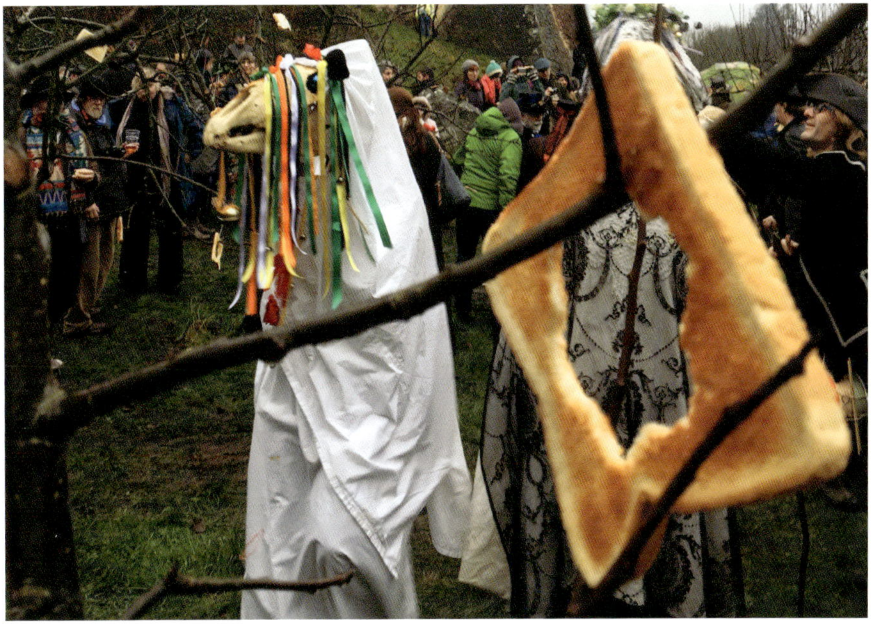

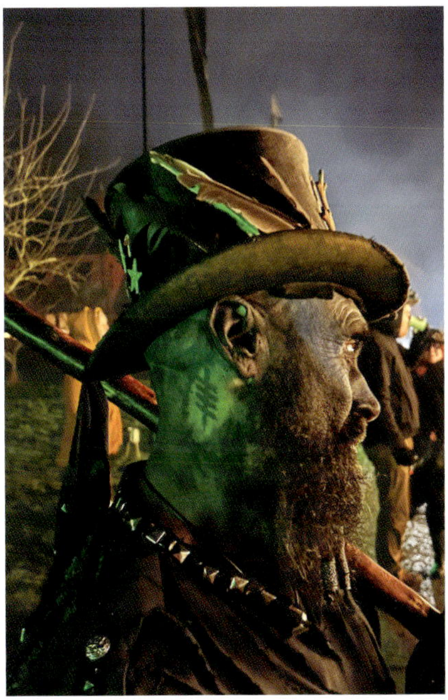

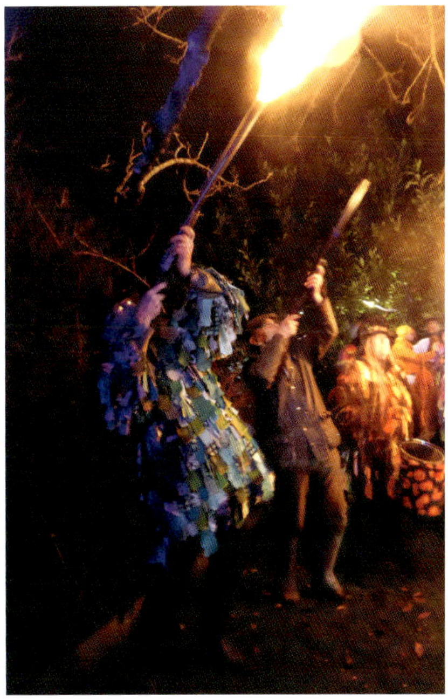

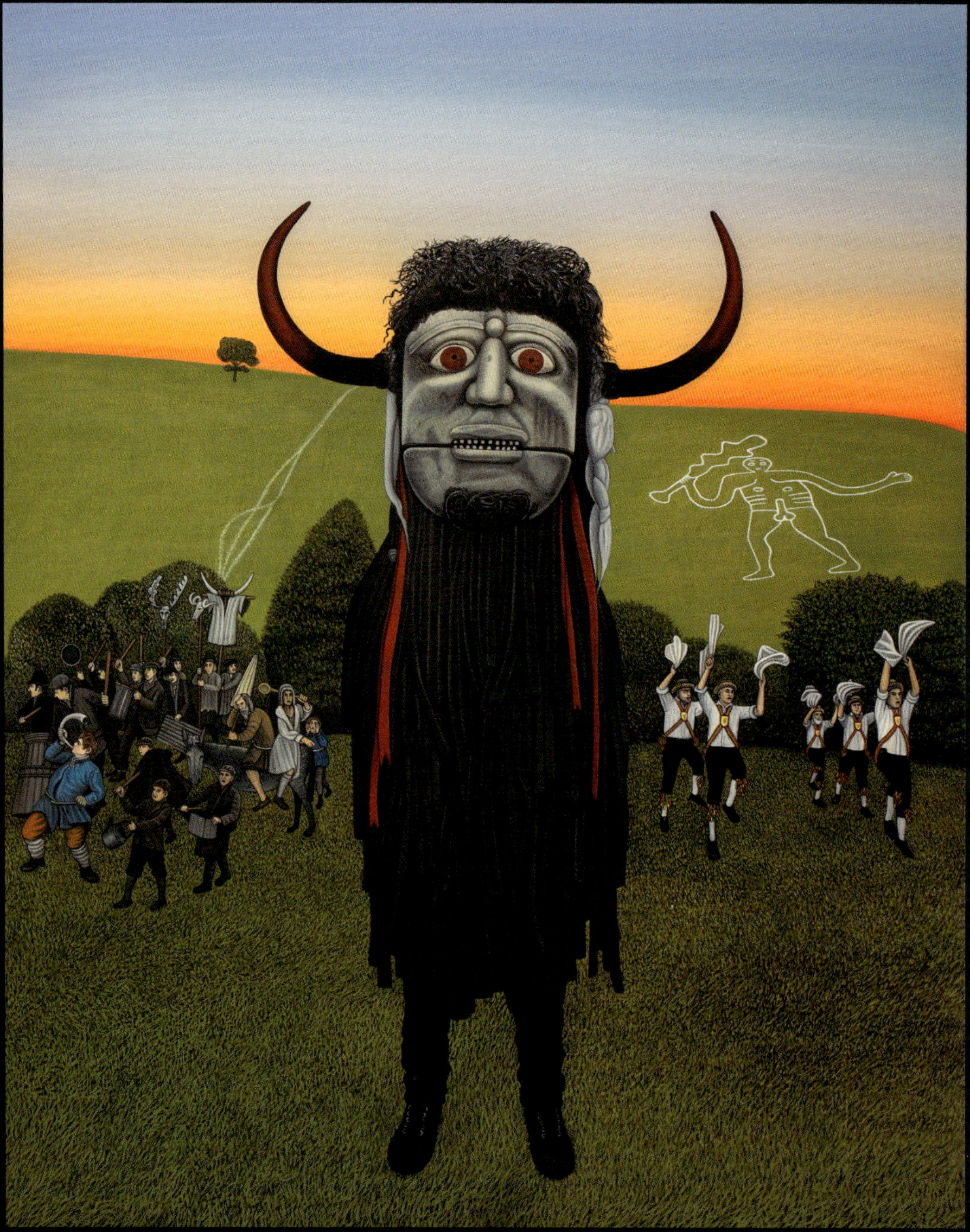

THE DORSET OOSER

Oil on Canvas, 100cm × 80cm

2020

The Dorset Ooser

DORSET AND HEREFORD

JANUARY VISIT

Ever since seeing the gold-embossed face of a horned mask on the front of the iconic 1973 Reader's Digest book *Folklore, Myths and Legends of Britain*, I'd been intrigued to know exactly what it was that I was looking at. After some investigation, I discovered it depicted a mask called the Dorset Ooser, now lost to the ages, and of which there are only two surviving photographs in existence, taken sometime between 1884 and 1891. The image of the mask is genuinely terrifying: with its two large eyes bulging from the page and its demonic half-smile, tufty hair and big sharp horns, it immediately gives you the impression that it has some sort of connection with the occult, maybe black magic. Perhaps this is the reason that this image has endured and survived into contemporary consciousness. Its mystery is immediately intoxicating, terrifying and intriguing.

In January 2022, I attended a wassail ceremony in Herefordshire, arranged by the Blackthorn Ritualistic Folk (see page 86), whose founder Jamie had created a modern version of the Ooser mask and named it "The Darkest Ooser". This reinterpretation is now very much part of the side's entourage and appears at many of their performances throughout the year. When I first stood in the presence of this new Ooser, with its huge, carved white face and body of black rags, I was immediately struck by how it had the same haunting eyes as the original. This is a figure that most certainly horrifies –

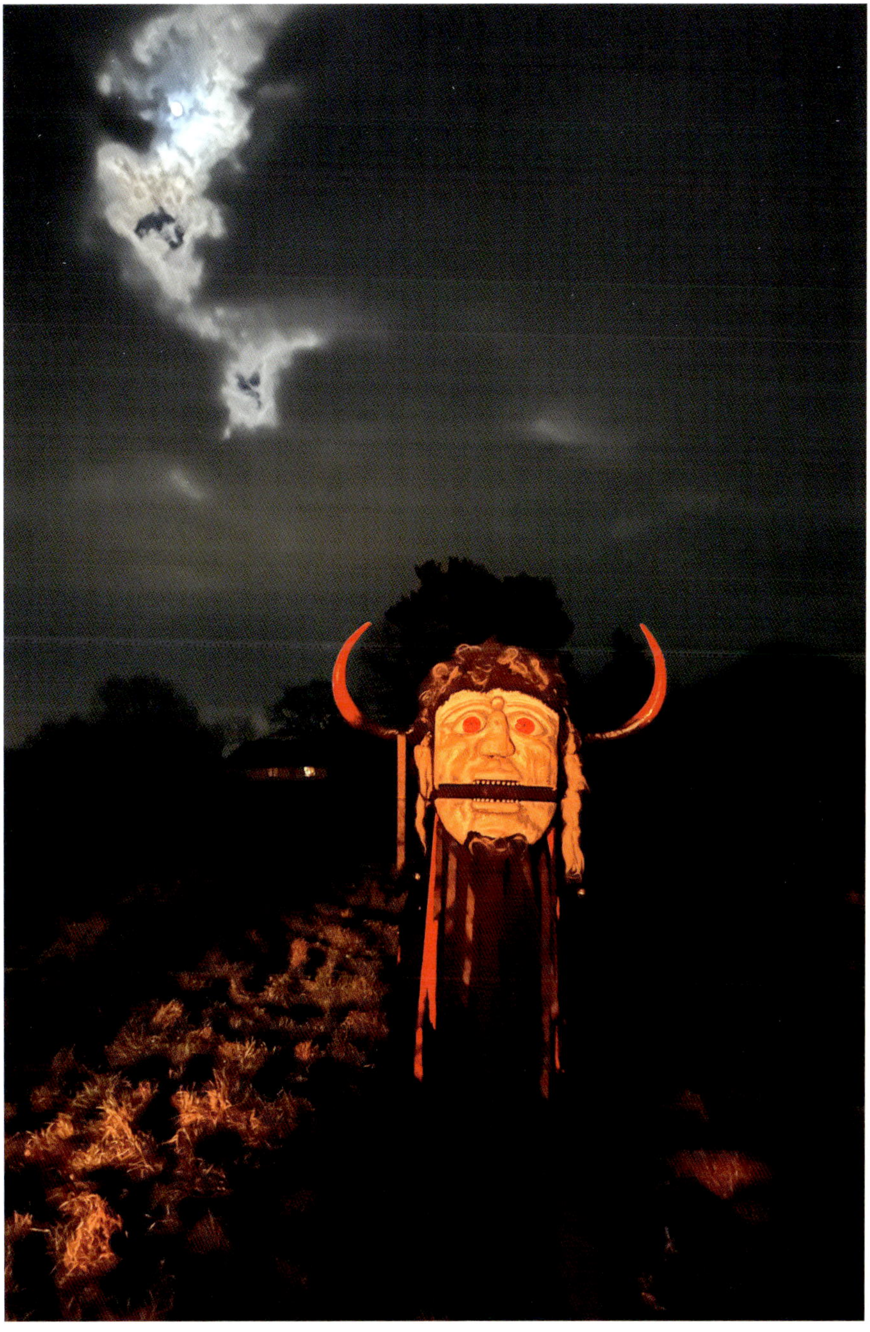

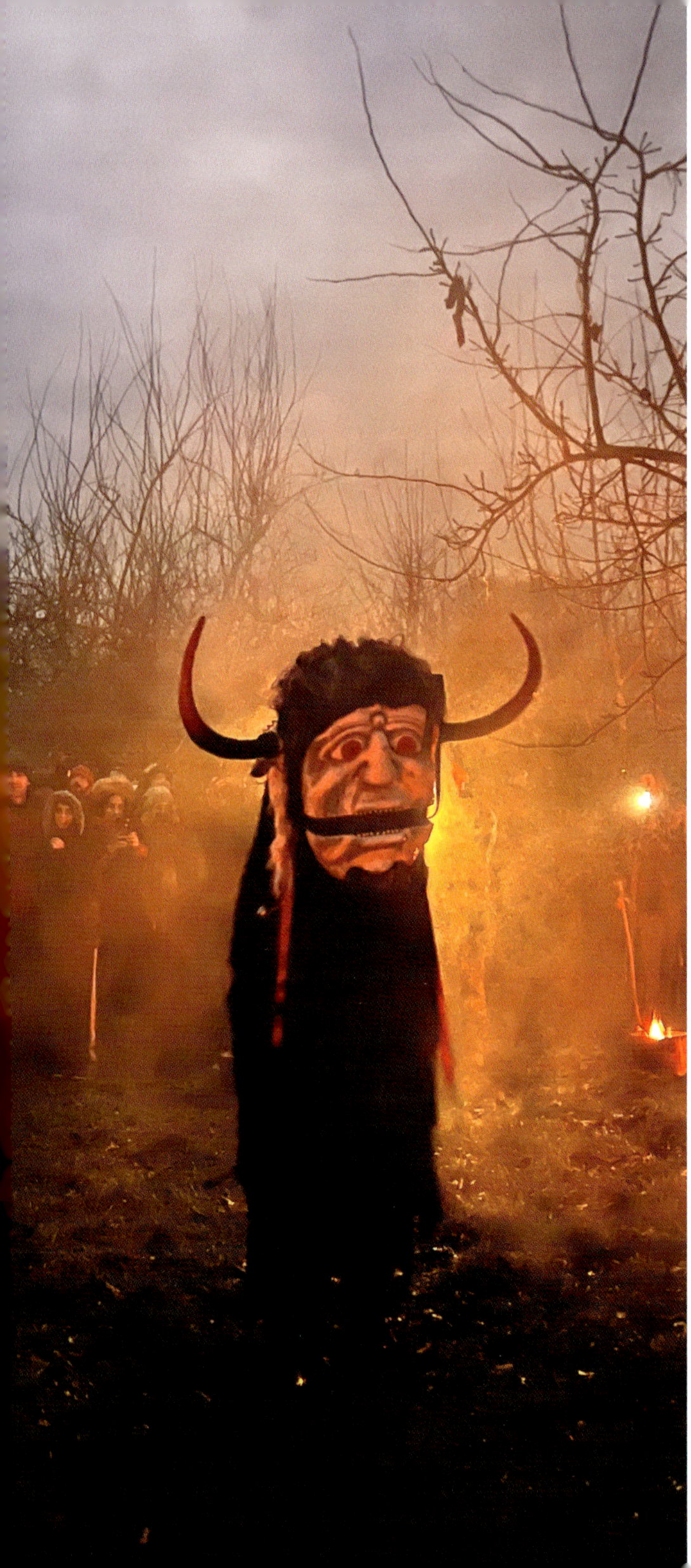

but what was it originally for? I decided I would investigate further, although one thing I did already know for sure: that I'd be using this most recent manifestation of the Ooser as the central figure of a new painting.

During the course of my research, one of the most remarkable and extensive of all the accounts that I came across was by the musician and author Daniel Patrick Quinn, who published an E-book titled *The Dorset Ooser* in 2021. In it, he describes how he embarked on a quest to discover the origins of this British mystery and managed to trace the mask back to the village of Melbury Osmond in Dorset, where the Cave family of Holt Farm used to own it. Much of the history of the mask is murky, with there being no sign of the original for over a century, and with various theories suggesting that it was sold to a stranger, lost or even said to have crumbled to pieces in a doctor's town attic.

However, I discovered that, like the Blackthorn Ritualistic Folk, the Wessex Morris Men have since made their own modern Ooser, with which they dance up the sun on May Day morning on Giant's Hill, the site of the Cerne Abbas Giant, also located in Dorset. While I've yet to see this ceremony with my own eyes, I knew I would have to include the equally mysterious Cerne Abbas Giant in any painting I did of the Ooser. The Giant is a chalk hill figure of a nude man with an erection and holding a club, which is believed to have been etched into the Dorset hills as early as 700 CE. And if I included him, then I would have to include the Wessex Morris Men's May Day ritual, too, as this was all an important part of the ongoing enigmatic story of the Dorset Ooser and of the custodians who keep his legend alive.

One of my favourite theories touched upon by Daniel Patrick Quinn is that the Ooser may once have been used in a popular form of moral protest, not uncommon in nineteenth-century Dorset, known variously as "skimmington", "skimmity riding" or "rough music". This consisted of a noisy procession, the aim of which was to humiliate publicly an unfaithful or badly behaved spouse. Often, two stuffed figures or real human impersonators were dressed up to represent and ridicule the couple, and seated back to back on a donkey or horse, accompanied by villagers or townsfolk who would beat tin pots and pans to make a din. If effigies were used, these might be shot, buried, burned, or thrown in a pond at the end of the procession. This seemed remarkably similar to the Hunting the Earl of Rone ceremony that I witnessed in Devon (see page 30). Which got me thinking … had the Earl of Tyrone been subject to skimmington riding and driven out of town in the month during which he went missing from the accounts of his life? That made total sense to me.

But to get back to the Ooser – I was intrigued by the idea of mob justice, in which the law was taken into their own hands by the village folk, and perceived wrongdoers were driven out through this terrifying ritualistic procession, which in some instances might last for days on end, while perhaps lurking within the procession, that horned figure of horror the Dorset Ooser could be found. That'd be enough to drive me out of any town or village! A vivid vision of this menacing procession and long-lost custom etched itself within my imagination, and I knew it would have to feature within the final composition of my painting, completing the jigsaw in my mind.

The original Dorset Ooser mask will probably never be found, and his original purpose may never be known, but through the power of storytelling, and as new meanings, theories and freshly crafted masks continue to spring up and attach themselves to this enigmatic figure, the Dorset Ooser remains very much alive and as relevant today as he has ever been. I wished for my own painting to be a celebration of this and part of the lineage of the telling and retelling of his legend.

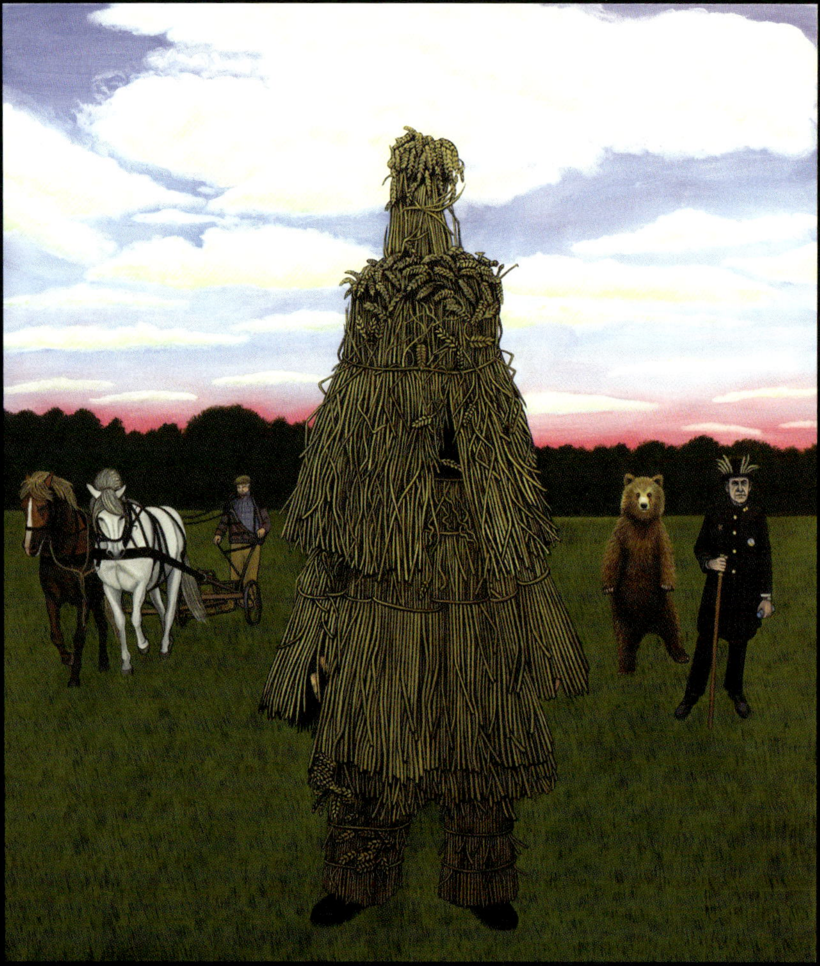

THE STRAW BEAR

Oil on Canvas, 80cm × 70cm

2019

The Straw Bear

CAMBRIDGESHIRE

PLOUGH MONDAY (FIRST MONDAY AFTER JANUARY 6)

I was particularly excited that day; I'd come across the Whittlesea Straw Bear in books such as Homer Sykes's *Once a Year*, and its image was already firmly imprinted in my mind. It's an unnerving sight, like something out of a folk-horror film – as though it's a kind of willing sacrificial victim. To be honest, I'd become slightly obsessed by it and spent hours on YouTube searching for any footage I could find.

After a difficult train journey where I stood most of the way, and had to travel from London all the way up to Leeds, before travelling back down to Peterborough, I arrived in the city to find football fans had caused further delays, with a fight breaking out on the platform. So I had to catch a bus to Whittlesey, which would take even longer. Despite my anxiety, I made it by a whisker: I'd missed the dressing of the Bear but had arrived just in time to see the Bear and its two cubs dancing around the corner onto the main stretch of the High Street.

It was pure magic to see them skipping along, with the earthy sounds of their straw-covered bodies swishing and rustling as they danced through the ram-packed streets. A man in a hat and long black coat was guiding the large Bear and two baby Bears (both concealing children) with a stick. The stress of my journey dissolved and I tuned in to the hypnotic tune played by an accordionist and trumpet player, with a drummer banging away to create the heartbeat of the procession. The tune played repeatedly throughout the day is slow and otherworldly, with an old fairground dream-like quality, and sinks right into your subconscious, humming in your head for weeks on after.

I followed the procession through the market square, where a Straw Bear effigy looked down from a thatched roof, passing morris sides that had already started to perform. There were morris dancers literally everywhere, in all sorts of weird and wonderful costumes; some in black-and-white checks, holding brooms; some dressed like demonic woodland spirits and others in more traditional attire, waving handkerchiefs as their giant cockerel mascot roamed among them. I spotted one of my favourite sides banging their sticks, the Red Leicester Morris Men, who resembled dancing birds showing off their plumage.

A mother with a young baby went up to the Bears, but the child looked terrified so the mother quickly took him away. Then the adult Bear broke into a wild dance in a sort of bear-pit area cordoned off with traffic cones, while a car alarm went off in the distance. The whole spectacle was a feast for the eyes.

The Straw Bear processional tune started up again and the Bears and their party made their way through the streets, passing a Barclays Bank and a Pound Shop. A bakery had created a whole themed display around the Straw Bear. We crossed the road as the lights went red and the green man shone brightly. Now we'd reached a residential part of town, and the Bears danced frenziedly, hopping and skipping, with their straw outfits swooshing. People were peeping out of windows, some smiling, some watching expressionless, some clutching smart phones.

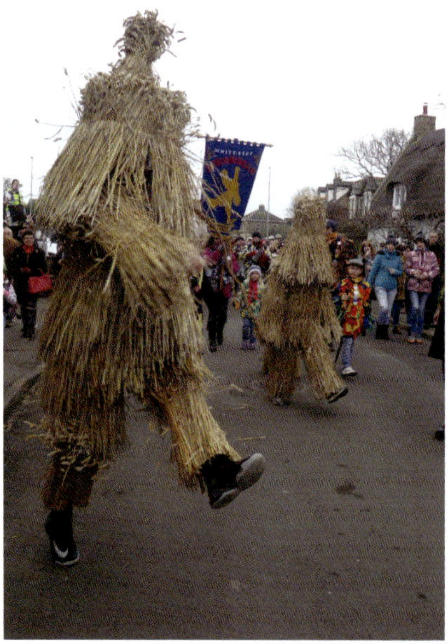

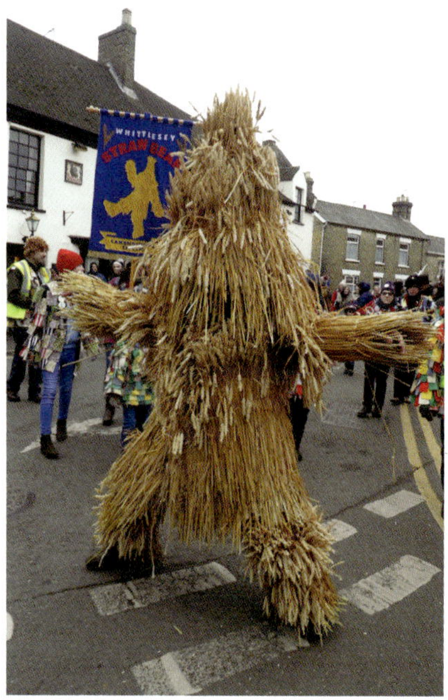

We arrived at a community centre with a bar and stage, where I noticed a man dressed in a bowler hat and Crombie coat. I recognized him from some old footage; he was the predecessor to the current Keeper of the Bears. I went up to him and he seemed flattered that I knew who he was. When I asked him about the Straw Bears, he replied, "Well, it started with the plough boys that used to plough the fields. They'd be out of work from Christmas up until Plough Sunday, so during that period they didn't get paid at all, and to get money they dressed someone up in a straw outfit that resembled a bear and they went around people's houses, begging for money basically, like with the old dancing bears that they used to have on the continent. And if people didn't give them food or whatever else they were asking for, they would plough up the ground in front of their houses."

I imagined what it must have been like hundreds of years ago, seeing these Straw Bears and plough boys approaching your house. It must have been quite a scary sight, and it sounded like very menacing behaviour, with the threat of damaging your land if you didn't give them what they wanted. A definite folk-horror element to it. The story was also reminiscent of so many other winter customs I encountered: whether it's the Mari Lwyds, mummers, hooden horses or the Straw Bear, up and down the country, people used their initiative and creativity, and took to animal guising as a form of entertainment to get the money and food they needed when times were scarce.

Next, we headed back toward the town square. When we reached the crossing, the Straw Bear danced comically in front of a stationary police car, while everyone laughed at the anarchic moment. Back at the square, a whole host of morris dancers were still performing. There was a skirmish in the local Weatherspoon's; the daytime drinking was taking its toll on some. The Bears and their party started to weave their way through the streets once again, passing a church and through a small alleyway. Here, a hobby horse appeared and jokingly lunged at them.

When we stopped off at a working men's club, the adult Bear had to duck down low to fit through the doorway. As we were leaving, children rushed out of the house opposite, shouting, "He's here, he's here!" before being joined by the whole family. More pub stops, more waving hankies, banging sticks, clinking of glasses, and on we went, till we reached a pub carpark where a group of mummers, all members of Red Leicester Morris side, were waiting to perform. Here, the Straw Bear joined in, lying on the floor and comically dying, while an onlooker's pet husky started howling and tried to investigate the strange pile of straw on the floor, before the Bear was resurrected by the Doctor character. The play ended, the crowd cheered, and I loved the hybridity of these customs all coming together. That's how new ones get made.

Back in the town square, the current Keeper of the Bears was standing by himself, so I took the opportunity to talk to him. He told me the same origin story as his predecessor about the plough boys, but added, "When they got the beer, they got drunk and started getting abusive and the local police started to step in and ban them, eventually bringing the tradition to an end, so it died out for a time." He advised me to talk to the festival organizer, who was responsible for bringing the tradition back. When I managed to catch up with Brian Kell, the organizer, later, he said, "Yes, I revived the tradition, being very interested in folklore, because we didn't really know why the event was stopped, but we suspect it was because people were demanding money with menaces. The last time (before the revival in 1979) that we had a Straw Bear on the street was around 1909." He agreed that there might be a connection to medieval times when street performers with dancing bears would tour the country.

The image in my mind of plough boys and Straw Bears dancing with menace, ploughing up people's property, got more and more vivid as the day continued. I could see a ploughed field with a Straw Bear and plough boy emerging from it; I also imagined a dancing brown bear in the party, being led by today's keeper. As I walked to the station to catch a train to where I was staying, there was a green glow over the horizon. I'd never seen a sky quite like it. This completed the composition and I could see the painting coming alive.

The following morning, I headed back in to Whittlesea for the final part of the ceremony, which was taking place at a school. Here, the Straw Bear was to be burned, a sacrifice of sorts. Thankfully, there would be no human being under the costume today, although as it was set alight a child screamed, making me think I'd been mistaken for a second. As the Bear lit up in gold and orange flames and slowly collapsed, I couldn't help but think of *The Wicker Man* and the final scene where the outsider is sacrificed to ensure a good harvest. I got out of there quick. But then I did have a train to catch, honest.

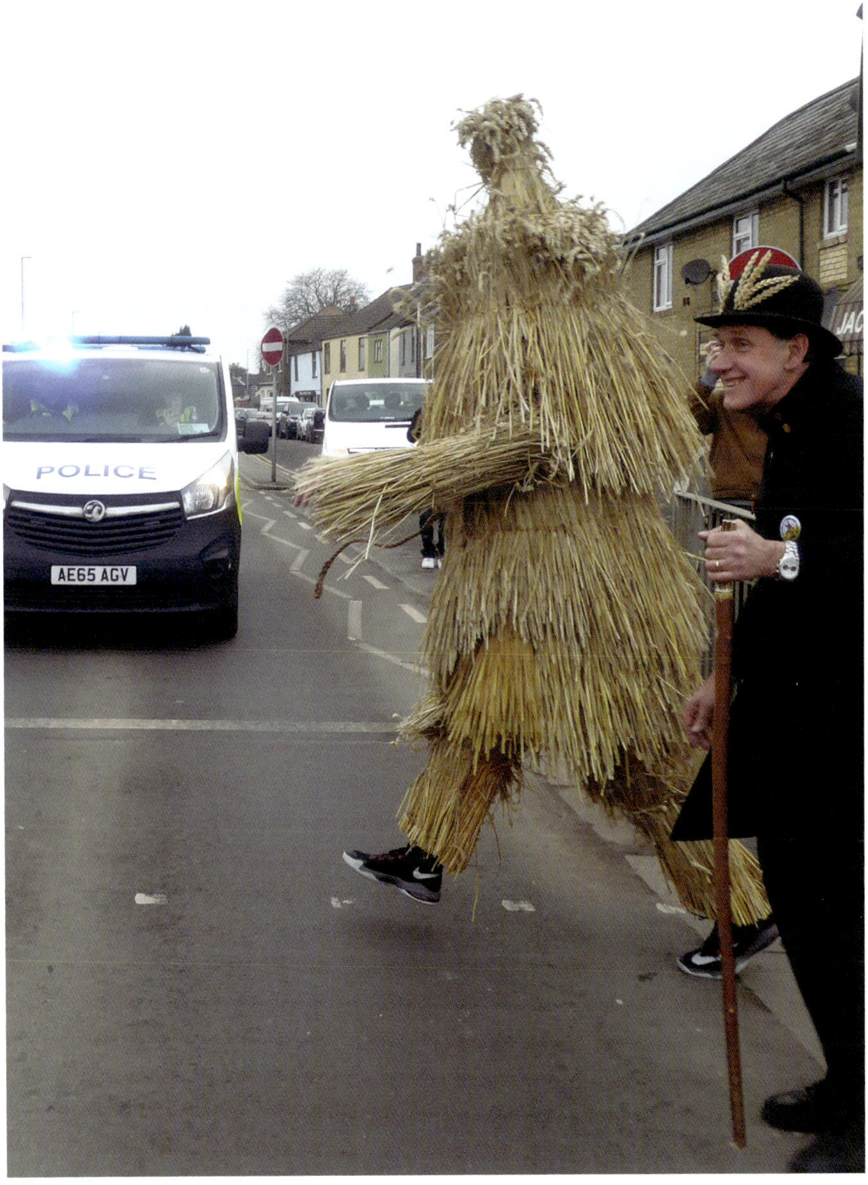
POLICE
AE65 AGV

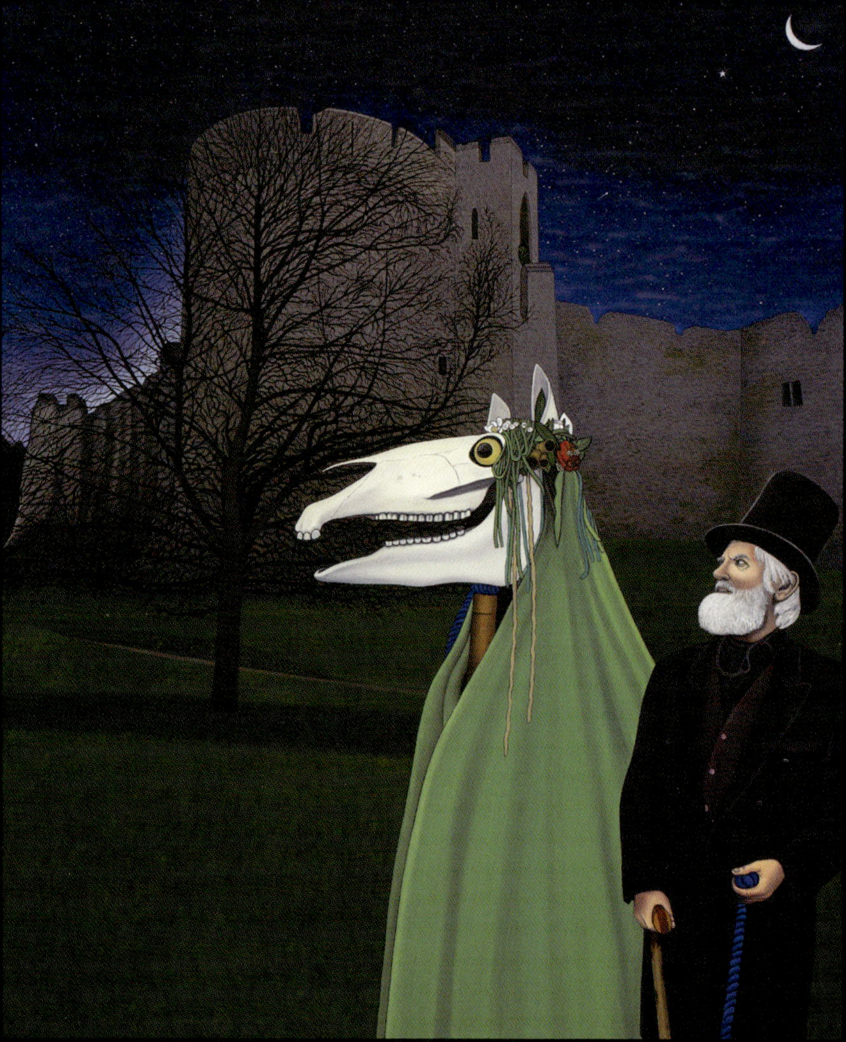

THE MARI LWYD

Oil on Canvas, 125cm × 100cm

2019

The Mari Lwyd

MONMOUTHSHIRE

LATE JANUARY

The first time I ever saw a Mari Lwyd, my friend Anton and I had just arrived in Chepstow and were walking down the hill toward the castle. From the distance came the sound of bells, a noise I was growing increasingly familiar with on my folk adventures, although this was different: the bells sounded larger and the ringing more sporadic. As we approached, we could see a woman leading a strange creature by a rope. There it was, the Mari Lwyd, mischievously peering into the windows of houses. The woman playing the part of its Ostler shrieked, "Naughty Mari!" and playfully tapped the shoulders of the beast to move it on. Before we knew it, we were face to face with its harnessed horse's skull and snapping jaws, mounted on a pole with its carrier hidden beneath a white sheet.

It was quite a sight to see – the living dead, winter personified. This was January, a time when everything has died or seems to be dying, yet will regrow and live on. The Mari Lwyd seemed like a reminder of the cycle of life and death that's part of the wheel of the year as the seasons turn. Later in a pub, another Ostler would tell me with a chesty cackling laugh that, "In the Gower they used to bury the skull every year at the end of the season and cover it in lime to keep it white, and then dig it up again the following season."

As we carried on down toward the castle, past pubs and terraced houses, we were met by more Maris and their Ostlers. There were all shapes and sizes, jaws snapping in every direction; some decorated in ribbons and fairy lights and some with balls for eyes. One Ostler with a white beard and top hat especially caught my attention, and I knew I want him in my painting.

Behind him yet more Mari Lwyds appeared. It was a spooky, hellish scene, but fun, tapping into the enjoyable side of feeling scared, like a ghost story. There was an element of childhood regression and adult play too, as the Ostlers, the people who guide the Maris on reins, were having a great time telling them off and treating them like misbehaving pets. As well as the Maris, there was of course morris dancing, but with an added competitive element: if you crossed the nearby bridge you'd leave Wales and find yourself in England, so at the end of the day morris dancers from England would march over to the centre of the bridge, where they were met by the Welsh Maris and morris dancers for a "morris off".

I later learned that this was a record year, with thirty-five Maris Lwyds in attendance, potentially the largest gathering ever. There was a Maris Lwyd whose mouth was wide open, head tilting to the sky, and another with white eyes and Celtic patterns, which moved in a way that reminded me of the velociraptors in *Jurassic Park*. There was a particularly haunting one draped in green instead of the traditional white. I'm fascinated by how traditions evolve over time, and learned that some people feel that unless a Mari is draped in white, then it's not a proper Mari Lwyd but a separate tradition. I found myself drawn now to the idea of depicting a Mari that represented the tradition's evolution, keeping things fresh and relevant to new generations and, in my opinion, ensuring the custom's survival.

I began making a mental collage and imagined the bearded, top-hatted man standing with the green-clothed Mari in front of the looming castle. I could already see the painting that I needed to make. Like the Mari Lwyd tradition itself, it would need to be a timeless yet modern image, eerie yet fun.

Afterwards, I was to discover that even though the event was so popular, it wouldn't take place again for another five years. The reasons were the Covid lockdowns and because the town didn't having the facilities to handle all the people (or the Maris) that the festival attracted. However, in the winter of 2019 I was lucky to be invited to show my now-completed painting of a Mari Lwyd at Chepstow Museum in an exhibition curated by Mari Lwyd enthusiast John Exton, who'd arranged for a traditional Mari Lwyd ceremony to take place for the exhibition's opening.

It was a particularly dark night and when the herd of Mari Lwyds met up by the castle entrance, you could see the glow of fairy lights inside some of their skulls, like they'd come to take you to the underworld; as we walked to the museum, the snapping of their jaws accompanied the sounds of the fiddler. The top-hatted man appeared, although now without his beard. I learned he'd already seen my painting and seemed pleased with my depiction of him. As we approached the entrance, where a lady in a black hat and bonnet waited, acting the part of the mistress of the house, the party collectively started to sing in Welsh. The song was the Mari Lwyd Carol, which translates into English as:

Here we come,
Dear friends,
To ask permission to sing.

If we don't have permission,
Let us know in song
How we should go away tonight.

I have no dinner
Or money to spend
To give you welcome tonight.

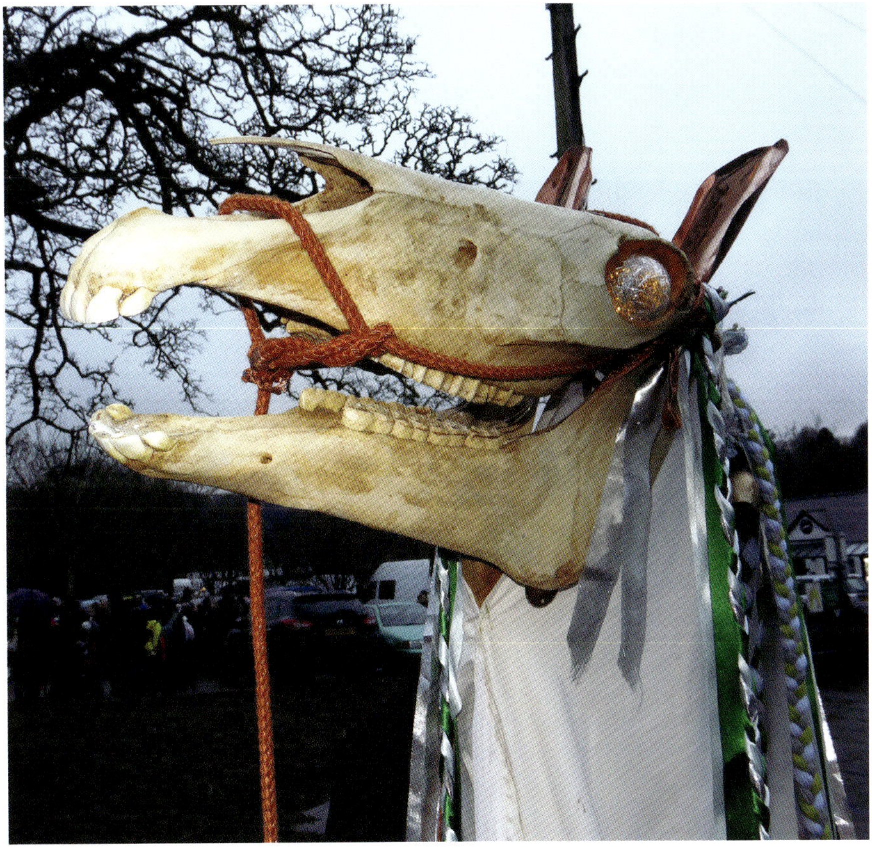

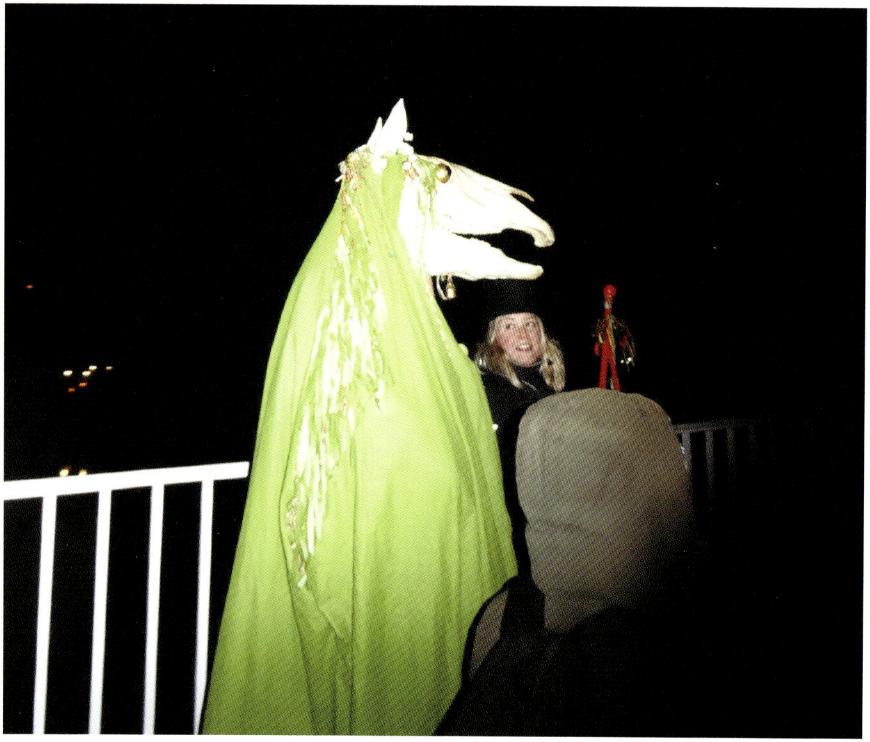

There followed a battle of wits of sorts where the Ostlers, their Mari Lwyds and the rest of the party would poke fun at the woman and vice versa, like an ancient kind of rap battle. Eventually the Maris Lwyds' party won and was invited in for food and drink, which is what still traditionally happens across the Welsh valleys whenever the Mari Lwyd goes from door to door.

When we got inside I approached George, the subject of my painting. As we looked at it, he jokily said, "Do you want me to grow my beard back?" We got on to the subject of the tradition itself and he explained, "The Mari tradition itself goes back a great many years. It was the means by which agricultural labourers, when they were at their poorest, went around begging at the big houses. What happened was what they call the Mari party, which consisted of the Mari, some poor soul who couldn't see a thing heaving around this very large horse's head, and an Ostler who would lead it round from place to place.

"There were other people in a Mari party, whose purpose was to sing and when they went house to house, they would bash on the door and ask the people inside to let them in, 'cause obviously they wanted a little bit of refreshment, and perhaps a little bit of food as well. And as well as sing a song, they would compliment the people in the house on how marvellous they were, pillars of the community, and rich. But then the people inside the house would sing back "Clear off"! And so it would go, back and forth, what they call the *pwnco*, between the Mari party, who are singing a version asking for entrance, and those inside doing everything to stop them, until eventually the party inside relents and lets in the Mari party. The Mari party would then entertain them for a bit of food, a bit of drink and money, and job done, the party cleared off to the next big house." It sounded remarkably similar to carol singing, perhaps its ancient predecessor.

I was curious to find out about the symbolism of the horse's skull, and why people first began using one. When I spoke to John Exton, the curator of the exhibition, who also has a Mari Lwyd, he said, "Well, there're lots of theories. One of them is about Epona the Roman horse goddess, and Rhiannon the Welsh horse goddess; you know, the Romans slaughtered horses in the field for fertility. To the ancient world, the horse was like an HGV: it transported things, people, and was used in war. In Ireland, they'd have horse skulls underneath floorboards, which acted as a soundboard when they were dancing, and in a couple of churches horse skulls were put beneath or close to the altar to amplify the sermon. At Portway in Herefordshire, there's a pub where 'a couple of wagons' of horse skulls were put under the floor. The other main reason for embedding them under floors and in walls is for protection against evil/witches, etc. So there were lots of reasons why the horse was important."

I also spoke to Vivian, the Ostler of the Mari that'd reminded me of a velociraptor. She told me, "You know, it goes way back in history, it could be as far as Druidic times. Really the horse tradition is worldwide, but the Mari Lwyd itself is a grey mare [which is what the name means], and that traditionally meant a white sheet or a table cloth often held up by a pitchfork. It was traditional in the darkest nights of winter, and it's supposed to frighten away the bad spirits from the previous year by creating chaos."

Horse symbolism like that of the Mari Lwyd sits at the heart of many of the traditions I've visited, where the ideas of death, rebirth and fertility seem to be embodied by the horse, whether the 'Obby 'Osses of Padstow or the various hobby horses that take part in customs ranging from the Abbots Bromley Horn Dance to the Hunting the Earl of Rone, or in ancient monuments such as the Uffington White Horse. Could this all be interconnected and related to ancient fertility gods and surrounding rituals? I'd like to think so.

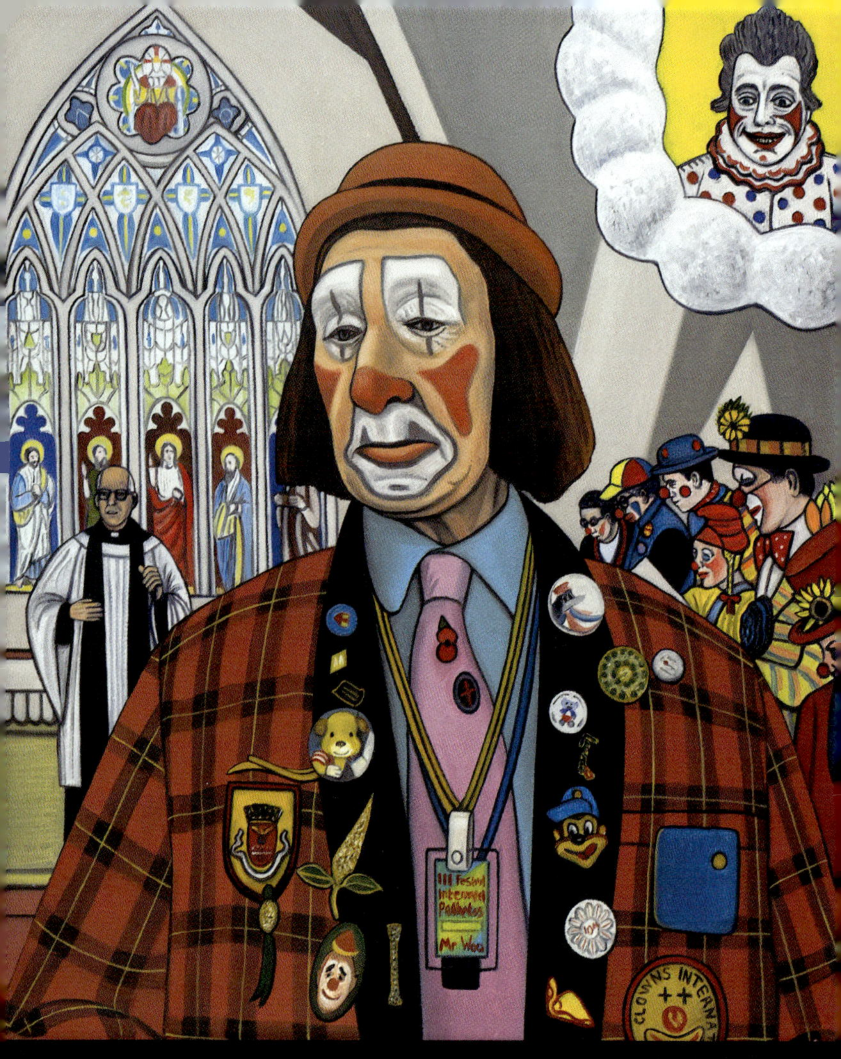

THE CHURCH OF THE CLOWNS

The Clowns' Service

EAST LONDON
FIRST SUNDAY IN FEBRUARY

Circus tunes were pumping out from a large musical box, as a man in a Union Jack jacket and bowler hat wound the handle. In front of it, a whole heap of clowns were joking around and performing tricks for groups of children and their parents, stealing their noses, and chucking rings of artificial sausages. But I wasn't at the circus. This was All Saints Church in Haggerston, East London, where clowns gather from all over Britain and even abroad to remember the life of the pioneer of modern clowning, Joseph Grimaldi (1778–1837).

Starting in 1946, the service originally used to take place at Grimaldi's graveside at the old St James's Church on Pentonville Road, Islington, and then moved to the Holy Trinity Church in Dalston, now also known as the "Clowns' Church", which up until recently housed a museum and archive, including the Clown Egg Registry, a custom whereby clowns trademark their individual clown face designs by painting the patterns on to eggs. (The Registry has since moved to the Clowns-Gallery Museum in Wookey Hole.) Over the years the service has grown in popularity and had to be moved to its current venue to accommodate the growing numbers of clowns, worshippers and members of the general public who wish to pay their respects to Grimaldi.

Before entering the church, I bumped into two clowns who'd come all the way from Normandy. Taking puffs on hand-rolled cigarettes, they opened pots of bubbles and started blowing smoke through the plastic bubble-makers to create smoke-filled bubbles that floated up and burst in the air. Next, I met a clown with fake buck teeth and a fireman's uniform who wandered over and said, "I'm Fireman Sam, eat your heart out." When I asked him what was going on, he explained, "This is the Grimaldi day, the Clowns' Service to commemorate the life of Joseph Grimaldi, who was the originator of clowning. He was a pantomime clown, and he's called the father of clowning as we know it today." Then a clown with a feather duster began lightly brushing my face, but when I tried to speak to him, he comically pointed to his mouth and shook his head, implying he was mute.

I turned to find even more clowns, including an elderly clown sitting on a fold-out chair who I went to stand beside. He said he was called Salvo. "We're here to give thanks to Joey Grimaldi," he explained, and added, "We're here for the privilege we have of entertaining as clowns and also for meeting up with our chums."

I decided it was time to go into the church, stepping past a clown with a toy rabbit in his hat that popped out at me as I went by. Inside were the two French clowns, so I took the opportunity to have a chat with them before everyone else sat down. Curious why they'd come all this way, I asked whether they thought Grimaldi was a saint. "He's a spirit," they said. "We have come from France for the spirit, we want to take the spirit with us back to France, and enjoy the spirit, and after give it back to England."

People started to take their seats, with the front rows consisting purely of clowns in full dress. The organ began to play "The Lord of the Dance" and soon the church was full to the brim. While the clicking of cameras could be heard throughout the service, I kneeled down close to the wooden pews on the front row to ensure I got some good shots of the service. I'd been to this service on numerous occasions and now had a small archive of material, including a great portrait of a clown called Mr Woo, who has an incredibly expressive face that speaks of both tragedy and comedy, a tradition that goes all the way back to the masks of the Ancient Greek theatre, where clowning most probably evolved from. So with enough source material to work from, today was more about re-experiencing the service to allow the painting I was yet to make to reveal itself to me.

The clowns sang along to the organ music comically and I was taken back to my days at St Gregory's Catholic Comprehensive in Tunbridge Wells, where we used to sing along to hymns in funny voices, much to the annoyance of the teachers and "Fathers" that led the services. There's something fantastic about witnessing a joyful, light-hearted church service, without all the fear and damnation, and the clowns bring an element of joy and even

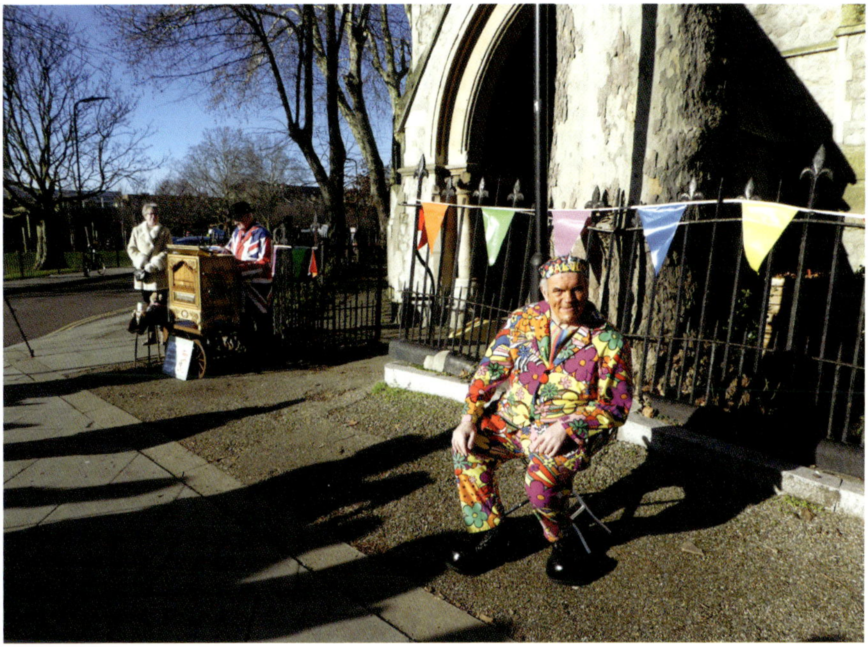

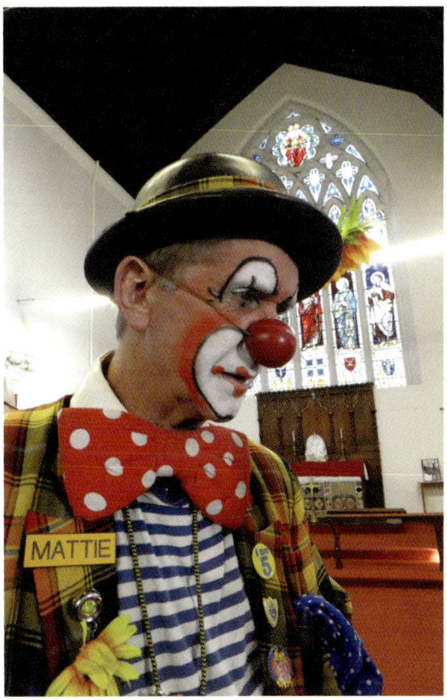
MATTIE

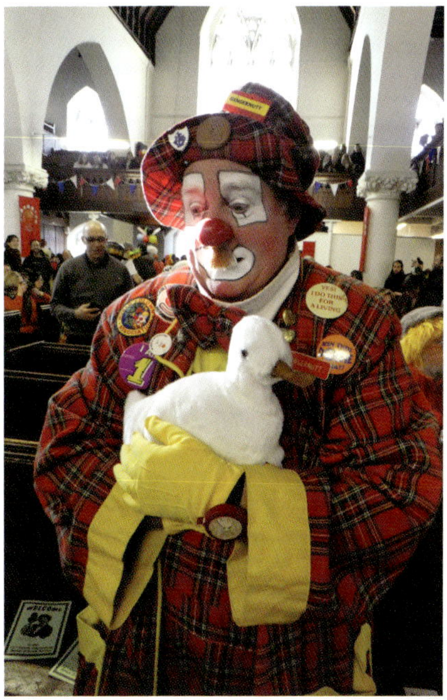

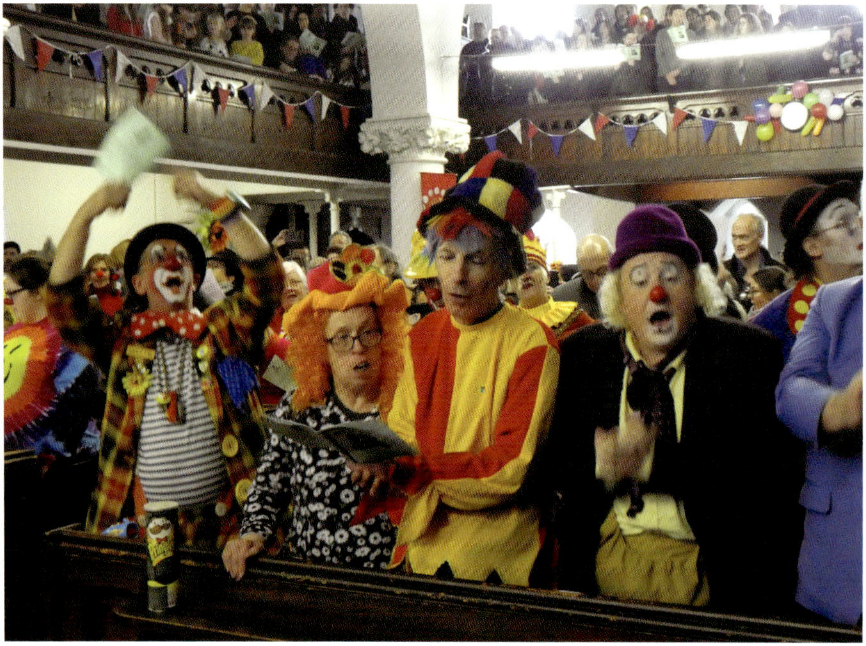

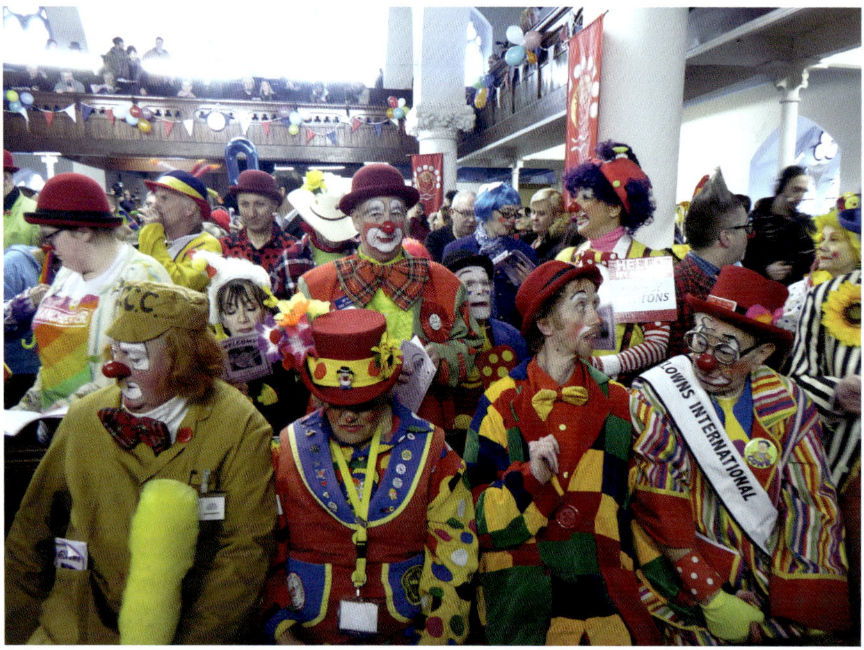
LOWNS INTERNATIONAL

emotion as they give thanks for the joy of laughter. It's nice to be where people celebrate the artistry of their industry like this. It doesn't feel disrespectful to those of faith, it just works, makes sense even. The whole day feels like a celebration of all the people who have shared laughter and joy in their lives.

The vicar began a reading in which she gave thanks for the profession of clowning and reflected upon the gifts that clowning brings to the world: "Sometimes they laugh by getting it wrong, imagine; sometimes they make us laugh and feel something 'cause we feel sorry for them, and in this respect aren't they the bravest of performers, because they show what it is to be human, to embrace a tear in order to make room for pure joy. And I wonder if that is why some people are a bit scared of clowns, they just can't make them out, these people that really engage with humanness instead of worldly ambition and success. It's a frightening thought for some of us to get rid of all those things, the shiny successes, and to be frighteningly unique, so frighteningly vulnerable, in order to encourage others to smile."

There was an added layer of emotion and thoughtfulness to the service when candles were lit in memory of all the clowns who'd died over the past year, including a poignant moment in which the "Unnamed Clown" was remembered, as a harrowingly moving tune was played. Then a wreath was laid for Joey Grimaldi himself. I could imagine the roof opening, with Grimaldi watching down from the clouds and approving of his enduring influence. Mr Woo the clown would be at the centre of the scene, stepping away after placing the wreath for Grimaldi upon the altar. The clowns were standing peacefully in the church pews and the Vicar was delivering the rest of the sermon. My composition had now fully revealed itself to me.

As the service came to an end, there was a reading in honour of Grimaldi: "Our Father, we remember before you the life of your servant, known as Grimaldi the clown. His artistry, his skills and invention, we thank you for the many lives blessed through his ministry; we thank you especially for all those inspired by this ministry, who have brought and sought to bring laughter to others, amen." The service ended, squeaky noses were pinched, kazoos blown, there were cheers, clapping and laughter as the organ music reached a crescendo. And then I went out into the waiting London street with its block of flats as the clowns dispersed in all directions.

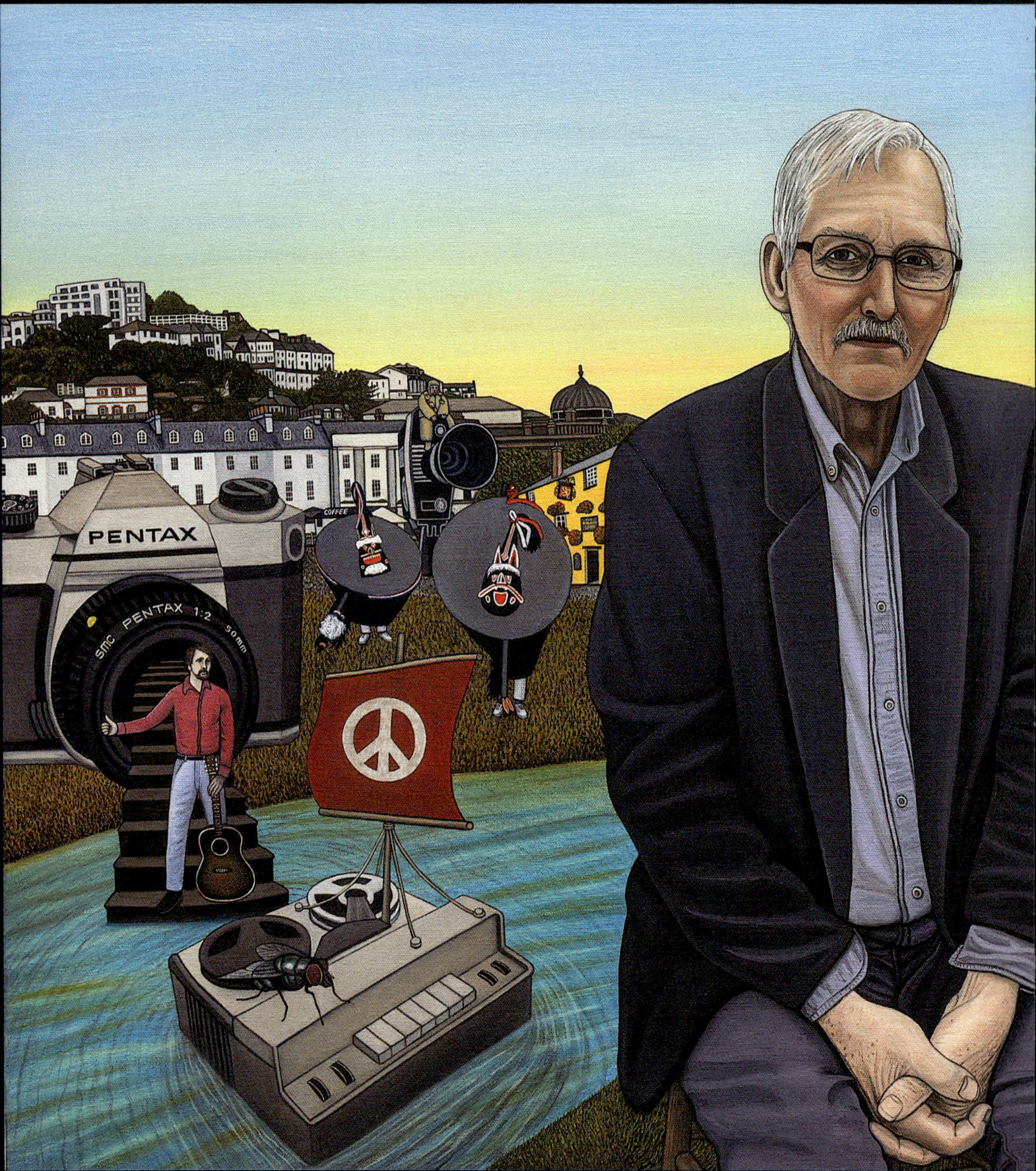
PENTAX
smc PENTAX 1:2 50mm
COFFEE

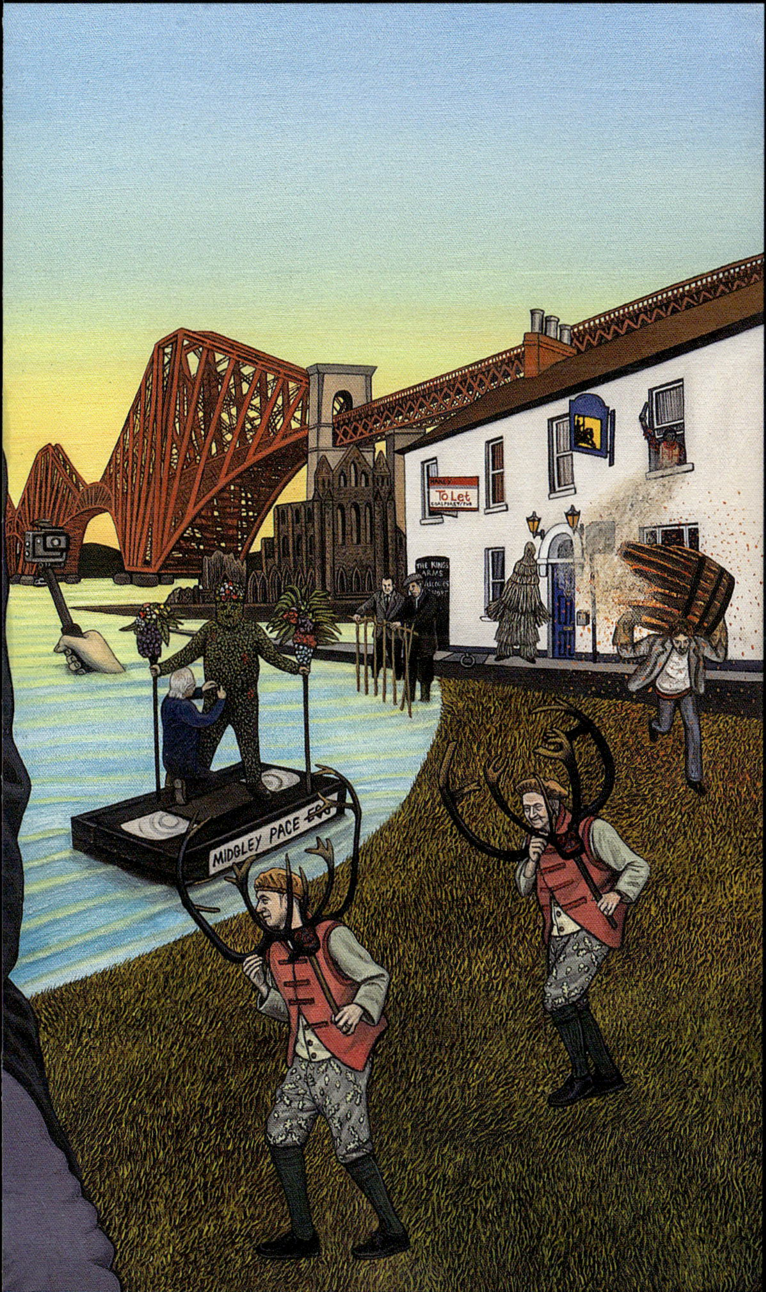

THE ISLE OF DOC ROWE

Oil on Canvas, 65cm × 100cm

2024

Doc Rowe

NORTH YORKSHIRE

EARLY MARCH VISIT

As soon as I started visiting local celebrations of folk customs, I began to collect books, pamphlets and any kind of printed matter that I happened to stumble on about British folklore. Very early on, I noticed that one name came up time and time again in the photo credits for these publications. The name itself sounded like a character out of folklore – "Doc Rowe" – and I began to wonder who this person was.

It felt like it would only be a matter of time before our paths crossed, and as mentioned previously, we did in fact meet very early on in my folkloric journey, at the Horns of Ock Street ceremony in Abingdon, Oxfordshire. After this first encounter, Doc Rowe and I quickly became friends, and Doc has since been incredibly generous with his time and expertise, opening doors for me that would have potentially taken me years to open by myself, such as witnessing the private dressing ceremony of the Burryman in South Queensferry.

Doc was also very encouraging about the video side of my work. When I first began to film customs, it was simply for the purpose of sending clips back to Rose, so that she could share what I was experiencing. At the time, I was filming in portrait mode, and it wasn't until I started uploading the videos online and Doc said to me, "For goodness' sake, turn the camera round – you're getting some good stuff here", or words to a similar effect, that I actually took his advice and flipped the camera to landscape.

Once I got to know Doc, I was amazed to discover that he has been obsessively documenting the seasonal customs of Britain ever since the 1960s, and has accumulated an incredible archive of material that is currently housed in what has become known as the "Doc Rowe Archive" in Whitby, Yorkshire, close to where he lives. For years, I kept meaning to journey up there and visit it. Then, because I was working on a portrait of Doc, depicting his colourful life at the heart of British folk culture, and the filmmakers Tim Plester and Rob Curry were filming my process for their documentary *The Isle of Doc Rowe*, I finally made my way up to visit him and to view the archive that I'd heard so much about but still hadn't seen with my own eyes.

It was a grey and windy day, and I had arranged to meet Doc outside the business centre where the archive is kept, which is just a short walk from the gothic ruins of Whitby Abbey. Once inside the building, we signed in at reception and made our way down the barren, white corridors. Doc's keys jangled when he pulled them from his pocket as we reached the archive's door. As soon as I entered the archive, I was struck by the layers and layers of material, along with cameras and equipment, which span the decades that Doc has been researching British folklore. What also caught my eye were the black and white photos lying around, which looked old yet somehow familiar, documenting customs that I had recently visited and which hadn't really changed, although the world around them had altered so much, with people's clothes and hairstyles and the settings marking the passage of time.

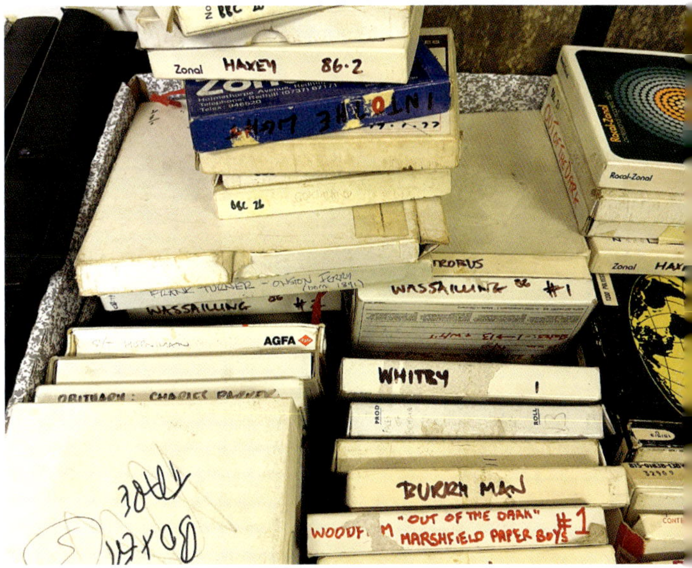

After sifting through shelves packed to the brim and the equally full drawers in the metal cabinets, containing video tape after video tape, and clippings and piles of publications in which Doc featured or which he had collected, I noticed a set of shelves that were pretty much empty, which looked strange given that everything else was so full. Doc explained that this was connected to the recent crowdfunding campaign that I was proud to be involved with, which had been set up by Tim Plester and Rob Curry, and aimed to digitize a huge chunk of the archive, ensuring its survival as a vital resource for future generations. We'd all thought that a good amount of money could be raised, but had no idea the general public would respond in such an explosive manner, with an incredible £60,000 being achieved.

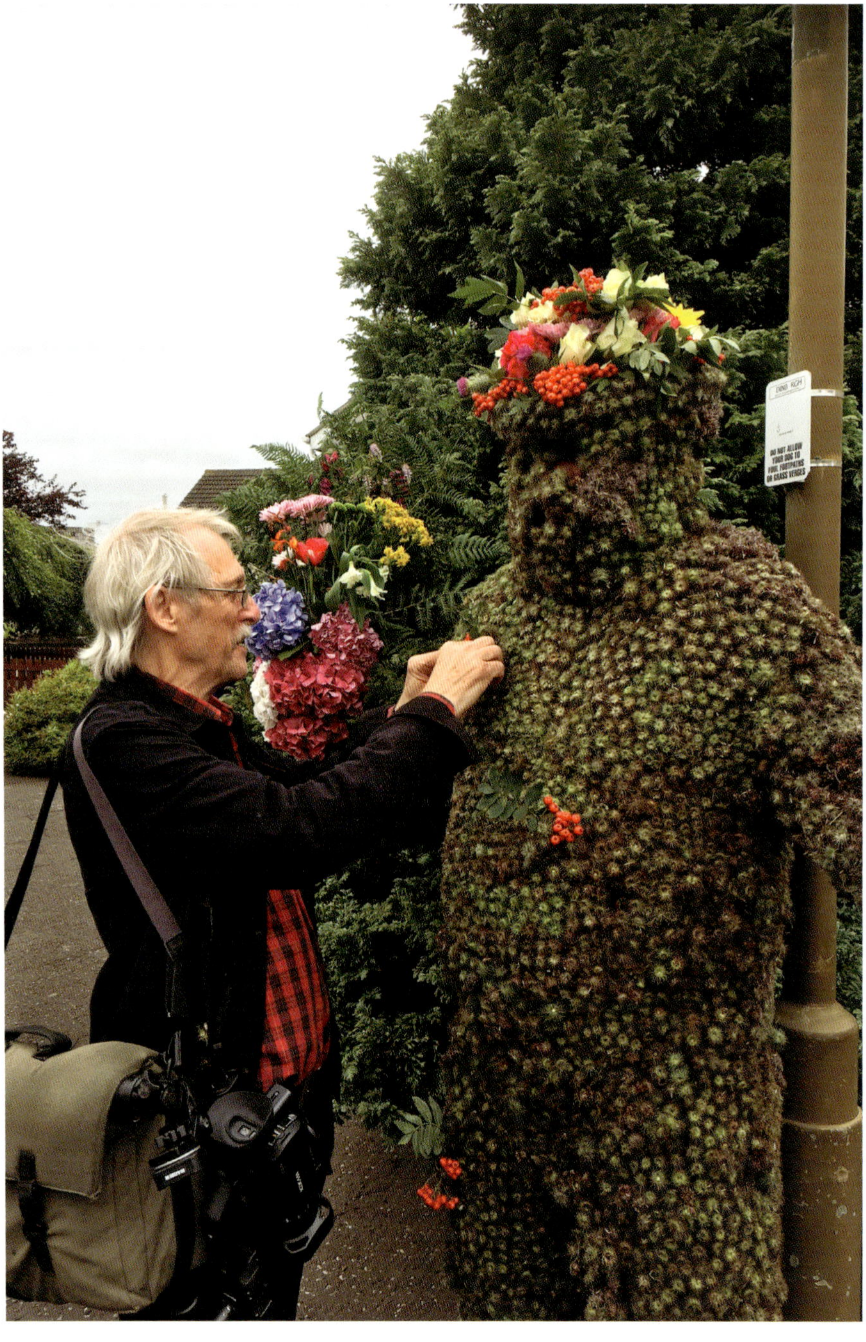
DO NOT ALLOW
YOUR DOG TO
FOUL FOOTPATHS
OR GRASS VERGES

After I'd enjoyed a good look round and come across one of the Burryman's original masks, we sat down to talk about Doc's life. I had interviewed Doc once before, when he visited my studio to sit for the study shots for his portrait. Then, he had told me his full life story and that sitting became the basis for my painting. Doc's tale is a fascinating one: he has dedicated his life to immersing himself in the folk culture of these isles.

Sitting against the backdrop of an old reel-to-reel machine, the steel filing cabinets and the now empty shelves whose videos were being digitized, Doc explained that the archive currently houses 23 tons of material; it took the equivalent of three furniture removal vans to bring it all here, and of course he'd added to it since then.

He admitted, "You know, I never consciously set out to document or record anything. I went to Padstow in 1963, and it's just an extraordinary event, amazing – something that was happening on the streets, created by real people. It was very emotional, and I went back the following year, 'cause I really couldn't believe that I'd seen it, quite honestly, and I've been doing that ever since."

The way Doc described his journey resonated with my own: there was an element that sounded like serendipity, like this was the path meant for him. Ever since his first visit to Padstow, an obsession had been born within him that would last a lifetime.

He continued, "It was about ten years before I went to another seasonal event, as I would call them, and that was at Abbots Bromley. It was almost like the big finger in the sky was nudging me toward the right people: I always remember how Maid Marion came up to me and almost took me by the shoulder, and said, 'You need to meet this man.' And I met the guy who was the leader of the horn dancers in the 1930s, and it sort of went from there."

From the very beginning, you can see Doc's fascination with the people involved, and he soon created a sort of formula that he started to apply to documenting other customs as well. He explained, "I started collecting some of the older photographs and then recording people talking about the detail in them. If you like, I brought the same technique, the same device I should say, to other events – of collecting older photographs and going back to the older residents and getting them to talk about their memories. And I suppose it then grew. Whatever book on folklore tradition you picked up, it had Padstow, Haxey, Abbots Bromley, and so on. So the natural order was to actually go and see some of these."

He elaborated, "And I still go annually – it seemed rude not to in a sense, as these people became my friends. And so, very casually, it was pointed out to me that I was documenting the changes year after year after year. In the late seventies, early eighties, I suddenly I realised what I was doing."

After spending a lot of time with Doc at various events, I have found it particularly inspiring to see how he is far more interested in serving the actual communities in which the folk traditions take place, than in any commercial opportunities. In fact, he sees the commercial side as an immense distraction from the work that matters most to him, which is about documenting and celebrating Britain's regional traditions, which exist not because of the establishment, but in spite of it.

To go back to Doc's life story, in my portrait you will see that on the left-hand side of the painting we begin in Torquay, Devon, where Doc grew up. In the background, there're also the Golden Lion pub and the 'Osses of Padstow. This is his "second home", as he describes it, and where he first witnessed the May Day celebrations that kick-started his passion for documenting the folk culture of Britain.

The portrait also shows some of the early equipment that Doc started out with, such as the SLR Pentax, his first camera, from which emerges a staircase with a young Doc Rowe and his guitar, as Doc was also a musician and heavily involved in the musical side of British folk culture. He hitchhiked a lot at the start of his travels, and here he's about to board another piece of early equipment, an Uher reel-to-reel tape recorder, which forms a sort of raft. Another thing that Doc has been consistent about is keeping up to date with the latest equipment, which has acted as a kind of portal through which he can fulfil his drive to document and travel. The raft's sail, with its symbols and socialist colours, represents the period when Doc went to art school and took part in mass sit-ins. He was also part of the folk club scene, worked with the singer-songwriter Ewan MacColl and was active in left-wing politics. The fly on the raft symbolizes a story Doc told me, about how he hopes to be like a fly on the wallpaper within the communities that he documents, but on one occasion he was told, "You aren't a fly on the wallpaper, you *are* the wallpaper!"

You can also see an 8mm Bolex camera in the background, another of Doc's early cameras, which the Earl of Rone is riding in this instance. As the Earl's a Devon-based tradition, I thought he'd fit in nicely as a nod to Doc's origins. The river that runs through the painting is a metaphor for Doc's life, and as we reach the right-hand side of the painting it's flowing off into the horizon, while along the way we can see some of the customs and communities that have meant the most to him. The raft has evolved with the times and now takes the form of a VHS tape. On it, Doc is dressing the Burryman, which shows what an insider he has become over the years in the communities that he documents. In the background, you can see the Forth Bridge, a representation of South Queensferry, which is a very special community for Doc.

In the foreground, there are two Abbots Bromley horn dancers from two generations, Jeff Bradbury and his son Jamie, to represent the passing down of the customs between the generations. The recent sad passing of Jeff, who is also at the centre of my painting about the Horn Dance, also represents the loss of people who Doc has encountered along the way and who he often speaks about. Jeff, I know, was particularly important to Doc.

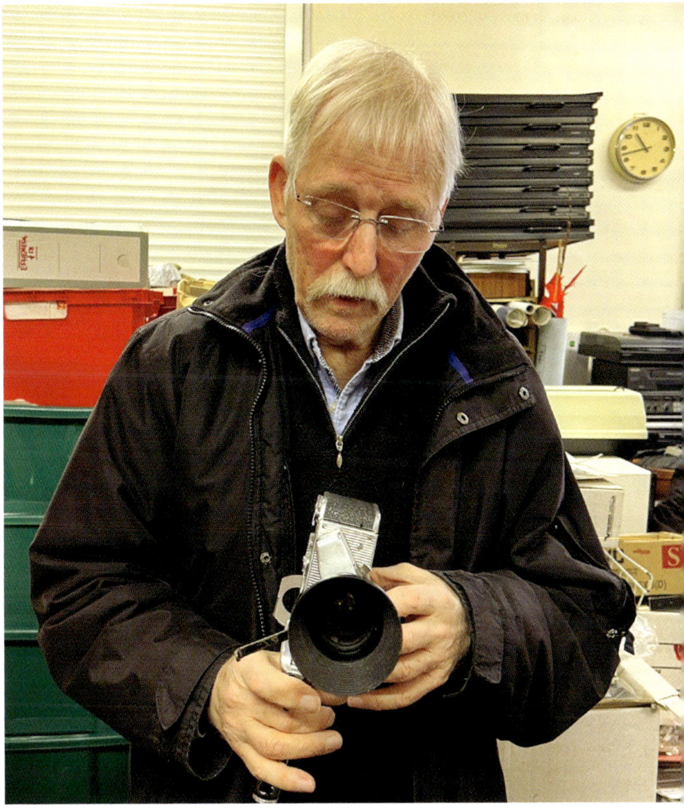

We then have Whitby Abbey and the tradition of the Penny Hedge, a local custom that Doc has been involved in for decades and which represents where he lives today. You can also see the Kings Arms of Haxey, one of the main pubs (aka "goalposts") that Doc is very vocal about keeping as part of the tradition, despite landlords trying to turn buildings like these into flats. You can also see the Fool with the "hood" leaning out of the top window.

Next, there's a Straw Bear wandering about and a barrel runner who unknowingly smokes the Fool in the window, further highlighting the creativity and uniqueness of Britain's ever-evolving, living and breathing regional traditions. Then, to finish things off, we have a GoPro camera and gimbal, representing Doc's open mind and his desire to keep up with the latest equipment. Here, his hand rises up from the meandering river of his life like a mythical sea creature heading to the horizon, as his journey continues, equipped with the latest technology. I think it's safe to say that Doc's contribution to British folklore is unlikely ever to be matched and there will never be another quite like him.

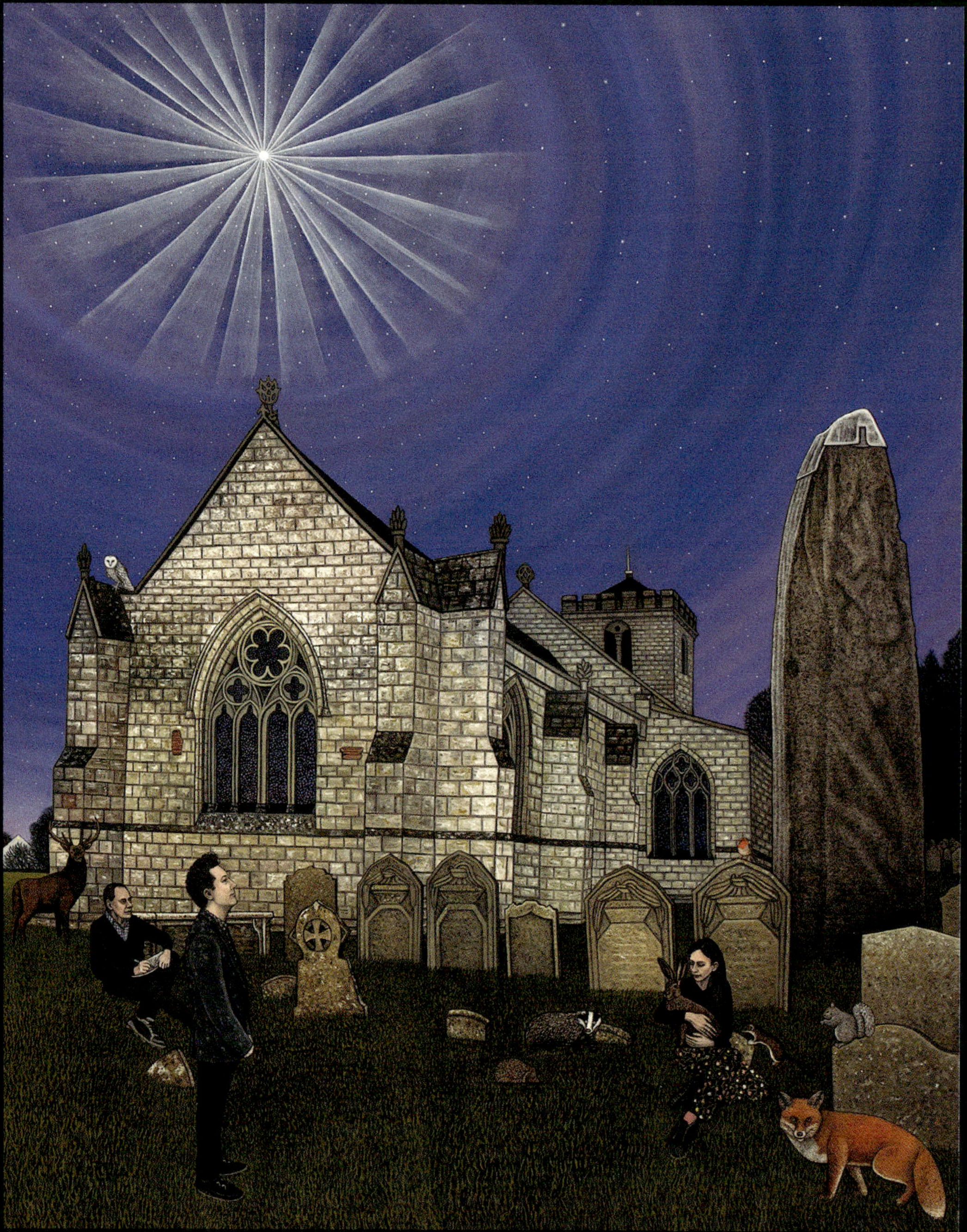

DREAMING AT RUDSTON MONOLITH

Oil on Canvas, 100cm × 85cm

2024

The Rudston Monolith

EAST YORKSHIRE

EARLY MARCH VISIT

It was time for my next stop in Yorkshire and I was on my way to Rudston, where the tallest standing stone in Britain has stood for over four thousand years; and where the world has shifted and changed beyond recognition all around it, so that today it finds itself surrounded by gravestones in the local churchyard.

From the moment that I first saw pictures of the monolith standing triumphantly next to the church, I'd dreamed of visiting it. For me, it said so much about religion: the fact the two stand side by side, both rooted in humankind's attempt to understand the great unknown, the cosmos and creation itself. However, this strange combination of distant relatives begs so many questions: how did the Christians accept this Pagan monument within their churchyard? Was there some kind of local legend, some tale of black magic associated with it that meant people were too afraid to take it down? Maybe it was incorporated into Christian worship? I'd heard stories that a cross once sat on top of it.

As I contemplated these questions, I thought about the ancient community who'd lived here for centuries on end, most likely worshipping multiple gods before eventually converting to a new religious idea – that of the one God of Christianity. Despite this, I couldn't imagine that it was a case of them tearing everything down: surely some of the old ways crept into this new way of worshipping under a different guise. Who knows? But what is known is that this same site has been spiritually significant to countless generations over a period of deep, deep time. A sense of this is further heightened by the four cursus earthworks that lie nearby. These Neolithic structures suggest that the location was perhaps part of a larger complex and its significance was once so great that people felt the need to go to the effort of marking the site with this towering monolith.

The stone itself is believed to have been originally transported from Whitby, from where I myself had just travelled, a journey that had involved a long bus ride, a train and finally a taxi; so however the stone was transported here, it would have taken an immense amount of labour and organization to cover the distance.

I'd first become familiar with this part of the country from the landscapes of David Hockney, who has strong connections with nearby Bridlington and who returned to paint the area in relatively recent years. Today, there was a peacefulness to Rudston. The hand-painted tourist information board gave the village a wholesome, welcoming feeling, while birds chirped from the hedge rows. I decided to head straight to the church while there was still daylight. When I wandered up the narrow path, I was immediately confronted by the giant monolith, which is 7.6 metres (over 25ft) tall. It was awe-inspiring, demanding full attention and respect. Looking at the church and stone together, thousands of years of history seemed to flash before my eyes. Despite having known I would find them together here, I could hardly believe what I was seeing and it took me a moment to process this most unlikely of pairings.

When I walked over to the monolith and peered up at it, its immense size made me think about the work that went into erecting this thing, especially bearing in mind that only prehistoric technology would have been available at the time. As I stared up at it, I couldn't help but perceive it as something phallic, something very masculine indeed, the biggest one in Britain, standing at full attention, telling the universe, "We've arrived and progressed as a species and are ready to start shaping Mother Earth to suit our needs, and are no longer at her mercy!"

It marked the start of something, all these megaliths: it marked the moment when after thousands of years of living like a feather on the land, leaving only ephemeral footprints, people switched to farming and started sculpting the landscape, physically demarcating the domesticated from the wild in an attempt to control it. Nature was othered, especially around the time of the construction of this monument, which dates to the late Neolithic and the early Bronze Age, when people began meddling with the elements and creating new manmade materials by mixing copper and tin to make bronze tools. As much as I feel that a deep sense of spirituality emanates from these monuments of the early farmers, and admire the way in which they honoured the seasons and were far more connected to Nature than our own modern existences are, this was the start of the world in which we live today. A world where we have become severed from Nature to such an extent that we have been taking far more from the land than it can handle, and offering very little back to repay the debt owed.

With all this in mind, I began thinking about the need to return to the nurturing spirit of Mother Nature, and how this lack of balance between the masculine and feminine has gone hand in hand with the destruction of the planet over the past few hundred years. My visit coincided with the very tail end of winter, when Easter and spring were approaching, and I'd been reading about the disputed existence of the Pagan goddess Eostre, who is mentioned briefly by the Anglo-Saxon chronicler Bede and is thought by some to be the deity from which the festival of Easter would later get its name. It has also been speculated that she was derived from a Germanic deity, Ostara, a goddess of fertility who was associated with that magical animal the hare, the predecessor to the Easter bunny. As my mind drifted, I realized I'd received a text from Rose, asking how I was getting on. Still deep in thought and half daydreaming, I imagined her as Eostre sitting at the foot of the monolith, as woodland animals made their way to her and she cradled a hare in her arms.

A short while later, I went into the church where there was a small wall display with information about the monolith, mentioning a dinosaur footprint that some people think exists on one of its surfaces. It also noted that a study of the gigantic monolith during the eighteenth century conjectured that it may be the same length underground as above it.

As I wandered back outside, I received a phone call from my great friend and patron, Stephen Baycroft. Stephen is a writer and philosopher, and we sometimes spend hours on end speaking about the concepts behind my work. He is not much of a traveller, but I always feel his enthusiasm and presence when I am doing my field research. On this occasion, I told him about the stone and its towering presence, and we discussed the idea of the masculine and feminine in Nature. I could hear his pen scratching on paper as I said goodbye.

When I passed in front of the stone again, I imagined him there with me, writing down our conversation and gazing up in awe as the ideas cooked in our heads. I then imagined Rose once more, surrounded by animals that she was nurturing. It was nearly dark by now, and I became slightly spooked by the sounds of breaking twigs and the presence of life in the bushes around me, as I gazed up at the strange piece of lead that had been placed on the stone's tip and which pointed up at the sky. This in turn directed my eyes further up into the cosmos, the great unknown. I imagined the universe, the endless galaxies and stars and everything else. It's the same sky that the people who erected this stone would have been looking at, but what did they make of it all? What was their explanation? As four thousand years of time dissolved, my composition was ready.

The painting itself I have called *Dreaming at Ruston Monolith* and it completes a polyptych of four paintings that will be displayed as one work under the collective title of *In The Weave Of Being*, and which also includes the pieces *Boss Morris at Spring Equinox*, *The Dorset Ooser* and *John Barleycorn Must Die* (pages 266, 218 and 84 respectively).

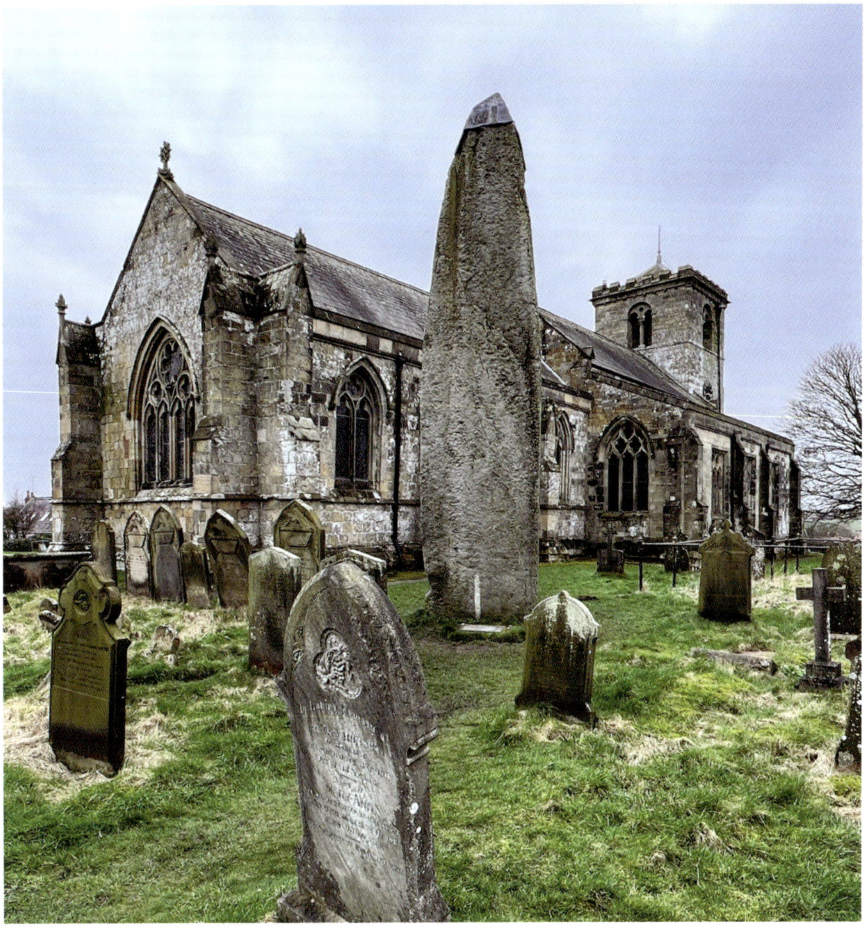

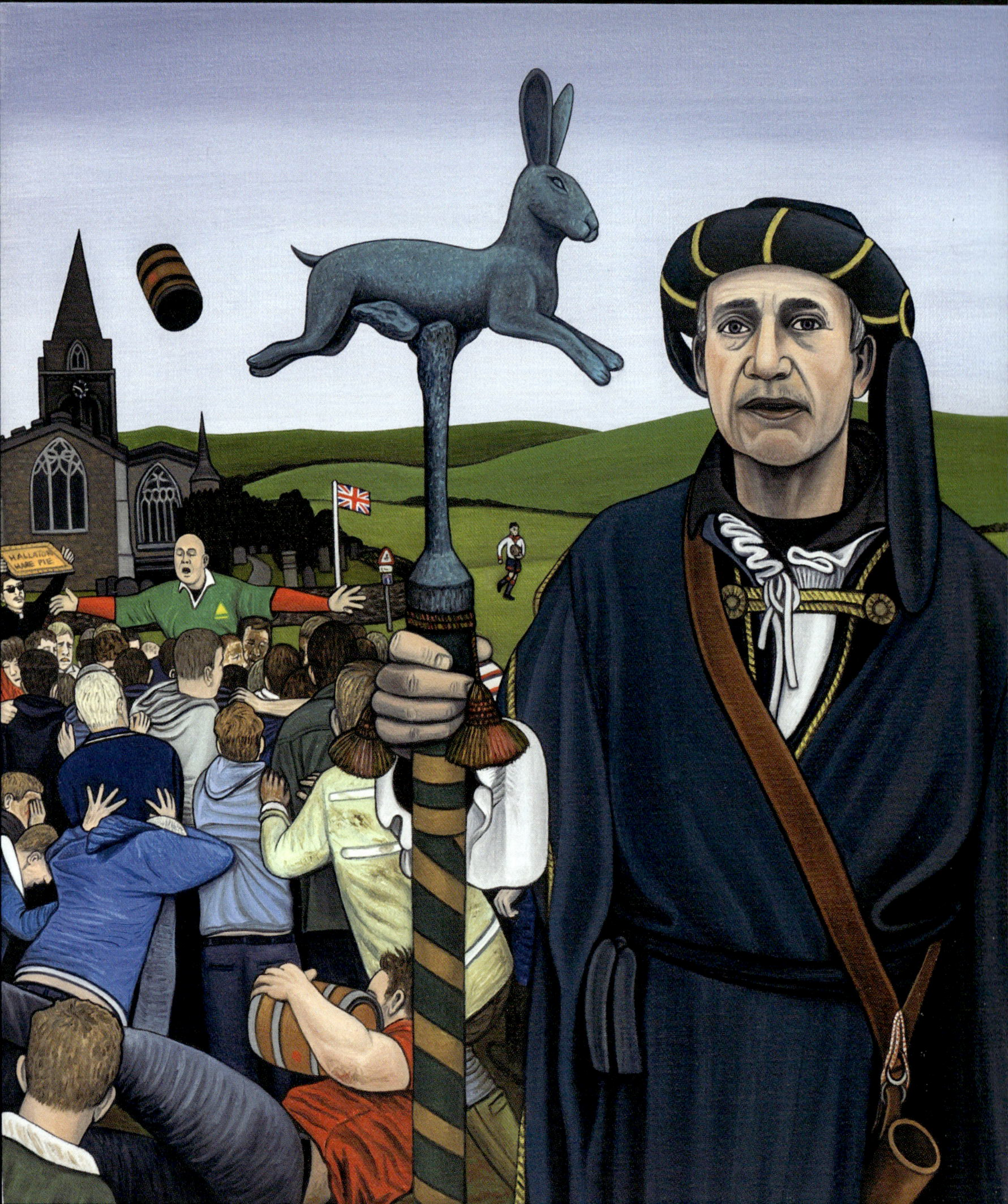
HARE PIE

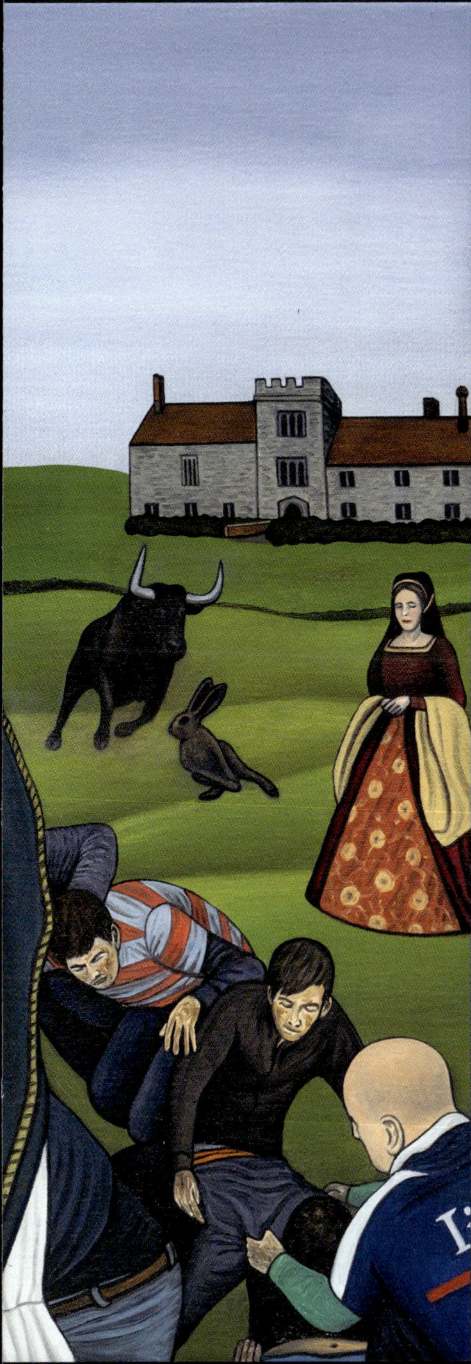

THE HALLATON HARE PIE SCRAMBLE AND BOTTLE KICKING

Oil on Canvas, 50cm × 40cm

2020

Hallaton Hare Pie Scramble and Bottle Kicking

LEICESTERSHIRE

EASTER MONDAY

When I arrived in Hallaton, I followed people heading to the Fox Inn at the top of the village. It was here the procession would begin and a large marquee had been put up, where the band inside were blasting out rock 'n' roll classics. There was also a pop-up bar where a queue had formed, with the vast majority of those in it being broad-shouldered men in rugby shirts, some already holding plastic pint glasses. However, one figure didn't fit this description and that was a man dressed in Tudor costume with a long green robe, a large medieval-style hat and a puffy-sleeved white shirt. He was also carrying a long staff with the figure of a hare on top.

I approached him and, with his permission, began to take pictures. When he smiled, I asked him to please keep a straight face, explaining I wanted to use the photos as references for a painting and he'd be an ideal central figure for my composition. He seemed pleased and told me his name was John Morrison, and that he was the "Warrener" who'd be leading the day's procession. It turned out he was also a local historian and had written a book on the tradition. As the band broke into a Jimi Hendrix song, we walked somewhere quieter and he told me what he knew about its origins.

"What you see today I've traced back to about 1600," he said. "Previous to that, I think it was a religious ceremony, which goes back two thousand years, to the time of the Hallaton Treasure found on the hillside.

"But the tradition we see today came about some five hundred years ago, when there was open land rather than the fields we see today. One day, two ladies were out walking, when they realized that they were being chased by a bull. They started to run and of course the bull ran after them. But luckily a hare jumped up. The bull became distracted by the hare and chased after it instead, forgetting about the ladies, who got away.

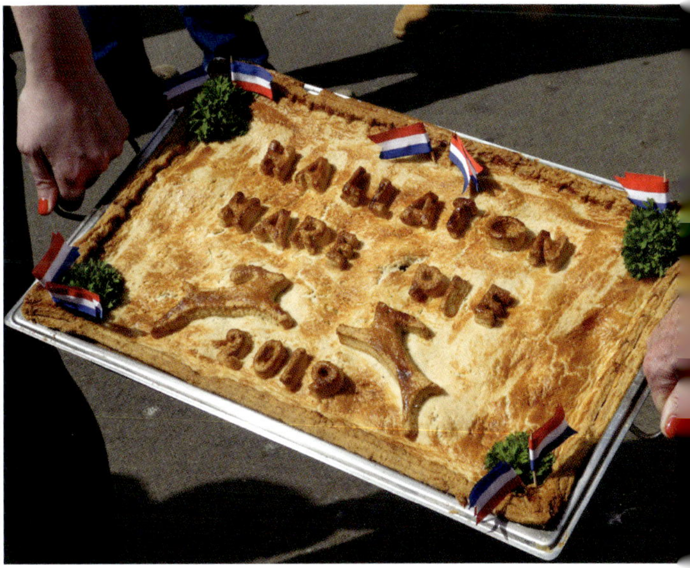

"Well, they were relieved that by the grace of God they'd escaped from what looked like certain death, so they wanted to commemorate this in a befitting way. They persuaded the lord of the manor to give a bequest on their behalf to the church of Hallaton, which was a portion of land that now we call Hare Crop Lees. It's on the hill where the game's going to start in about an hour's time.

"The bequest was on condition that the rector supplied two hare pies on Easter Monday, a quantity of ale and two dozen penny loaves, and that he preached a sermon, which is exactly what we have today. That ceremony started then and melded itself with a religious ceremony that was already in existence, and there was free food and free booze in these two little barrels that we call 'bottles' in this part of the world.

"Nowadays, there's three of them: the middle bottle is actually a solid bit of painted wood. It was introduced in about 1835, because the lads of Medbourne, the neighbouring village, started thinking, 'Oh, there's free food, free beer going!' And they came over and started scrapping for it, so the challenge between Hallaton and Medbourne was born about

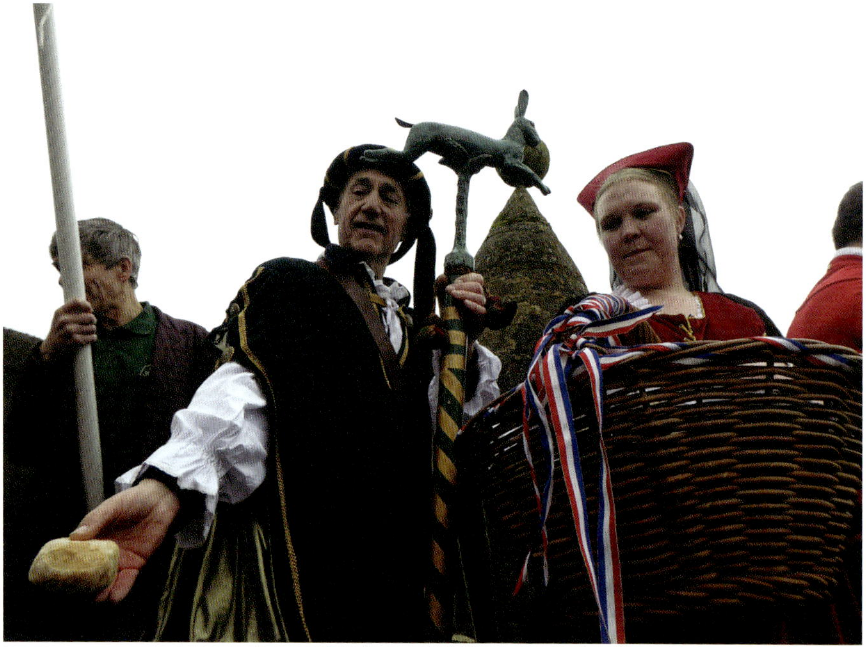

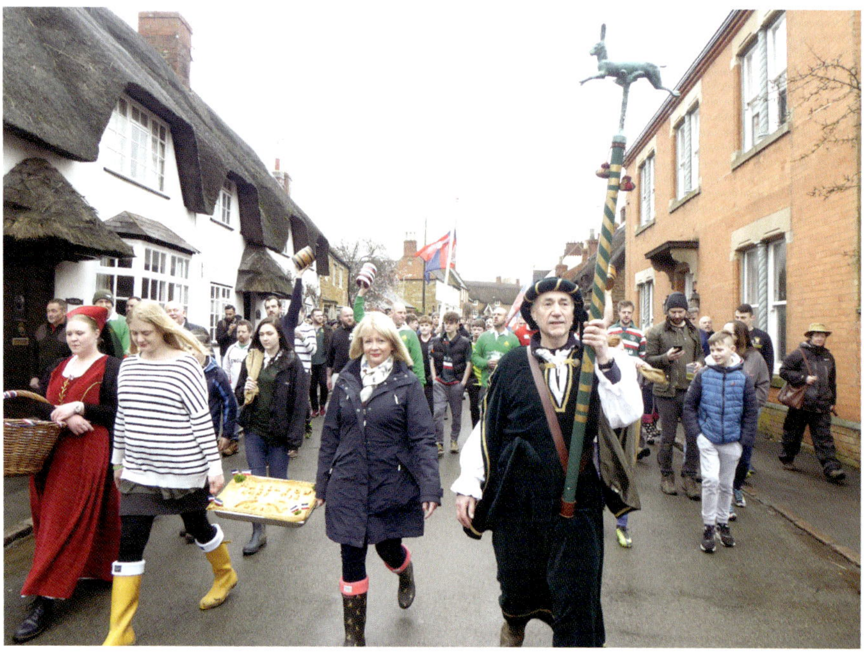

then. But of course you can't win the best of two and the red and white dummy bottle was made, so you could win the best of three.

"When you start at the top, the first of the three barrels is thrown up in the air three times, then someone tries to run off with it and of course they end up being rugby tackled. A big crowd gathers and you might have five hundred or even a thousand people all trying to scrummage for the bottle. To win, they have to get the bottle down from the top of the hill, across their brook – in our case, it's across Hallaton Brook, in Medbourne's case it's across Medbourne Brook – and if you do that then you've won that bottle. And if you can do that with two out of the three bottles, then you've won the contest for the year, and you get to keep the bottle, or at least the village does.

"Then they come back on to the green, climb onto the Butter Cross – that's the conical thing down by the Bewicke Arms – and they get the right to drink the beer, and that's the procession and the ceremony you see today."

When the Warrener finished his explanation, someone handed him a pint and told him the event was about to start, so we headed into the road, where people had begun to gather. A lady in a red medieval costume, holding a basket of penny loaves, stood next to the Warrener on a raised platform. In front of them, three thickset men held aloft a barrel a-piece in one hand. A man with a thick mane of hair and bull-like shoulders in a striped rugby shirt seemed particularly focused, there to win. Bagpipes struck up, as did a marching drum, the Union Jack was waved alongside the local Hallaton flag, and the procession began to wind its way through streets of thatched houses and new-builds. It felt like a march to war, and for some people that's exactly what it was.

The procession stopped at the village monument of the Butter Cross, where the penny loaves were handed out. We set off again and approached the church where the historic hare pie lay waiting. It seemed harsh that the pie was made using the same animal that'd saved those two ladies on the hill. Later, I got chatting to a New Age traveller type with a stained front tooth, curly hair and wide-open eyes, who told me, "It's sacrifice, all this: the hare symbolizes the old Pagan goddess Eostre. They used to sacrifice hares to her and all sorts up on the hill. It's actually beef, though, now in the pie," he added, breaking into laughter.

At the church, where the vicar stood waiting, the huge pie was blessed and then cut into pieces. "Who wants some hare pie, then?" came the shout, and the pieces of pie were launched into the air over the crowd, who grabbed chunks and ate what hadn't fallen on the floor. With the pie now dispatched, the procession started its way up the hill.

After passing hedgerows busy with nesting birds, we entered a field. Some of the pie had been put in a sack, which was now ritually emptied. As bits of pie were chucked once more in the air, someone shouted, "Oi, that went in my pint!" A huge crowd had gathered by now; at the centre, a bald man holding one of the bottles yelled, "Let's get bottle kicking! Bottle one, bottle two, bottle three!" As he threw the bottle on the ground on the count of three, a huge scrum piled in, with people pushing, pulling and thumping each other out of the way.

Men roared like wild animals, with the occasional panic when somebody got trampled. I saw a guy's shirt torn from his back, another being nearly knocked out and walking hazily away from the crowd, while another spat out a tooth. Some were shouting the name of their village: "Come on, Medbourne!" The crowd was forced down a slope, the momentum was out of control as bodies slammed into bushes and fences. The scrum was locked, with arms trying to burrow beneath it to grab the bottle, run with it and make some ground.

The crowd then bulldozed through a hedge, left flattened onto a neighbouring field. Back in the open, the scrum was moving quickly again, and I found myself right in front of the barrel. As I stepped back, concerned for my safety, a man was knocked out cold; his friends pulled him out of the fray, hoisted him up and dragged him off. Every now and then, a fist came flying, with old feuds being settled on a day where lawless violence was allowed.

I got chatting to one of the Melbourne team as he caught his breath at the side of the field. He spat out his gum shield and smiled. "You know the crime rate's lower here 'cause of this: if we have a problem with someone we save it for today." He stuck the gum shield in again and made his way back to the centre. Nearby, girls were getting involved on the edges, some egging on their partners while others were getting properly stuck in. The scrum fell again, and this time some people seemed seriously hurt. When they got up, one whose trousers had been partially pulled down swore loudly, before rolling on his front and nursing his head.

I kept moving with the scrum, and imagining the origin story playing out alongside the game. I could picture this fine woman walking, as the bull charged at her and the hare sacrificed itself to save her. Is she the goddess Eostre that the New Age traveller was talking about? Maybe a Christian variation of her; fun to think so.

It was getting even more violent now. Next to me, a man was crawling along the top of the hedge and waiting to receive the barrel. With a nod at the scrum, he said, "Watch out, mate, you see that crowd – they're about to flatten this bush, and you." I took his advice and he wasn't wrong, so I followed the game through the new gap in the hedge. Tops were off now and expletives flying as layers of injured players were peeled back like an onion by people helping others up. Eventually just a teenager remained flattened at the bottom, gripping his knee in agony.

The game moved back on to open terrain with a constant roar like a choir of rampaging Vikings. The more I immersed myself, the more I couldn't quite believe what I was seeing; there's that feeling of imminent danger, which is almost addictive, and it's a time- and worry-dissolving moment, where you're just caught up in the now. I didn't think I'd like it, but I was having a great time, getting as close as I could to take pictures. Then it happened – hands shoving behind me, it was too late, I was at the centre. "Heave!" came from all around, the crowd collapsed and I was stuck. I could see the barrel, then a pair of muscular arms came in and scooped it up. Someone knocked it out of his hands, there was a fight for it, everyone was up apart from a few of us; they came my way and I took about three or four boots to the chest as I was run over. The wind had been knocked out of me, but someone kindly sat me up and made sure I was OK.

The bottle kicking had travelled quite far by now and I wondered where we were in relation to the goalpost. "Hallaton are making good ground," someone told me. The crowd was now

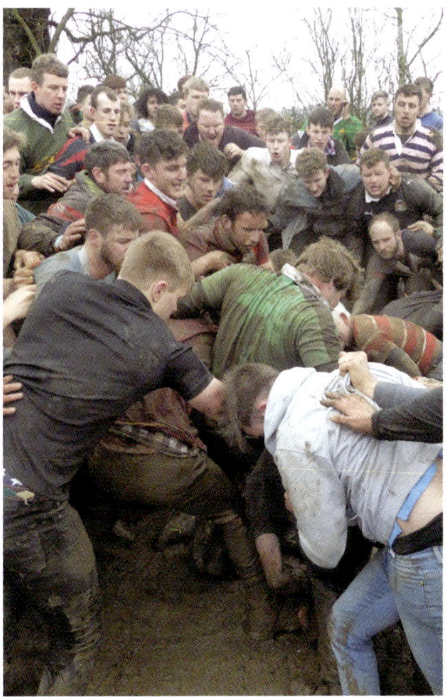

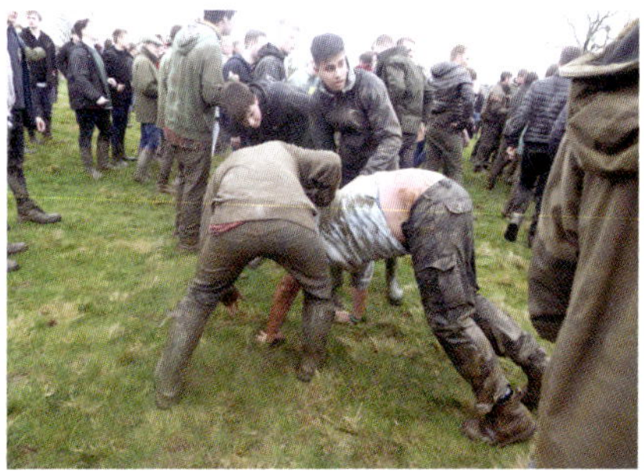

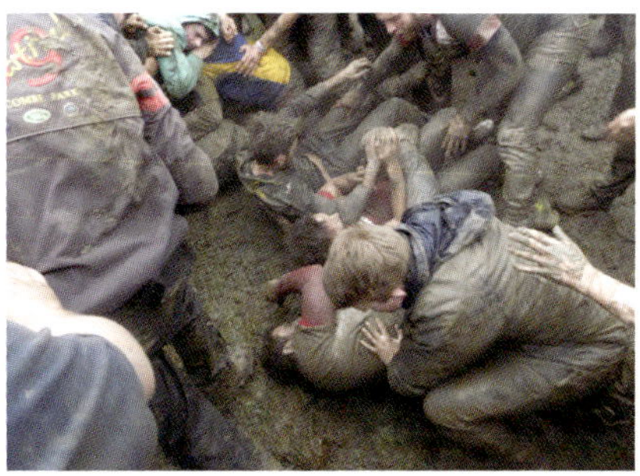

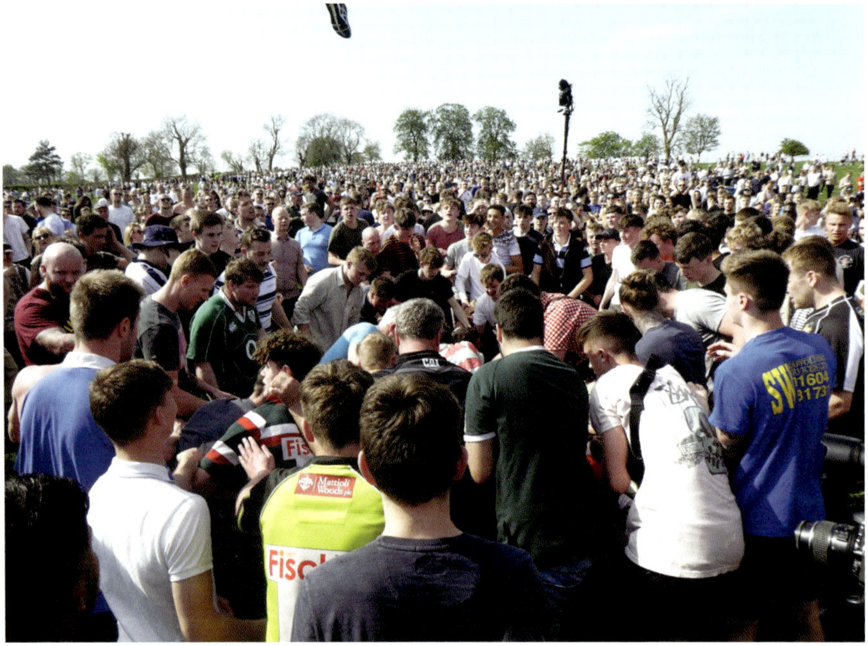
Mattioli
Woods plc
CAT

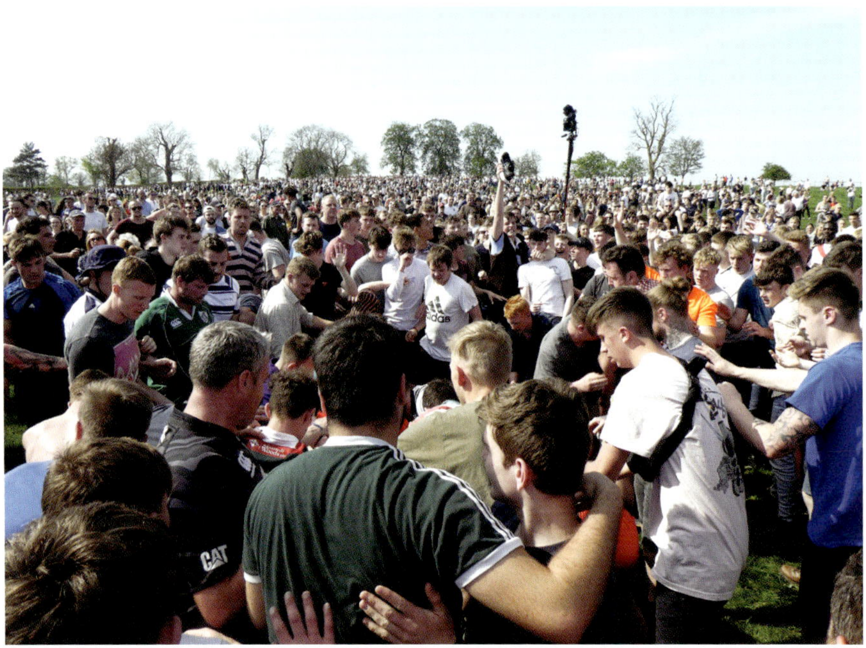
adidas
CAT

literally hanging on a barbed-wire fence, shirts were torn, there were black eyes, cuts and bruises; this was hard core and only the serious players remained. Someone shouted, "Come on, show me your bollocks!"

We entered the next field, with a fenced-off slope at its edge and a stream beneath it. The Hallaton boys were doing all they could to force the crowd toward it. The bull-shouldered man in the striped rugby shirt was still going strong at the heart of it, blood dripping from his nose. Another man walked away grinning, his grin fading as he felt his mouth and realized he'd lost a tooth. The crowd was now being pushed against the barbed wire next to the slope. The bull-shouldered man then suddenly forced his way through and got his hands on the barrel and gripped it with all his strength. As twenty pairs of arms tried to snatch it, he managed to tip it over the fence, where an older man with white hair grabbed it and fell backward down the slope, tumbling while gripping on tightly as a Melbourne player rolled down with him into the stream and Hallaton cheered. The first barrel was theirs.

It'd been incredible, but I wouldn't be sticking around for the next two games. I'd seen enough and my chest and ribs were throbbing. Nevertheless, I managed to chat to a few of the players, including the burly man in the rugby top who'd pretty much steered the bottle home. He told me, "William Web Ellis was the vicar's grandson and he came back every Easter, saw the game and the rest is history, I think." He was referring to the famous incident when William Web Ellis of Rugby School picked up a ball and ran with it, thereby inventing the game of rugby. If that was is true, wouldn't that be an incredible lineage?

For the game to have been started when two ladies were saved by a hare, and who then donated two pies, penny loaves and "bottles" of beer to the church to be divided among the village folk; a gift that was then merged with what some believe to be a very ancient religious festival, and which the neighbouring village, Melbourne, then got wind of; so their men came and fought over the food and "bottles" in what became a refereed mass brawl, which in turn inspired a vicar's grandson called William Web Ellis at Rugby School to pick up a football and run with it … If that doesn't demonstrate how traditions merge and evolve, I don't know what does. This was a story that had be retold and commemorated in the form of one my paintings.

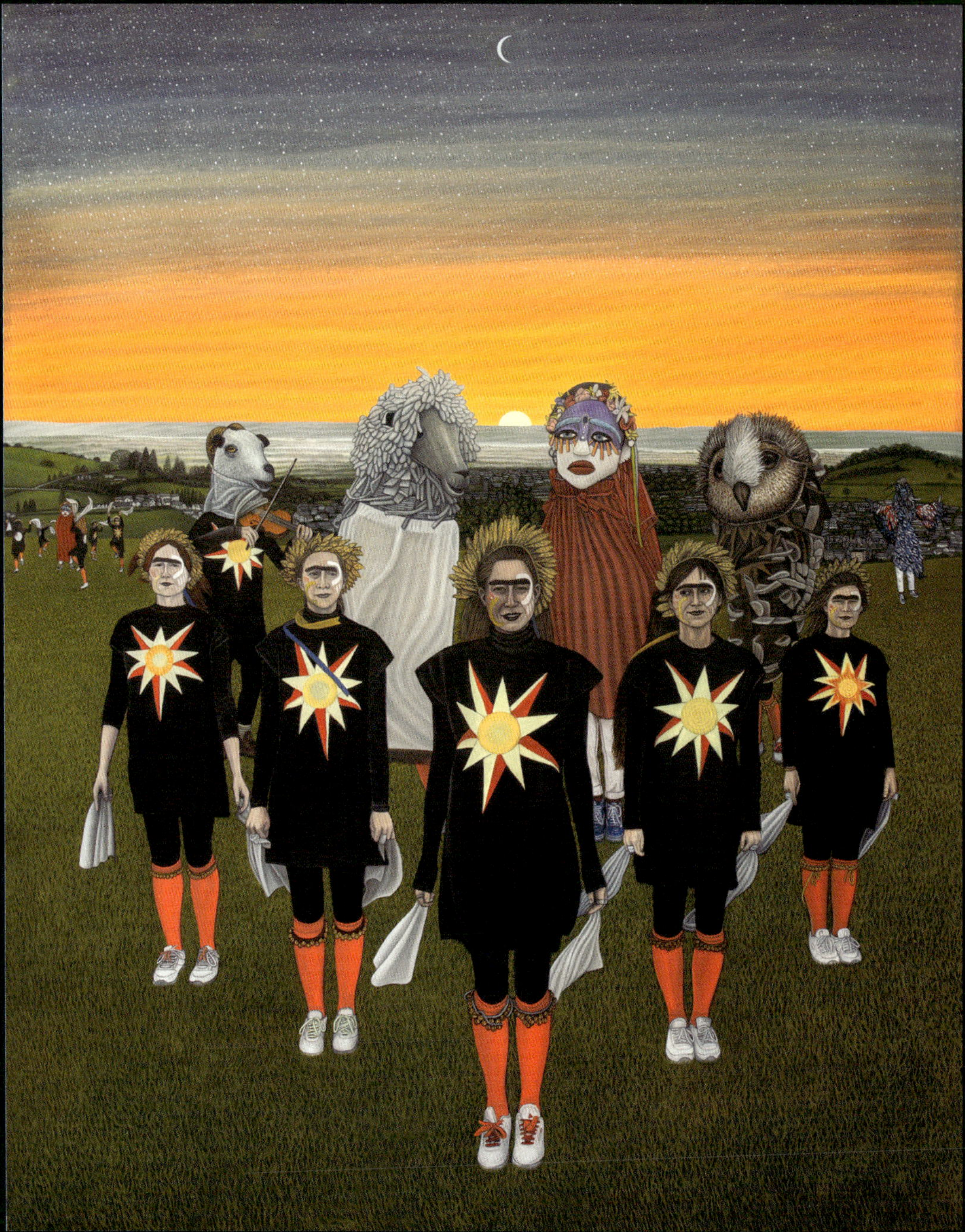

BOSS MORRIS AT SPRING EQUINOX

Oil on Canvas, 100cm × 80cm

2023

Boss Morris

GLOUCESTERSHIRE

SPRING EQUINOX

I arrived in Stroud, Gloucestershire, to meet Boss Morris on the day of the spring equinox, where they would be performing their own private ritual, to which I'd been invited. I first came across this all-female morris side around the same time that I began my own folklore adventure, when I saw a YouTube video in which the group were dressed in red with florescent socks and tassels, face paint, garlands in their hair, and with some hauntingly beautiful handmade masks that included a sheep, a goat, a monkey and a Mother Goddess-like figure that mirrored the group's collective look, as if they were worshipping some kind of female deity. The video had elements of folk horror, the occult, dance culture and dramatic cinematic music that broke out into a rave song. It's safe to say this wasn't something I'd ever seen before; it was fresh, new and exciting. This wasn't just another traditional morris side formed of men in white; this group was a pioneer of what has come to be known as "prog morris".

When I asked her about the group's origins, founder Alex Merry told me, "We're first and foremost a friendship group. My sister instigated setting something up in 2015; she'd seen I'd done morris dancing before, and she really wanted to give it a go. We were ready to start something new, and it felt right to do our own thing, in our hometown. We were keen to draw inspiration from things that excited us and not feel constricted by tradition."

What I found to be different about this popular side was they were a group of female creatives who weren't afraid to adapt traditional dances in unique ways that help make morris dancing seem more inclusive, forward-looking and relevant today. Their outfits were a mishmash of influences, inspired by both traditional morris as well as contemporary fashion and pop culture. Somehow they managed to evoke a sense of nostalgia for simpler times, while appearing to be free of the shackles of tradition. This combination left me questioning the importance of an unbroken lineage within traditions. Since the beginning of time, people have expressed themselves through ritual and ceremony in order to make sense of and to celebrate life, and align themselves with Nature; from what I could see, Boss Morris represented one of the most contemporary manifestations of this very human instinct, and I could immediately tell that what they were doing was important, so I invited them to appear in a music video for the song "When I Leave" by the band Fat White Family, which I worked on the art direction for.

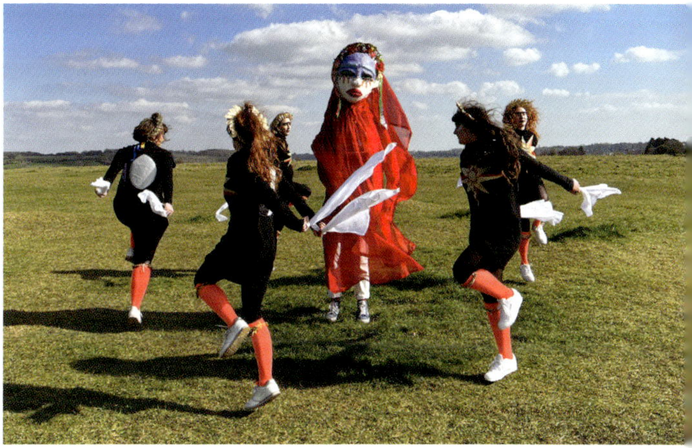

But now it was time to celebrate the spring equinox with them. As the door of Alex's house swung open, I could already hear the excitement and jingling of bells as the Boss Morris dancers got ready, pulling up their bright orange socks and tying bells around them like garters, before slipping on white trainers. It's no surprise to discover that the majority of the group are fellow artists; the creativity was pulsating around the room. You could see it in the attention to detail in all the costumes, made from local wool, on which symbols had been lovingly handstitched by members of the group: a red and yellow sun on the front, and a moon on the back, to represent the equinox as a time of equal day and night. Each outfit depicted a different moon phase, so the whole group represented the entire moon cycle, highlighting how individual chemistry and creativity comes together in one collective force.

Boss Morris member Rhia Davenport explained, "We were all working professionally as artists, makers or craftspeople, utilizing our skills as a means to make money, so it felt like we had this pent-up creative expression that we needed to find an outlet for. It organically became the perfect way for us to channel all our wilder artistic energies, especially as we were feeling a bit frustrated as creatives having to toe the line of turning our passion into a trade to make money. Boss is a way for us to do what we didn't realize we needed to do to cope with being grown-ups and re-discover creation as a means of pure joy."

Then it was time for their face paint, the finishing touches you could say. This involved a spontaneous discussion, with everyone chipping in ideas. The final design also mirrored the symbolism of the equinox, with the sun on one side of the face and the moon on the other, finished off with a giant black mono brow, the reasoning being, as one of the group said, "I don't want to look pretty."

Upstairs came the clunk of a metal ladder being unfolded from the attic, as the "beast" heads were brought down carefully, ready to celebrate this day of balance. It was now time for Boss Morris to assemble on Rodborough Common, a beautiful strip of land high up on rolling hills with a spectacular view of the Severn Vale below. It was the perfect spot on this bright and sunny day to watch Boss Morris mark the equinox. A series of dances were performed as the group joyously laughed, whooped and skipped their way around one another, waving crisp white handkerchiefs in to the air, while their fiddle player dressed in a goat's mask played along to the sounds of the jingling morris bells.

Aware that I was witnessing perhaps the most contemporary version of morris dancing currently on the planet, I was particularly struck by the appearance of a beast called Ewegenie, whose large sheep's head gently swayed in the breeze: juxtaposed against the view of the valley where the wool industry once thrived for generations, it reminded me that Boss Morris are very much a product of the surrounding landscape and regional culture. As dancer Lily Cheetham put it, "What we do and make and how we think about things has evolved to relate to the place we live in, to the land and culture that we're interested in." With this in mind, I knew this view would have to feature within the painting and so would Ewegenie. And I didn't want to miss any of the dancers out as the chemistry of the group is so strong; it's very much a coming together of the right personalities that seem to complement each other and create this feeling of joy, community, family and collaborative creativity.

Above all, for me the importance of Boss Morris is the feeling of female empowerment that they seem to harness and release into the world. Our folk culture is undoubtedly still very male-dominated, and for that reason I also felt that the equinox, a time of balance where day and night are of equal length, was the perfect metaphor for how Boss Morris can inspire us to realign ourselves with Nature, ritual, creativity and a much needed feminine energy.

Around the same time that I completed my painting *Boss Morris at Spring Equinox*, the group were invited to dance at the Brit Awards as part of a performance by the band Wet Leg, highlighting the recent boom of interest in British folk culture. It was also probably the first time that the relatively new phenomenon of "prog morris" had been shared with a mainstream pop audience, marking a culturally significant moment in the history of morris dancing and British culture as a whole.

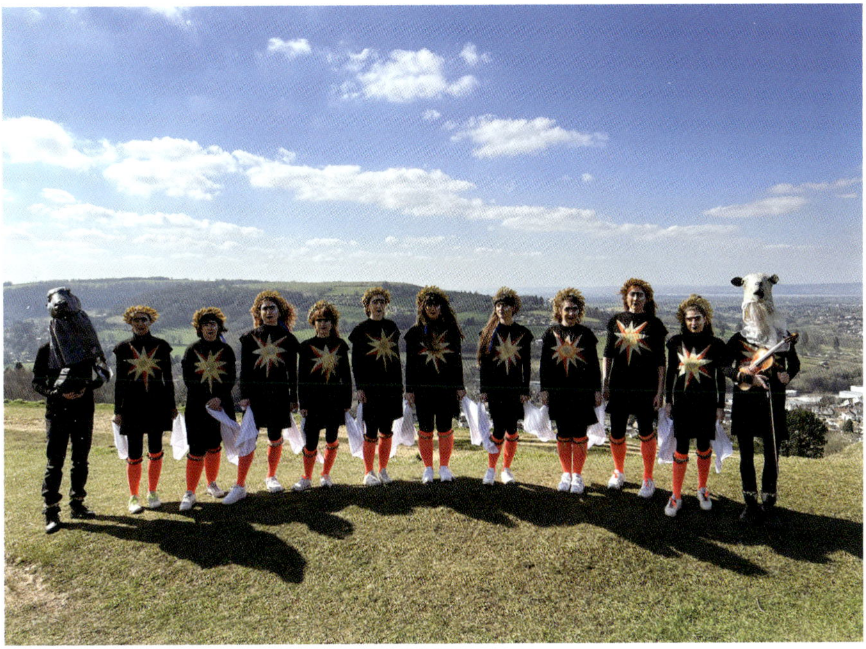

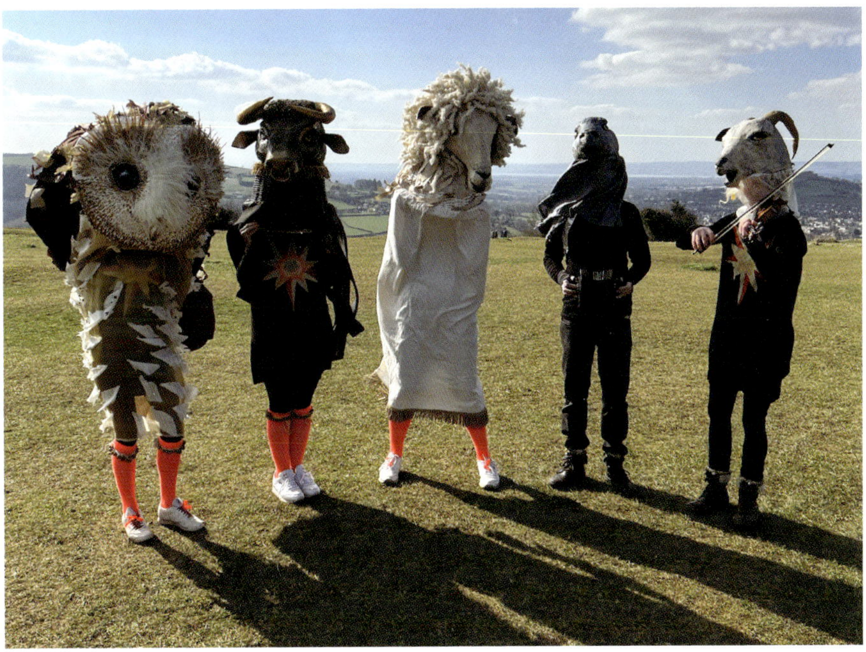

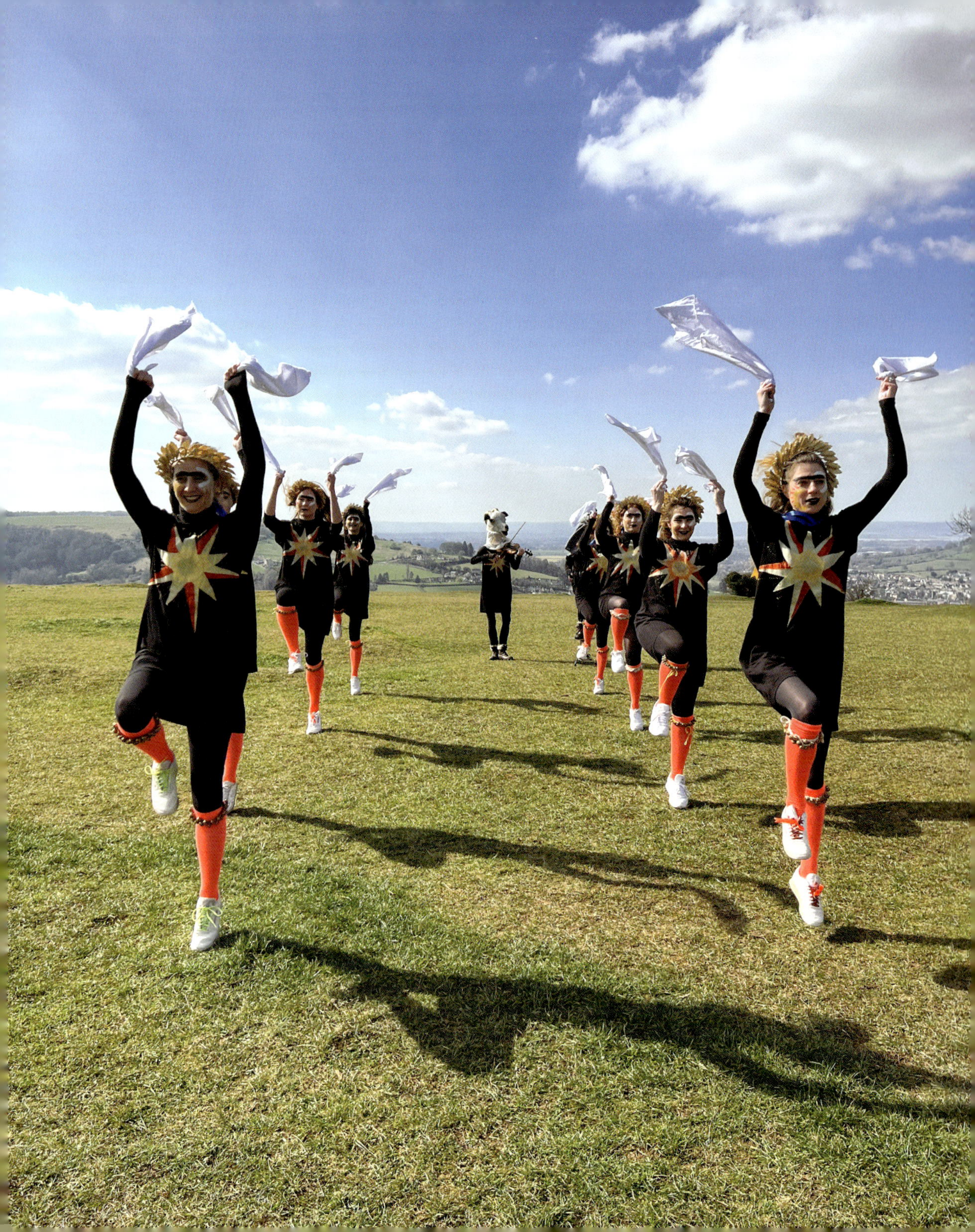

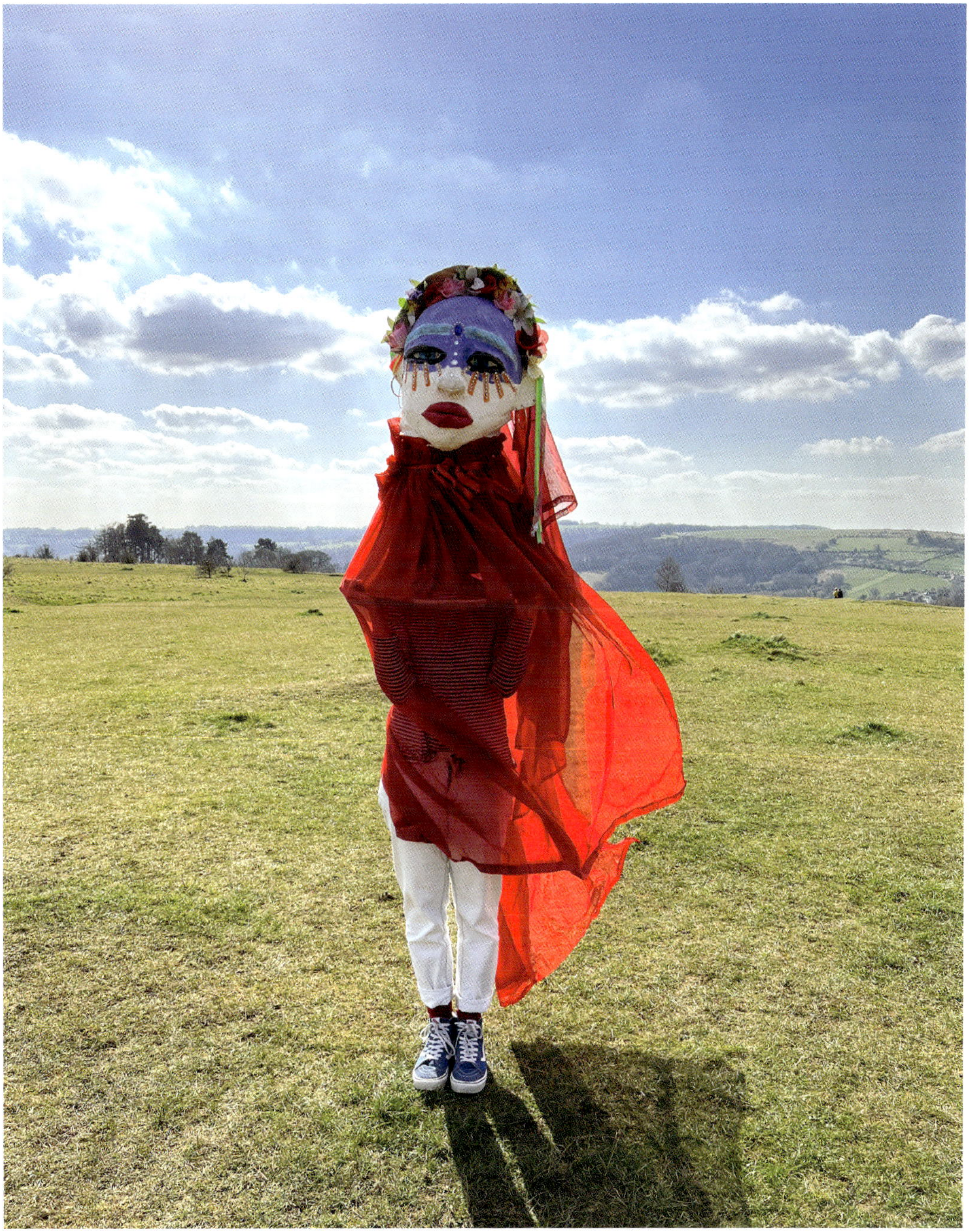

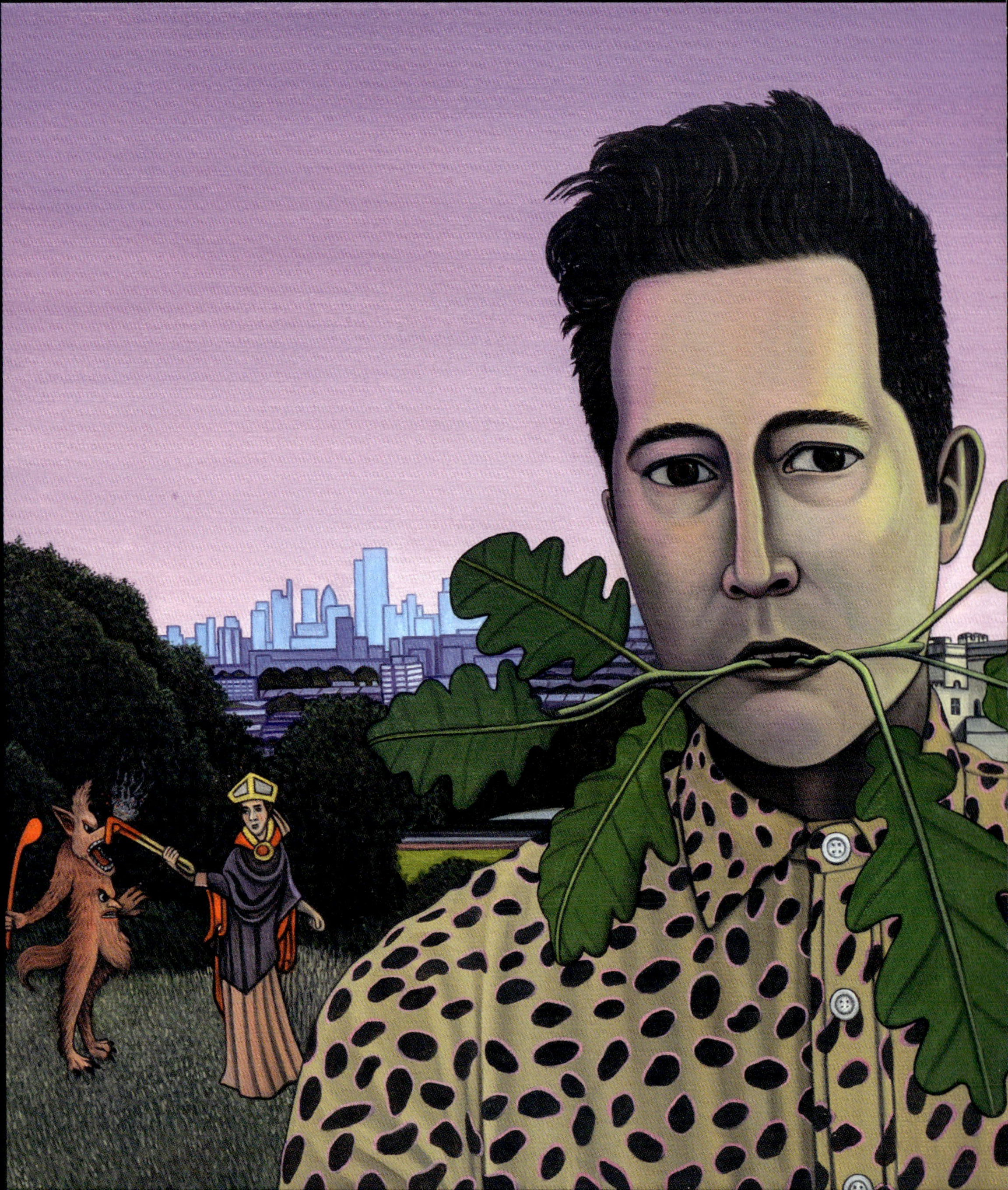

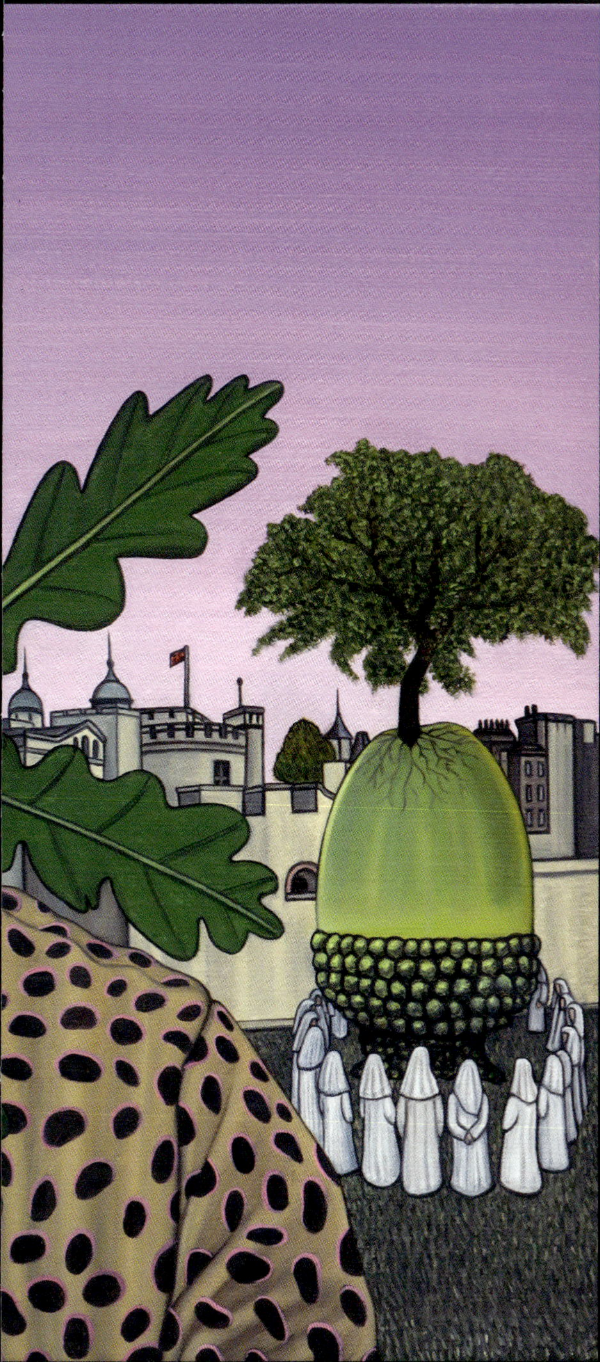

IN MY NATURE (SELF-PORTRAIT AS THE GREEN MAN)

Oil on Canvas, 55cm × 40cm

2021

Conclusion: Ritual Britain

The wheel of the year turned once more from equinox to equinox, and I had now spent what felt like a lifetime on what I'd come to call the frontline of folklore. I had thrown myself headfirst into a serendipitous, life-changing project and created a series of twenty paintings, completed in the winter of 2020, which I duly named *Frontline Folklore*. There was an accompanying film of the same name, which my friend and collaborator Angelica Jopson, who'd joined me on some of my field trips, edited with my assistance during the first lockdown.

With this body of work now complete, I was ready to exhibit it to the world. I decided to approach Simon Costin, having become familiar with his nomadic Museum of British Folklore collection. Despite various attempts, it had yet to find a permanent home, highlighting the lack of value placed on folk culture by the British establishment, and I wanted to see whether Simon would be interested in showing some of his vast collection of costumes, Punch and Judy dolls, and many other weird and wonderful artefacts alongside my work. I thought it'd make the ideal partnership: having been so inspired by the participants in the customs, the folk artists themselves, I felt it was important for them to be represented in my exhibition through the actual ritual objects and costumes that they had used and worn, not just through my depictions of them. To my delight, Simon agreed and I set out to find a suitable venue to house the exhibition.

This proved to be more difficult than I'd imagined. After approaching well over a hundred potential collaborators and receiving only a handful of replies, with the general gist being "thank you for sharing your work, we enjoyed looking at it but the subject matter is to niche for our audiences", and now realizing that it'd be hard to come across mavericks who were willing to take a chance on an exhibition that championed the culture of everyday people, we followed our gut feeling that this show just had to happen. Undeterred, Simon, Mellany Robinson (also part of the Museum of British Folklore) and I decided to hire a space ourselves and put on the exhibition no matter what. Again, this was another challenge, with the prices to hire spaces in London being extremely high and in some instances plain ridiculous. However, when we found the Crypt of the St Pancras New Church, somehow it made total sense.

When I turned off Euston Road, and entered a gate onto the gravel carpark of St Pancras New Church, I was confronted by a line of caryatids, architectural figures directly inspired by the giant female figures that support the roof of the Erechtheion temple in Athens. I placed the clunky key in the heavy metal door, turned it and pushed the door open. Inside, as I walked down the stairs, the smell of trapped damp air from the crypt hit me. When I wandered through the arched cave-like tunnels, alcoves and dark brick rooms where the dead were once laid to rest, it was absolutely clear that this was the ideal venue, and the fact that it was a church inspired by a Pagan temple made it seem all the more fitting. We all agreed this had to be the place for the show that we would call *Ritual Britain*.

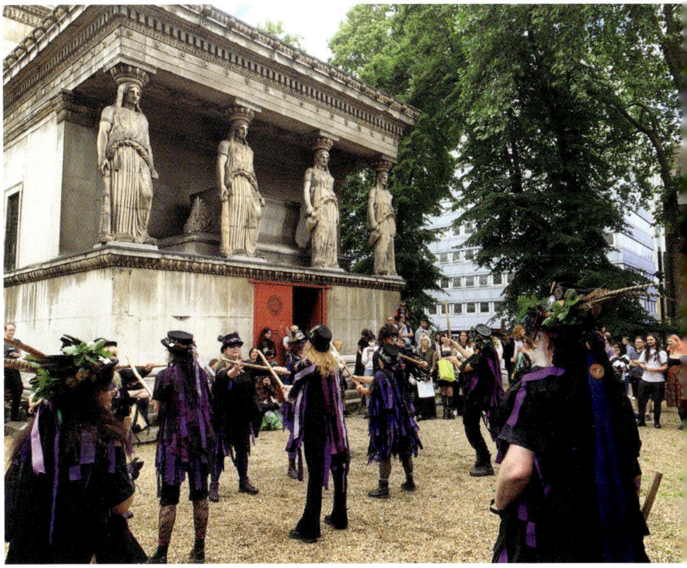

Simon's a renowned set designer and curator, which made me feel in very safe hands when taking on such an unconventional space. The venue now confirmed, we were booked in for the summer of June 2021, but then Covid cast a cloud of uncertainty over everything. Somehow the stars aligned and the exhibition took place between the two main lockdowns of 2021, when an art- and culturally starved nation were ready to re-immerse themselves in the world. Serendipity had come through for me yet again.

I had spent the months prior to the exhibition on the rampage, contacting everyone and anybody who I thought might be interested, including the press, who were remarkably responsive. Angelica helped me make a press video, in which I spoke of my Druid epiphany and how the exhibition came about, which proved to really catch the imagination of anyone who opened my emails. And my follow-up messages, in which I abbreviated "*Frontline Folklore* Series" to "FFS" in the subject line, seemed to work a treat for those who'd missed my email the first time round. Simon also used his platforms, including the Museum of

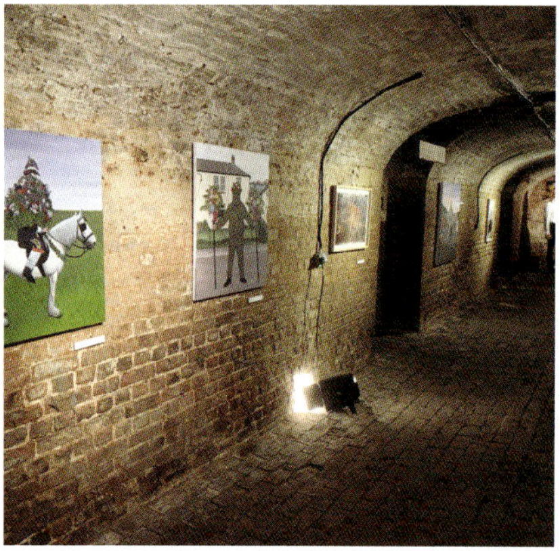

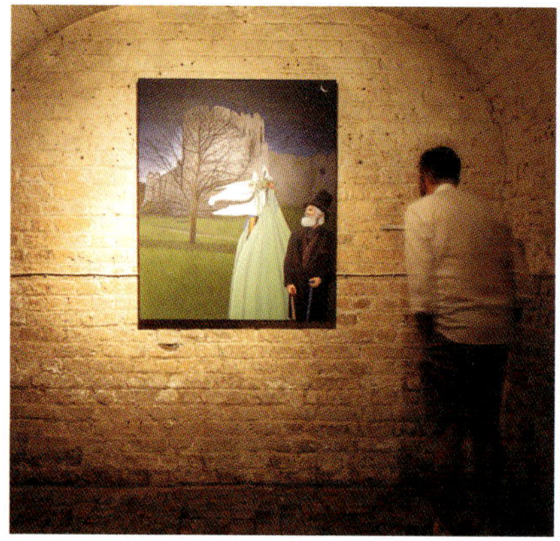

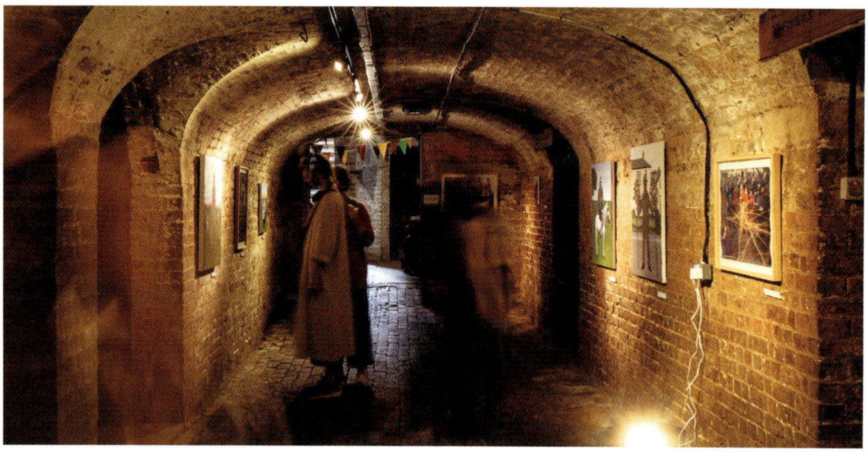

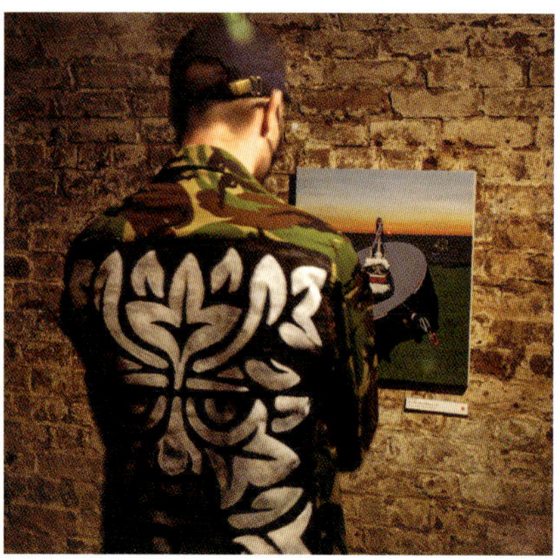

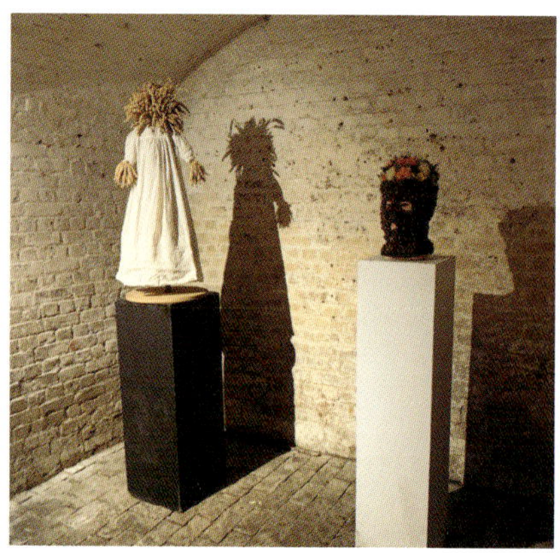

Witchcraft and Magic, which he's the director of, to spread the word.

Once set up, the show looked spectacular: the combination of the various mediums and the immersive setting of the crypt made it a visual feast that tantalized the senses. It was now opening time and after having three huge banners made to advertise the show, which we attached to the iron railings around the church, we were ready to open the doors. The banners proved to be a godsend, as many people on their way to the nearby Wellcome Collection, or coming out of Euston station saw them and were overtaken by curiosity.

On the first day that we opened our doors to visitors, little did we know what was in store for us in the month ahead. From then until the show's closing, there would never be a moment when the venue was empty. We created a rota but I couldn't keep myself away and spent every day there – and I'm glad I did, as it proved to be one of the most exciting and life-affirming experiences I've ever had. Word spread, people started sharing pictures on social media and the show went viral. We never knew what to expect or who would arrive and large queues started to form, as people from all walks of life waited patiently to be admitted, including on one occasion a group of modern witches who performed purification rituals before entering the crypt. Eventually the queues were so long that they wound all the way up Euston Road.

Over the weekends we invited special guests, and staged a discussion between Simon, Mellany, me and the broadcaster, writer and DJ Zakia Sewell, whose four-part series *My Albion* had recently been broadcast on Radio 2. We then had a celebration of morris dancing, in which Boss Morris danced and spoke, and there was a screening of the film *Way of the Morris* by Tim Plester and Rob Curry, who also took part in the discussion. The writer and folklorist Jeremy Harte of the Folklore Society gave a talk, and there were talks, too, by Simon and me throughout.

Toward the end of the show, visitors had begun arriving from as far afield as Scotland, and the crypt itself was getting more and more packed, with queues forming inside too. This came to a head on the final day, when the Black Swan Border morris side performed outside and the vicar of the church tried to close the exhibition early because of concerns about the Covid restrictions. Thankfully, this didn't happen as we settled on a "one in, one out" policy, which made the queues stretch to the point where I was amazed at people's patience and perseverance to get into the show.

When we finally closed the doors, I held back the tears. I felt shell shocked – I think we all did. This was the first time in my life I had completely followed my instincts and fully committed to doing things DIY. It was life-affirming, to say the least: like folk culture itself, this exhibition existed completely outside the establishment, and any claims that it would be too niche were most certainly disproved by the overwhelming response of the ten thousand or more people who'd visited the show. I've also received numerous emails since from people who say the show was a huge influence on them and a great help with funding applications, as they could now point to clear proof of the thirst for, and interest in, Britain's criminally unsung and neglected cultural heritage. It was undoubtedly my proudest moment and one it's taken me a long while to recover from; in fact, I'm not so sure that I have to this day.

There followed a period of deep self-reflection. As described earlier, when I started my adventures in folklore, it had been at a very dark time in my life, in which I'd been very depressed, experienced family tragedy and lost my job as a labourer. I knew wholeheartedly that things couldn't get any worse than that dark night of the soul, and I'd burned any boats and bridges that could lead to any other way of life for me than that of an artist. It was what I truly wanted to do and I'd never, ever considered the possibility of not going full-time with it one day, although what I'd imagined had been an easy transition with my work suddenly being championed by a major gallery and me making loads of money. But despite the lack of financial stability, I found that once I'd made that decision lots of serendipitous moments kept occurring all around me. I was at my own kind of inner equinox, you could say; somewhere between the darkness and light.

This has been a journey of healing, self-discovery and finding my life's purpose, and I have never looked back since. And I've continued to experience inexplicable coincidences that highlight to me that I'm on the correct path and exactly where I should be. Although I don't subscribe to any specific belief system or organized religion, one thing that I do know for sure is that I believe in the great unknown – and that's enough of an explanation for me.

I've come across the symbol of the Green Man almost everywhere I go – in my grandfather's woodcarvings, in plaques on the houses and doors of the communities I've travelled to, as characters in rituals and processions, and, of course, staring down at me from the dark corners of ancient churches, including right at the very beginning of this story, when his leafy face watched over me and the Druids from All Hallows-by-the-Tower at spring equinox. He is even incorporated in the Victorian houses in the part of London where I live, where I've found over two hundred representations of his face, including four on the front of my own building. Everywhere I go, it seems that the Green Man is watching me and, as you'll be aware by now, I've come to think of him as a kind of sign.

Whenever I finish a series of works, there's always a feeling of relief; but you can't help but look forward to what will be next, and I always take this transitional period as an opportunity to paint a self-portrait, with the Green Man and his symbolism sitting very much at the forefront of my mind when I go to work. For me, the Green Man is not just a symbol of ancient religion, death and rejuvenation, but a symbol of recovery; from within him new life grows, represented by the foliage that appears from his mouth. He also reminds us to be at one with our own nature and to accept who we are as individuals, and that we are part of the natural world and not above it: by abusing it we are abusing ourselves. These sorts of ideas led me to write the "Art 4 Folk" and "Folklore Activist" manifestos (see pages 284–5), sets of principles that I hope will inspire others, too, to awaken their own inner artist and set out on their own creative folklore adventures.

With all these thoughts in mind, I considered my folkloric journey so far and what it has done for me on a personal level. I saw that I had followed the wheel of the year and moved from the darkest days of my own winter into what had begun to feel like psychological summer, in which the light returned and the joy of being alive came back to me. It was no coincidence that this story began on the spring equinox, which sits in perfect balance between the dark depths of the winter and the bright, long days of midsummer.

I had found my life's purpose; I had found myself, my true self. I felt good about who I was and where I was – a feeling that I could not have imagined before all of this. And as I reflected and sat down to paint my self-portrait, I felt something rising from the pit of my stomach; I choked slightly as my lips were forced open and the tips of leaves began sprouting up through my throat and out from within my mouth.

I should have been terrified but it felt as natural to me as breathing; the tormented soul that once stood on Primrose Hill in my last self-portrait was now unrecognizable to me. Everything around me made sense, I knew where I fitted in within it, the leaves had unfurled and I was at one with my inner nature, my true self revealed.

I was reborn.

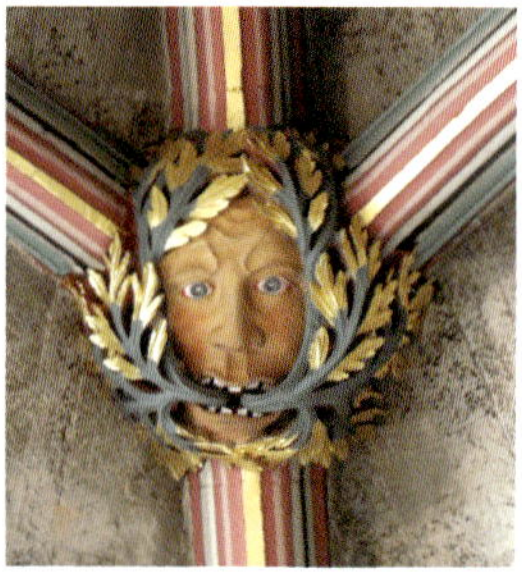

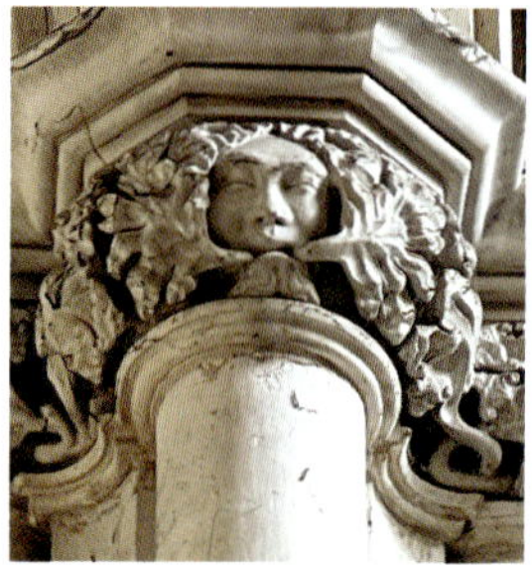

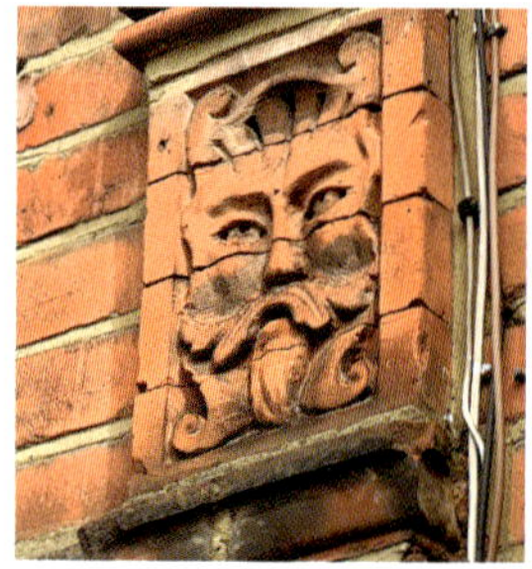

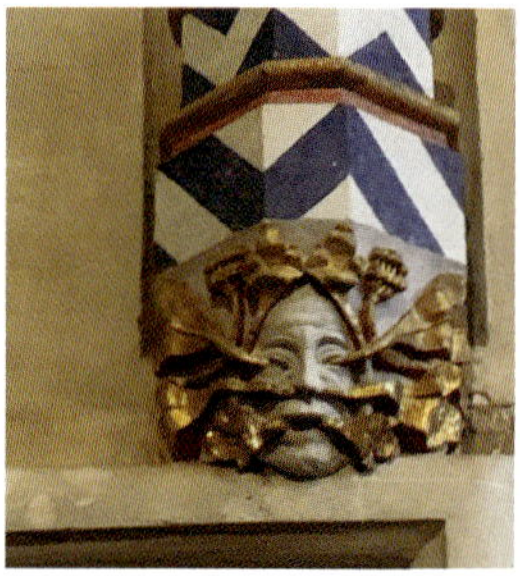

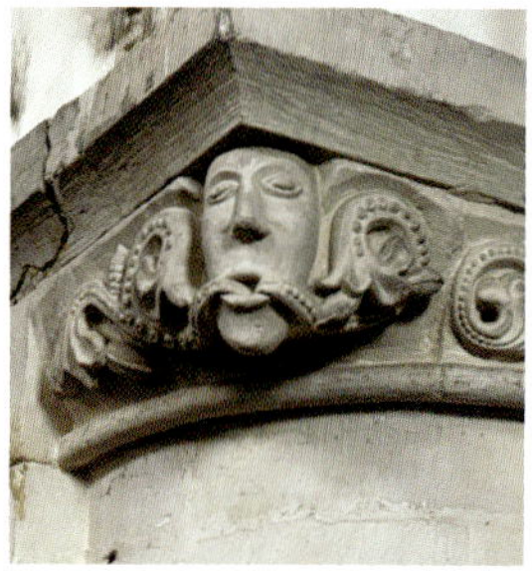

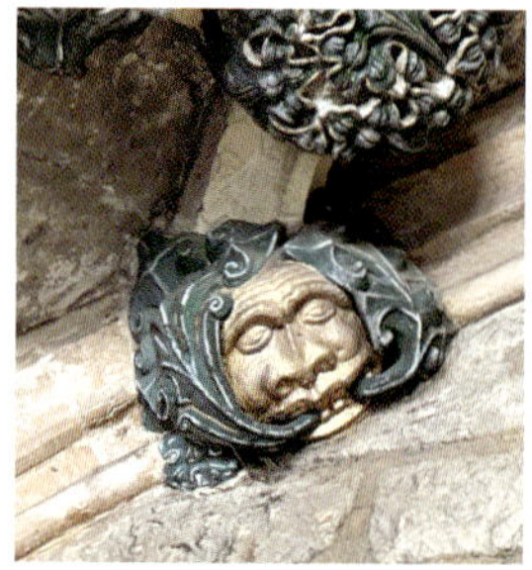

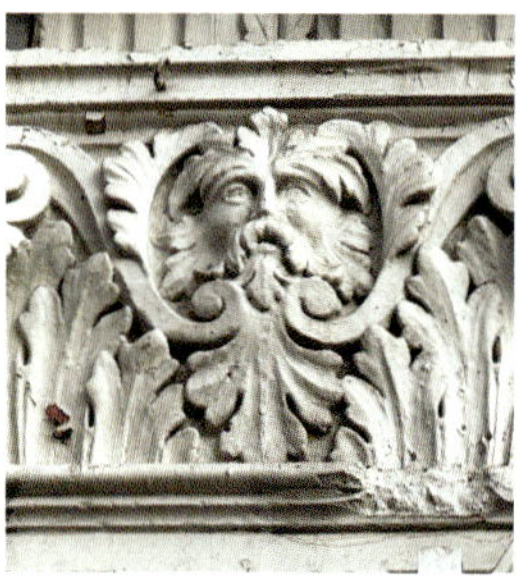

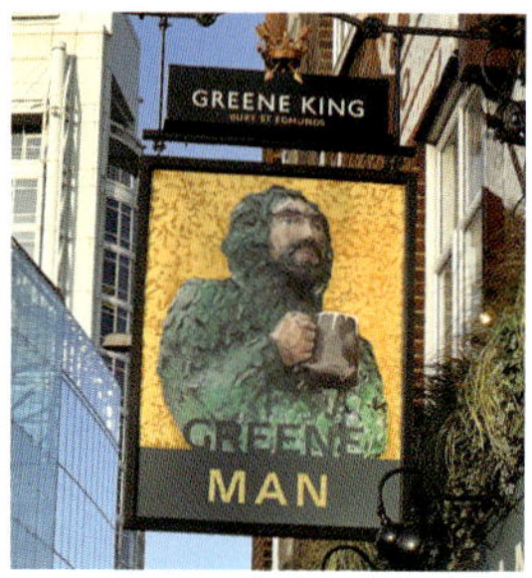
GREENE KING
MAN

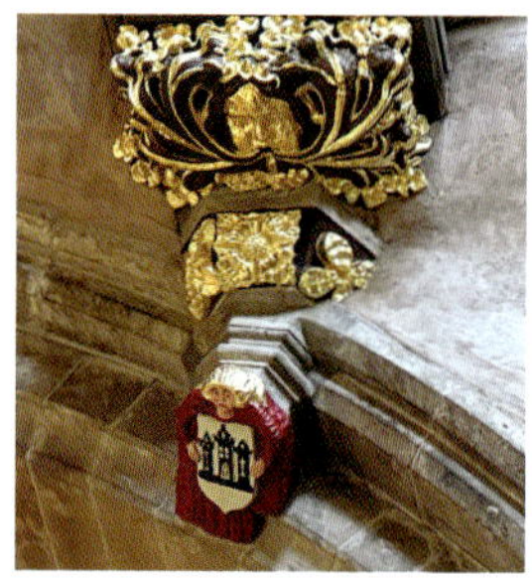

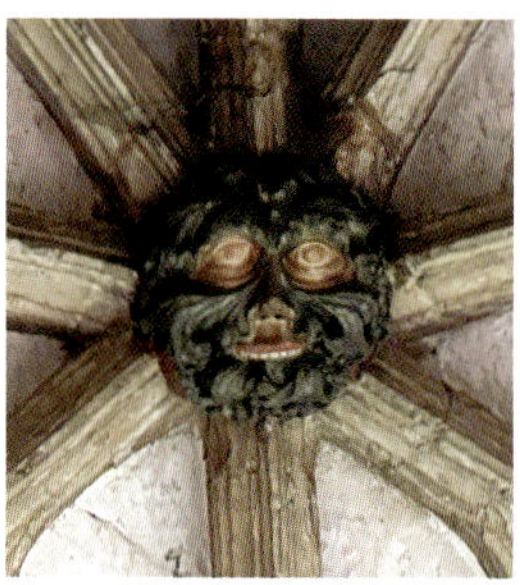

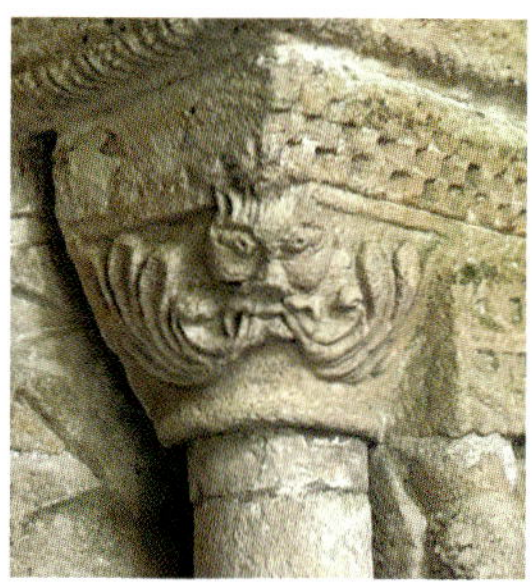

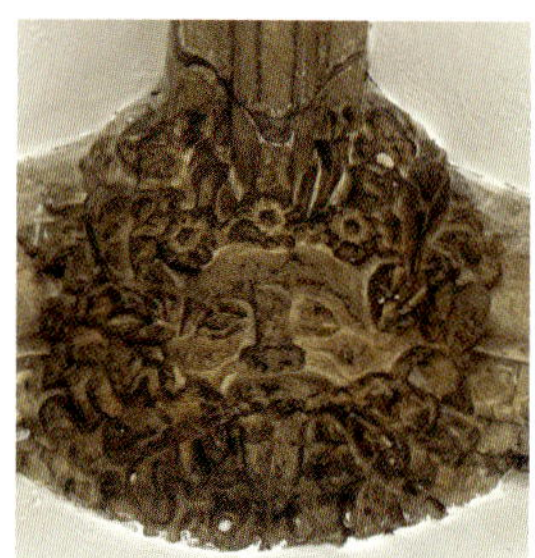

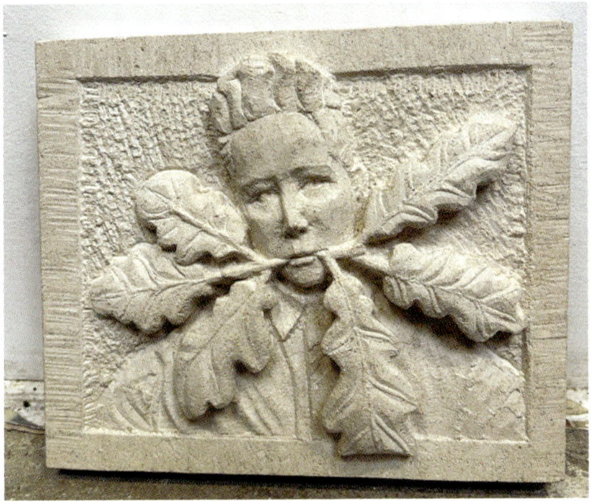

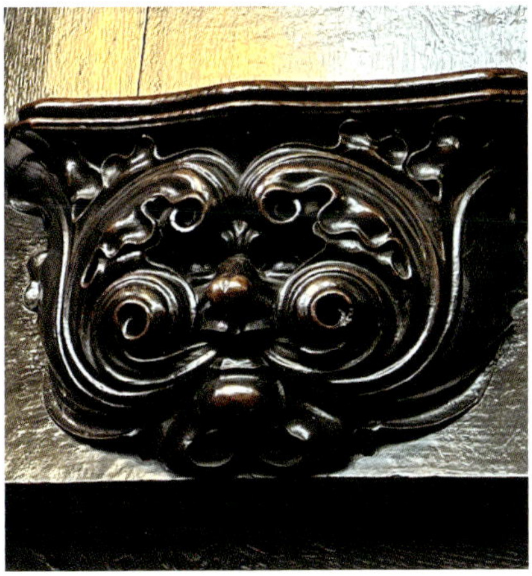

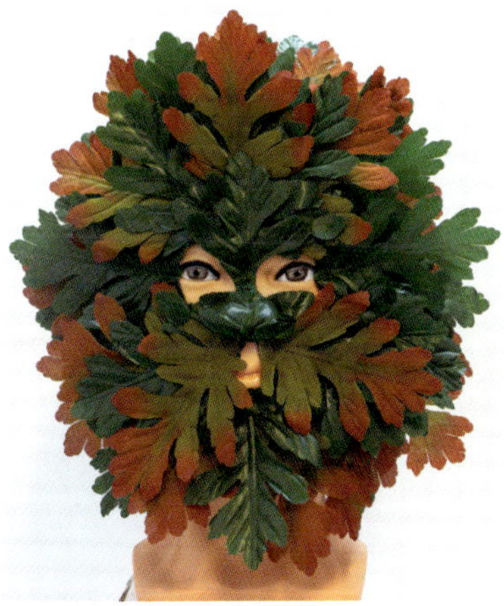

GREEN MEN

Opposite, in order of appearance: Exeter Cathedral; York Minister; Shoot-up Hill, Kilburn, London; Ottery Saint Mary's Church; St Nicholas-at-Wade Church; Magdalen College, Oxford; Cricklewood Broadway; Greene Man Pub, Euston Rd, London; St Mary's Cathedral, Edinburgh, Scotland; Canterbury Cathedral; St. Swithins Church, Quenington, Gloucestershire; St. Cuthbert's Church, Wells, Somerset
Above, in order of appearance: *Self-Portrait as the Green Man Corbel Carving* (crafted by Cats Eye Carving); Westminster Abbey; *Foliate Head* by Ben Edge, 2021

Appendix: The Folklore Rising Manifestos

FOLKLORE ACTIVIST MANIFESTO

* Folklore is the traditional beliefs, stories, songs, customs and art passed down orally by ordinary people, whose voices have survived against all the odds in spite of attempts to eradicate them from history.
* Folklore questions the colonial mindset to only see historic truth and value in the accounts of the educated classes and oppressive regimes who had the privilege of the written word.
* Folklore is a universal phenomenon, in which we celebrate our collective shared humanity and joy of being alive while simultaneously celebrating the never-ending uniqueness, individuality and creativity that can be found within regional cultures around the world.
* Folklore reclaims art and creativity as necessary human endeavours for everyone and not just for the select few.
* Folklore manifests itself through skilled craft and regional culture and by doing so is an antidote to capitalist mass-produced, mono culture in which the value of the individual is disposable and all high streets are the same.

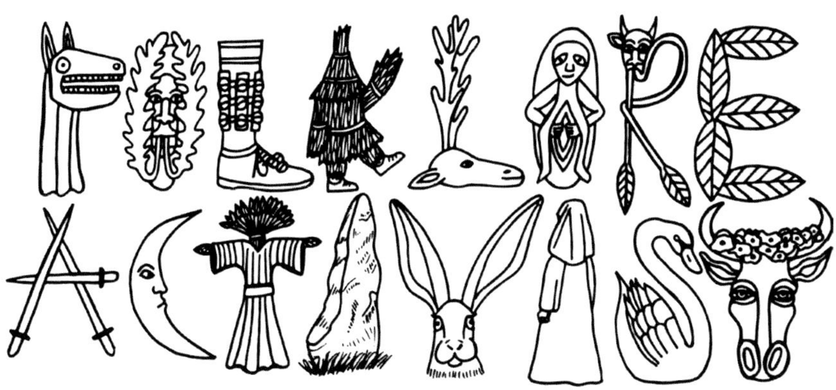

* Folklore encourages us to actively remind ourselves that we are part of Nature and most importantly not above it. Taking the time to celebrate the wheel of the year is a radical act of reconnection and defiance in the face of climate change.
* Folklore proves that we don't need gods to be spiritual, and that creation and destruction are forces that lie within each of us.
* Folklore, much like the history of Britain itself, is an ever-evolving mongrel that contains the ephemeral remnants of everyone that has ever told it, retold it, lived it and breathed it. A living entity that connects us to the past, present and future, constantly changing and adapting through time.

ART 4 FOLK MANIFESTO

* Art is an extension of Nature.
* Art is not just for white walls and the privileged.
* Art is the messiah within. Obey the messiah within ...
* Art for one, art for all, art for folk.
* That is all ...

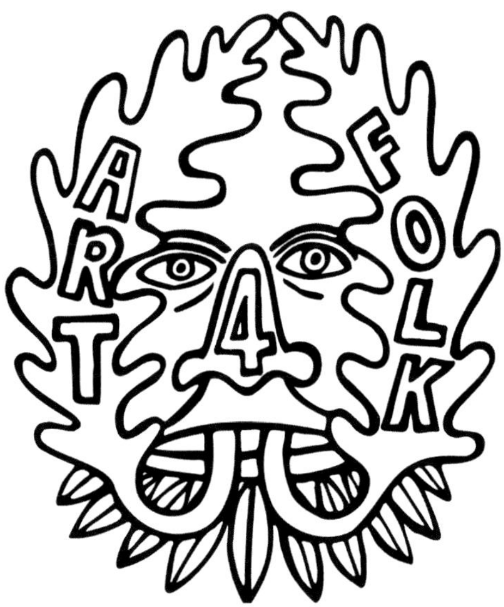

Acknowledgements

I dedicate this book to my wonderful wife, Rose Spencer. Her never-ending love, encouragement and companionship continue to inspire me to grow and become a better version of myself on a daily basis.

I would also like to thank and acknowledge the following people in no particular order:

Stephen Baycroft, for his time, generosity and regular discussions of the intellectual ideas around my work. David Harrison, for reminding me to always look up and notice the magic of everyday moments. Anne Ryan, for my first proper studio, giving me the space to take my work to a new level. Patrick Couderc, for seeing something in me that no one else had, bringing me out of my comfort zone, and for taking me to Le Palais Idéal, a life-changing trip. Anton Forward, for being my first companion in visiting the folk customs and for the healing camper van holidays. Angelica Jopson, for editing the *Frontline Folklore* film and on-going collaboration. Kathryn Roberts Parker, for the musical collaborations, academic knowledge and stimulating discussions. John Spencer, for the writing retreat in the Vale of the White Horse, where I wrote this book. Patrick McArdle, for being an early enthusiast of my work, bringing me over to Pittsburgh, USA, and for his infectious love of art and outsider culture. Doc Rowe, for cultivating the film side of my work and for opening many doors along the way. Simon Costin and the Museum of British Folklore, for the opportunity of *Ritual Britain* that has been a turning point in my career. Sharon Ament, for the encouragement, guidance and generosity. Sylvie Tata, for documenting my work from the very beginning, and for the photographs of my art in this book and the additional photos of the *Ritual Britain* exhibition and profile picture. Weird Walk for collaborating and championing my work. Fiona Robertson, for approaching me to create this book and without whom this book would not exist.

I would also like to thank the full team at Watkins who have been incredible and seamless to work with, and this includes: Alice Coleman (Designer), Rebecca Wright (Cover Designer), Karen Smith (Head of Design), Daniel Culver (Watkins Editorial Manager and Head of Digital), Sue Lascelles (Copyeditor), Steve Williamson (Proofreader), Lisa Footit (Indexer), Christiana Spens (Publicist), Hayley Moss (Marketing Assistant), Laura Whitaker-Jones (Head of Marketing and Publicity), Monica Mistry (UK Sales Manager), Lauren Strange (US Sales Manager) and again Fiona Robertson (Publisher).

I am grateful to Holly EJ Black, Charlotte Mullins, Jerry Saltz, Jarvis Cocker, John Higgs, Dr Jennifer Wexler, Dr Neil Wilkin, Maxine Peake and again Weird Walk and Sharon Ament for endorsing this book and for all the individual encouragement that each of them have shown.

I'd also like to thank my Dad, Steve Edge, for the art of storytelling. My Mum, Fiona Edge, for the independence of spirit. And them both, for the creative childhood, love, laughter and encouragement to follow my own path and vision. I'd also like to thank my brothers and sisters, family and friends and all those that have believed in me and been a constant source of inspiration. Lastly, and importantly, I want to thank all those who keep their traditions alive.

About the Author

Ben Edge is an artist, songwriter, film maker, author and folklorist, whose work depicts the extraordinary lives of ordinary people. Ever since serendipitously stumbling on a Druid ceremony at Tower Hill, London, Edge has been obsessively documenting the seasonal customs of Britain and beyond, establishing himself as a rising star in both the art world and as a leading voice in what he describes as the "Folk renaissance". In 2021, Edge displayed his *Frontline* series at the Crypt gallery of the St Pancras new church, in an exhibition titled *Ritual Britain* that attracted over ten thousand visitors with extensive media coverage and viral exposure across social media. Find out more at benedge.co.uk and on Instagram @ben_edge_art

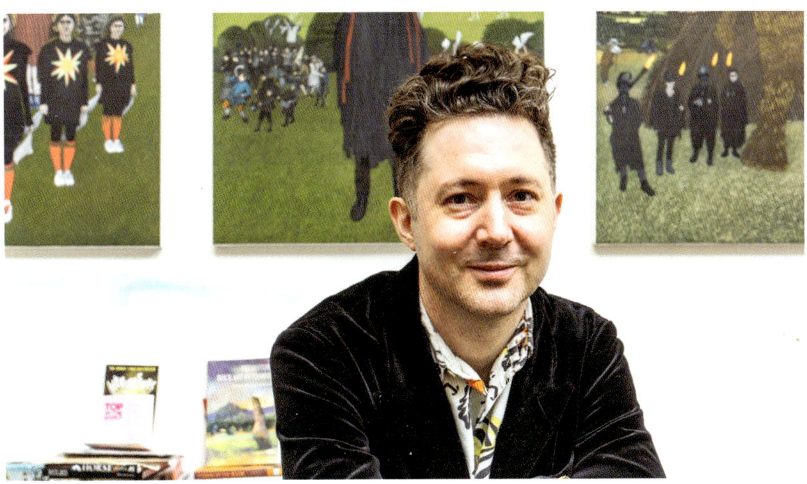

Index

Note: page numbers in **bold** refer to illustrations.